Horst Gerlach • The Power of the Roman Catholic Spirit

Horst Gerlach

The Power of the Roman Catholic Spirit

and the Vatican's Claim to the Leadership of a
Unification of Religions
with the Aim of achieving a "perfect" Humanism

"weighed in the balances and found wanting"

FOUQUÉ PUBLISHERS NEW YORK

Copyright ©2012 by Fouqué Publishers New York
Originally published as *Die Kraft des Römischen Geistes, 2010*
by August von Goethe Literaturverlag

All rights reserved,
including the right of reproduction,
in whole or in part,
in any form

First American Edition
Printed on acid-free paper

Library of Congress Cataloging-in-Publication Data
Gerlach, Horst
Die Kraft des Römischen Geistes / Horst Gerlach
1st American ed.

ISBN 978-0-578-10468-3

Dedicated to the martyrs and spiritual victims of Western religious tyranny and to the courageous heroes of faith, who were liberated from Roman spiritual tyranny.

This book including all of its parts is protected by copyright law. Every utilization outside of the narrow limits of the copy right law without permission of the publisher is illegal and liable to prosecution.

This applies especially to copying, translating, and processing in electronic systems.

The Author

Horst Gerlach has been an active church leader and pastor of an Protestant Free Church for almost thirty years. He feels obligated to the "Theology of the Reformation". Horst Gerlach is the author of many smaller books and also of "Life out of Life, or Life out of Death?" He is also the founder and leader of "Sebulon Zuflucht – (Zebulon Shelter International)", a center for Biblical counseling and Biblical redeemership, and Protestant mission organization. Through the work as a therapeutic counselor and through international cooperation with other counselors, he helps people who have experienced traumatic and other psychological damage through strong bondage to the Roman system to find a new identity. For this purpose a place of refuge is necessary in order to be safe from all psychological persecution.

"*The people of Zebulon, however, risked their very lives.*" (Judges 5: 18).

Translators: Anne Ulman (Canada)
Achim Kemmesies (Canada)
Peter and Susan Wallace (England)

My special thanks goes to all those unnamed helpers who worked in the background and without whose help this book would not have been possible.

Introduction

"Weighed in the Balances and found wanting"
(Daniel Ch. 5 v. 27)

About the origin of this book

Since 1982 the author has been grappling with the practices of the Roman Catholic Church. He asked himself this question: What kind of power keeps the Roman system together? Consequently many study trips were undertaken to approximately 120 most important, cult locations of Rome in Europe and also in most of the southern parts of the USA and the Caribbean all the way to Mexico. The author collected much evidence for his thesis, that Rome uses occult-magical practices in order to regain religious-political world domination.

The latest popes since Vaticanum II worked intensely to unite the religions with their transcendent power sources as effects of synergy under Rome's leadership. These demonic, magical synergies will be handed over to the expected "world authority" for the purpose of world domination which they pursue. The New Testament calls this "personified world authority" the Antichrist.

Religious Rome cannot give up putting its religious, sacramental stamp on world politics. These Roman lusts for power are dangerous fundamentalisms which make a peaceful co-existence of divergent cultures impossible. An unrestrained and fair competition among world religions and world views can only exist in a democratic context of our pluralistic society.

It is no longer enough that we, as a Bible believing world wide church of Jesus, merely write about was is doctrinally unbiblical and therefore wrong and dangerous for true faith. Without a change of approach we can hardly expect to reach out beyond those who belong to our circles anyway. Neither it is sufficient to sit back in the comfort of our living rooms and discuss how bad times are, if we even do that. This will usually end in depression or even a further withdrawal into the intimacy of our families.

Not retreat, but attack is the command of the hour! Why? Because the fate of believers cannot leave us indifferent, about those in danger of falling away from the faith in their Savior and becoming badly damaged. And it also should not leave us unconcerned, that decade after decade here in Europe as well as in North America less and less people convert to Jesus Christ, and miss out on receiving eternal life, in spite of conflicting "reports of victory" of rebellious charismatics. The whole secular world as well as the so-called Christian world seem to become completely caught up in rebellion against God – whom many call contemptuously "the weak Judeo-Christian God".

We should not get paralyzed by the worldwide rebellion against the Holy God. Let us stand up against the enemy of people's souls! We should not give in to private comfort!

Therefore, resistance against the enemy of life-giving faith is the command of the hour – and not ecumenical assistance. However, we have to mention one thing: The Charismatic movement has completely perverted "spiritual warfare". It has to be rejected as an imitation of the Biblical original of the spiritual struggle of faith (Eph. 6: 10-17) because it contains elements of white-magical witchcraft.

But we should not go to the other extreme and deny the spiritual battle of faith. For whoever does not engage in this spiritual struggle of faith will not be able to resist the ever increasing pressure of the spirit of unbelief in the future, and will be in danger of falling away from the faith. Even Biblically justified fight needs training.

This is what Paul means when he admonishes his young brother in the faith, "Also if anyone competes as an athlete, he does not win the prize unless he competes according to the rules." (2 Tim. 2: 5).

Basically Paul's challenge is also for us: *"Fight the good fight of faith ..."* (1 Tim. 6: 12).

So for twenty-seven years we have been fighting the spiritual battle in three directions:

1. Against the lie about the supposedly same roots of any faith in any god. The means of the fight is apologetic discussion with the Ecumenical movement and other antichristian spiritual groups.

2. Against the spirit in the macrocosm (the fallen world of the great cosmos; comp. Eph. 6: 12). The means is the worldwide practical action against certain destructive places of spirit power.

Introduction

3. Against the mirror image of this spirit in the microcosm of certain people who, however, have turned away from their perverted past life (comp. 2 Peter 2: 10-19ff) and become believers. The means are mission oriented proclamation, individual counseling, and Biblical redeemership. This is the realization of the Biblical command of spiritual struggle against the flesh, the world, and the devil. In this book we grapple apologetically with the spirit of the Roman Church. Especially Rome's views and actions were observed, e.g. through studies of publications of the Vatican as well as through trips to Roman places of spirit power during the years of 1982-2009. We are only obligated to the truth in Christ. Therefore, we do not hesitate calling this spirit with prophetic clarity diabolical, coming out of the antichristian spirit.

"Finally, be strong in the Lord and in his mighty power. Put on the full armor of God so that you can take your stand against the devil's schemes. For our struggle is not against flesh and blood, but against the rulers, against the authorities, against the powers of this dark world and against the spiritual forces of evil in the heavenly realms. Therefore put on the full armor of God, so that when the day of evil comes, you may be able to stand your ground, and after you have done everything, to stand. Stand firm then, with the belt of truth buckled around your waist, with the breastplate of righteousness in place, and with your feet fitted with the readiness that comes from the gospel of peace. In addition to all this, take up the shield of faith, with which you can extinguish all the flaming arrows of the evil one. Take the helmet of salvation and the sword of the Spirit, which is the word of God. And pray in the Spirit on all occasions with all kinds of prayers and requests. With this in mind, be alert and always keep on praying for all the saints."
(Eph. 6: 10-18).

The Author

Preliminary Remarks

A spirit from transcendency is always a forerunner and pioneer of a philosophy, ideology, or theology, which are developed by people, then taught with conviction at universities, and finally practiced by the majority of the population.

If this spirit is especially tied to its time and the milieu of society, its temporal (immanent) content is called spirit of the age-philosophy.

Many people find it hard to imagine "spirit" as being something personal. In general, "spirit" is depersonified and is used symbolically, e.g., as "influence", or "trend". These humanistic interpretations however do not answer the question from where these so called trends suddenly come at any specific and limited time. The readers will understand the present book better if they understand this "spirit" as being a personal, transcendent and invisible reality. As the Holy Spirit , the Spirit of Jesus Christ works in a person like way in the "children of light", so the demonic spirit also works in a person like way in the children of darkness (Eph. 2: 1-2). An interpretation that is too limited distorts the truth and turns into a myth.

So, according to my judgment, the non-Christian Sigmund Freud is assessed inadequately by us Christians and is too quickly rejected as being wrong in all of his statements. The fact, however, that Freud equated Christianity primarily with Western Catholicism is not appreciated enough. Therefore, is Freud's statement completely wrong when he says correspondingly, that the Western "idea of the one great God" is basically only the distorted reminiscence of a once really existing "founding father" and his absolute power?

If one substitutes "idea" with myth and "distorted reminiscence" with perverted truth, one has understood Freud's ideas more correctly – because one has looked more closely at what he wanted to say. For all real Christians – which are those redeemed by Jesus Christ – words like "great God", or "lovely God" are religiously Western, empty word shells. These are used primarily by conservative humanists.

And at this point I agree with the non-Christian Freud: The myth of the great, lovely God – or this idea – is the basic substance of all religions. This idea has a range which reaches from compulsion to delusion (from legalism to chaotic fanaticism). When this "myth of distortion" is overcome and is lead back to its "precursor, to the thing in the past", when we return to the truly existing God, who has the Biblical name Jesus Christ, which means something like: God helps through the Redeemer, then the campaign for the truth stops!

The essential point is: To obtain life through truth rather than death by lies, deceit and delusion.

So I argue resolutely concerning the distortion of the Creator, the Upholder and the Redeemer by the Roman-Catholic religion; but not in the spirit of a Sigmund Freud, but in the Spirit of Jesus Christ as he has revealed himself in the Holy Scriptures, the Bible. The distortion of God, which makes up the Catholic religion, we call disrespectfully perversion of the faith. True faith in the one and only holy God started with Abraham (Gen 15: 6; John 8: 39) and was perfected by Jesus, the Christ (John 8: 58; Hebr. 8-9; 12: 2).

Therefore we fight with "spiritual weapons" against the delusion of the Roman religion, which created the delusion in its religion through deformation out of the death powers of the spirits which fell away from the God of the Bible.

In this sense, even the non-Christian Freud is correct when he says, that the deformation of the true God by the religions is the medium (here: transmitter) of displacement. And displacement appears again in a transformed, changed form – as mythological religion. This means in Biblical terms: If the true God is argued away through reinterpretation and ignorance, life giving faith disappears. It appears in an altered shape after displacement as ritual "faith", as religion. Therefore truth disappears and with it intellectual soundness. The delusion of death spreads and finds its form in myth.

Out of this "demented" arrogance the Roman Catholic Church receives its life.

If the Roman religion "killed" the God of the Bible in Jesus Christ by so misinterpreting His word that He has been turned into a religion founding god, then the true Christ has been pushed out leaving the way open for their changed and disguised God to appear as the

God of this world and occupy the position that became vacant.

The non-Christian Freud says it like this, "The defaced return [Roman religion, the author] of the displaced fact [Biblical God, the author] constitutes a fiction" [a fabrication, here the myth, the author]. The fiction, or the myth of "faith" is also the religion of the Roman Catholic Church.

So this book shall substantiate my thesis, that through the "replacement of the true God", by distorting religion, Satan, as the "god of this world" (2 Cor. 4: 4) has reached the throne of power in the Roman Church. Together with the Babylon Harlot (Rev. 17: 1-8; 18) the mediatrix of death powers, he emits streams of spirit power which come out of the seven sacraments through the sacramentaries of images, statues and relics, etc.

These spirits of Rome impart to religion the demonic powers of witchcraft, which pull people into the spell of delusion.

Rome is indeed the church out of the spirit of the Antichrist, because it uses every Biblical symbol, in order to misuse them through reinterpretation. The spirit of Rome also created the myth or fiction of being the "only saving world church", which supposedly contains the complete truth.

We should rather get into the clear and true, personal fellowship of will and love with the Biblical God, which he established through Christ's work of salvation, and which he offers to us now. This acceptance of the covenant of friendship: *"You are my friends if you do what I command (...) I have called you friends ..."* (John 15: 14-15) is what the Bible calls faith. Whoever wants and does something different, wants and does the perversion of it.

Our contribution as redeemed people consists of liberating ourselves from the deformation of faith into delusion and myth through a spiritual battle of faith. It will be often necessary to rob the macrocosm, e.g. the Vatican with its worldwide churches and other cult places of religious delusion, of its great spiritual powers, so that life giving faith from Jesus Christ, who is the way, the truth, and the life (John 14: 6) becomes possible again for people who search for unadulterated truth. *"You diligently study the Scriptures ... These are the Scriptures that testify about me."* (John 5: 39).

This book has been written out of responsibility to Jesus Christ, "... in whom are hidden all the treasures of wisdom and knowledge"

Introduction

(Col. 2: 3) so that life giving faith can lead to victory by revealing the powers of evil which obscure the truth. We want to promote healing through sound teaching (1Tim. 4: 7; 2Tim. 4: 3-4) instead of mental-spiritual delusion of Western religion. Therefore this book is also an aid for living, because it does away with many a myth, for:

Teaching, which does not create life, creates a void!

The Author

Chapter I

The Activation of Invisible Powers for an Ecumenism derived from Worship of Relics and Saints

1. The Catholic Worship of Relics, Saints and Beatified Persons Today

First of all, let us look at the clarifying statements that God makes on this subject:

"God is spirit, and those who worship Him must worship Him in spirit and truth." (John 4: 24)

"These things occurred so that the scripture might be fulfilled (Ex 12: 46) "You shall not break any of its bones!" (John 19: 36)

"He buried him in Moab, in the valley opposite Beth Peor, but to this day nobody knows where his grave is." (Deut 34: 6)[1]

I would like to describe two events that took place in Germany during May and June of 1996: the "Holy Coat Pilgrimage" in the two-thousand-year-old city of Trier, Western Germany and the beatification ceremony undertaken by Pope John Paul II in Berlin. According to the understanding of the organizers, both events were supposed to represent milestones on the way to a unified Europe and the unification of all Christian churches.

Trier, the oldest city in the antique Roman Empire north of the Alps, was the imperial capital where Constantine the Great resided in the 4th century A.D. His mother, Helena, was a native of Trier. After the victory over Maxentius in 312 A.D., Constantine went to Rome and let himself be celebrated as the liberator of Christianity. His mother followed him there.

2. The Beginning of Relic Worship in the 4th Century

In 327 A.D., Helena travelled to Jerusalem with a great entourage, but without her, in many respects, dubious son. Her purpose

---

[1] For further information on and treatment of this subject, we recommend the book: "The Two Babylons: The Papal Worship: Proved to be the Worship of Nimrod and his Wife" by Alexander Hislop.

was to bring back relics for him and the nation. As we can see, Christianity in its faith-based substance was already endangered by the rise of relic worship in Constantine's time. Helena played the role of the "great mother", as precursor of the Marian spirit and its multiple Madonna statues. The mediation of demonic spiritual powers out of the cosmos began. Soon after, "Mary" was acknowledged as mediatrix, a mediator to God, by the Ecumenical Council and in 431 A.D., the beginnings of Marian worship prevailed with intrigue against the biblical theologians. At the "Robbers' Synod" in Ephesus (449 A.D.), wild hordes of monks used violence to assist the supporters of Marian reverence. The first Pope in the modern sense, Leo the Great (440-461 A.D.), was decisive in the move away from Augustine's theology of grace. Instead, the lesser cults of Marian, saint and relic worship became central in theology and religion.

Unfortunately, many Protestants do not know that the mediation of Mary refers to the gathering and provision of demonic spiritual powers from the realm of the dead, the natural forces of the Earth and the powers of the universe (cosmos). As well as this, it is largely unknown that the hidden or esoteric meaning of the Roman Catholic version of "Trinity" relates to the utilization of demonic spiritual powers from these same three areas: the realm of death, the Earth and the universe (cosmos). The Bible describes the antichristian system as cosmic and Satan, the ruler of this world, is also called cosmocrator (see Eph 6: 12; Mt 4: 8-10).

The Catholic Church, born out of the Roman spirit, owes its continued existence to these cosmic spiritual powers and not to the Gospel of grace.

A Roman Catholic Church would be unthinkable and no longer Catholic without relics in its church buildings. An altar in a church is only referred to as an "altar of honour" if it contains remnants of the corpse of so-called "saints" i.e. a relic.

In order to understand the "Holy Coat Pilgrimage" of Trier and other processions, we must take a look behind the scenes at the hidden, esoteric goals of the Roman Church. Practitioners of responsible pastoral care trying to help Catholics find the truth, need to recognize the true proceedings and nature of the Catholics institution. For this reason, we need to consider more than just the open self-portrayals of the Catholic Church which are meant for the public. Otherwise, we could neither help someone who wants to break free from the spiritual tyranny of Rome nor fight against this invisible spirit.

3. The Classes of Relics

Let us come back to the relics. Besides the actual relics of body remnants (bones), there are touch relics of first and second class.

Torture instruments or the clothing of Jesus and other persons belong to the first class.

The second class includes copies of first-class relics, which have been put into a state of demonic cosmic spiritual effectiveness through official consecration. For example, the cloth relic of Trier, the Holy Coat, is regarded as a cloth relic of second class. These are the official statements out of Rome's mouth. Before we deal with the esoteric, that is the spiritual, concealed meaning and its consequences, we will go deeper into the story of the alleged "Holy Coat".

4. The Story of the "Holy Coat"

When Helena arrived in Jerusalem, she was mostly interested in the construction site of the Church of the Holy Sepulcher and gave instructions to search for relics of Jesus everywhere.

According to the historical accounts of the Catholic Church, discoveries were made while digging around the "Holy Tomb". The coat of Christ, nails of the cross and a piece of the cross were brought to Trier as relic booty.

5. Problem-Solving for the Roman Church in the Face of Danger: The Pilgrimages to the "Holy Coat"

For centuries, this so-called consecrated "Coat of Christ" lay enclosed by brick under the altar of the cathedral of Trier. In 1196, the coat was transferred to the newly erected high altar. There, it rested untouched until 1512, when Emperor Maximilian wished to see the coat, because of the miraculous powers that he believed it

Chapter 1: The Activation of Invisible Powers for an Ecumenism

possessed. Around this time the first pilgrimages started. In situations of discord or quarrel in the Church, the coat was allegedly used as a symbol for church unity and displayed to fight against the break-up of the church. "When the Holy Coat was publicly shown on different days in 1512, even hard hearts were moved."[2]

6. The Dangers for the Roman Church in the 19th Century

During the time of the cultural battle between the German Protestants and the Catholics in the 19th century, two pilgrimages took place with over one million pilgrims.

7. The Dangers for the Roman Church in the 20th Century

The Third Reich (1933-1945)

In the past century the dangers for the Catholic Church did not diminish. And so the first pilgrimage of this century took place in the „holy year of redemption" in 1933. The name originates in the Vatican. In the same year Adolf Hitler took over power in Germany. For the Nazis it was the year of their „redemption". In the same year, the so-called "Reichskonkordat", the concord with the German empire was signed by the Pope. It basically constituted a pact of silence between the Catholic Church and Hitler, giving him a free hand to eradicate the Jews. In this fateful year, 1933, the next pilgrimage took place with over two million people. To the embarrassment of the Roman Church, many Catholics participated in their brown SA-Troopers uniforms, showing their allegiance to Nazi-Germany as well. The statement in the official brochure of the Roman Church, that "many people in those times experienced a decisive strengthening of their faith and their loyalty to the church"[3], is pure hypocrisy. After all, the overwhelming majority of Catholics felt as little moral conflict as the Protestants. Both united with Hitler to unleash World War II and fight the most scandalous of all wars:

---

2 „Holy Coat Pilgrimage of 96", 1995, p. 35.
3 Ronig, Franz, „1933: Over 2 million pilgrims". In: ibid. p.38.

the war against the unarmed Jews. Could it have been mere coincidence that the culturally Catholic Hitler and his devoutly Catholic Foreign Minister, von Papen, made the "Konkordat" with Nuntius Pacelli, who became later Pope Pius XII. It should make us suspicious that the SS Commander Himmler and the chief destroyer of the Jews, Eichmann, were Catholics as well. The main danger for the church was the defection of Catholics to the Nazis, who better represented their nationalistic German interests.

The Liberalism and Socialism in the 50's and 60's of the 20th Century

After the Second World War, a new era (New-Age) began with a new attempt to unite all religions and nations. Achieving one unified antichristian world religion and government through world wars seemed less and less likely. This was also ensured by the military deadlock between the USA and the Soviet Union.

To gain political and religious world domination through peaceful means became now the hidden slogan and political tactic. Out of this, the Vatican Council II of the years 1962-65 arose, with the main goal of unifying all Christian churches by the year 2000 under the primacy of the Roman Church. Vatican II merely represented a new peace tactic to neutralize the impediment of Protestantism, which stood in the way of the "peaceful" antichristian spirit of the age. At the climax of preparations for the Council in 1959, they initiated a new "Coat Pilgrimage" visited by 1.8 million pilgrims. The Catholic "Jesus Christ" was beseeched in prayer to join again a divided Christianity.

In the following two decades, ecumenism was actively promoted through the WCC (World Council of Churches) in Geneva, Switzerland, especially by the Protestant Churches and the Eastern European Orthodox Church bodies. The collaboration of the WCC with world communism, however, froze completely ecumenism with the Catholic Church.

Pope John Paul II, the Most Capable Integrator and Organizer of Cosmic, Catholic Spiritual Power

This only changed when Pope John Paul II took over his pontificate in 1978. He will likely go into the annals of history as the greatest carrier of hope for unity and, at the same time, as the most tragic pope of the 20th century. He seemed to be successful in everything. The Protestant resistance ceased more and more. Even when he did something completely uncatholic and met to pray with representatives of all world religions as well as with Shamans in Assisi, Italy (1986), there was no power of the reformation left to help the Protestant churches to oppose. His spirit out of the "cosmic Christ" seemed to disable and paralyse them. The resistance against his restless gathering of cosmic demonic spiritual powers grew weaker and weaker. He, like no pope before him, beatified and canonized the deceased by the dozens. Even the canonization of criminals and murderers from the time of the counterreformation met no real opposition. His build-up of spiritual "secret armies", like Opus Dei and other secret orders, who set out to infiltrate Protestant societies and fight their enemies with demonic spiritual power, went unopposed as well. Almost unnoticed by the Protestant world, he succeeded in building up demonic-cosmic spiritual power in forgotten Marian places of pilgrimage. No pope before him managed to gather so much cosmic power for the antichristian ecumenical movement and met so little resistance.

But in those years, the real LORD Jesus Christ called people to fight and reduce these gathered and organized cosmic forces, in the power of His cross and resurrection. Therefore, Pope John Paul II acted more and more as being on the retreat. His tragedy existed in the fact that he massively challenged the true Christ, assuming that He would always remain silent. Then the tide turned: This pope out of the antichristian spirit became the most tragic figure in the 21st century. God exercised judgement! Neither his "cosmic Christ", nor his "Mary", nor his secret associations could save this pope. They were not able to carry him to victory.

Meanwhile, an atmosphere of bankruptcy had started to reign in the Protestant churches of Europe. Submissiveness to this Pope on the part of several representatives was already the embarrassing norm. In the meantime, new, strong forces in the Vatican were brushing off the ingratiation. These forces of tomorrow do not even want the bankrupt Protestant potential! Although the Protestant circles are begging to participate in the magical Catholic communion, which they call the Eucharist, Rome has steadfastly refused. The Protestant theologians know very well that the Eucharist, believed to be the transubstantiation of the blood of Christ, is not the sign for the Last Supper of the Lord. Yet they deceive their churchgoers by claiming that Rome must not deny them full participation in the Lord's Supper.

The Stagnation of Ecumenism since the Middle of the Nineties in the 20th Century

In reality, the current crisis of ecumenism constitutes itself twofold. It is a crisis caused by the failing abilities of Pope John Paul II to integrate all powers and a revelation that the Protestant churches in Europe have totally exhausted their faith having already turned away from biblical truth! In the middle of this crisis, the third "Holy Coat Pilgrimage" of the century took place in April/May 1996. For the first time, it was to be an ecumenical pilgrimage, expressing the hopes that ecumenical unity would gain by it the necessary cosmic spiritual powers. The German national Protestant churches were represented, as well as several independent church bodies. An ecumenical service was held. Although such great ecumenical importance had been attached to this pilgrimage, only 700,000 pilgrims participated, according to official statements. Even I, although a strong opponent of any belief in magic, mingled with the pilgrims. All around us were Polish Catholics. I asked myself: what would this dangerous magical spectacle still be worth without these Polish Catholics who were willing to give their lives for this pope? The motto of this pilgrimage was:

"Walking with Jesus Christ."

People were further seduced by key statements like:

"The aim of the pilgrimage is to deepen the personal relationship with Jesus Christ."[4]

"In this world situation, we, as Christians, want to set an example for hope and peace. It has to do with a special devotion to Christ and a special endeavour of contemplation, of prayer and of actively taking responsibility for each other."[5] "This endeavour should come from the devotion to Christ."[6]

---

4   Ibid. p. 3.
5   Ibid. p. 41.
6   Ibid. p. 41.

Chapter 1: The Activation of Invisible Powers for an Ecumenism

No traditionally raised Catholic really understands the meaning of these expressions. They come from Protestantism and are used by the Catholic church to deceive Protestants. Catholics do not have a personal relationship to Jesus Christ. This would give them assurance of salvation, something which they are denied by Roman doctrine!

The hundreds of people around us, who had queued for over one hour, did not really want to experience Christ. How could they? All they came to was a piece of cloth, more like a rag than a coat. In actual fact, the people went there to profit from the cosmic power-field of the touch relic. These people had the same expectations as those observed in sects and esoteric movements.

Nevertheless, the brochure promoted the pilgrimage with the seductive words: "The Holy Coat Pilgrimage is to be a special **exercise** of faith. The Christian who makes a pilgrimage to the Holy Coat, exercises his/her faith in Jesus Christ. With his/her heart, he/she approaches Christ in worship, obedience, trust, devotion and love. In faith, he/she grasps Him, from whom alone salvation comes (see Acts 4: 12)".

The closer we got to the coat under the pyramid-shaped glass dome, the more we felt the so-called cosmic spiritual energies surging against us. Let us call them demonic powers. The pilgrims around us were seized by these demonic energies and became inherently filled with them. It was similar to the "Toronto blessing", except that everything here took place in a peaceful and reverent manner. The pilgrims went like sheep to the slaughter. Some changed instantly, several became fearful, others had a fanatical expression of pathological insanity in their eyes for a short time.

What did we do? From the start to the finish at the "Egyptian death-pyramid" covering the cloth, we prayed against these demonic forces in the power of the cross and the resurrection (see Eph 6: 12).

The Esoteric Significance of the "Holy Coat" Touch Relic

With that, you, dear reader, have recognized the nature of relics: relics of people or touch relics have been consecrated through powers of death, i.e. spiritual powers, and surrounded by invisible cosmic-demonic forces. When a person looks at remnants of material objects with fascination and reverence, that person's spirit is opened. This worship of material and the identification with the alleged owner or carrier of the relic leads to a hidden and supernatural identification with the true carrier: DEATH. Demonization to varying degrees results from this sin of idol worship. For this reason, the people of faith in the time of the Old Testament were to destroy the high places and stone pillars, because a material identification with the demonic had taken place. Similarly, being God's people of the New Testament, we destroyed the invisible powers around the Coat. We were not interested in the rag of material.

In principal, the same holds true for the worship of saints:

The image or figure is revered through genuflection, bowing the knees. The spiritual forces of death, concentrated around the figure through consecration, feel attracted by the identification and literally enter into the body and soul of the people who worship them. Death enters the lives of such people in part. The affected person breaks into many small pieces like a shattered water-glass. These pieces now belong to the realm of death. There, they do slave labour by forming para-material elemental substances which are often surrounded by a massive concentration of cosmic forces. These substances are then programmed by the cosmic powers to function as weapons of attack and seduction against other people. Through this symbiosis of human and demonic spirit created by the devil, the forces of darkness gain immense powers.

This was also the aim of the "Holy Coat Pilgrimage." Many reverent worshippers bring lots of "spiritual raw material" for transformation by cosmic-demonic forces. Since it concerns a "Christ"-pilgrimage, these newly organized forces are naturally under the supervision of the "cosmic Christ".

I think that it is clear to all readers: The "Jesus Christ" named by Catholics is not the wonderful Lord and Saviour proclaimed by the Bible. It is an imitation created by the father of lies to alienate true Christians from their real Saviour. The Catholic Christ is a forgery, born out of blasphemy. If the atrocities through the unimaginable Catholic idolatry were not so great, the demonically acting powers would not be nearly as strong as they are today.

The sinful human, himself, in effect produces the power of the demons in every age and provokes the wrath of God!

Chapter 1: The Activation of Invisible Powers for an Ecumenism

The relic powers described in Trier were to be used to speed up the ecumenical unification process. They also serve as seductive forces against true Christians, to cause them if possible to fall away from the true faith.

It is a crime against God and humanity, when many weak people are destroyed in their souls through mystic seduction. That is what this pilgrimage, and in principal, all pilgrimages, spiritual exercises, etc. amount to do.

We belong to the real Christians who do not allow themselves to be intimidated by the Catholic Church. If necessary, we will bring back stolen life out of the Roman Church from every place on Earth, insofar as Jesus Christ, in his mercy, has ordered it. I am writing this as a warning, well aware that our publications are carefully read by the Vatican. After all, we do the same with theirs.

Now let us come to the second event we mentioned, which consisted of a series of ecclesiastical and political meetings.

8. The Intentions of Pope John Paul II during His Visit to Germany from June 21st-24th 1996 (Paderborn and Berlin)

First of all the statements and clarifications given by God on this subject should be mentioned:

"You shall have no other gods before me. You shall not make for yourself an idol in the form of anything in heaven above or on the earth beneath or in the waters below." (Ex 20: 3+4)

"When men tell you to consult mediums and spiritists, who whisper and mutter, should not a people inquire of their God? Why consult the dead on the behalf of the living?" (Isaiah 8: 19)

The Anti-Pope Trip

Being spiritual opponents of the pope, it was our task to "take the same route as planned by John Paul II." A small company recruited from our ministry set out to be at the designated places, which had been specially consecrated by the Vatican before our spiritual and theological adversary arrived. That also took us to the Cathedral in Paderborn. It was the common concern of the Roman Church to prepare an enthusiastic welcome for their pope in Germany. The

German Cardinal Meisner expressed it like this: "We must give this pope a welcome that he will not soon forget."

9. The Blasphemies Hidden from the Protestant Public

One of the groups most subservient to the pope is the "Community of the Beatitudes" of Mary of Medjugorje. In their brochure, they promoted the participation of faithful Catholics with the following words: "You are Peter, the Rock. (...) In the turmoil of the current time, many people can only come to believe through our and his witness. (...) Brothers! Come to the Lord, the living stone, rejected by people but chosen by God and precious to Him (1 Peter 2: 4)." It is obviously very important to the pope to let himself be honoured as the "Vicar of Christ". But when it came to impressing the Protestants with bible-based statements and quotations, all tracks of this idolatry and blasphemy were carefully covered up.

Yet, Protestant supporters of ecumenism suggest that the pope preaches the same biblical Jesus Christ as the national and independent churches born out of the Reformation.

10. The Recognizable Goals of the Papal Visit

The pope had set two goals for his visit to Germany:

To promote the unity of all Christians, i.e. Catholics, Protestants and members of independent churches, so that by the year 2000, the "birthday of the Lord", a united Christianity could be laid to the feet of this "Lord" as a birthday present.

To complete the union of Europe under the primacy of a strong and united Roman World-Church. As a Catholic-political world power out of the Roman Spirit, Europe would then be in a position to influence the future antichristian world government decisively.

11. The Deception Comes from the Falsified Source

The sermons of the pope were in no way traditionally Catholic, but very bible-based and interspersed with Protestant terminology. Similarly, the political speeches sounded very impressive and in some places even fascinating for us Protestants, when he dealt with areas of ethical responsibility for the state, the church and the citizens, for example.

This pope is likely the most clever, or rather, the most cunning theologian as well as politician in 21st century Europe. At the very least, he knew how to win the German hearts. The things he had to say about freedom were exactly what I wished for, along with many other Protestants. John Paul II: "As human beings, we are called to freedom. To all of you, who are listening to me now, I proclaim: The fullness and the perfection of this freedom has a name: Jesus Christ. It is He, who witnessed about Himself: I am the gate. In Him, the door to the fullness of freedom and life is opened for humans. It is He, who truly sets people free by expelling the darkness from the human hearts and revealing the truth. He completed his work in the sacrifice of his life for us. That is how He freed us from sin and death. (…) Christ is our Saviour, our freedom."[7]

It became difficult for us to deny the pope our natural human sympathies. When he said "that Christ is the truth and the centre of life" in the beatification ceremony, one can not help breathing a deep sigh of relief as a Protestant. How can that be deception, if said in such a biblically correct manner? We definitely do not want to "split hairs" by trying to find the anti-biblical mistake in partially liberalistic, modernistic theological terminology.

The point remains: Most of what the pope says to the public, addressing Protestants, is biblically correct. But, nevertheless, it is all wrong! Let anyone accept this who can!

In many of his statements, we can not use pure apologetics, the theological defence of faith, to convict this pope of lying. Whenever his Christian ecumenism is at stake, he rarely leaves himself open to attack. Therefore, many Protestants are impressed by him. Millions already recognize him as a moral leader. It is only a question of time until they accept him as theological leader as well.

What is wrong, despite so many correct words?

---

[7] Speech held by Pope John Paul II at the Brandenburger Tor in Berlin on June 21, 1996.

12. The Devilish Method to Seduce with Fragments of the Truth

In View of this, I would like to look at the story of Jesus' temptation according to Matthew 4: 1-11 and Luke 4: 1-13.

1. Jesus was literally starved and at the limit of His physical strength.
2. In this borderline situation the devil came and promised Him bread, by reminding Jesus that He, as the Son of God, is the Lord over all laws of nature and has the power to make bread out of stones.
3. The devil tempted Jesus again, this time with Psalm 91: 11+12 where the Scripture speaks about His protection.
4. The devil acknowledged Jesus as the Son of God and even used God's Word: He tried to seduce with the Word of God twice.
5. The devil does not reveal his motive until the last seduction attempt in Mt 4: 9: Jesus was supposed to worship him.

We are also starved by the liberalistic-modernistic Protestant theology with all its immorality, as well as the spirit of legalism, the theology of prosperity, etc. found in many independent Protestant churches. In the midst of this situation, the pope speaks biblical words that do good to many of us, only to mention his ethical directives that match very much with a bible believing Christian. How did Jesus recognize and overcome the address of the devil? By constantly keeping in accordance with the will of the Father in heaven! We, too, will only be able to differentiate the truly Christ-centred from the antichrist-centred if we stay within the will of Jesus, the Christ. It seems to us, that many Protestants are caught in an identity crisis because they have long fallen out of this accordance with the will of Christ, their Saviour. Why and how?

Because, in their hearts, they are looking for doctrines that agree with their flesh, i.e. human nature. However, God reveals Himself in Jesus Christ only to spiritual man, since only he searches everything in man, as the depths of God are searched by the Holy Spirit.

Having received the Spirit of God, we know what God has given us (1.Cor 2: 10-16). Simply said, even though some might stumble:

Whoever can not distinguish the Spirit of God from the spirit of this world (cosmos) has too little of the mind of Christ (verse 16).

Why? Because some statements of pseudo-biblical exegesis and ethics are so good, that no one cares about the source. Like in the story of Jesus' temptation, the pope may have made four fundamentally correct statements, but in the fifth, he let himself be worshipped as the representative of Christ and then incidentally, you might hear that he receives his power from the mediatrix of all forces of death, the queen of heaven, whom he calls Mary. Please read Jeremiah, chapters 7 and 44 for more information on this crucial issue.

Whoever ignores the actual sources of the pope, should not be surprised if he/she is fooled by the "right" words, spoken for the ears of Protestants.

Deeper understanding is the fruit of deep repentance, which goes on to recognize even the sins of our forefathers and our own culture.

When you read the chapters in Jeremiah mentioned above please read also Daniel, chapter 9.

In Daniel 11: 32b and 12: 10, we read:

„*but the people who are loyal to their God shall stand firm and take action.*" "*Many shall be purified, cleansed, and refined, but the wicked shall continue to act wickedly. None of the wicked shall understand, but those who are wise shall understand.*"

13. The Goal of Seduction with Fragments of the Truth: Neutralization of Spiritual Power

The sermons and speeches that Pope John Paul II delivers to the general public are meant to impress Protestants, hoping to bring them, if at all possible, under the influence of the "cosmic-eucharistic Christ". His aim is to neutralize or totally eliminate the function of true Christians as they restrain evil. This means that the pope would have succeeded in breaking all spiritual resistance and his wish to be the "Holy Father of all people" would be fulfilled. Once true Christians have been neutralized and eliminated by fascinating them with his personality and church, the pope believed it would also be much easier to force the secular, atheistic world under antichristian Catholic dominion through Marian power. That explains why he is willing to snub and offend the secularized world, including many liberalistic national churches, with his "biblical positions". The world, of course, does not see through this. And so the pope is depreciatively labelled "conservative". In truth, he is the most progressive "pope of all religions" of modern times and, therefore, the most dangerous pope out of the antichristian spirit.

14. The Dependence of "Babylon" on Successful Religion and Politics

Religion plays into the hands of politics. Without a religiously strong Rome, there is no politically strong Roman empire to exert European influence on the one world religion and government. We will later come back to the political contents of the political Babylon. With his visit to Germany, this pope had aimed to strengthen both.

15. Ecumenism as the Basic Prerequisite for the Religious Babylon

"Pope John Paul II was inspired by the idea of leading the church into the third millennium, and overcoming the offence of division played no small part in this."[8] Further quotations from this newsletter:

"Interdenominational commissions, acting on behalf of their churches, have long pointed out considerable agreement in matters of Christian faith."[9]

According to the pope, there is "a broad agreement in central, basic truths."[10]

Let us note the broad agreement with the pope regarding the "offence of division", especially in the Protestant Charismatic movement. No one on the Protestant side seems to remember that the division of the church was the fruit of the Roman Church's unspeakable lies and blasphemies as well as the absolute last resort to

8   „Name of journal for the catholic family", edition dated June 23, 1996, p. 4.
9   Ibid. p. 4.
10 Ibid. p. 4.

save people from Catholicism's death-bringing idolatry. If freedom is subject to the truth, then it must be proven in this matter. But instead, both sides are talking about overcoming the division through union. It is said to be the requirement for God to bless again. However, God will only bless if repentance results in a clear confession of sins, especially the lies of the papacy in the past and the present, e.g. the increased Marian idolatry in the last century. And God will only bless those who understand truth in Christ and for Christ's sake as the holy duty of a sanctified believer but not as an offence or stumbling block. The spiritual fruit of true unity in the spirit of Christ will only grow if the truth is said and done with love, and love is practiced in truth.

The religious ecumenical movement is not supported by the Holy Spirit, but by the spirit of Babylonian integration encompassing all antichristian religious-demonical powers.

The papal statement, "that efforts toward unity must be supported by the trust in the Holy Spirit", is pure hypocrisy from the representative of the (anti)-Christ. Here, only the name of God is the same, but the person represents the complete opposite.

The Liborius newsletter claims that the current Pontifex Maximus, John Paul II, is the most important buttress for leading all of Christianity into the third Christian millennium, united across all denominational trenches. Pontifex Maximus was a title given to the Roman emperors which means supreme bridge-builder.

We should be fully aware that this unity can only come at the high cost of losing the true Jesus Christ! The union created by the "supreme bridge-builder" will constitute a union with the demonic antichristian forces of the Roman Empire rooted in the Babylonian spirit.

16. The Attempt at Reviving, Activating, Reorganizing and Programming Neo-Roman Forces

We as Christians comitted to the spirit of the Reformation, were not willing to accept the pope's plan without resistance.

And so we arrived in Paderborn, Westphalia, Germany one day before him. This Westphalian city is a significant centre of ecumenism. The Johann-Adam-Moehler Institute there "has, over the last forty years, given trend setting impulses for overcoming the centuries-old division of the church".[11] That was one of the reasons why the pope, who attached great importance to symbols, chose to visit this particular city. A second symbol important for John Paul II was, as it was said, "the old Episcopal seat (Paderborn) from the 8th century which holds the memory of a historic meeting between Charlemagne and the Pope Leo III in the year 799 AD."[12] Charlemagne was a Frankish-German ruler in the 8th Century. He is considered the founding kind of a united Europe. The first Holy Roman Empire began under his rule.

At this meeting the co-operation was arranged between the European Cesar Charlemagne and the pope. "This was to influence and determine the history of Europe for centuries."[13]

It led to the establishment of the "Holy (Catholic) Roman Empire of German Nation", called the First Empire (Reich), which was forcibly ended by Napoleon in 1815. For over 1000 years, the Roman Church was in symbiosis with the Roman Empire of German Nation. For over 1000 years, the state and the church were united in the Roman-Babylonian spirit.

John Paul II wanted to build on this. But after the Second and Third Reich failed, he did not believe in a Fourth Reich of German Nation. The Second Reich is called the Roman Empire of German Nation. The word "Holy" Catholic is missing here, since it was a Protestant-freemason attempt at world dominion that lasted only for short time (1870-1918). Hitler's Third Reich, his version of a Roman empire, was mainly anticlerical coming from black-magical origin. It ended after only 12 years (1933-1945). Pope John Paul II no longer believed in a Fourth Empire (Reich) of German Nation but in a Holy Catholic Fourth Roman Empire made up of all European nations.

As a culture-conscious Polish man, the power from Catholicism was for him of utmost importance. He wanted a clerical Catholic empire in Europe rooted in the spirit of Rome. The pope though highly of certain German abilities that may have helped him

---

11   Ibid. p. 4.
12   „L'Osservatore Romano", No. 27, July 5,1996, p. 2.
13   Ibid. p. 2.

achieve his aims. For this reason he flattered Germans whenever it appeared opportune to him. He put second in rank behind him the German Cardinal Ratzinger who became his successor in April 2005 and is now known as Benedikt XVI. But Germany is also the country where only 7% of Catholics remain committed to the Vatican. Around 50% of the 80 million Germans are Catholics; however, 93% of them are secularized.

This does not hold true for Polish Catholics. Therefore, the pope was doing everything to bring the Catholics from Germany and Poland into a symbiotic union. He considered the Polish Catholics having the necessary "Marian bite". This pope was using the very tragic and atrocity-ridden history of German-Polish relations as a cover. Thus nobody noticed when he connected Roman Catholic demonic power-fields in Germany and Poland, paving the way for a unified Europe under Catholic-clerical leadership.

What does this revival of Catholic-demonic forces out of the Roman spirit look like? To begin with, let us consider again the pope's deep belief in symbols.

17. Symbols being the Reality for Esoteric Spiritual Powers

All organizations who believe in supernatural powers, such as Freemasons, Catholic secret orders, and esoteric institutions, see mysteries behind their symbols. This distinguishes them as religious or esoteric systems. Insiders of the respective circles know how to decipher the mysteries. Some talk about spirits, which they call holy and name them gods, while others simply describe them as impersonal powers or energy sources or the like.

Every antichristian system, every religion believes that symbols are more than just signs to remember like a monument, for example. They assume that all symbols are surrounded by the spiritual power of gods or impersonal energies of transcendental nature. They can and must be made available or useful to their system through gifts or sacrifice, reverence and worship. Only this makes religion in the widest sense conceivable and is also the reason why specific rituals are followed. Whoever observes the rituals, will have experiences based on the mysteries, which the believer then integrates into his immanent life. Therefore, the Roman Catholic Church, as a religion of mysteries, also belongs to the esoteric system rooted in the antichristian spirit.

18. The True Faith in the Triune God is Not a Religion

The above observations could possibly alarm those readers who have accepted the biblical Jesus Christ as their Lord and Saviour from sin and death. Such people need not be worried. In my critical assessment, I have spoken about demonic transcendence, from which all religions and pseudo-religious systems, i.e. esotericism, have originated. They are, without exception, counterfeits of the original Godly transcendence. Faith in Jesus Christ, on the other hand, is based on the trust of the immanent human being in the triune God, who is transcendent.

God is Spirit, i.e. transcendence according to John 4: 24. What does it mean, that a person can only worship God in his spirit and out of the truth? Whoever has been born anew (John 3: 5), has received transcendent abilities as a renewed part of life along with his salvation from sin and death. Therefore, a person redeemed by Christ can believe, understand, pray and act without using rituals! A true Christian does not "recite" a prayer, but instead prays, i.e. communicates with the God of life in Jesus Christ. In contrast, religion utilizes special mediators, often called "holy", such as priests or the Marian spirit. In Romans 8: 15, the relationship between the true God and people redeemed by Him through Jesus Christ is likened to the intimate relationship of a good father to his child. Such people can address God with "Abba! Father!"

For this reason, the Bible always speaks of faith as the key to an undisturbed relationship between man and God. Consequently, "symbols and rituals" are expressions of the falsification of "religion" which do not suit real faith. Man wants to assert himself and appeases the transcendental forces with rituals.

The one and only true God, the Creator and Sustainer of all people and His Redeemer Jesus Christ, can only be experienced in His transcendence if one invests trust and love in Him. God reveals Himself to such people, above all through his word, the Holy Scriptures. He gives them knowledge about his will and also the power to put this Godly will into practice through his Holy Spirit.

In summary, biblical faith is the original out of God's transcendence and the counterpoint to the "self-assertion-faith" of a religion or esoteric system. This biblical faith does not believe in the necessity of symbols, which gain great power through the magic of rituals. God has immense spiritual power ready for those who put their faith in Him, without symbols having to be "set in motion."

19. The Demonic Reality of Spiritual Forces out of History

One could ask: are forces not released through ritualistic activation of symbols in various religions and mystic movements?

Indeed, hidden or esoteric, transcendent demonic powers are released and utilized by the ritualistic believers, if they follow the prescribed "cosmic laws" , i.e. rituals. This results in the reception of the power of those forces, through which they intensify the efforts to reach their goals.

Now we understand why this ritualistically religious pope visits deeply symbolic places. He hopes to revive the demons concentrated in such places through the atrocious sins that happened there, in order to pursue his goals more vigorously. That was also the case in Paderborn, Westphalia.

For this purpose, he visited the location where Charlemagne and Pope Leo III met to found the "Holy Roman Empire of German Nation" in 799 A.D. There, John Paul II revived the historic spiritual forces of the Roman state and medieval papalism out of the antichristian spirit which had been laid dormant by the many other spirits of the ages. The re-awakening again takes place through ritual consecration. Our spiritual task was to prevent the revival of these old Carolingian and papal "Western European spirits". We were standing against these spirits of the empire in the power of Jesus' cross and resurrection. This is done in contrast to ritual prayer, since Christ is called upon not to allow the strengthening of these deceptive spirits. Consequently, they could not be revived by the pope when he arrived one day later.

We also prayed against the spirit of ecumenism in the cathedral where an ecumenical service was to be held the next day.

Unfortunately, many Protestants believe that the papal Curia works only with human powers of persuasion. Such thinking is, however, a sign of another demonic spirit: the spirit of Greek Humanism and Enlightenment. This sin exists through ignorant arrogance of rationalism. With rationalism, of course, no place for spiritual effects, neither Godly-positive nor demonically-negative, can be found.

Only repentance can help here. This means changing your mind and starting to think in accordance with biblical principles.

20. First Results of the Spiritual Binding and Powerlessness of Demonic Forces

The pope celebrated the Eucharist in Sennestadt near Paderborn, where 100,000 Catholic believers had gathered. Then he flew to Berlin, Germany for the beatification celebration of two German Catholic theologians in the Olympic stadium.

We passed up the Mass in Sennestadt, in order to be present in Berlin before the pope's arrival. Later, we followed the Mass on video. It struck us that in Paderborn/Sennestadt and later in Berlin, the pope seemed very nervous and unfocussed. The famous charisma was gone. His so-called "charisma" that thrived in the past seemed no longer present. We even felt a bit sorry for him, as he read every speech and sermon word for word and obviously did not even notice when he was applauded. He recited his notes like a robot. A man speaks like that who has been coping with a severe personal blow. He can only adhere to the text already prepared in the Vatican like a lecturer. He delivered words without his proverbial power, which had made him famous. Spiritually, we rejoiced, despite the pity that sometimes arose. The secular press tried to explain everything by pointing out that the pope was very sick and suffering from numerous afflictions of old age. But this was not the decisive truth.

21. The Intended Publicity Effect for Two Notable German Nazi Opponents

The publicity effect for the German Catholics was very well chosen. Two theologians, the cathedral provost, Lichtenberg, and the priest, Leisner, were to be honoured for their resistance against the barbaric National Socialist movement in the 40's of the 20th century.

Both died as a result of the criminal acts inflicted on them. In my view, these two were used to generate German sympathies for the Vatican and especially for John Paul II. Their cases follow a very typical pattern: The Roman Church leadership abandoned both of these humanely notable people while they were still alive. They did not receive support from the Vatican in their resistance against the Nazi-Regime. But in 1996 the church decorated itself with these men of the resistance movement, who followed their conscience and not the politics of the Catholic Church manifested in the concordat treatment with the Nazi-State. Honouring these two deceased was supposed to impress the Protestants in Germany and help reduce ecumenical reservations.

Let us now look at the Catholic-theological side of the beatification act.

22. The Theological Process of Beatification and the Papal Act

It was amazing to see the unusual haste of the pope, who literally convinced the commissions in charge of numerous beatification processes. Even members of the Curia accused him of operating a "saint factory". Indeed: John Paul II beatified and canonized men and women in a number like no pope before him. The reasons behind this are found in ecumenical significance.

Since 1234, only a pope can bestow such honours according to Catholic law. In order to make an arbitrary selection process more difficult, Pope Sextus V established a "Congregation for the Causes of Saints" during the Counter- reformation in the 16th century. It still exists today. In 1983 John Paul II radically reformed this system, making everything easier and faster. A candidate must be dead for at least 5 years, before such a process can be initiated. The following prerequisites must also be fulfilled:

Either such a deceased person is recognized as a martyr, as the two beatified in Berlin or this 'person' must have worked a healing miracle after death. It happens like this: A very seriously ill person must beseech the deceased for help in prayer. If the patient becomes well again, physicians from the Vatican are employed who must determine that the recovery is scientifically inexplicable. Theologically, this observation delivers proof that the deceased miracle worker is indeed in the presence of God; because miracles supposedly can only be worked from there! Such an assumption can only come from arrogant and ignorant hearts. Once a deceased candidate has been beatified, all Catholic believers in his or her diocese may pray for help! Beatification is the prerequisite for that person to possibly be canonized later. For canonization, an additional condition has to be fulfilled: miracles of healing must be demonstrable, even for martyrs.

If such a "beatified" person later becomes a "saint", the entire Catholic world, not just the diocese, may worship, pray to and call on him/her as mediator. A spiritual assessment of these spiritistic proceedings seems unnecessary, as they already speak for themselves.

23. The Ecumenical Significance of Papal Beatification and Canonization

As we mentioned, Pope John Paul II canonized exactly 477 deceased persons and beatified 1317 (including "Mother Theresa") from the time when he took over the Pontificate in late 1978 until October 19, 2003.[14] Of the beatified persons, 550 of the deceased came from Asia alone. The mass beatifications carried out by Pope John Paul II are new too, such as 120 Chinese martyrs, 103 Korean martyrs, 106 primarily Vietnamese martyrs, 16 Japanese martyrs and 25 Mexican martyrs[15]. And so it went on. Up until his death on 02. April 2005 John Paul ll had altogether canonized exactly 488 deceased persons and beatified 1338 people (Internet http: www.zenit.org4/2005). Why was he doing this? Why was he burdening himself with this enormous additional workload? During our spiritual assessment, I became involved in an unplanned controversial discussion with a Catholic church-leader. He became angry, lost control somewhat and barked that the pope was in the process of gathering powers from everywhere to overcome the last Reformational

---

14 www.de.news.yahoo.com/021020/12/30ozt.html. In: Internet Associated Press News. Service of Oct. 20, 2003.
15 Compare „L'Osservatore Romano", No. 30/31 of July 27, 2001; Nr. 32/33 of 10.08.01; No. 34 of Aug. 24, 2001.

resistance. If you have followed until now, dear reader, you will be able to understand better what we wrote in the section about relics. Every beatified or canonized person signifies an increase in demonic spiritual power. Through the atrocious sins of consulting the spirits of the dead, demonic forces are literally attracted and only need to be organized by the Catholic institutions. People who worship "beatified persons" or "saints" lose their lives in part, which are then programmed to form a symbiotic union with the demons in the cosmos. They perform slave labour with the concentrated demonic force as invisible spiritual beings which take the place of the beatified persons or saints. This concentrated demonic force demonizes the corresponding worshippers and robs them of even more power of life.

Just try to lead such a regular saint-worshipper to the real Saviour Jesus Christ! Surely, you all know how hard that is! You can only lead a living person to Jesus. Therefore, it is extremely difficult to save someone from death through the One who is the life, Jesus Christ, when that person has already lost his/her life as described above. But those of us practicing pastoral care still fight for the lives of the "living dead" and gain victory.

24. The Celebration of the Eucharist in the Olympic Stadium in Berlin on June 23, 1996

130,000 Catholics were expected to attend the beatification mass, but, in fact, only 70,000 people came, according to generous estimates. From this figure about 20, 000 came from neighbouring Poland. The entire faculty of German Cardinals and Bishops was present. 600 communion-helpers alone marched into the stadium. The visible spiritual army of the pope, various secret orders such as Opus Dei and many restored fascistic orders of knights, marched through the stadium with runic banners and took their places on the sports-lawn of the stadium. Spiritual-demonic force exuded from this "power place", even if those unfamiliar with the scene may not have noticed. Everything was shrouded in a veil of decent conservatism.

We opposers of this idolatrous, demonic spectacle seated ourselves 10-15 meters below the politicians' box with the former president

Chapter 1: The Activation of Invisible Powers for an Ecumenism

of the Federal Republic of Germany, Roman Herzog, the former chancellor, Helmut Kohl, as well as several former state presidents of the old and new federal states.

Then the climax: the (Roman) gates of the stadium were opened and Pope John Paul II made one trip around the stadium in his bullet-proof "Pope-mobile" accompanied by cheering applause. Next came the announcement and appointment of the candidates for beatification. First, the pope preached about Matthew 10: 28-32 and described the beatified persons as models because they had found the centre of their lives in Christ. Tears stung in our eyes, knowing that Leisner, in particular, had not received his strength for resistance from Christ, but instead from the militant Marian order of the Schoenstatt movement near Koblenz, by totally surrendering his life to the Schoenstatt "Mary".

Then Pope John Paul proceeded to Jeremiah and said: "Jeremiah is the model of Christ and through Christ the model of all, who do not allow themselves to be deceived (see Jer. 20: 10); all, who put their faith in the power of God and hence bear away victory."[16]

That sounds good, but is not good, because the mouth of this pope serves the ancient serpent. This is another example of how the pope abuses God's Word with the intention to deceive. In Jeremiah 7 and 44, the cited prophet talks about the background reasons for apostasy from faith. It concerns the worship of the queen of heaven, who is called "Mary" in the Roman Church and continues to be praised and adored.

Jeremiah says to the Roman church today:

„*But they did not listen to me or pay attention. They were stiff-necked and did more evil than their forefathers. ... Truth has perished; it has vanished from their lips.*"

(Jer. 7,26.28b).

In the mouth of the highest representative of the Roman Church, God's Word is truth when it appears opportune to him. He, too, lives through the demonic power of the queen of heaven, not in the strength of the true Christ. The impressive words of this pope could not deceive us, even when he said the following with regards to the Catholic martyrs:

---

16 "L'Osservatore Romano", No. 26, June 28, 1996, p. 7.

"Christ is the way. B. Lichtenberg and K. Leisner bore witness to this in a time when many had left the right path and gone astray out of opportunism or fear. Whoever considers the way of these two martyrs, knows: Their martyrdom was not an accidental mishap on the paths of their lives, but instead the last and inevitable consequence of a life lived as a follower of Christ."[17]

These words of K. Leisner in his witness for Christ at a youth gathering in 1943 sound like a contradiction to his Marian devotion:

"We must serve – proclaim Christ to the youth."[18] "Karl entrusted himself to Mary. He made a bond of love with her in Schoenstatt, i.e. he devoted his life to her and she protects, promotes and supports it. She protects his life in her immaculate heart ..."[19]

In Catholicism, this is not a contradiction. Essentially, "Mary" and the Catholic "Christ" are interchangeable. Mary is seen as the "star of evangelism" and the carrier of all graces. A Catholic can only come to Christ through her.

This blasphemy makes it clear to us, as bible-based Christians, that the "Christ" to whom "Mary" leads is Satan's "redeemer" and that the Roman Church saves people from life into death, while the biblical Christ redeems the people that believe in Him from death into life!

This criticism of the Marian faith does not prevent us from having great respect for the courage of the two beatified persons, in a human sense. Unfortunately, there were only very few on the Protestant side who equalled them morally. But the fact remains with regards to the Vatican: "Mary", the queen of heaven, is always present, where Christ or his word is concerned, whether she is named or not.

25. Our task during the Celebration of the Eucharist

Although the four-and-a-half hours in the stadium were primarily dedicated to the appointment of the beatified persons by the pope, the Eucharist was the centre of attention, as always. The theological term is transubstantiation. According to Catholic doctrine, the "body of Christ" must literally be sacrificed anew with each mass,

---

17 "L'Osservatore Romano", No. 27, July 5, 1996, p. 2.
18 „Fire and Light", special edition, No. 24-IV. 1996, p. 5.
19 Ibid. p. 7.

the transformation of elements or the celebration of the Eucharist. Thus, "Christ" is said to be truly present as the crucified Lord. We will deal with this central Catholic-christologic subject later in detail. But it is already discernable, that this Eucharist has nothing to do with the Lord's Supper. During the celebration of the Eucharist, a conversion is brought about through transformation, or in other words, magic is practiced. When the pope then held up an especially large "suncake" (wafer) and showed it to the 70,000 people present, an enthusiastic excitement swept over the crowd. Several Catholic members of government demonstratively accepted the Eucharist.

In the total 4 1/2 hours, we found ourselves in a battle of prayer against the "eucharistic Christ" and his human representative. We experienced a lot of victory later in counselling. Praise and thanks be to the true Jesus Christ. We could see that the Catholic transcendental forces, which were also employed against us, became more and more ineffective, the longer the battle lasted.

The shaking of the pope's left hand increased and he appeared more and more frail, tired and absent-minded. Many believers worldwide prayed with us against this magical deception.

26. The Speech of the Pope at the Brandenburg Gate

In the evening of the same day, the pope bade farewell to the Berliners with a speech at the Brandenburg Gate, as it was said officially.

The pope also stood there as the political chief of the Vatican. In fairness, it must be acknowledged that few politicians in the world would have been able to give such an outstanding political speech, peppered with Christian ethics. This speech was published everywhere and can be referred to. To save space, I will repeat only those parts which are decisive for us.

It became apparent how well the pope of the world-church and the conservative, Catholic ex-chancellor Kohl had synchronized their speeches. Both talked about religious unity as the foundation for a strong European state, in which the three revelation religions, Christianity, Judaism and Islam, should make up leading elements. The German ex-chancellor thanked the pope for his merits in overcoming the division of Germany. The impression deepened:

John Paul II obviously anticipated that Kohl, like Charlemagne in 799, could be the partner for the Vatican to bring about the political union of Europe once the religious union had been achieved. After the political downfall of Kohl in January 2000, this hope bursted like a soap bubble.

Despite all these thoughts, we did not forget our task at the Brandenburg Gate. The transcendental, nationalistic and Catholic forces dispersed like fog after the battle of prayer. A very irritated pope left the speaker's desk.

We would like to encourage all those, who are reformation-minded for the sake of Christ, to take up the spiritual battle against the political as well as the religious Babylon.

We need free space worldwide, so that many people can still get to know the gospel of grace and find the salvation from sin and death through Christ Jesus.

Chapter II
The Roots of the "Cosmic Christ"

1. The Historical and Trend-Setting Situation at the Outset

The antichristian spirit has chosen the "cosmic Christ" to be the "redeemer" of the Roman world empire. The division of the Catholic Church into West and East Rome occurred in 1054 A.D, and the final political separation took place in 1453, through the fall of Constantinople. Today, we find ourselves on the threshold of a third phase of the Roman world system, namely the reunion of Western and Eastern Rome.

In this chapter, we will show our readers how the Roman Catholic Church has activated powers of cosmic blood-magic since the 9th century, the age of Charlemagne. Today they are bringing these old demonical forces into the new ecumenical movement. Furthermore, the Catholic Church and other ecumenically-minded churches are working towards a return to the old gnostic heresy that Jesus Christ became in one moment God, the second person of the Divine Trinity, that is the moment of his spiritual incarnation! This results in the depersonification of the Divine Trinity. The foundation of the early Christian teaching is to be destroyed and room made for the Catholic doctrine of three powers, or three aspects of power in the Trinity. This removes one of the main stumbling blocks for Judaism and Islam, i.e. that Jesus Christ is true God and true man in one person.

2. Salvation only through the Roman Church?

Justification through the grace of Christ and faith alone, in accordance with the Holy Scriptures, is not adequate in Rome's view. Additional grace must be conferred by Mary, the "mediatrix of all graces", through the seven Catholic sacraments. Their usage is claimed to be necessary for the personal salvation of the believers. Let us look at baptism as one example of additional sacramental salvation. Without baptism, there is no "candidacy" for redemption

Chapter II: The Roots of the "Cosmic Christ"

and inheritance of heaven available. Without baptism into the Roman Church, no one can become a child of God. In the 1960's Vatican II confirmed this doctrine, which had been adopted as a dogma by Pope Boniface VIII in 1301:

Extra Ecclesiam Nulla Salus: no salvation outside of the Catholic Church.

Another statement of this Vatican Council was "that the Catholic Church possesses the wealth of all revealed truth as well as all mediums of grace, and it is impossible to allow others a similar status." Therefore, mission in the Catholic sense means that all people of all confessions must be brought into the "one true church which is founded on Peter, the Rock." All seven sacraments of the Roman Church are necessary for the salvation of Catholics.

Under the authority of the former head of the "Congregation for the Doctrine of the Faith", once known as Holy Inquisition Authority, Cardinal Joseph Ratzinger published the pamphlet "Dominus Jesus" as a declaration on Sept. 8, 2000. Today Ratzinger has been chosen to be Pope Benedict XVI. Such a declaration is binding for the Catholic Church worldwide. It repeats the claim of the Catholic Church to sole representation of Jesus above all other confessions. This claim is even widened to rule over all non-Christian religions because the Roman Church exclusively contains all truths in perfection. We are citing here from this declaration, published unabridged in the L'Osservatore Romano No. 36, Sept. 8, 2000.

First, Ratzinger shows his reverence to the alleged common roots of all religions referring to the Vatican Council II from 1962-1965 with the following quotation:

"In the Council's declaration about the relationship between the Church and the non-Christian religions, it is stated openly and positively: The Catholic Church does not reject anything that is true and holy in these religions." Some rules and lifestyles do differ from what the church "itself holds true, but not rarely they (the non-Christian religions) show rays of the same truth that illuminates all human beings." The inter-religious dialogue is cultivated because it accompanies the "missio ad gentes." "on account of that mystery of unity of all redeemed people who supposedly share through varying forms in the one and same secret of salvation in Jesus Christ through the Holy Spirit." This dialogue is now an important aspect of the missionary work of the church. It allegedly leads to an enrichment and is supposed to be an act of obedience to the truth and an expression of "the respect for freedom."

Despite this "Jesuit truth", Ratzinger maintains that the declaration should help "reject certain wrong or ambiguous positions." In typical Jesuit dialectic style, he abruptly shifted into the reverse gear of Catholic conservatism, after going full speed ahead in the spirit of universalism to impress the non-Christian religions with the goal of one world religion. He talks about the "universal mediation of salvation by the Church, the subsistence of the one church of Christ in the Catholic Church." With this, he unmistakably said that the Roman Church does not even need the others because it exists or subsists through itself und is, therefore, independent of and superior to all other religions.

Ratzinger then turns critically to the Protestant denominations. He categorically states the sovereignty and control of the Roman Church over the interpretation of the Holy Scriptures, just as it was done in the past:

The Catholic tradition functions as the control for the understanding of the Bible.
- The Bible is subordinate to the tradition and follows the principles of a "dynamic exegesis of tradition."
- It is complained that "there is, after all, a tendency to read and explain the Holy Scriptures without consideration of tradition and the ecclesiastical lectureship."

Furthermore, the document argues that the doctrines of other religions do not supplement the sum total of religious revelation to attain the fullness of the truth.

"The opinion that the revelation of Jesus Christ is limited, incomplete, imperfect and complementary in relationship to those in other religions opposes the faith of the church."

If considered independently, i.e. without the control of the Roman tradition, this sentence about the biblical revelation of Jesus Christ appears correct. But, nevertheless, it is wrong because the statement refers to the mystical body of Christ, meaning the Catholic Church with its tradition. The Roman Church understands itself as the immanent, the visible procurator of Jesus Christ. The title of the Pope as "Representative of God", the title Pontifex Maximus, or supreme bridge-builder comes from this understanding.

In light of the unchanged self-image of the Roman Church, it is more than surprising that almost everybody is seeking "dialogue" with the Catholic Church. A dialogue with the goal of unification must be described as absurd and meaningless under these circumstances. The purpose of this absurdity is that Rome is attempting to integrate the Christian denominations, the non-Christian religions and the philosophical religious systems into the "fullness of their perfect truth." This can be called religious globalization and hostile takeover of all other religious systems, to use the fashionable words of capitalism.

The declaration also observes that the convictions and religious experiences of other religions are only fragments of truth. From the perspective of Rome they never can be the whole truth. Therefore, the absolute revealed truth of the Roman Church can not be equated with the religious experiences of other religions since they "are still in search of the absolute truth" and also lack "their approval (confession) of the self-revealing God".

It is said that God wants to call all people to Himself in Christ and give them the "fullness of his revelation and his love." According to Rome, God also discloses Himself in other religions through the "wealth of their spirituality", even if these contain "gaps, shortcomings and errors. So, the holy books of other religions, which, in fact, lead and nourish the lives of their followers, receive **from the mystery of Christ the elements of the good and the grace that they contain."**

Ratzinger states that the mystery of Christ lives out of its inner unity. God is said to have "established the church [Roman Church] as a mystery of salvation. He, Himself, is in the church and the church is in Him." Consequently, if you believe in the unique role of Jesus Christ as mediator of salvation, then that is only valid in conjunction with the faith of the Roman Church. Jesus Christ expects faith and, therefore, the world must "firmly believe in the uniqueness of the Church founded by Him and in the (perfect) truth of the Catholic faith." As a result of this reasoning, the Roman Church is the "only perfect and true Church of Jesus Christ." Further, it must be acknowledged "that there is a historical continuity between the

Catholic Church and the Church founded by Christ, rooted in the apostolic succession."

Hence, the true church is believed to exist only in the Roman Church, while merely "varied elements of sanctification and truth can be found" in the other Christian churches and communities. Because these Protestant churches have left the fullness of the truth and grace, they must be brought back to recognizing the primacy of Rome, "its apostolic succession and the valid Eucharist." That is the only way for them to "become true partial (participating) churches again." The recognition of the primacy of Rome is, of course, inseparably bound to the primacy of the Pope, rooted in the apostolic succession and the continuity of salvation.

As long as the other Christian churches have not adopted these Catholic essentials, they are not counted as "partial churches" and must content themselves with the status of communities which only contain pieces of the truth and grace. They are pushed into the same corner where non-Christian religions are found. The Roman Church sees itself as the "comprehensive sacrament of salvation" and therefore has "**an indispensable relationship to the salvation of each and every person, according to God's plan.**"[20]

3. The Sacrifice of the Mass – The Eucharist

In order to understand the character of the Roman Eucharist, we have to look at the decisive roots of the eucharistic or cosmic Christ. If we understand the Eucharist in its very nature as an instrument of the Roman Catholic revelation of Christ, then we will also understand that the Jesus Christ preached in the Catholic Church and the Christ revealed in the Bible are not the same. Due to its very nature, the Eucharist is not the same as the Lord's Supper celebrated in the Protestant Churches. It is instead the magical scheme of an Anti-Church. It is the deliberate forgery of the Lord's Supper. At the end of the words of institution in 1 Cor. 11: 25+26, we read: "This cup is the new covenant in my blood. Do this, as often as you drink it, in remembrance of me. For as often as you eat this bread and drink the cup, you proclaim the Lord's death until he comes."

---
20 „L'Osservatore Romano", No. 36, Sept. 8, 2000, p. 7-11.

This biblical admonition stands in irreconcilable opposition to Roman Catholic teaching. The Catholic doctrine states that Christ is truly and **bodily present in the sacrament of the Eucharist.** The consecration of the bread, also called sun-cake or wafer, and the wine transforms the substances into the real body and the real blood of the Lord Jesus. The immanent, material objects intended for remembering and proclaiming Jesus' sacrificial death for the sin of man are transformed into a mystic-demonical transcendence. The demonic power is brought into real existence and exhibited through arbitrary repetition. That is what the Latin word "Mass" means. In other words, Jesus Christ is supposed to be transformed back into the Saviour dying on the cross in each Mass through transcendental consecration. Therefore, he is sacrificed anew in each celebration or sacrifice of the Mass, as it is called in most languages! In Heb. 6: 6 and 10: 12-14,26,29, we are warned against such machinations. God calls them abominable sins out of the realm of magic and witchcraft. The transformation happens through the magical act of consecration. This transformation is called "transubstantiation" in theological terminology. Why does it need to take place again? In Heb. 9: 24-10: 18, we are taught that Jesus, as the sacrificial lamb without blemish, offered Himself for our sins once and for all times, so that it can never be repeated. Please read Heb. 7: 27 as well. For this reason, our Redeemer, Jesus Christ, was able to proclaim triumphantly, "It is finished" (John 19: 30), shortly before His death on the cross. This leads to the conclusion that the Eucharist is an expression of rebellion against the clear statement of God emphasizing the single and unique sacrificial death of Jesus. Indirectly, the Roman Church says that the salvation through the single and unique sacrificial death of Christ is unfinished and, therefore, incomplete.

There is no reliable redemption from sin through the sacrificial death of Christ found in Catholic theology, but only a possibility of redemption through the acceptance of the Mass-sacrifice received as sacrament. In reality, every Mass a Catholic hears will only be consolation to him, a plea for forgiveness. According to them every Mass will reduce more or less the punishment for his or her sins. Through the Mass and the holy sacrifice, Jesus Christ does something for sinners. With each Mass, the time to be spent in purgatory is shortened.²¹ **So the purpose of the each Mass is to work off or reduce sins through the celebration of the "sacrament of salvation."** The Roman Chatholic Eucharist is not a remembrance of The Last Supper where Jesus Christ`s complete sacrifice for all sin is made quite clear and is not to be repeated. But the Roman Eucharist belongs to the area of occult magic as it is believed to be the holy sacrifice itself, the mass or in theological words the transubstantiation. The single and unique sacrifice of Christ is denied through this so-called sacrament. In Gal. 1: 8, the Apostle Paul tells us that anyone who preaches a different gospel is accursed. The Mass is a different gospel! More precisely it needs to be said that in the Roman Church no gospel in the sense of the good news of grace and complete forgiveness is preached. In order to fake a Bible believing faith Rome cites the passage in John 6: 53 and takes it out of the context of Jesus' sermon: "... *unless you eat the flesh of the Son of Man and drink his blood, you have no life in you.*" Through its magical understanding of the Scriptures and the seduction to "transcendental cannibalism", the Catholic Church proves itself to be a magical church once again. The one who believes in Him and lives through Him can only "eat and drink" Christ. Please read the whole context starting with John 6: 35ff. The Eucharist or the Mass is the unimpeachable foundation for the activities of the "cosmic, eucharistic Christ." Here lie the roots of this antichristian spirit which, in turn, is charged up or strengthened by such magic. In the Eucharist, this spirit appears in transcendental reality. After the Mass, the consecrated alter bread is placed in the tabernacle, the tent of the most holy, for safekeeping as the Host. At this place the "sun-cake" can be worshipped. We can recognize that this Christ is indeed a different Christ, a forgery by the spirit of the Antichrist. Through invocative consecration, Roman Catholic magic and mysticism produce a Christ from the kingdom of darkness. In other words, the entire Roman Catholic Church is a mega-sect-institution which builts up its transcendental power through witchcraft and magic. In case some of our readers might think that we are only relying on old Vatican views which are of lesser importance today, we will quote John Paul II the predecessor of the present Pope with regards to his beliefs on the sacrament of the Eucharist.

---

21 See Hunt, „Global peace and the coming of the antichrist", 1990, p.311.

In a sermon concerning the alleged grave of the Apostle Peter in the Roman Basilica, the Pope spoke about the "cup of salvation" landing in the hands of Rome.

Pope John Paul II said: "This cup came to us from the Room of the Last Supper. We received it through the intervention of an apostolic successor of Christ, Himself, the only and eternal priest." Further, he explained that the sacrifice of Jesus "in a bloody manner was executed only once in history [on the cross, the author]. But He [Jesus, the author] wants this decisive event to remain present for all times, so that every generation of people on the face of the Earth can experience it in their time to a certain extent." Then the Pope quoted the words of institution from Luke 22: 19+20 and came to the following conclusion: **"The apostles receive his body in the form of bread and his blood in the form of wine** from the hands of Christ, Himself: That is how the first and original eucharistic consecration was performed!" This magical understanding of the Word of God has lured the Western World away from the Supper of the Lord or Holy Communion, and replaced it with the everlasting Mass-sacrifice in the Eucharist.

"In a mysterious, yet real way, we, too, take part in the Last Supper of the Lord when we raise our hands over the bread and the wine and pray: send your spirit down upon these gifts and bless them that they become for us the body and blood of your Son, our Lord Jesus Christ. The Holy Spirit thus causes the human gifts of bread and wine to become the body and blood of Christ, just like in the room of the Last Supper back then. In this way, the community of believers receives the great sacrament of salvation through the priest in the form of bread and wine when they celebrate the great **mystery of faith.**"[22]

4. The Magic Word – The Fragmentary Dilemma

Magical actions require magical thinking. The transcendent world reveals itself to the magician as soon as he takes the Word of God "literally", i.e. tears it out of context to use only word fragments. Through the fragmentary use of the Bible verses, the con-

---

22 „L'Osservatore Romano", No. 47, Nov. 22, 1996, p. 11.

textual coherency is nullified. A completely different understanding of the written Word develops and becomes a theological pillar in the church tradition. A fragmentary use of the Word of God always leads to heretical doctrines or false theology. The magical use of words is not restricted to the Roman theology. Even Protestant biblicism can become heresy through fragmentation of the Bible, when allegedly biblical doctrine turns out to be an abuse of God's Word. According to such heresy, power is attributed to a single word or spoken sentence, in itself. For example, a Protestant bible-adhering Christian may suddenly become fearful of an attack by powers of darkness. Then one often hears an expression which is similar to a magical invocation: "I place myself under the blood of Christ!" Such a practice can not be found anywhere in the biblical context. A sentence in the Bible can be taken literally as a fragment, only to reveal magical piety in the end. Let us look at another example for better understanding:

In Phil 2: 12+13 we read: "... work out your own salvation with fear and trembling, for it is God who is at work in you, enabling you both to will and to work for his good pleasure."

In the first part of verse 12, the responsibility for the perfection of salvation is placed on the believer. This is what the Catholic Church puts special emphasis on. If considered fragmentarily, verse 13 tells us that God takes full responsibility for the completion of salvation, without any contribution by the saved person. That is how it is primarily taught in Protestantism. Now which is correct? According to true biblical understanding, the grace that comes from God works together in every situation with the faith of the redeemed person. Please read James 2: 22. One is incomplete without the other and has more of a juridical than a practical meaning. Verses 12 and 13 must be considered in the whole context of Scripture if we want to understand correctly God's intention mentioned here. Fragmentary consideration of a biblical text finally leads to apostasy. In addition, the danger of falling into the anti-faith of magic appears. The fragmentary use of a text forms the basis for magic. It is typical for this thinking that the reader looks only at one sentence or one word to which spiritual, or more precise transcendent powers are attributed. To receive more power in a life crisis, these words must be recited repeatedly in order to unfold the desired power.

In such a case, a believer is definitely not acting in the sense of delegated responsibility for the completion of his salvation, according to verse 12, because he is being unwilling and disobedient to God's word. If this believer is asked about his lack of zeal in faith, he cites verse 13 for his personal protection. His conscience is placated every time he repeats verse 13. Power flows to him from this word. This power "helps" him, so that he does not need to change in accordance with the whole biblical standard! This thinking is found in Charismatic circles as the same song verses are often repeated many times. The "power" becomes greater with every repetition of the song. That is how a certain song or word creates power. As a result, Christians hungry for magical power are unable to learn. They only need their word, their biblical promise, which they use like a Hindu Mantra or magic formula. Such believers dismiss all comprehensive learning as "Catholic justification by works." But, in fact, these believers are closer to Catholicism, which is built solely on magic, than to their Protestant tradition of the reformation.

5. The Magic of the Roman Church

Let us turn our attention back to the magical theology of Rome. When Jesus was joined by his disciples during the Last Supper, none of them thought of taking Jesus' words literally, or magically, when he said: "this is my body. (...) this is my blood of the covenant" (Matthew 26: 26-28). Neither the bread nor the wine that Jesus shared actually became His body or his blood during this ceremony that took place so many years ago in history. Jesus never said that the shared bread would turn into his real body later when His Supper would be celebrated by the believers. The Roman Church insists on "taking Jesus at his word", instead of understanding Jesus through his Word by understanding the meaning **and** context of his words. This spiritual pride and arrogance is a kind of biblicism of the worst possible magical form. The practice of such a "Lord's Supper" occurs as a magic ritual which is based on tradition and contains invocation formulae. The Mass or Eucharist is theologically known as transubstantiation and called by the Catholics consecration or even literally change of element. It is a biblicistical and magical spectacle which releases demonic, cosmic powers and demonizes its participants.

It needs to be concluded that the Roman Eucharist is a counterfeit of the Lord's Supper. The true ceremony is meant to be a remembrance of his unique, never-to-be-repeated sacrificial death for our sins. Mysterious doctrines around the Eucharist are supposed to lead to devotion and personal union with God. However, they create the "mystical body of Christ" through witchcraft. For this reason they stem from the dark world of magic. The consequences for the people are inevitable. Such occult practices are subject to punishment and, hence, the curse of God. Therefore, the Mass or the Eucharist constitutes an abominable sin of magic that falls under the curse of death. Because the Mass portrays the incessant sacrifice of Christ, its practice and theology stand in irreconcilable opposition to the one and unique sacrificial death of Christ, as proclaimed by the Holy Scriptures (Heb 10: 14, 9: 25-28).

Since this Catholic Christ is continuously sacrificed every day around the world, he is symbolically portrayed as hanging on the cross, i.e. as Corpus Cruzifixus. The thought behind this tradition is the rebellious assumption that Jesus did not fully complete the work of salvation. The blasphemy of scorning and belittling the non-recurring and completed sacrificial death can be seen clearly in the following statement of the woman who was known as Mother Teresa of Calcutta during her lifetime. She was beatified after her death and is revered by many Protestants too. She said once: "It is beautiful to see the humility of Christ (…) in his permanent state of humility in the tabernacle, where He degrades himself to such a small piece of bread, that the priest can hold Him in two fingers."[23]

That is why Martin Luther spoke of the Eucharist as an "unspeakable atrocity, completely contrary to the principle of justification through faith alone."[24] Calvin expressed himself even more clearly and without theological flourishes: "It is Satan's attempt to falsify the Holy Communion of Christ and to shroud it in thick darkness."[25]

The book by Michael de Semlyen, already cited, gives further explanation on page 46:

---

23 „In der Stille des Herzens", Mutter Teresa, 1983. In: Semlyen, „All Roads lead to Rome", 1993, Ch. 2.
24 Semlyen, „All Roads lead to Rome", 1993, Ch. 2.
25 Ibid. p. 42.

Chapter II: The Roots of the "Cosmic Christ"

"The English Reformers flatly rejected the doctrine of the real presence of Christ in the Mass and insisted on the key words in 1.Cor. 11: 24 "in remembrance of me." As a result, many of them were burned at the stake. (...) They died because they rejected a doctrine that, according to their conviction, darkened or even destroyed the whole system of Christian truth."[26]

6. The Holy Blood and the Magic of the Blood

If we have followed so far, the next question arises about what sources the blood-magic of the Eucharist feeds on. Every reader has surely noticed that the crucified Lord is depicted with a bleeding wound in the right side throughout Western countries. In many Catholic Churches, especially Italian ones where the so-called "Holy-Saturday-Christ" is shown, a blood-covered "Christ" lies in a glass coffin. Occidental Catholic history is always a history of blood. A conspicuous trend developed at the Carolingian court of Charlemagne in the 9th century that reached its climax in the glorification of the holy blood. Worship of relics and saints were part of this as well. The fragmentary consideration of salvation unavoidably led from the practice of "literalistic faith" to blood-magic. This had very practical consequences for the Western Cultures. No value was attached to the blood of humans as the carrier of life. Therefore the history of the Catholic Occident is a history of bloodthirstiness in every respect.

The Abbot Waldo of Reichenau (Lake Constance) was the historian who wrote about these theological blood trends at the court of Charlemagne. We have no doubts about the historical assessment which says that the beginning of the anti-church, i.e. the church out of the antichristian spirit, dates back to the 9th century under Charlemagne. Therefore, it is not surprising that in this century magic, witchcraft and blood-cults took the postition of Christian faith and turned everything upside down. During this time, the Germanic blood-cult was revived in Germany and integrated into the rising "Holy Roman Empire of German Nation." Fragments of the true faith in Christ replaced the bloodthirsty heathen gods. The power of the shed blood, produced by magic rituals in the consecration, was

---
26 Ibid. p. 46.

Chapter II: The Roots of the "Cosmic Christ"

already praised back then. For the deception of the people, it was furnished with the attributes of the death of Jesus on the cross, in accordance with several fragments of true salvation. That is called exoteric representation, which people are supposed to believe. But, inside this anti-church, completely different laws reigned and still reign. Since this 9th century, the Roman Catholic Church has become increasingly a typical secret organization or mystery religion. Only insiders can decipher the mysteries, and only they know that the Roman Church has turned into the world organization of an esoteric, i.e. hidden system. Further, this blood-magic is the source for the "cosmic Christ" arisen out of the realm of magic. Without hesitation, we can also call him the "instead-of-, anti- or against-Christ" because he is the "alternative" out of Satan's counterfeit factory. Let us come back to the abbot mentioned earlier, the historian of Charlemagne. When he writes "about the precious blood of our Lord Jesus Christ through which the human race was saved from the power of its archenemy", truly redeemed people should not allow themselves to be deceived by these biblical words. These statements were exoteric, i.e. meant for the public. Somewhat later, we are told by the abbot that he is not speaking about the historical Jesus Christ whom he supposedly praises for his sacrificial death. Instead, he is referring to the pictorial representation of the cross in Niedermünster which he praises and worships as a "relic of the first bloodshed of Christ."[27] This is typical of all kinds of esoteric systems. The secret motives or intentions and the true background as well as the dynamic cosmic powers are kept hidden from the outside, only accessible to those who have climbed several steps up into the hierarchy. For the outsiders, the cross of Jesus is depicted as the salvation from sins in this world. However, when a believer reveres and worships a secretly, i.e. occultly, consecrated cross in any given location, he comes under the spell of esoteric, cosmic forces. These powers are not recognizable to our natural senses. Such a cross is indeed not the cross and the body of our Lord Jesus Christ, our Saviour, who died for our sins. In these powers the roots of the everlasting sacrifice, the never-ending suffering, i.e. the incomplete and unfinished sacrifice are found! In blood-magical theology, the

---

27 Stein, Weltgeschichte im Lichte des Heiligen Gral", 1986, p. 14.(World History in the Light of the Holy Grail The Ninth Century).

sacrificial death of Jesus Christ in our place and his perfect salvation is ignored. Instead, the substance of the "blood" itself, brings salvation, but only in the sense of "relief and hope", of course!

And yet, Jesus the Christ has brought us the one and only atonement for all of our sins through the blood He shed, once and for all times (Heb. 9: 12). The one and unique sacrifice of Jesus was in our place. It does not need to be repeated because it is final and has brought about salvation for humankind. This Jesus is alive! He is risen from the dead. *"He is the image of the invisible God,"* (Col. 1: 15). *"... and through him God was pleased to reconcile to himself all things, whether on earth or in heaven, by making peace through the blood of his cross."* (Col.1: 20) *"... he has now reconciled in his body of flesh by his death, in order to present you holy and blameless and above reproach before him"* (Col.1: 22). Our worship, our reverence and our love belong to the living Jesus Christ, both God and man. He bore vicariously the sins of all people on the cross. He revoked through His resurrection eternal death as the consequence and punishment of sin. Thus He destroyed the works of the devil by His complete and final salvation.

„[...] he forgave us all our trespasses, erasing the record that stood against us with its legal demands. He set this aside, nailing it to the cross. He disarmed the rulers and authorities and made a public example of them, triumphing over them in it." (Col. 2: 13b-15)

In the cited biblical passages, we can clearly see the past tense used. The original Greek text uses the Aorist which describes past occurrences as completed actions and finished processes.[28] Jesus has completely borne our sins and conquered our eternal death,

---

28 The historic aorist (tempus) is sometimes used in the New Testament to describe overwhelming facts, for example:
· He made himself nothing (Phil. 2: 7)
· He humbled himself (Phil. 2: 8)
· He died (1. Cor. 15: 3)
· Christ was raised from the dead (Romans 6: 4)
· He gave him (His son) up (Romans 8: 32)
· He offered himself without blemish (Hebr. 9: 14)
· He glorified his servant Jesus (Apost. 3: 13)
compare. Hoffmann, Siebenthal, „Greek Grammar in the New Testament", 1985, p. 325.

Chapter II: The Roots of the "Cosmic Christ"

if we have confessed our sins, repented from them and therefore experienced forgiveness through Christ (1.John 1: 9). In light of these biblical observations, how can an institution which sees itself as the successor of the apostles claim that the Lord's Supper signifies a continuous dying of Jesus without the characteristic of finality? And, with respect to salvation, how can it allege that the punishment for sins is "more or less" reduced through Jesus' death? How can salvation be only a matter of pleading for forgiveness as the sins of the believer have not been forgiven yet?

Here is my answer, without flourishes:

They can do this because their institution is the biggest secret, esoteric organization of the world, originating from the spirit of the Antichrist. As we are obliged to love the truth, we are on the side of the Reformation and state bluntly:

The Roman Catholic Church is the work of blood-magical, cosmic-demonic spiritual powers. In truth, it is a power-hungry, religious world organization which holds the baptized Catholic people in degrading dependence through blood magic. In the end, there is no forgiveness. Therefore, it is implied that Jesus Christ died for them in vain!

In this "church", the salvation-bringing signs of the cross and Jesus' blood are declared to be salvation in themselves. The constantly exposed sign is the salvation for this anti-church. The historical person, Jesus Christ, is no longer the Saviour. That explains why one needs consecrated crosses, called Corpus Crucifixus, everywhere that are supposed to bring salvation to all worshippers. In the hidden reality of the Roman Church, these magically consecrated crosses restore the harmony with the cosmos or fallen world.

This church belongs to the world and the world belongs to this world-church!

The magical theology of the blood must also preserve the substance of the "blood". For this reason it is brought to holy places as a relic in order to keep it through the sorcery of transubstantiation. These atrocities began with Charlemagne in the 9th century and the Abbot Waldo of Reichenau. The paintings depicting the dying keeper of the blood relic handing the vessel with Christ's blood over to the abbot, as well as the passing-on of the blood relic to Charlemagne, can still be admired today in the church of Reichenau – Mittelzell an Island on Lake Constance, Germany.

7. Faith as Motive for Acting According to the Demands of the Law

In the Old Covenant, all invisible, spiritual facts of salvation were shown to the People of God through material images. By living out of faith, as Abraham did, and fulfilling the natural material demands of the Mosaic law, they became righteous in the eyes of God, having satisfied the legal ordinances of Yahwe. The invisible spiritual world of God entered into their lives as a preliminary, not final, shadow image. A visible translation of the invisible was created, to be seen and touched by the believers. Out of invisible motivation, i.e. out of faith, they had to physically fulfill the visible demands of the Mosaic law and all other legal orders (James 2: 17+21-26). Jesus' repeated confrontations with the theologically educated Pharisees stemmed from their desire to fulfill the visible law in the flesh, but without the invisible aspect of motivation which is faith. Jesus reproached them for confirming their authority by the fact that they are Abraham's children by the flesh. But because they wanted to carry out the visible letter of the law without the spirit of the law, i.e. faith (John 8: 37-45), they changed sides, perhaps without even noticing. "*And without faith it is impossible to please God*" (Hebr. 11 v.6). Because they did not want to believe, they were given Satan, as their father (punishment for sin), in place of God (John 8: 44). Jesus states the reason in Verses 37 and 39: "because there is no place in you for my word. If you were Abraham's children, you would be doing what Abraham did." Abraham worked deeds out of faith (James 2: 21). The people of old did not come into the righteousness and salvation of God despite adhering to the law: "but Israel, who did strive for the righteousness that is based on the law, did not succeed in fulfilling that law. Why not? Because they did not strive for it on the basis of faith, but as if it were based on works …"(Rom. 9: 31+32). Jesus Christ fulfilled the law, as the visible framework of faith, which is invisible. "For Christ is the end of the law so that there may be righteousness for everyone who believes." (Rom. 10: 4). What is now left for the follower of the law? **He needs to believe in Jesus**

Chapter II: The Roots of the "Cosmic Christ"

Christ as the personification of the <u>fulfilled</u> law and put his faith in Him as the Godly person, according to Abraham's model of faith. How has this become possible? **"Christ redeemed us from the curse of the law by becoming a curse for us," (Gal. 3: 13)!** Jesus has taken the punishment for sin, the curse of all people, upon Himself, instead of laying it on us. This caused His death as He gave his life, and shed his blood for us. As a result, we are saved from sin and the punishment of sin, eternal death, if we believe in Jesus as our Redeemer. This salvation from eternal death happened in the past on the cross and is valid for the present, the future, and for all eternity!

This uniqueness of Jesus' sacrifice on the cross must not be weakened. The Roman Catholic Church says that the sins of man are merely reduced by this sacrifice[29]. But in John 19: 30 we read "It is finished". This final satement of Jesus shows that he took the curse of our sins upon himself for all time. Those who do not believe this must carry their curse for themselves as Jesus cannot carry the curse for disbelievers. Rome magically transforms this past occurrence and finality of Jesus' death on the cross into a "continuous dying out of humility" into the present through the worship and reverence of consecrated crosses and relics. Those who do this, as Catholics do, cannot really be saved.

We are redeemed through faith. No law, no tradition, and no work of salvation conjured into the present is necessary as a supplement!

The Roman Catholic Church finds itself in the deepest curse of the holy and righteous God through its insistence on self-assertion. It is the incarnation of "Babylon, the great whore", mentioned in Rev. 17: 1, who shed the blood of the true martyrs and is entangled in the curse of blood-magic! It scorns the blood that Christ shed once and for all time for our salvation!

For the joy of our believing readers, I would like to mention several biblical passages that tell us about the uniqueness and the complete, final salvation of faith through the voluntary sacrifice of Jesus' life in the shedding of his blood:

Mat. 26: 28: The blood of the covenant through Jesus' sacrificial death.

---
29 See Hunt, „Global peace and the coming of the antichrist", 1990, p. 311.

Chapter II: The Roots of the "Cosmic Christ"

- Acts 20: 28: Obtained through his blood.
- Rom. 5: 9: Justified by his blood.
- 1 Peter 1: 18+19: Redeemed through his blood.
- 1 John 1: 7 His blood cleanses us from all sin
- Heb.9: 14 the blood of Christ cleanses our conscience
- Rev.1: 5 he washed us from our sins by His blood

8. The Holy Grail – the Magical, Esoteric Blood Relic

Another source of Catholic blood-magic, which lies even deeper, is the story of the Grail. Before we deal with it, let us look at the history, or rather, the legends surrounding the Grail.

The following story is told: [30]

A famous man from Palestine had heard of the unparalleled battles and miracles of Charlemagne in the 9th century. He glorified the blood that Charlemagne shed to promote the rise of the Occident and saw in him the incarnation of the cosmic Christ. This man from Jerusalem wished to be allowed to see "the dear features of the imperial face." He wanted to give the emperor "such a treasure, the likes of which had never been brought into the Franconian Kingdom."

Pope Leo II was asked to act as a mediatory between Charlemagne and this mysterious man. The pope sent messengers to the imperial palace in Aachen (Aix la Chapelle), today in Germany, with an ardent plea to accept the gift: "If you are the man the whole world and the universe think you are, the very most Glorified and Celebrated, then you should not spare your life until you have acquired such a treasure."

In this story, we see how Charlemagne was supposed to be made a "redeemer". The papacy of the 9th century became the agent of the Antichrist. The Roman religion and the Roman Empire co-operated with each other for the purpose of integrating religion and worldwide political power to reach the goal of one world government.[31] Charlemagne refused to go personally to receive the treasure. "The emperor was afraid of the dangers of the sea." Rome's

---

30 See Stein, „Weltgeschichte im Lichte des Heiligen Gral", 1986, p. 13+. (World History in the Light of the Holy Grail).
31 See Chapter I.

esoterics immediately declared "that Charlemagne had too little faith to rule the 'sea of nations' and therefore did not travel on the sea of the emotional spiritual world." Thus, this 'Christ-to-be', this carrier of Christ in the sense of incarnation had not enough faith, even though he "possessed the sceptre through the powers of the heavens".

Charlemagne finally decided to travel to Rome by land. The mysterious man from David's City travelled by sea to meet him and came as far as the Island of Corsica. Charlemagne was afraid to board the ship bound for Corsica. Then the enigmatic carrier of the treasure became seriously ill and was therefore unable to ferry across the sea to meet the emperor. The Pope was getting nervous, insisting that the treasure must be obtained at all costs. Charlemagne sent two men to Corsica in his place, one of which was the Abbott Waldo of Reichenau. The treasure was brought to Sicily. After making a pilgrimage there, barefoot and in a penitent's gown, Charlemagne found the treasure venerably arranged. "As an ardent worshipper of God he took it to his chapel." The sanctity of the treasure was kept with great reverence. The sick carrier never recovered from his illness and died. He had not found a worthy successor for the treasure since the candidate for the incarnation of the "cosmic Christ" had too little faith. What did the mysterious treasure consist of? It included an "ampoule of onyx, filled with the blood of the Redeemer as well as a small golden cross with tiny diamonds, which enclosed the blood of Christ with its four arms and also carried a sliver of Christ's cross in the centre. The treasure also contained the crown of thorns that had adorned the head of our dear Saviour and one of the nails in addition to wood from the cross of the Lord (…)." This blood relic of the first order, allegedly from the Lord, landed on the island of Reichenau on Lake Constance and was hailed as "the salvation." The treasures were kept locked up in the tabernacle or shrine, the Holy of Holies. This is the shortened version of what the historian Waldo of Reichenau reported.[32]

---

[32] See Stein, „Weltgeschichte im Lichte des Heiligen Gral", 1986, p 13+ (World History in the Light of the Holy Grail).

9. The Esoteric Fraction of Roman Catholicism in the Century of Charlemagne

Waldo belonged to the clerical, esoteric fraction of Grail-searchers at the 9th century court of Charlemagne. For the ears of the public, the "treasure" is officially or exoterically called the "blood and cross relic", not "Grail". Similar legends exist outside the church, such as "King Arthur's Round Table" in the Celtic culture. According to this series of legends, Charlemagne would have been an unworthy Parzival. Here, the sick grail-keeper passed on the magical power of "Christ's" blood. He died because he could not find a successor worthy to take over the rule of the world, i.e. the Antichrist. For the Celts, the grail-keeper was a sick fisher-king. It may only be coincidence, but the mitre of the Pope also originated from the fish-god Dagon. Was this, or could this have possibly been, to identify the Pope as the esoteric fisher-king?

Now we will leave the esoteric legend behind and turn to the biblical account. It is a historical fact that Jesus shed his blood for us on the cross! The salvation-bringing effect of his voluntary sacrificial death in our place happened in the past but reaches into the present and the future. Therefore, the mere "mention" of the blood shed 2000 years ago in the sacrifice of Christ's life is history! However, the salvation produced by his death remains effective until the end of time in a transcendent spiritual way. Whoever wants to add to this once only sacrifice betrays this truth! He inevitably ends up caught in the demonic power of blood-magic. Due to their "theology of the holy blood", it is logical that the Roman Church must preserve the blood as a "substance" and bring it to a "holy place". It inevitably followed that Rome also carried out in the course of history transcendent, esoteric transformations of other substances, such as bread and wine, using magic and rituals. This is familiar to all occultists as it originated from the system of witchcraft.

10. The Close Association Between the Grail and the Eucharistic Chalice

The Chalice of the Eucharist has a history of its own. We have all surely seen representations of the cross in Catholic churches showing the crucified Christ with a wound in his right side just under the ribs. According to John 19: 33+34, the soldiers did not break his legs, but instead "one of the soldiers pierced his side with a spear and at once blood and water came out." Based on this, the esoteric Catholic tradition has created a lung-wound on the right side. The so-called Catholic folk-piety as well as the secularized esoteric circles concocted legends like the following:

A Roman soldier, named Longinus, is said to have pressed the spear into Jesus' right side, causing the "holy blood" to flow into a bowl. Interestingly, this must have been the blood of the dead body of Christ since the Bible reports that Jesus was already dead when the soldier pierced his side (John 19: 33+34). It was not the blood of the dying Lord who was still alive.

"Grail" is derived from the old French word for "container or bowl." In the old Latin language, "gradalis" means stepped chalice. It is conspicuous that the chalice for the magical celebration of the Eucharist, which started in the 9th century, was shaped like a bowl with a stem. The bowl-chalice or stepped chalice and the subject of the Grail seem to be inseparable. One thrives on the other. Further, the legend reports that this Grail with the "holy blood" from Jesus' right side, his lung wound, was brought to Europe by Joseph of Arimathia. Whoever is in possession of the blood, i.e. the Grail, has power over everything. Under certain circumstances, he is even worthy of becoming the incarnation of the returning "cosmic Christ", (and this is always the Antichrist).

Image 1:
Eucharist Chalice

Besides the Grail being seen as a sign of religious world dominion, historical legends also developed around the "holy spear" of Longinus as a symbol of political world power. Hitler for example, sought to obtain this "spear of fate." It was in the possession of the former Habsburg dynasty, but he claimed it for himself. Today, the spear belongs to Austria and is displayed for reverence in the Hofburg in Vienna.

Chapter II: The Roots of the "Cosmic Christ"

This should be mentioned for the sake of completeness. The minnesinger, Wolfram von Eschenbach, who lived in the 12th/13th century, was the first to treat the theme of the Holy Grail in poetry, with reference to the knight Parzival and Arthur's Round Table. For all esoteric carriers of the antichristian spirit, a decisive factor of their own self-image was the quest to gain possession of the Holy Grail. The blood relics of both bowl and spear make up the blood-magical roots of the "Holy Roman Empire of German Nation." To this day, they were and still are magically transcendent symbols of the quest for world power in the antichristian spirit. The greatest "honour" for the person who receives the holy grail consists in the fact that he will become the ruler of the world (Antichrist). Therefore, all blood-magical systems, such as the Roman Catholic Church with its white magic and Adolf Hitler with his black magic, or rather, his satanic successors out of the black magic New-Age fraction are searching for the 'receiver' of the Holy Grail, the bowl relic of the holy blood. This 'receiver' (Antichrist), is not the administrator of the grail, but is the incarnated body of the "cosmic Christ." The "holy blood" turns into a transcendent image with magical power. How can these images, common to all types of blood magic, be deciphered? In truth, the "relic of the holy blood" or the "Grail of the holy blood" is a representation of the Whore of Babylon described in Revelations 17:

"Then one of the seven angels who had the seven bowls came and said to me, 'Come, I will show you the judgment of the great whore who is seated on many waters, with whom the kings of the earth have committed fornication, and with the wine of whose fornications the inhabitants of the earth have become drunk.' So he carried me away in the spirit into a wilderness, and I saw a woman sitting on a scarlet beast that was full of blasphemous names, and it had seven heads and ten horns. The woman was clothed in purple and scarlet, and adorned with gold and jewels and pearls, holding in her hand a golden cup full of abominations and the impurities of her fornication; and on her forehead was written a name: ' MYSTERY BABYLON THE GREAT THE MOTHER OF PROSTITUTES AND OF THE ABOMINATIONS OF THE EARTH' *And I saw that the woman was drunk with the blood of the saints and the blood of the witnesses to Jesus. When I saw her, I was greatly amazed."* Revelations 17: 1-6

Chapter II: The Roots of the "Cosmic Christ"

Verse 5 speaks about Babylon's antichristian system and the procuress or mediatrix of all abominable sins. In the Roman Church, this mediatrix of all consequences of sin is called Mary. The consequences consist of the demonic powers of death from the Cosmos, the Earth and the kingdom of Death. The blood- magical chalice is a symbol for all atrocious sins committed in the past. It is the perversion of the blood that Jesus Christ shed when He bore our sins. In the blood relic, the darkness triumphantly portrays the power it has gained through all the abominable sins committed. This demonic capacity of the power of sin, mainly built up through atrocious sins of people in blood-magical systems, is made available to religions, pseudo-religions, esoteric systems, and/or political systems. The Catholic Church, born out of the Babylonian spirit, plays the leading role in all of this. The Grail or "chalice of the Lord" in the Eucharist of the Catholic mass is the symbol for the possession of the transformational power of sin. Whoever possesses the sin-power of the entire world, the death power as the consequence of all the atrocities ever committed, will become the Antichrist! This has been the hidden message for over 1200 years and is still sent out today. Therefore, everything is now being done to combine the sinful potential of all esoteric systems and religions through Ecumenism, according to the motto: "strength through unity!" Many people do not consider the Roman Church to be one of these esoteric systems, but there is plenty of proof of this classification. For years, Rome and worldwide Satanism have been working hand-in-hand with the New-Age movement at the helm.

Not far from Nürnberg/Ansbach, Germany, is a small town called "Wolframs-Eschenbach." The name stems from the minnesinger mentioned earlier. Its parish church, the "Liebfrauenmuenster", shows today's tourists how the Grail theme was integrated into the Catholic Church and is identified with the Eucharist. The official tourist information reads: "The stone sculpture, created by the sculptors Sonnleitner of Wuerzburg and Erl of Munich, portrays the Holy Grail, a miracle-working dish, standing on a tiny altar with a dove hovering above, the host in its beak, the old Grail-King Anfortas to the left, the new one, Parzival, to the right, and an inscription underneath saying that the remains of the great poet lie buried

Chapter II: The Roots of the "Cosmic Christ"

Image 2: Sangraal Knights

under the cathedral."³³ This is the description in the official pictured pamphlet of this town.

The Grail pictured standing on the altar is the chalice of the Eucharist! The dove, an old image of the esoteric Catholic Grail-fraction, brings the, through magic, eternally crucified Jesus in the form of the host to the chalice. To the left the mediator of the magical blood relic, the old Grailking Anfortas, is worshipping and on the right, Parzival, the knight who was found worthy of attaining complete union with the power of the blood joins him. This knight symbolizes the world redeemer, the world teacher or Antichrist who receives the whole power of sin from Satan in order to rule the world with it (Rev. 13: 2+4). Thus we can see that Satan had already tried to bring the Antichrist to power in the Middle Ages. Through the grace of Christ this did not happen, but this does not mean that he will never appear. We know that only the one particular person out of the antichristian spirit whom Christ appointed to be judgement for the world will come to power as the Antichrist (Rev. 17: 17). It needs to be concluded that the source of the transubstantiation doctrine, which developed in the 9th century and formed the basis for the Eucharist, can be traced back to Lucifer, the satanic master-forger. No one can seriously claim that the Eucharist and the Lord's Supper are the same. Whoever takes part in the Catholic Eucharist literally eats or receives the death demons of the "cosmic Christ" born out of the antichristian spirit and brought forth by magic. If a Catholic wants to gain true salvation in the biblical Christ, he must ask the true Christ to forgive him these abominations. Forgiveness is promised to him on the basis of sincere repentance. Even after the person has received forgiveness through grace, many blockades to grow spiritually often

---

33 Besner, "Wolframs-Eschenbach", 1983, p.17.

continue to exist. They must be understood as the consequences of blood-magical sins and can be overcome through faith.

11. The Heart of the Mass – The Holiest Sacrament of the Altar remains central

In 1564, the Roman Church Council of Trient saw the centre of power against the Reformation in the Mass and in the doctrine of transubstantiation, the heart of the Eucharist. Here lie the roots of the Counter-Reformation that resulted in its incomprehensible crimes against the Protestants. The Reform Council Vatican II from 1962 to 1965 reaffirmed this core of the blood-magical Eucharist.

The Church Council states very openly. "If anyone should say that no true, real, reconciling sacrifice for the **living and the dead** is presented to God in the Mass, or that what is offered for consumption is anything other than Christ, let him be accursed (anathema) ... If anyone should say this with the words, 'do this in remembrance of me,' let him be accursed (anathema)."[34]

The following statement of the late Pope John XXIII, who has now been beatified, is characteristic of this Council's blood-magical spirit: "Our voices trembled with inner excitement ... (during) ... the central, decisive, shining climax of the assembly. Our consecrated and holy hands lifted up the sacrifice of the Eucharist: Jesus, our Saviour and Redeemer."[35]

At Vatican II, the Mass was described as the "source and climax of the entire Christian life"[36], confirming the position of the 1564 Anti-Reformation Council. We are sometimes reproached that our criticism of Rome is outdated and that the Council of Trient in 1564 is no longer binding for the Catholic Church today. These assertions are ignorant. Even after AD 2000 Rome has not revoked a single point from 1564. More evidence can be found in the publications and sermons which are absolutely binding for every Catholic. In the year 2000, the "L'Osservatore Romano" published a documentation on the occasion of the Eucharistic World Congress that had taken place in Rome. We will cite several of those issues on the subject of

---

34 Semlyen, "All Roads Lead to Rome", 1993, Ch. 2.
35 Ibid. Ch. 2.
36 Semlyen, "All Roads Lead to Rome", 1993, Ch. 2.

Chapter II: The Roots of the "Cosmic Christ"

the Eucharist expressing the official doctrine of today. The Lord's Supper, founded by Jesus in Mt.26: 26+27, is interpreted as the Eucharist since the bread and wine, "given as a sacrifice, became his body and blood in his holy and venerable hands."[37] "In the room of the Last Supper, the sacrifice on Calvary was made in advance,"[38] according to Roman deception. The one time historical death on the cross for the sins of the world is re-interpreted into salvation for the suffering of all people! "Through the suffering of Christ, there is salvation for the suffering of each and every person." "Through his Passion, human suffering receives new value. Through his death, our death is conquered forever."[39] The cross of Christ embodies the Catholic hope for the elimination of all pain and sorrow that man who is considered the victim is suffering. Because all suffering leads to death in the end, Christ has conquered all just and unjust suffering through his resurrection, based on the Catholic deception. It is not the one time, historical, sacrificial death of Jesus that brings us forgiveness of all sins and reconciliation with Him through his blood. Instead, the Eucharist gives the Catholic believer strength in life, freed through the forgiveness of sins.

This is a form of rebellion against God! Through Roman deception, people see themselves as innocent victims of the many kinds of human suffering. Jesus declares his solidarity with them and dies for their suffering, so that their pain can be transformed into life through his resurrection. According to the antichristian spirit, the cross and resurrection of Jesus are nothing but acts of solidarity by a good person in whom the "cosmic Christ" could become incarnate.

But the Holy Scriptures tell us in stark contrast to these ideas that we are sanctified and freed from sin once and for all times only through the historical sacrifice of the body of Jesus Christ,:

"But when Christ had offered for all time a **single** sacrifice for sins, 'he sat down at the right hand of God'" (Heb.10: 12).

"For by a **single** offering he has perfected **for all time** those who are sanctified" (Heb.10: 14).

"For Christ **did not** enter a sanctuary made by human hands ..." (Heb. 9: 24). Yet, the Catholic Church talks about the holiest sacrament of

---

37 "L'Osservatore Romano", No. 26, June 30. 2000, p.7.
38 Ibid. p.7.
39 Ibid. p.7.

the altar. **"Nor was it to offer himself again and again ..."** (Heb.9: 25). This is exactly what supposedly occurs in the Eucharist. *"For then he would have had to suffer again and again ..."* (Heb.9: 26a).

"But as it is, he has appeared once for all at the end of the ages to put away [or do away with, the author] *sin by the* [historical, the author] *sacrifice of himself. And just as it is appointed for man to die* **once** [because of the sin since the fall of Adam, the author], *and after that comes judgment, so Christ, having been offered* **once** *to bear the sins of many ..."* (Heb.9: 26b-28).

Jesus Christ did not die and rise again for humans as victims, but instead for humans as perpetrators. He did not take death upon himself just to show solidarity with the suffering of humanity. Out of his own free will, He died as the only One who was truly pure, innocent, and sinless before God. Therefore, God the Father could accept his sacrifice in place of sinful humans. On the other hand, God's judgment over humanity as a whole remains valid:

"There is no one who is righteous, not even one ... There is no one who seeks God. All have turned aside, together they have become worthless. There is no one who does good, not even one" (Rom.3: 10-12).

Consequently, the one-time, historical sacrifice of Christ was necessary. For all those who believe in Him, it was also the prerequisite for death and suffering, the wages of sin, to be done away with through the resurrection of Christ. "For the wages of sin is death ..." (Rom.6: 23).

According to antichristian Roman deception the sacrifice that constantly recurs in the Eucharist through transubstantiation is the way to salvation. But the historical cross of Jesus merely portrays the sympathy of God for humans, coupled with the false promise of an end to all suffering through the resurrection of Christ.

Cardinal Schoenborn of Vienna, Austria said:

"In the Easter mystery, the Lord has given us two incomparable gifts: The Eucharist in the night before his suffering and the forgiveness of sins on the evening of his resurrection (John 20: 23)."[40]

Based on this demonic doctrine, a Catholic receives the gift of life through the Eucharist. But Jesus would not have had to suffer the gruesome death on the cross for its accomplishment. But how

---

40 Ibid. p. 8.

does a Catholic receive forgiveness of sins according to their own understanding? It is mediated by the authority of the church to forgive sins. Eternal life is created by the constant sacrifice of Christ in the Mass through transubstantiation and the Roman Church's authority to forgive sins! Therefore, the permanently crucified "Roman man", the so-called Corpus Crucifixus, must always be pitied and bemoaned. In fact the Catholic bemoans his own suffering as a victim and feels sympathy for the man on the cross by identifying with Him. "Through the Eucharist, the communion with the body and blood of Christ, Catholics grow into that mysterious deification which makes them become children of the Father through the Son in the Holy Spirit" as the official Vatican documents tell us.[41] The goal is the "deification" of humans, an ambition shared by all religions and esoteric cults. As a result, the Pope can say something which is blasphemous by biblical standards:

"We have become the Christ."[42]

John Paul II published his last doctrinal writing on this subject on Thursday, the eve of Good Friday in 2003. He defends the "cosmic Eucharist" as irrevocable in 62 chapters. The American author Flannery O'Connor, a devout Catholic, delivers a short and drastic defence of the Eucharist in a debate with an Anglican, summarizing the Catholic viewpoint concisely: "If the Eucharist is nothing but a symbol of Christ [in remembrance of Him, the author], then I say: To hell with it."[43] With a wholly different motivation I need to answer: To hell with the Eucharist!

For a believer in Christ, taking part in the Eucharist is incompatible with the truth of God's Word, personified in Jesus Christ. *"No, I imply that what pagans sacrifice, they sacrifice to demons and not to God. I do not want you to be partners with demons. You cannot drink the cup of the Lord and the cup of demons. You cannot partake of the table of the Lord and the table of demons"* (1.Cor.10: 20+21). The Vatican Council from 1962-65 (Vatican II) has dared to condemn all those who insist that the true Supper of the Lord should be celebrated in remembrance of Jesus' sacrificial death and not by means of transformation in the Eucharist. We answer with the Word of God:

---

41 "L'Osservatore Romano", No.40, Oct. 6, 2000, p. 2.
42 "L'Osservatore Romano", No.43, Oct. 27, 2000, p. 2.
43 "Die Welt" May 24, 2003.(The World, Newspaper).

Chapter II: The Roots of the "Cosmic Christ"

"Then the Lord knows how to rescue the godly from trial, and to keep the unrighteous under punishment until the day of judgment ... They [the unrighteous, the author] have eyes full of adultery, insatiable for sin. They entice unsteady souls. They have hearts trained in greed. Accursed children!"
2. Peter 2: 9+14

12. God became Flesh – same words different meanings!

God coming in the flesh means that the Son of God, Jesus Christ, accepted human nature. Doing so he remained within the fullness of God. It could be seen that neither his Godly identity nor his Godly characteristics have ceased or were reduced in power. All divine glory remained with Him from the beginning of his earthly life to the end and beyond. When the Son of God "humbled Himself" (Phil.2: 6-11; John1: 14) by "becoming flesh", He voluntarily abstai-ned from this divine glory during his life on Earth, because his mandate of salvation necessitated it. This is the line of thought how the fathers of the Reformation expressed this divine truth. The so-called Lutheran "Formula concordiae" describes the fact of Christ's humbling Himself with words like "keeping secret" or "not using" His glory. In reference to his exaltation however they speak about "revelation" or "usage" of His Glory. In this section, we will focus primarily on his "humbling." The Protestant Reformers considered the beginning of his human person in the first moment of life to be the foundation for the abasement and the exaltation as well. From the moment of his conception by the Holy Spirit, Jesus was the humbled Son of God. The conception of Mary is described: "... she was found to be with child from the Holy Spirit" (Mt.1: 18), "for the child conceived in her is from the Holy Spirit" (Mt. 1: 20). "The Holy Spirit will come upon you, and the power of the Most High will overshadow you; therefore the child to be born will be holy; he will be called the Son of God" (Lk.1: 35).

In light of this, it is impossible to understand Mary's conception through the Holy Spirit as the result of sexual intercourse between a male god and a female human. The conception of Mary does not imply a symbiotic connection between God and man to create a new kind of hybrid being. However, with the Antichrist a hybrid being will be the case. He will be transformed from a Homo sapiens into a Homo noeticus[44] through the complete incarnation of Satan's spirit in a human. When the Bible talks about God coming over her and overshadowing her with his power in Luke 1: 35, it tells us that there is no rational explanation for this Godly "conception." This overshadowing was a divine occurrence which can not be compared to the usual process of conception. Instead, it marked the beginning of Mary's pregnancy. Of course, Mary was pregnant! Everyone could tell. She carried her child for nine months. But does not a pregnancy involve more than just "the carriage of a child"? The cause of a normal pregnancy is the union of a male sperm cell with a female egg cell. The body of the woman bearing the child usually produces the egg cell. If this is not the case, i.e. where no identification between the fertilized egg cell and the mother exists, we have what is called a surrogate mother. She only offers her womb as a protective place for the development of an egg cell fertilized outside of her body. A normal pregnancy involves the participation of a man and a woman in the process of fertilization. This was not the case with Mary. According to Mt.1: 18, Joseph did not have sexual intercourse with Mary before the birth of Jesus, which might have led to the fertilization of an egg cell. Since the Holy Spirit did not fertilize Mary as a male God, so to speak, the Bible uses the term "overshadowing" to symbolize the supernatural process of Jesus becoming flesh. Because there was no biological fertilization of one of Mary's own egg cells, God, in effect, deposited a fertilized egg cell in her body. This fertilization was beyond Mary's biological means and can only have occurred outside of her body. Her pregnancy was as real as the pregnancy of any surrogate mother. For this reason, Jesus was born without any inherited sin! The process of that "overshadowing" remains rationally inexplicable. It is a secret of God which we should not try to unravel further. Jesus, who possessed the glory of God, was with God from the beginning (John 1: 1-3), and carried divine names like Jehoshua which means "Yahweh saves" in Hebrew, Immanuel or God with us (Isa.7: 14), Wonderful, Counsellor, Mighty God, Everlasting Father and Prince of Peace (Isa.9: 6). Before all creation, the glory of Jesus was with God (Col.1: 15+16). Jesus is God and, therefore, not part of creation. Jesus is the Christ (1.John

---

44 Homo noeticus: In contrast to Homo sapiens, this refers to the "enlightened human" (Gnosis), who has transformed into a spirit-person.

2: 22), just as the Christ is Jesus. Whoever splits these two names into two different persons, works lies in the antichristian spirit. We will come back to this later.[45] As a result, the "overshadowing" of Mary, which led to a natural birth, refers to the deepest abasement of Jesus, the second person of the Godhead. *"Who, though he was in the form of God* [before his earthly life and remained God in secret during his life on earth, the author] *did not regard equality with God as something to be exploited, but emptied himself, taking the form of a slave, being born in human likeness. And being found in human form, he humbled himself* [voluntarily, the author] *and became obedient to the point of death – even death on a cross"* (Phil.2: 6-8). When He "emptied Himself", it was based on his own free will. The acceptance of "human form or likeness" indicates that, unlike us, Jesus had no inherited sin and remained without personal sin throughout his earthly life. The "conception through the Holy Spirit" marked the beginning of Christ's humbling.

13. The Divine Glory and Pre-existence of Jesus Christ

The Lutheran systematic theologian Franz Piper describes the fact of Christ's abasement as remaining fundamentally in His glory: "Because of his personal unity, Christ, in his human nature, is in the possession of his Godly majesty from the point of conception. In reality, Christ renounced the use of his divine majesty, so that he could develop as a human."[46]

This indicates that Jesus Christ did not use his Godly glory when He died on the cross. If He had made use of it, He could not have died for the sins of the world. Christ saved us by voluntarily not using his divine glory! He did not come as God, but as a human, taking the form of a servant or slave. We have already talked shortly about Jesus Christ becoming a human with hidden Godly glory, which He renounced because of the work of salvation given to Him by the Father. Now, we must briefly consider the pre-existence of Christ as well. "Pre-existence" means that Jesus Christ existed before He was born. He exists through all eternity. "Before Abraham was, I am"

---

45   See Chapter II.
46   Piper and Mueller, "Christian Dogmatics", 1946, p.381. Concordia Publishing House.

(John 8: 58). Therefore, Jesus Christ is not part of creation, but instead, the second person of the Godly Trinity. According to "Major Bible Themes"[47], we can conclude that the Son of God, Jesus Christ, is eternal on the basis of the following:

1. **The works of creation in Jesus Christ.**
   Scripture passages: John 1: 3; Col.1: 16; Heb.1: 10.
2. **Jesus Christ appeared as an angel or a human in the Old Testament.**
   Passages: Gen.16: 7; 18: 1; 22: 11+12; Dan.7: 13.
3. **The titles of the Lord Jesus Christ are indications of his eternal existence:**
   Son of God, the unparalleled and unique Son, the only begotten Son (John 1: 14), the First and the Last, Alpha and Omega, Lord, the Christ, etc. These titles also show the association with the God of the Old Testament who revealed Himself as Yahweh.
   Passages: Mt.1,23 and Isa.7: 14; Mt.4: 7 and Deut.6: 16; Mt.22: 42-45 and Ps.110: 1; Mark 5: 19 and Ps.66,16.
   Furthermore, the names of the Son of God in the New Testament are linked to the titles of the Father and the Holy Spirit.
   Passages: Mt.28: 19; John 14: 1; 17: 3; Acts 2: 38; 1.Cor.1: 3; 2.Cor.13: 13; Eph.6: 23; Rev.20: 6; 22: 3; Isa.9: 6.
4. **Jesus Christ is called God.**
   Passages: John 1: 1; Rom.9: 5; Titus 2: 13; Heb.1: 8+9; 1.John 5: 20.
5. **Jesus Christ has the characteristics of God.**
   Passages: Mt.28: 18+20; John 1: 4; 3: 16; 5: 26; 14: 6; 1.Cor.4: 5; Col.1: 17; 2: 3; Heb.1: 8-12; 7: 26; 13: 8; Rev.1: 8.
6. **Jesus Christ is worshipped as God.**
   Passages: John 20: 28; Acts 7: 59+60; Heb.1: 6+8.

14. Jesus Christ: True Man and True God in One Person

When Christ became flesh, it is essential to understand that He remained a single person with two different natures: "unmixed and undivided, unchangeable and non-split", true man and true God.

---

47 Chafer, Walvoord, "Basis of Bible Teaching", 1974, p.60 German Edition.

After long quarrels, even the Council of Chalcedon in 451 professed this truth about Jesus Christ as one single person. However, they also adopted the heresy passed at the 'Robbers' Synod' of Ephesus in 449 that Mary is the Mother of God.

"We follow our holy forefathers and unanimously teach everyone to confess one and the same Son, our Lord Jesus Christ. The same is perfect in his Godliness and perfect in his human nature, true God and true man. Made up of one intelligent soul and one body [and one spirit, the author]. He has the same characteristics as the Father with respect to his Godliness and the same characteristics as we do with respect to his human nature, similar to us in every aspect, with the exception of sin (...) We confess one and the same Jesus Christ, the Son, the Lord, the only Begotten, revealed in two different natures, unmixed, unchanged, undivided, and inseparable. Under any and all circumstances, the difference in the two natures is not cancelled by their unity. The uniqueness of each nature is preserved. Both unite to form one person and one hypostasis [manifestation, the author]. We do not confess someone split or torn into two persons, but instead one and the same, the only begotten Son, the Godly Logos [Word, the author], the Lord Jesus, as the prophets and then Jesus Christ, Himself, taught us and as it has been handed down to us from our forefathers in their confession of faith."[48]

Through faith, our forefathers in the Reformation defended passionately this creed and rejected all other theological interpretations as heresy.

15. The "Incarnation" of God in Jesus Christ

At first glance, this heading may look as if we are splitting hairs. The literal translation of this Latin word is: to become flesh. However, as with all words, we are not only interested in the origin of a word or how it was originally used, but also what meaning this word has today!

Let us look at the following example:

The relationship of the true Christian with the invisible God is on a 'spiritual level'. The word 'spirit' comes from the Latin word 'spiritus' from which we derive the word 'spiritual'.

---

48 Steubing, "Bekenntnisse der Kirche", 1985, p.27, 28.(Confessions of the Church).

Chapter II: The Roots of the "Cosmic Christ"

Those dealing in the occult, such as Hinduism, Budism etc., believe that under the influence of a 'spirit', and here we are talking of a demonic spirit, a personality change takes place because the 'spirit' lives in them and the person involved speaks and acts accordingly. Here the non-Christians use the word 'incarnation' meaning that the spirit becomes inherent in the person involved or moves into the 'flesh' of this person. Used in a Christian context, the word incarnation describes Jesus Christ's first coming in the flesh as the son of man.

Interestingly, Protestant theologians who had turned their backs on the Reformation re-introduced this term into theology and filled it with an esoteric-philosophical meaning. Indeed, bible believing, Reformation-minded Christians should be very careful when using the word "incarnation" with respect to Christ becoming flesh. We need to make it very clear that this word is well understood as described in John 1: 14. What exactly does this word mean in modern esoterically influenced theology? One characteristic of the "antichristian theological incarnation doctrine" is that Jesus Christ consists of two separate persons. Andreas Roessler, representative of the syncretistic fraction of the Protestant church in Germany, writes: "It must be distinguished between the cosmic Christ and the human, Jesus Christ. This does not harm the close connection [between the two] established by the cosmic Christ becoming human in Jesus of Nazareth."[49] These are old Gnostic heresies. Roessler says that "according to Christian doctrine, the Logos became flesh and blood in a single person, in Jesus of Nazareth."[50] This sounds Christian but is not at all. It is misleading for from a Gnostic perspective God is thought of as a threesome. The second godly person, the eternal Christ, the Logos, was sent to Earth to find an ethically suitable human out of the nation of Israel. He found him in Jesus of Nazareth and the spirit Logos, or the Christ, then entered or incarnated into this man. Early Christians recognized such "Christian doctrines" as heretical and combated them. As seen before, even the Protestant Reformers based their theology on the Council of Chalcedon. They recognized and confirmed the characteristic of the two distinct na-

---

49 Roessler, "Steht Gottes Himmel allen offen?", 1990, p.8. (Is God's Heaven open for all?).
50 Ibid. p.20.

Chapter II: The Roots of the "Cosmic Christ"

tures of Christ as the truth. If we want to advocate biblical points of view successfully, we need to stay on the theological foundation of our forefathers laying the foundation anew during the Reformation. The neo-Gnostic separation of Jesus Christ into two persons, Jesus, the human, and Christ, the God, is just another method of promoting a universal antichristian world religion. By now, the reader will have discovered that both the Roman Catholic and the Protestant state churches in Germany are deeply entangled in the heresies of the Gnosis. Both are, in fact, worshipping a false Christ, an Anti-Christ, whom they call "cosmic Christ." The differences have become very minor. Just like the Roman Church, such heretical Protestant theologians use passages from the Apocrypha as biblical evidence! According to this literally "cosmic" heresy, the "eternal Christ" comes to Earth and enters into Jesus, who dies on the cross. God then uses his **death to "reconcile to Himself all things" citing** Col.1: 20. But they believe that people as well as the cosmic powers are meant here.[51] Here, Paul's letter to the Colossians is abused to support the doctrine of apocatastasis. All "spiritual" beings, even the fallen angels that have become demons, are reconciled through the cross of Christ according to this heresy. For them, Jesus is just the vessel for the "cosmic Christ, who captures his rays like a burning mirror."[52] This doctrine of incarnation about the "Christ in two persons" can then proceed to say that Jesus Christ rose from the dead, but only in an insincere, figurative sense. Jesus, the human person, died. The eternal Logos, the Christ, arose, and now rules the cosmos and dwells in the believers through the Holy Spirit. The Catholic church feeds their ideas from this Gnostic background. Jesus' death is glorified by bemoaning it, as manifested in the pictures of the Corpus Crucifixus or in Pietà statues and other figurines of lamenting women. Jesus is dead. That remains the message of Rome. Therefore, all of us humans should cry because He died for our pain! This also explains the other gory, blood-magical "Jesus statues" which show a blood-covered Jesus in a glass coffin, the so-called "Holy-Saturday-Jesus." Because Jesus has not risen in the Roman church, He is permanently hanging on a cross as a reminder to mourn Him and his innocent suffering. When the Catholic church

---

51   Ibid. p.23/24.
52   Ibid. p.27.

proclaims his resurrection on Easter morning, they are not talking about Jesus, but about the "Spirit Christ", the cosmic Christ who returned to the cosmos after the death of Jesus. It is not difficult to see the parallels between the incarnation doctrine of the "two-person-Christ" developed by the Protestant supporters of Ecumenism and the Catholic Gnosis of Rome. As a result, the crucifixes are surrounded by hordes of demonic-cosmic spiritual forces, brought forth by the heretic worship of death. The doctrine of Jesus Christ "in two persons" is paving the way for the anti-Reformational, anti-biblical Ecumenical movement.

The doctrine of the two natures has degenerated into the Ecumenical dogma of two persons, which the universal Antichristian spirit is using to build its one worldwide religion.

16. The Cosmic Spirit – Another Characteristic of the Incarnation Doctrine

Since Ecumenical Christology sees itself as a cosmic theology, let us now look closer at the word "cosmos." It has eight meanings in the Bible. One of them refers to the immanent world, i.e. the entire universe created by God, which is the meaning that the advocates of "cosmic Christology" like to cite. We accuse them of ignoring the fact that this world, once created by God, has fallen twice through sin. The first time, a third of the angels fell by rebelling against God. God threw them out of the heavens, into this world, the cosmos (please read Isa.14: 12+13; Luke 10: 18; Rev.12: 4). The second fall was Adam's. God had plans of salvation from sin and its consequence of death for him and his descendents. Jesus Christ died for the sins of humans as the flawless sacrificial lamb and also overcame the consequence, death, through his real, bodily resurrection. Therefore, the biblical passages using the word "cosmos" in this context are all of a negative connotation. The world is hostile to God, lost and in need of salvation (Rom.5: 12; 1.Cor.11: 32). It is under the control of the ruler of this world (John 12: 31b; 14: 30; 16: 11). This world or cosmos lies under the power of Satan (1 John 4: 4; 5: 19), the fallen "morning star" (Isa.14,12). The world of God's adversary (Satan) and the world of humans belong together. But it has to be made sure that this in no way reduces the responsibility of humans for their sins. As a result, the world or "cosmos", is excluded from Jesus' intercession (John 17: 9+25). Neither Jesus nor those saved by Him belong to this world, because they have been rescued from the world (John 15: 19; 17: 14,16,25; 1 John 2: 15; 4: 5). All true Christians make up the ecclesia, a Greek word meaning "those called or summoned out." They suppress the world system through faith until the rapture. They stay in the world, without belonging to it (John 16: 33; 17: 11-18; 1 John 4: 4; 5;4). According to Eph.6: 12, the demonic archangels are called "cosmocrators" and have networked the world into their dark system. Consequently, it is dishonest to apply the term "cosmos" to Christ, since it stands for the creation that has fallen away from God through sin. A different name applies to this fallen 'cosmos': Satan, the supreme cosmocrator. When citing biblical evidence, one can not pretend that the term "cosmos" is only used to describe God's good creation, such as in John 6: 33+51 where it refers to the living space for humans, or in 1.Cor.4: 9 where it encompasses all beings who have or are a spirit. For Jesus Christ came into this fallen world to redeem it. Jesus Christ is the pantocrator, the master and Lord of everything, the Almighty (Rev.1: 8), not the fallen cosmocrator (see John 12: 31). Therefore, "cosmic Christ" is an antichristian term and, in effect, a disguised name for the Antichrist, whose spirit will incarnate in a human and transform him into homo noeticus, the Gnostic knowing man.

17. The Trinity and the Fathers of the Reformation

We need to look a little deeper at this difficult subject since the Ecumenical supporters of "cosmic Christology" also use this area in their seductive attempts to establish a one-world-religion. If we do not want to have the rug pulled out from under our feet, we must briefly consider the biblical position of the Reformation. In the Word of God, we find clear indications about one God as three persons, called the "Trinity" in the early church. Martin Luther shows "that the Christian church has always been involved in a struggle around the Trinity doctrine, against enemies from the outside as well as erroneous spirits coming from its own midst. The Christian church had to fight two groups in particular: firstly, those who denied the three persons, and secondly, those who denied the one God or the one

Godly nature."[53] Mt.28: 19 speaks for the three persons of God: "[...] *baptizing them in the name of the Father and of the Son and of the Holy Spirit.*" These three persons are three "Identities." According to Piper, the Bible pronounces the Father, the Son and the Holy Spirit to be real as well as different persons. A person consists of an identity and is not just a piece, a characteristic, or a manifestation, i.e. hypostasis. That was the understanding of the Reformers. As a result, the three persons are not three divine beings, or three Godly natures. Luther wrote that there is no graduation or multiplication of the divine nature. This means that "God is one (1.Cor.8: 4) and exists only once, and each person possesses this single and unique fullness of Deity ... the Father, the Son as well as the Holy Spirit each have the whole, undivided Godly nature (Col.2: 9; Acts 5: 4; Mt.28: 19).[54] In the Holy Scriptures, the same characteristics apply to all three persons. It is important to remember what the fathers of the Reformation confessed after they recognized this truth in God's Word:

There is only one Godly nature or Deity, the divine characteristics and deeds exist only once, wholly and undivided. Each person is the whole God! There are orders of precedence, but human understanding of time and rank do not apply. "So the Father is the first person, the Son, the second, and the Holy Spirit, the third person of the Trinity."[55]

The Bible tells us that the Father has not received the divine nature from anyone else, while the Son has received the Godly nature from the Father, and the Holy Spirit has received the divine nature from the Father and the Son (Mt.28: 19; 2.Cor.13: 13; Heb.1: 3).

18. Ecumenical Cosmic Christology and the Trinity of God

As we have already heard, the heretic system started with the idea that "the cosmic Christ united with the human, Jesus of Nazareth, and used him as a means of revelation."[56] Here is exposed the irreconcilable difference between Ecumenical theology on the one

---

53 Piper und Mueller, "Christian Dogmatics", 1946, p.182.
54 Ibid. p.184.
55 Ibid. p.187.
56 Rössler, "Steht Gottes Himmel allen offen?" 1990, p. 66.(Is God's Heaven open for all?).

Chapter II: The Roots of the "Cosmic Christ"

side and the early Church, the fathers of the Reformation and the Bible, on the other. To summarize what we have already discussed **Jesus Christ is <u>one</u> person with two natures, real man and real God, unmixed and inseparable, unchangeable and undivided.** As already quoted, the supporters of Ecumenism argue that Jesus of Nazareth, the human, is one person, and that the cosmic Christ, a second person, is God. The second Godly person dwells in or incarnates the other person who is human. Out of this symbiotic relationship, the Godly human, Jesus Christ, arises. This is rooted in the ancient mystical and antichristian religion of Babylon. Consequently, it can be depreciatively described as "Babylon" because it represents the exact opposite of biblical salvation. Here lie the roots of all the destructive developments which will and must inevitably lead to the one single world religion out of the antichristian spirit. For this reason, the doctrine about the "two natures" of Jesus Christ is abandoned in favour of the "two-person-doctrine" founded on the incarnation concept out of the Babylonian spirit. Of course, they maintain a pseudo "two-naturesdoctrine" in order to deceive. They say: Jesus and Christ are two natures: man and God. But by creating two persons, they have left the biblical foundation of the Reformation. In giving up the "two-natures-doctrine", they deny that Jesus is God. If Jesus is no longer God, his resurrection is just a proclamation of faith (kerygma), and therefore not a reality of salvation. Death the consequence of sin would not have been conquered (Rom. 6,23). In 1.Cor.15: 14, Paul writes that if Christ has not been raised, our preaching is in vain and our faith is also in vain. Out of the whole context of chapter 15, it is easy to recognize that "Christ" refers to Jesus Christ. To say it with the fathers of Chalcedon: Jesus Christ is one person with two natures, unmixed and inseparable, unchangeable and undivided, who died for our sins and all their deadly consequences. He conquered death with his bodily resurrection since his tomb was empty!

Speculation beyond the creed the Trinity doctrine is softened and torn away from its hard, fundamental core, like we have already seen. In order to unite all religions, the Trinity is dissolved piece by piece. The established stumbling block, Jesus, the fate of all of us, appears to be overcome. Another stumbling block on the road to a single world religion in the Babylonian or Roman spirit is the one

Chapter II: The Roots of the "Cosmic Christ"

God in three persons. Why? "Jews and Muslims feel offended by the doctrine of the Trinity because they suspect it to be a doctrine of three Gods, a remnant of polytheism."[57] According to Roessler, the Christians violate the uniqueness of the Creator. For the sake of adaptation to non-Christian thoughts, the three persons, as personal identities, are denied. God is "put in concrete form" by changing the three persons the Bible testifies about into three manifestations, hypostases or aspects of God. The fathers of the Early Church, who warned that the Trinity should not be misunderstood as a doctrine of three Gods are hypocritically cited. The perpetrators can be charged with dishonesty because they arrogantly ignore the doctrinal struggles of early Christianity and also the clear and uncompromised profession of the Trinity in the Reformation.

One God in three persons!

But according to the demonic doctrines, Jesus has been eliminated as Saviour. In their Trinity, there is only a second divine aspect, the hypostasis of the "cosmic Christ", the third hypostasis of the "Holy Spirit" and the "Father" as the "basis of creation." A God with three aspects or manifestations is supposed to replace the God in three persons. These hypostases can be summarized as: creation, salvation and perfection. In this heretic doctrine, one God in three persons completely disappears. A single god in a single person is brought into the cosmic religious spectacle as the basis of creation in order to unite all religions. If they conclude that all religions have the same god, they are right in a totally different sense. By removing the fundamentals and making it empty of purpose, a system becomes an anti-system. An antithesis is further developed into a synthesis which is the united one world religion.

The opponents of God stem from the god of the cosmos the ruler of this fallen world, who is called Satan! In our Western culture, his hypostasis of salvation is called "cosmic Christ." To summarize: Ecumenical theology has one "Father" as a continuous, universal Creator. Everything is evolving out of him. Therefore, the theory of evolution has not only come into fashion in culturally Protestant circles, but also the Catholic Church. In October 1996, Pope John Paul II told the press that evolution no longer contradicts the

---

57 Ibid. p.67.

Christian faith. After all, the theological basis of "continuous evolution" is found in the cosmic, eucharistic Christ as well. His continuous death is celebrated because a constant transformation is evolving out its mystery. This "cosmic Christ", with the Catholic name of "eucharistic Christ", is a universal Christ who unites all religions through their "Holy Spirit."

19. The two cosmic levels through their Hypostases and the results of praying to pictures

The dimension of the immanent fallen world is considered to be interchangable with the transcendent fallen world. The worshippers of the cosmic Christ look at the visible and the invisible world synomously. Through mysticism both levels of creation are attempted to be brought systematically into an equivalence of quality. The Roman Church is thinking in terms of analogy between the visible Church and invisible powers. The one and only God is no longer adressed as a person in practical theology, as all other powers play a much more important role. For this reason the theology of the Trinity is no longer serving as a bulwark against the unification with the religions of revelation, Judaism and Islam.

Let us take a quick look at the history of theology to show the explosiveness of this step by step "de-personification" of God. By adhering to the Trinity in three persons, union with the so-called religions of revelation is impossible. In order to make this union possible the Christian Ecumenical movement even goes so far as attempting to eliminate the three persons of the Trinity. The Greek term "hypostasis" refers to "mode of action" or "form of realization." Influenced by Greek philosophy, the theologian Basilius, called the Great (d. 379), brought this term into theology at the Synod of Alexandria, Egypt in 362 A.D. This initiated the unfortunate further developments of de-personification ideas. Classical Greek philosophy differentiated between the nature or being of a person and the manifestations or forms of realization of that being. The very nature of the person is considered according to his or her gender while the characteristics or qualities of the person are thought to be neuter. This means that a person can be thought independently from his or her actions. This philosophical thought process stems from Plato.

Basilius demanded that the results of this differentiation be applied to the "divine doctrine." The three persons of the one God were not eradicated, but instead received an interchangeable, neutral set of characteristics. After some time, the Godly characteristics developed a pseudo-personal nature by understanding and were worshipped as forms of realization. As the types of effect were separated from the person the hypostases of the person are worshipped and no longer the person of God.[58] For a true believer, this is impossible, because worship and prayer always have exclusively a personal character reflecting a real communication with the person of God. Prayer requires the transcendent person of God and the redeemed person acting in a personal relationship to each other. Therefore, faith in the deepest sense is the faith in a person and deals with the trusting relationship of humans as persons to their God as a person. Faith is not the belief in manifestations, saying I believe in the Bible or I believe in miracles. Instead, it encompasses the understanding of the actions of God. True faith opens the way of knowing God, who possesses certain characteristics and acts in accordance with them, such as according to his holiness, righteousness, grace, or mercy. This faith is the consequence and tangible expression of the personal relationship of a human person to his God. Consequently, biblical faith in the deepest sense is not a religion.

By linking the terms person and hypostasis interchangeably, Basilius said in 362 that God, as the Father, is also a hypostasis because of his lack of origin or state of being. Now the synonymy becomes clear: "The second hypostasis is Christ", since He has the characteristic of being the Son of Godly nature. The third hypostasis is the Holy Spirit as the sanctifying power. For Basilius, the word "person" was the common characteristic of all three hypostases of the Trinity."[59]

In the practice of faith, the following happened: Man as part of the immanent fallen world or cosmos created a picture, an icon or a statue which was set up for worship. To begin with this was just a material object that could be discussed about on the basis of art. The churches of Western and Eastern Rome however called it a

---

58 The worship of wisdom (Sophia) was very popular in the Greek church, as seen in Constantine's Basilika Hagia Sophia, which means "the holy truth."
59 Adam, "Lehrbuch der Dogmengeschichte", 1985, p. 236-237. (Textbook of History of doctrine).

representation to be adored. The good characteristics captured in the picture were supposed to serve as examples for the believers to emulate. By revering the depicted persons, they revered the characteristics and vice versa. The believer could choose what to worship because one was the equivalent of the other.

In his standard book on the history of dogma, Adam explains this way of thinking: "The pictorial representation of Christ [picture or Corpus Crucifixus, the author] is not hypostatically different from Christ. He, Himself, portrayed in the picture, is actually invisibly present."[60] This doctrine of the hypostasis of the Trinity has lead the Roman church as well as the Orthodox church into the abomination of idol worship. **The symbols, pictures, and statues are revered and worshipped, because they are understood as hypostases, as manifestations or forms of realization, and are equated directly with the personal existence of the depicted being!** The hypostasis in the form of a picture or statue is considered to be the visible component corresponding to the original. The picture of Jesus Christ is seen as having the exact same qualities as the person himself. A Roman church building becomes the mystical body of Christ by means of its hypostatical objects installed there to worship. The devilish heretical assumption that Christ and the "saints" are personally present in the pictures through hypostases drives people to worship the material objects in the various church buildings. Even in the Protestant camp of Christianity the question should be raised whether some believers have not celebrated the Lord's Supper "hypostatically" on some occasions. Danger looms when the Lord's Supper no longer proclaims the death of Christ *"until he comes"* (1 Cor.11: 26), but becomes interchangeable with the presence of Christ. However, true believers can assume that the living Christ is always personally present through his Spirit whenever something is done through faith, not just during the Lord's Supper!

Ecumenical Protestant theologies feeding on the roots of rationalism also see the manifestations or aspects of God as hypostatic expressions of Him. These characteristics are then given the names of persons, without a person-to-person relationship existing with the personal God of the Trinity.

---

60 Ibid. p.379.

The only difference to the Roman church is that they worship the manifestations of God, such as reason, wisdom, love, etc. abstractly, without the need for material objects like pictures. The idolatry exists just the same, because the Godly Trinity is not revered in person.

20. The Immanent and Transcendent World

Besides the Greek philosophy of hypostatic equivalency, there is a second reason why the supporters of Ecumenism want to abolish the personal nature of God. They view the world in a double way. The visible world is corresponding with the mystical world. Of course, the idea of the existence of the immanent material and the invisible spiritual, is biblical. If someone sins in the visible world, this deed not only has corresponding consequences in the immanent realm, but also has an equivalent effect on the transcendent world. A sin against a human in the immanent realm is simultaneously a sin against God in the transcendent world (Ps.51: 6). *"Father, I have sinned against heaven and before you"* (Lk.15: 18). The sins of humans result in the spoilage of all creation. Therefore, the entire living and non-living creation awaits the final salvation of humans (Rom.8: 1922). Through the sins of mankind, huge armies of cosmic spiritual powers of death are so to speak produced or strengthened by sin (Rom.6: 23). The fallen immanent realm, or cosmos, creates reflections of the actual sin in the invisible, transcendent fallen world. Through Scripture, we know that the first fall came from the transcendent world of angels, when Lucifer and his followers were brought down. As a result, humans in their cosmos, the immanent realm, were tempted into death (Gen.3: 1; Isa.14: 14-21; 1 John 5: 19; Heb.2: 14+15; Rom.6: 23; 5: 12). This should suffice to show that the Bible clearly teaches us about dependencies and equivalencies to the invisible fallen world. Jesus, the Christ, fought against the sinful works of the devil in the fallen immanent realm as well as in the fallen transcendent world. He made a proclamation to the spirits in prison (1 Pet.3: 19; 4: 6), captured demons (Eph.4: 8-10) and triumphed over everything by his resurrection.

The Roman Catholic and Orthodox churches perceive these fundamental thoughts only through the mystical mindset of the fallen transcendent world. Western mysticism is a counterfeit of true spirituality. They also see this cosmos through the natural eyes of the flesh and discover a double world. For them, spiritual mysticism is reflected in the immanent material world.

The thought paradigm of Rome – a summary:

The first level of the cosmos is the visible, immanent, material world. In this realm, pictures, statues, relics, etc. are set up before the eyes of the worshippers. Through consecration, these objects become hypostases, or reflections of the second cosmic level, the spiritual, invisible world of the transcendent.

According to this theology, the spiritual world is the original of all hypostases of God. Because one exists within the other, the material world is within the spiritual realm and vice versa. The first level leads to the second level and back. Meditating on, revering and worshipping material pictures leads into the transcendent world and back from there into the visible. As a result, the two levels become interchangeable. Based on this heresy, a picture of Christ for believers to worship, does not lead to Christ, but is Christ, and Christ is the picture.

In contrast, true faith remains within the biblical paradigm and considers the visible world, or cosmos, to be a totally fallen world. This was also recognized as important by the Reformer Luther. In the false faith of Catholicism, the sinful human in the fallen world is only considered to be partially sinful. The redeemed person with true faith, on the other hand, has drawn the right conclusions from his totally fallen condition (Rom.3,10-12+23). He has allowed himself to be made righteous through repentance, forgiveness, and faith (Rom.3: 24-28), out of the grace of Christ. On this foundation, he has spiritual access to the reality behind his faith, the Godly transcendence (Eph.1,3-14). In the counterfeited faith of Rome, Catholics act like a burglar. Their repentance is false because they have not even recognized their condition as fallen creatures. Thus, they also lack forgiveness, as we have already discussed. This false repentance and forgiveness only serve to mark their lost condition in the eyes of God. Hence, they break into the transcendent world as unredeemed individuals, through the worship of pictures. The Catholics consider those pictures to be hypostases of the Godly Trinity and revere them as God, Himself. At its core, this is rebellion against God. He punishes it with partial death and, in the end, with eternal death because they are not saved. The holiness of God is infringed upon and tarnished. Such people end up in the hands of the god of this world, Satan, and his "cosmic Christ", along with the whole army of the fallen cosmos, the demons. Essentially, the characteristics of God and the "saints" supplant the three persons of the divine Trinity, i.e. God, Himself. True worship never takes place. Instead, God is used as a box number for "divine" hypostases and characteristics. God is reduced to a type of effect or an impersonal demonstration of power. The same applies to the mysticism of the Protestant Charismatic movement. A Catholic refers to the person of God as Father or Christ, although he is really talking about the mode of action or effect. Even the worship of Mary occurs interchangeably because of the multitude of Madonna-statues with many different helper-characteristics, or hypostases. Formally, Rome adheres to the dogma of the Trinity of God and confesses belief in the three persons of God. **In reality, however, Rome is referring to the hypostases of the cosmic powers, mediated through the many different Madonnas.** Due to the acceptance of Basilius' ancient Greek philosophy, there is, in fact, no true adherence to God as three divine persons, neither in the Roman church, nor in the Orthodox churches, nor among Protestants who think and act ecumenically. In the course of history, the Roman Church has become a blood-magical anti-church out of the antichristian spirit, by abandoning the one person of Jesus Christ as true man and true God as well as abolishing the three real persons of God as Father, Son and Holy Spirit. The practiced facts need only be published as binding theology in order to remove the Trinity from Catholic theology entirely. A holism has long been practised that aims to make a "God" of man. Western Catholic mysticism provides ample proof. Through their hero mystics they endeavor to discover God in every human being. The connecting strands are the hypostases of "God", which prove to be cosmic powers out of the fallen world of the demons. God as a person is mutilated, de-personified, and abolished. This holistic New-Age view of the world is old and goes as far back as ancient Babylon. This anti-church out of the roots of Babylon together with the fourth Roman world empire is about to make possible a single world church that will lead the way for the Antichrist

Chapter II: The Roots of the "Cosmic Christ"

to take over power. The course is set. The train of religious developments is moving at an alarming pace toward a single worldwide religion; even though some extremely long hold-ups at the stations of various religions and cults can be observed.

In summary, blood-magical, mystical practices always lead to a different God. The true God, in his holiness, refuses to be subjected to such abuse and moves out. The cosmic spiritual powers trickle into the vacuum, establish themselves, and take over the wonderful names, but empty them of real meaning and fill them with the antichristian spirit! This has happened in the past, it occurs in the present, and will continue to happen in the future. Babylon, the great whore, is Rome! Her carrier is the "cosmic Christ" who will give his entire power to the beast. The worldwide rebellion against the faith in the Holy Trinity, namely God, the Father, the Son and the Holy Spirit, is close at hand.

Chapter III
The Eucharistic Cosmic Christ and the Sacraments

1. Sacraments as Substitutes for Faith

In the second chapter, we dealt with the blood-magical powers of Rome, especially the Catholic sacrament of the Eucharist. We showed, that from the 9th century onwards, the Roman Church has established a direct connection to the Grail through magic. It represents a "form of salvation" under the power of Satan. As an antichristian spirit, the cosmic eucharistic christ thrives on blood-magic and other "things deemed holy", i.e. the sacraments. Consequently, the word "faith" has been given a totally different fundamental meaning which stands in stark contrast to what is written in the New Testament. Faith in Jesus Christ has been replaced by faith in a religion of sacraments out of the antichristian spirit. This sacramental Roman Catholic religion wants to lead the way to unification, particularly with the Orthodox Church, Islam and Judaism, the religions of revelation. In the European Union, conservative forces see these three religions as the ideological basis for political union out of the Babylonian spirit. The European cosmic christ must be adapted to make him more acceptable to the other two religions. As explained in the previous chapter, Ecumenical theology is striving to eliminate all knowledge rediscovered during the Reformation. They hope to succeed by de-personifying God, getting rid of the three-person Trinity of God and applying the Hindu (re)incarnation doctrine to Jesus Christ.

We will now look more closely at the Catholic sacraments as substitutes for faith and their meaning with respect to the eucharistic cosmic christ.

2. Faith in Sacraments and the Eucharistic Cosmic Christ

"You foolish Galatians! Who has bewitched you? It was before your eyes that Jesus Christ was publicly exhibited as crucified! The only thing

I want to learn from you is this: Did you receive the Spirit by doing the works of the law or by believing what you heard? Are you so foolish? Having started with the Spirit, are you now ending with the flesh? Did you experience so much for nothing?— if it really was for nothing. Well then, does God supply you with the Spirit and work miracles among you by your doing the works of the law, or by your believing what you heard? Just as Abraham 'believed God, and it was reckoned him as righteousness,' (Gen.15: 6) so, you see, those who believe are the descendents of Abraham. And the scripture, foreseeing that God would justify the Gentiles by faith, declared the gospel beforehand to Abraham, saying, 'All the Gentiles shall be blessed in you' (Gen.12: 3). For this reason, those who believe are blessed with Abraham who believed. For all who rely on the works of the law are under a curse; for it is written, 'Cursed is everyone who does not observe and obey all the things written in the book of the law' (Deut.27: 26). Now it is evident that no one is justified before God by the law; for 'The one who is righteous will live by faith.' (Hab.2: 4)."
Gal.3: 1-11

We have already indicated that the seven Catholic sacraments are additional graces, deemed to be essential for Roman salvation. According to Catholic theology, Christ instituted these sacraments. The Latin word Sacramentum means "holy". The Catholic encyclopaedia describes the sacraments as: "... effective means of salvation, instituted by Christ, which allow people to benefit from Christ's act of salvation through the observance of certain ceremonies [rituals, the author]."[61] Based on this encyclopaedia, God has **linked the granting of his graces to outwardly visible signs** in compliance with human nature. Further, it says that the **supernatural effectiveness** of these means of salvation, or sacraments, was instituted "by the deified human [Jesus Christ as two persons, the author]", who gave the outward signs "their supernatural powers of graces."[62] Therefore, the supernatural powers depend solely on Jesus Christ "who instituted them as channels through which his grace flows to us."[63]

According to Catholic theology, the sacraments exist for the purpose of increasing faith and worshipping God by means of their

---

61 Fischer-Wollpert „Wissen Sie Bescheid?" (=Do you have wide-ranging knowledge?), 1982, p. 495.
62 ibid. p. 495.
63 Ibid. p. 495.

Chapter III: The Eucharistic Cosmic Christ and the Sacraments

supernatural effectiveness. The more earnestly God is worshipped through the sacraments, the more grace he can give to increase the faith of the believers through invisible powers. Because of the fundamental relationship between the sacraments received and the personal faith in them as well as the augmentation of faith trought them, they are called "sacraments of faith."[64]

Jesus becoming flesh means that Jesus Christ remained one person in two natures: unmixed and undivided, as true man and true God.[65] However the II Vatican Council abandoned the confession of Chalcedon by stating "that the Son of God, **in union** with human nature, conquered death, redeemed man an reshaped him into a new creation through his death and his resurrection."[66] In 451, the Council of Chalcedon had confessed that the Bible reveals Jesus Christ in two natures, unmixed and undivided, unchangeable and inseparable.[67] Rome, on the other hand assumes that Christ incarnated into Jesus and that **the Son of God then unified human nature with God** through death. The scheme of the antichristian spirit looks at it like this: Christ, the God, incarnated into the human, Jesus of Nazareth, who then became a "deified person". The "supernatural demonic powers" depend on this new species of "deified human", the antichristian homo noeticus. They can then "**flow as the life of Christ into all of those faithful, unifying them with Christ through the sacraments in a mysterious and yet real way.**[68]"

In other words, Catholics aim to "receive faith and grace through the faithful use of the sacraments and to be transformed into a new creation as a fruit [of these efforts, the author].[69]" When Rome says that "salvation of people comes through faith in Christ and his grace"[70], these terms are given a completely different meaning in the antichristian spirit of the eucharistic, cosmic christ. A believer who

---

64 II Vatican Council Lit. 59. In: Fischer-Wollpert, „Wissen Sie Bescheid?, 1982, p. 495 (Do you have wide-ranging knowledge).
65 see Chapter II.
66 II Vatican Council, In: Ibid. p. 496.
67 see Chapter II.
68 Fischer-Wollpert, „Wissen Sie Bescheid?"(=Do you have wide-ranging knowledge?), 1982, p.496.
69 Ibid. p.496,497.
70 Ibid. p.496.

Chapter III: The Eucharistic Cosmic Christ and the Sacraments

puts his faith primarily in sacraments is supposed to be transformed into "a new creation", but this stand in complete contrast to the message of the Bible. In Eph. 4: 15, we read: *"But speaking the truth in love, we must grow up in every way into Him who is the head. into Christ ..."*

From the context, we can gather that the Apostle Paul is talking about putting aside the old way of life, like a piece of clothing that is not longer in use. The new self, resulting from the new birth in Christ, should now rule the mind and deeds ot true believers (Eph.4: 24). However, the old self contiues to exist. It can only be kept in check and overcome trough faith. Genetically, nothing has changed in the life of a born-again believer. He has not mutated "into a new creation." *"So, if anyone is in Christ, there is a new creation: everything old has passend away; see, everything has become new"(2 Cor.5: 17)*! The "new creation" refers to the new self re-created by God through the new birth of His Spirit in us, raising us from spiritual death. It is our duty to live our lives according to this new creation, staying in Christ through faith and denying our old self daily.

3. The "New Creation" out the Roman Spirit: Homo Noeticus or the Enlightened Human

What do the representatives of Rome mean when they talk about "a new creation"? The Catholic renewal of man is based on the Gnostic idea of "homo noeticus", the enlightened human. When the cosmic christ incarnated into Jesus of Nazareth, God unified or harmonized humanity with himself. Jesus, the human, is deified and becomes a "human god." When Catholics ardently practise their faith in sacraments, they believe that "Christ's life flows into them" and they are unified with God in Christ. Such people mutate into sanctified "human gods." The goal of the Roman institution is indeed evolution. They want to change the human race through spiritual mutation. In Western Catholic mysticism, the human soul seeking union with God is one of the recurring themes. Through sacraments and the resulting process of transformation into enlightened humans, people are supposed to come to know God. In other words, humans created by God as homo sapiens allegedly have to

Chapter III: The Eucharistic Cosmic Christ and the Sacraments

abandon this nature and change into homo noeticus. This shows how well Western mysticism fits with the faith in sacraments and the cosmic christ out of the antichristian spirit.

How does the process of mutation into "a new creation" take place? Through worship, reverence and use of the sacraments, cosmic streams flow into the believers, in the form of de-personified, cosmic-demonic forces. Living pieces of the human soul or spirit are split away and changed into a mutated sense of consciousness called the "new creation." This mutated self receives an aura of cosmic-demonic energies, visibly portrayed in the Catholic "halo." The cosmic aura contains the "consciousness" of the cosmic christ, i.e. the darkness. Human consciousness and so-called "godly consciousness" have become one. An ungodly species is conjured up through the white magic of the cosmic christ. In the esoteric vocabulary of the New-Age movement, such mutation processes are known as "transformation into an expanded or higher consciousness." The cosmic-eucharistic christ changes these splinters of the human soul, spirit, or consciousness into a deified partial person. On the invisible, hidden side of the realm of the dead, this partial person must then do slave labour for Lucifer's cosmic christ. Some depictions of childlike angels in Roman churches are based on this idea of human spirits mutating into homo noeticus. When the true Jesus Christ came to Earth in order to fulfill God's plan of salvation, He suffered once for all sins. After His sacrificial death, Jesus Christ went to Hades, the realm of the dead, in spirit. "... *in which* [the Spirit] *also He went and made a proclamation to the spirits in prison* [Hades]" (1 Peter 3: 19)[71]. "*For this is the reason the gospel was proclaimed even to the dead* [in Hades], *so that, though they had been judged in the flesh as everyone is judged, they might live in the spirit as God does*" (1 Peter 4: 6). Jesus, the Christ, preached salvation in Him to the imprisoned human spirits in the invisible, transcendent cosmos, i.e. the realm

---

71 We must differenciate between the realm of death (Hades) and hell (gr. gehenna). Hell is a special place within the realm of death. It is final and underlies the power of God alone (Matth.10: 28). The charachteristic sign is fire (see Luke 16: 24, Matth. 18: 9). Hell is not under the ruling power of the fallen cosmos. For this reason there are no transformed people or demons there. Because of the finality of hell no preachings about Jesus took place.(Luke 16: 19-31).

of the dead or Hades. This proclamation only made sense if these former humans who had mutated into demonic spirits could indeed repent. Even today, the real Christ can still redeem from the genetic mutation into homo noeticus through His completed work of salvation. The de-transformation happened after Golgotha through the spiritual battle of the true Jesus Christ. In the Apostles' Creed, the time between Jesus' death and resurrection is described with the following statement: "… descended into hell." But, instead of hell, a more accurate term would be the realm of the dead or Hades in accordance with the passage from 1 Peter as well as Rom.10: 7, Col.1: 18 and Mt.12: 39+40.

This de-transformation still takes place today by spiritual battle through Jesus Christ. This is hope for many former catholics whose lives or parts thereof are trapped in the invisible realm of death (Hades) and have mutated to bad spirits. The abnormal "new creation" arising from Rome's antichristian spirit is a fruit of the fall of Satan and his angels in symbiosis with the fall of man in the Garden of Eden (Gen. 3: 4+5).

4. The Sacraments

In the 11th century, the Roman church laid down its seven sacraments, together with the Eastern churches.[72] These sacraments are baptism, confirmation, Eucharist, penance, anointing of the sick, ordination to the priesthood and matrimony.

According to Roman theology, God grants the "sanctifying" as well as the "helping grace"[73] to the believers through these seven sacraments. Moreover, every sacrament conveys a special blessing. The sacraments, themselves, **contain** the grace! They are **not** merely symbolic expressions of grace! Every sacrament is a channel of grace through which invisible and supernatural power flows. But for this power to flow out of the so-called grace, the prescribed ritual has to be followed meticulously. Except for baptism and penance, the Catholic must also be in the "state of grace,"[74] meaning that his

---

[72] See Fischer-Wollpert, „Wissen Sie Bescheid?"(=Do you have wide-ranging knowledge?), 1982, p. 496.
[73] see McCarthy, "The Gospel According to Rome", 1995, Part I, chapter 3.
[74] Ibid. Part I, Chapter 3.

soul must be in possession of the "sanctifying grace." Furthermore, the faith in the salvation-bringing sacraments has to be produced and the prayers as well as the corresponding penance exercises need to be completed. After fulfilling all of the above, a Catholic can expect the fruitful receipt of grace from God by means of the sacraments. The more preparation occurs through the exercises, the more generous God will be in distributing the graces, i.e. the cosmic powers. "The sacraments are absolutely essential for salvation."[75] As already mentioned, the Catholic must be in the "state of grace" in order to receive more grace through the sacraments.

What does this really mean?

5. The Sanctifying Grace in the Sacraments

According to Rome, the "sanctifying grace" is a gift of the Holy Spirit. It is granted with the sacrament of baptism and serves to make a Catholic holy. This lasting experience must be preserved in the soul. But, a Catholic can also lose the condition of "sanctifying grace" in his soul through conscious and deliberate sin. The sacrament of penance then renews the "sanctifying grace" and restores the "state of grace," the prerequisite for receiving grace through the other sacraments. It follows that the "sanctifying grace" has constant influence on the soul.[76]

6. Baptism

The Catholic "sanctifying grace" and the resulting "state of grace" can not be produced by themselves. Therefore, a person must receive the sacrament of baptism as soon as possible after birth. Based on the gospel of Rome, it grants humans the justification from all sin inherited through the fall of Adam! This sacrament, performed on an infant, is supposed to be the spiritual antidote against the deadly illness of sin. Because every baby is born with inherited sin in its soul, the sacrament of baptism becomes the foundation for Catholic Christian life and the entrance to the graces of the other sacraments. **The sacrament of baptism allegedly removes all inherited**

75 Ibid. Part I, Chapter 3.
76 see ibid. Part I, Chapter 3.

sin and allows the baptized person to become a born-again member of the body of Christ. "Baptism is the sacrament of rebirth through water and the Word."[77] According to Roman theology, a baptized baby will go to Heaven when it dies because it has become innocent and perfect through the sacrament. The baptized person is considered to be in the state of "sanctifying grace" and, therefore, redeemed for eternity. Based on Catholic doctrine, the soul re-obtains life in God. This life is "infused" into the baptized person. During the Counter Reformation, the Council of Trient (1545-1563) determined that the acceptance as children of God in the second Adam, Jesus Christ, occurs through baptism. The baptized child is said to be justified through grace! But in contrast to the biblical justification through faith, this justification title comes through the grace of sacramental baptism! These are two very different things. According to Rome, Catholic baptism constitutes the fundamental first step to eternal salvation. One could argue that personal faith is inevitably missing when an infant is baptized. But, in order to circumvent this reproach, Rome insists that baptism, itself, is a "sacrament of faith".[78] **In the Roman doctrine, a person is justified solely through the power of the sacramental actions: ex opere operato!** This sort of dialectic removal on inherited sin explains why Catholics talk about the flesh or the soul as something holy, given that the sacramental state of "santifying grace" is maintained. They know nothing about the danger of living and acting according to the flesh or the old self, the inherited cause of Adam's fall. **Ostensible, and often hypocritical, spiritual conduct in Catholics is produced by the justification through deeds, the transcendent spiritual effects of the sacraments as well as the reverent worship of crosses and so-called saints.** The concomitant supernatural occurrences, auditions and experiences of the soul being filled with spirit are nothing but satanic seductions of the flesh, arising from the spiritual burden of Adam's inherited sin and human culture, in general. In light of this Roman dialectic, one could ask why the Father in the Heavens chose the complicated process of "overshadowing" (Luke 1: 35) when He sent Jesus to Earth. Wouldn't it have

---

77 "Katechismus der Katholischen Kirche" (Catechism of the Catholic Church). In: McCarthy, "„The Gospel According to Rome", 1995, part 1, Ch. 1.
78 Ibid. Part I, Chapter 1.

Chapter III: The Eucharistic Cosmic Christ and the Sacraments

been easier to let Jesus be conceived naturally and then have him baptized as an infant in order to eliminate the inherited sin? Once baptized and free of inherited sin, God could have sent the spirit of Christ to incarnate into Jesus. It would have been much easier to deal with than the complicated truth of Jesus being true God and true man in two unmixed and inseparable natures. At least, this would fit well with the thinking of fallen man. Please forgive me if my remarks sound ironic. But the point is, Jesus was not baptized as a baby and He did not become the object of incarnation for a spirit. These demonic and unbiblical teachings come from the Roman Catholic and, to some extent, also the Protestant state churches. No one should think that modern-day Roman theology differs from these principles described in Catholic encyclopaedias. It becomes very obvious in a jubilee letter written by Pope John Paul II on Sept. 4, 1996. Under the theme "Reinforce the gift of the baptismal grace within yourself," he addressed the clergy on the anniversary of the first baptism in the Dominican Republic 500 years ago.[79] "The apostolic duty is organized such that everyone who has become a child of God through faith and baptism participates in the sacrifice, or Mass, and benefits from the meal of the Lord, the Eucharist." With respect to the jubilee, the Pope called on the clergy to "rediscover the infinite wealth of this sacrament and accept the resulting responsibility with new zeal ... Since all of you [Catholics, the author], who have been baptized into Christ, have clothed yourselves with Christ (Gal.3: 27). When they receive the sacrament of baptism, Christians are sanctified by being reborn of water and the anointment with the Holy Spirit. They join the church and become part of it. They are a chosen race, a royal priesthood, a holy nation, God's own people (1 Peter 2: 9). As true children of God, they share in the Godly nature and have therefore become truly holy" (Lumen Gentum, 40)."... Furthermore, on account of the rebirth [through the sacrament of baptism, the author], everyone possesses the same dignity, the same grace of being sons of God and the same call to perfection." The Pope continued that baptism is a gift and a commitment "to a new kind of evangelism which should include everyone and reach everyone." He wished for this evangelism "to incarnate into our culture, so that Christ ... could realize his kingdom

---

79 see "L'Osservatore Romano", Nov. 1, 1996, p. 9.

Chapter III: The Eucharistic Cosmic Christ and the Sacraments

among us." For the Pope, the great faith of the Latin American churches was proven by "the threefold great love which characterizes the Catholic faith of your nation; the love for the Eucharist, the love for the mother of the Saviour and the love for the church in the person of the Apostle Peter's successor." The article, itself, leaves no doubt that this is not the gospel of Matthew, Mark, Luke and John, but instead the gospel according to the Roman church. It names the crucial person who also mediates the sacramental cosmic powers: Mary, "the holy virgin, the star of the first and the new evangelism ... mother of God and our mother." Do the many ecumenical Protestants really still perceive these shocking antichristian goals arising out of the antichristian spirit? The actual theological problem is not the baptism of children, but rather, the "salvation-bringing" holy act, which is supposed to lead to rebirth. It should be recognized as demonic and, therefore, rejected. No holy act and no sacrament can reconcile humans with the holy and righteous God. There is only one way to gain reconciliation to God and that is through Jesus Christ. Trough Him we can receive salvation and become born again Christians but we must be willing to submit to the power of the true God in Jesus Christ, to repent and ask our saviour Jesus Christ for the forgiveness of all sins including inherited sin. A person becomes righteous before God by receiving forgiveness, and also reconciled to God, through Christ (1 John 1: 8+9). If it were possible to cleanse all ones sins, including that inherited, through the sacraments of baptism and penance, then no one would (or could) die. The fact that all people have to die provides the best proof that sin, especially the inherited sin through Adam, has brought death upon us as its fruit. *"For the wages of sin is death ..."*(Rom. 6: 23). Surely, we want to be on the side of the Bible and the fathers of the Reformation. In Rom. 3: 23, 24+28, we read: "*... all have sinned and fall short of the glory of God; they are now justified by his grace as a gift* [not on the basis of merit or sacraments], *through the redemption that is in Christ Jesus ... For we hold that a person is justified by faith* [in the complete salvation through the sacrificial death of Christ, the author] *apart from works prescribed by the law* [without sacraments, the author]." The so-called sacrament of baptism is a demonically inspired work of the flesh. It can never bring about the righteousness that is valid before God. Therefore, Rom. 4: 5 tells us: *"But to one* *who without works* [this includes alleged holy acts or rituals, the author] *trusts Him who justifies the ungodly, such faith is reckoned as righteousness."*

For further clarification, I would like to add that there is insufficient biblical evidence for the baptism of small children, even when it is not based on the faith in sacraments. Why? By its very nature, a baby can not yet have faith in Christ and be saved on this basis. The faith in Christ and His one and only sacrifice for sins (Hebr.9: 14+15) inherently leads a person to salvation and to becoming a born again christian by the grace of God. **What about baptism? It is not a sacrament. Instead, it is a public demonstration of the born-again believer in front of his church and the invisible world that he has died to sin and is no longer under its dominion (Rom.6: 3-14; 8: 12).** When a person redeemed by Jesus Christ decides to be baptized, he/she promises to break with the old way of life in the flesh, according to the biblical understanding. *"For in Christ Jesus you are all children of God through faith. As many of you as were baptized into Christ have clothed yourselves with Christ"* (Gal.3: 26+27). The phrase "clothed yourselves with Christ" can not apply to rebirth through baptism. Rather, it clearly refers to God's demand for a born-again child of God to live in the Spirit. This shows how important it is to read the Bible contextually, and not fragmentarily or magically. The so-called sacrament of baptism has become a weapon for the Ecumenical movement, wounding its victims and forcing them into apostasy.

7. Confirmation

"Through the sacrament of confirmation, the approximately twelve-year-old Catholics are more perfectly connected to the church and furnished with a **special power** of the Holy Spirit."[80] This special connection to the church obliges the children, or rather adolescents, "to spread and defend the faith both in word and in deed as true witnesses of Christ."[81]

---

80 Fischer-Wollpert, „Wissen Sie Bescheid?" (=Do you have wide-ranging knowledge?), 1982, p. 496.
81 Ibid. p. 496.

The cosmic powers of the so-called spirit are supposed to change these young people into militant Catholic fanatics. In other words, they receive strengthening from the cosmos through the sacrament of confirmation. The priest carries out the ritual by tracing the sign of the cross on the forehead of each confirmand with anointing oil, while saying: "Be sealed with the gift of the Holy Spirit."[82] The sacraments of baptism, confirmation and Eucharist are clearly and accurately described as the three sacraments of initiation. On these occasions, the spirit of Rome incarnates singularly but strongly into those young people who expose themselves to the above sacraments. The incarnation of this spirit, called holy in the Catholic church, is the ultimate goal of the initiation as well as Rome's version of sanctification.

8. The Eucharist

The Eucharist is somewhat like the sacrament of all sacraments. The others are all arranged around it as their common goal. Also known as Holy Communion, the Eucharist supposedly serves to unify those who believe in the sacraments more and more intimately with God. The New-Age esoteric movement talks about kindling and reviving the "focal point" or "light" within each person. These terms have the same content and purpose as those used in the Roman Church. Reconciliation, unification, and revival are terms found in all branches of Western mysticism, Catholic as well as Protestant. They always represent forgeries of faith, salvation and sanctification.

The Eucharist is also called the "holy sacrament of the altar." Through the cosmic power flowing from it, this sacrament burdens Catholics by letting cosmic spiritual powers incarnate into them. The Eucharist was first practiced from the 9th century onwards. But, to show that it is still a very current issue, we will quote comments on this subject published in "L'Osservatore Romano," the official paper of the Roman Church: "It has been given to us to consider [visualize or worship, the author] the sacrament which he has instituted in order to perpetuate the sacrifice of the cross through the ages until his return ..."[83]

---

82 McCarthy, „The Gospel According to Rome", 1995, appendix B.
83 "L' Osservatore Romano", No. 16, April 19, 1996, p. 9.

The sacrifice **has occurred** and can not be perpetuated! In Roman theology, the words "remembrance", "visualization", or "consideration" are linked with the real live presence of Jesus in the host, made transcendent through consecration. We need to realize the blasphemous character of the Eucharist and the continuously repeated sacrifice. That will help us understand the degeneration and perversion of faith from believing in Christ to believing in salvation through sacraments. Pope John Paul II said: "By the power of the act of consecration, the sacrifice for the salvation of the world is located on the altar."[84]

Consecration means that a certain thing or person becomes so sanctified through a ritual that it can be made into God. The deification of Julius Caesar in antique Rome is a good example of this. The act of consecration during the Eucharist supposedly transforms a wafer and some wine into the flesh and blood of a supernatural, invisible Christ by means of blood-magic. To put it bluntly, the wafer and the wine are enchanted to embody the so-called sacrifice of Christ through the sorcery of blood-magic. By now, it has become obvious that this "perpetual sacrifice of Christ" is linked to blood-magical demons. With respect to the night when the Lord's supper was instituted, the Pope observed: "He gave himself as nourishment. He gave himself with his own hands. He gave the body and the blood which were to be sacrificed in the bloody death on the cross for the salvation of the world. He gave himself to the church in the form of bread and wine for the bloodless eucharistic sacrifice through which the one-time sacrifice on the cross would remain present in the sacraments. He gave himself as sacramental food and sacramental drink for the people of the new and eternal covenant, the people on the journey ... Thomas put it like this: The word of the Lord [the words of institution] transformed bread and wine: the bread into flesh, the wine into blood for his remembrance. And he added: This truth is confirmed by faith, not the senses. Have faith! Believing is seeing! Open the eyes of your heart."[85] The Pope closed with the revealing statement: "We worship **the sacrament** that God, the Father, gave us – what a great sacrament ... **in the new custom from the 'upper room', the blood of the covenant**

---

84 Ibid. p. 9.
85 Ibid. p. 9.

is the blood of the Lord, that is the true sacrifice for deliverance which takes the place of the form of the Old Testament and opens the new – definitive, eternal – Testament where the slavery of sin is finally abolished ... by the power of the act of consecration, the sacrifice for the salvation of the world is found on the altar."[86]

As a result, Catholic theology insists that the bloodless sacrifice, i.e. the Eucharist, pertains to the New Testament while the bloody sacrifice relates to the Old Testament. This is nothing but Roman rebellion against God. These words show that the Roman Catholic doctrine separates Jesus' salvation bringing sacrificial death into **two** events:

1. The historical, bodily death of Jesus of Nazareth who died for the sin of the world. In Catholic terms, this means that human suffering finds salvation and human death is conquered forever through the cross of Jesus.[87]

The Bible, on the other hand, teaches us that the historical sacrificial death of Jesus Christ forms the basis for the salvation of humans. It was sin that had seperated us from God. Now, on the cross, **He took the sins of all people upon Himself, and made reconciliation possible. His victory over death was evidenced by His rescurrection.** Now as believers, thankful for our redemption, we **celebrate the Lord's supper, as an act of our obedience and in memory of Him, but never in and through a sacrament!** For all who believe, the historical event of Jesus Christ's sacrificial death has brought about eternal salvation. As true man and true God, Jesus Christ has conquered sin, all works of the devil and death through His death and His resurrection (1 John 3: 5+8; Rom.4: 25; Heb.2: 14).

2. According to Roman theology, Christ, the spirit, transformed bread and wine into real transcendent flesh and blood of Jesus through transubstantiation. The covenant of blood that saves people is not found in the historical fact of the sacrificial death. **Instead, the redeeming blood of Christ must be experienced continuously by participating in the sacrament of the Eucharist. This blood of Christ, that supposedly sanctifies and saves from sin, is created through transubstantiation or consecration in the ritual of**

---

86 Ibid. p. 9.
87 See Chapter II.

Chapter III: The Eucharistic Cosmic Christ and the Sacraments

the holiest sacrament of the altar. What does this mean? Jesus of Nazareth gave one unique bloody sacrifice for the sin of the world. Rome does not challenge this historical fact. They acknowledge it in a juridicial sense. But in actual practice, people are saved by the bread and the wine transformed through transubstantiation. "The sacrifice for the salvation of the world" **literally** lies on the altar of a Catholic church, based on Roman theology. Rome has a magical understanding of John 6: 50-56, where Jesus talked about receiving life from and out of Himself. In their view, Jesus was transcendently transformed into a spirit, the cosmic christ. The spirit of the so-called "eucharistic christ" enters into and surrounds the wafer and the wine during the consecration in the Mass. As Catholics eat the transcendent or spiritual flesh and drink the blood, they commune with the spirit of the cosmos, wrongly called Christ. They receive falsified life from the cosmos! The historical Christ is only mourned because of his death on the cross. "He died for the **suffering** of all people, giving it a purpose from now on." But one does not receive salvation from him! According to Roman theology, a Catholic receives salvation, eternal deliverance, through the "new custom of the upper room" which was made into a sacrament of salvation. Catholic salvation comes from the sacrament of the altar, the Eucharist! The eucharistic christ brings salvation, while the true salvation wrought by Jesus Christ on Calvary has degenerated into the Catholic lifestyle of a mendacious piety. They talk about Jesus Christ as a person, even though the Catholic form of salvation comes from the cosmic eucharistic christ who incarnated into Jesus of Nazareth. The close connection to Ecumenical theology and Protestant liberal theology can clearly be seen here. In practice, Rome has long created two persons with the nature of a divine human: Jesus of Nazareth and the eucharistic christ!

We want to stay with what the fathers of the Reformation professed on the basis of biblical truth: Jesus Christ, true man and true God, unmixed and inseparable, unchangeable and undivided. In our day and age, the Roman Catholic heresies about faith in sacraments must be mercilessly exposed to save people from eternal damnation and keep them from deserting the faith in the sole and unique saviour, Jesus Christ.

9. Penance or the Sacrament of Reconciliation

Penance is carried out within the framework of the so-called "sacrament of reconciliation." Before we deal critically with the sacrament of penance, let us take a quick look at the two kinds of sins in Catholic doctrine. I would also like to refer to the apostolic writing of John Paul II "Motu'proprio." In it, he left no doubt about his authority, beginning with the words: "I declare the following ..." and describing the new "Catechism of the Catholic Church" as infallible. He closed with the words: "I declare that everything I laid down in this present apostolic writing in the form of a "Motu'proprio", has full and lasting validity and should be observed from this day onwards regardless of every other order to the contrary."[88]

1. **The "Deadly Sins"**: "We commit a deadly sin when we violate a commandment of God in a serious matter, with full knowledge and of our own free will. Examples of a serious matter include lack of faith, hating our neighbour, adultery, major theft, murder, etc."[89] A "deadly sin" terminates the divine life which entered into the life of a Catholic during the sacrament of baptism. Such a sin leads to the death of the soul, hence the name. If this "deadly sin" is not regretted and forgiven, it leads to "eternal punishment." It basically constitutes a death-blow for the soul of a Catholic since he loses the "sanctifying grace" he received through the sacrament of baptism. He also forfeits the grace of "justification." For all practical purposes, the disobedient Catholic becomes a pagan who is under the wrath of God. In order that the now "dead" soul may be revived, the transgressor must turn to the church which then mediates "sanctifying Grace", that is new life, to his soul through the sacrament of penance and reconciliation commonly called confession.[90]

2. **The "Venial Sins"**: These can be forgiven without confession. This is the case when one of God's commandments is not seriously broken and when a transgression occurs without complete

---

88 „L'Osservatore Romano", No. 19, May 10, 2002, p. 7-8.
89 Premm, „Dogmatic Theology for the Laity" (Rockford IL: Tan Books, 1967), 373. In: McCarthy, „The Gospel According to Rome", 1995, part 1, ch. 4.
90 In: McCarthy, „The Gospel According to Rome", 1995, part 1, ch. 4.

knowledge and without complete consent.[91] Such transgressions are petty theft, white lies, laziness, lacking of love etc.[92] From a Roman Catholic point of view it is easier to forgive such sins when true repentance is shown. "Venial sins" do not kill the soul but weaken it.! The difference here is comparable to dying and having a light illness. These 'Venial sins' do not carry the burden of eternal punishment.

The Sacrament of penance is to restore the justified relationship between God and the disobedient Catholic, thus the second name: sacrament of reconciliation.

"Those that have fallen through sin from the height of jusifying Grace which they had received can be jusified anew."[93] Justification occurs through confession and the subsequent "sacrament of penance". Often this sacrament is simply called "confession". The confession of "venial sins" is advised, but not obligatory. Catholics are only compelled to confess "deadly sins." During "confession", it is necessary to show repentance and the determination to avoid "deadly sins" in the future through a prayer of penitence. After this act of repentance, the priest acquits the sinner and grants "absolution." As with other sacraments, the power of the "absolution" lies in the execution of the ritual, which includes the exact wording of the absolution formula. Thus, Rome insists that **the church** forgives **all** transgressions because it understands itself to be in the role of the judge.

In the biblical context, the word "repentance" means turning one's life around or changing one's way of thinking. Rome, however, attaches a different meaning to it. The Catholic receives absolution from sin, and thus forgiveness, through the authority of the priest, i.e. the church. But with respect to God, the sinner must try to make amends and compensate for his sin. He must atone for it himself. That is the Roman Catholic meaning of "repentance." Therefore,

---

91 Premm, "Dogmatic Theology for the Laity" (Rockford, IL: Tan Books, 1967), 373 In: McCarthy, "The Gospel According to Rome", 1995, part 1, ch. 4.
92 Ibid p. 83.
93 Council of Trient 6. Sitzung, 14. Kapitel; in Neuner-Roos, a.a.O., No. 812. In: McCarthy, "The Gospel According to Rome", 1995, part 1, ch. 4.

the priest imposes a work of penance on the sinner. It can consist of a donation or exercises of piety. Repetition of the Lord's Prayer, Ave Maria or the rosary may also be included. The work of penance provides atonement for the sin. Through the ritual of the sacrament, reconciliation with God is accomplished and the Catholic is brought back into the state of justification. We can see that this understanding of repentance and forgiveness has no biblical basis, to say nothing of the underlying extra-biblical and antichristian sources of power in the ritualistic sacraments. Real forgiveness only occurs when a believer puts his trust in Jesus Christ as the life-giving Lord and Saviour, bringing Him his sins with remorse and the earnest will to change. He will then receive forgiveness from his Lord Jesus Christ through His unique and **historical** sacrificial death (1John 1: 9). This is the biblical way to be justified before God and to live in a state of reconciliation with God. For the sake of completeness, it should be mentioned that **every sin** against God leads to death, provided that it is not forgiven by Jesus Christ (Ezek.18: 4; Rom.6: 23). In contrast, the Roman church puts itself on the same level as God, since it offers forgiveness, while saying that God demands compensation or restitution, according to their doctrine. Essentially, the Catholic church does not take sin and its consequences with respect to God seriously. After all, a Catholic can supposedly attain rejustification by working off his sins and not through the blood of Christ alone.

10. Anointing of the Sick

By anointing the sick person and speaking a ritual prayer, the priest entrusts him to "the suffering and glorified Lord." The patient is admonished to "**identify** himself consciously with the suffering and death of Christ."[94] As always, this identification with the "death of Christ" is carried out in the form of a ritual. It allows the cosmic spiritual power out of the sacrament, the sanctifying and helping grace, to reach the person who would often be approaching death. The cosmic power of death now flows to the patient through this channel, the sacrament of "grace." In other words, fragments of

---

94 Fischer-Wollpert, „Wissen Sie Bescheid?"(=Do you have wide-ranging knowledge?), 1982, p. 497.

the patient's soul are demonically transformed and disappear into the realm of the dead to become part of the cosmic spiritual power (1.Peter 3: 19). This constitutes the Catholic perversion of James 5: 13-16, where the church of Christ is called upon to pray for its sick. This prayer is centred on true faith, i.e. the trust in Jesus Christ. The confession of sin and forgiveness through Christ are important prerequisites which should not be overlooked. In order to fulfill these conditions, the mind of Christ must be in us (Phil.2: 5). It also includes the willingness to break with every sin (1.Peter 4: 1). As experienced by the Apostle Paul, a longing for the heavenly call arises from this spiritual mindset of faith (Phil.3: 14+15). It allows the believer to confess with Paul: *"I want to know Christ and the power of His resurrection and the sharing of His sufferings by becoming like Him in His death, if somehow I may attain the resurrection from the dead"* (Phil.3: 10+11). Obviously, the confession of Paul has a totally different content than the Catholic "identification with the suffering and death of Christ." But even after the ritual of the sacramental anointment has been completed, the dying person is still not sure if he will be saved by God. "In death, the separation of the soul from the body, the body of the person is subject to decay, while his soul goes to meet God ..."[95] There, the person finds out whether he has attained eternal life. It is the point in time where God decides about the final fate of a person."[96]

Even if a Catholic has lived in the state of "sanctifying grace" and has also been brought into and held in this state through the sacrament of the "last anoiment", he leaves this earth without the assurance of salvation. According to the sacramental rule, the sacrament of the anointing of the sick also includes the sacrament of penance, i.e. confession, and the celebration of the Eucharist with the sick or dying person.

11. Purgatory

In fact, only two groups of Catholic people can hope to be saved by God. Small children who die shortly after receiving the sacra-

---

[95] „Katechismus der Katholischen Kirche" §997. „Catechism of the Catholic church" In: McCarthy, „The Gospel According to Rome" 1995, part 1, ch. 4.
[96] „Council in Florenz, 6. Sitzung". In: ibid. p. 101.

ment of baptism make up one of these groups. The other consists of those who have worked hard on Earth in their "state of sanctifying grace." They have drawn heavily on the so-called "good in themselves" to help others and earnestly sought the "helping grace" against the temptation of sin through regular participation in all sacraments. This applies especially to those who have endured great suffering, either due to external circumstances or self-chastisement. Good examples are the Catholics who were 'beatified' or 'canonized' after their death.

For the majority of Catholics, this "conditional assurance of salvation" has no relevancy. Even if they only committed "venial sins", the Catholic God demands compensation **after death**, unless indulgences were obtained beforehand. The biblical passage in Mt. 5: 26 is wrongly applied to this: "... *until you have paid the last penny.*" These Catholics are seen as neither good enough for Heaven, nor bad enough for hell. Consequently, "there must be some degree of cleansing or punishment after death, depending on the debt of sin."[97] Yet, even the Roman Catholic theologians don't know how long such a Catholic needs to stay in purgatory. He must pay for his sins and his soul is cleansed through the purifying pain there. "Some venial sins tend to cling more strongly than others, just as the soul has more affection for them and is more deeply bound to them. And because it takes longer to cleanse what clings more strongly, it follows that some are tortured longer in purgatory than others, depending on how deeply their soul is entangled with them."[98] However, living Catholics can shorten the purification period of the deceased in purgatory by:

1. Having Masses read and the Mass sacrifice offered for them.
2. Reciting prayers.
3. Giving alms and doing other good deeds.
4. Trying to obtain vouchers for indulgences.

The Catholic church claims to have an immense supply of good deeds in reserve. Its demonic Roman doctrine assumes that each Catholic, who lives in the "state of sanctifying grace", earns merit with every good deed. This merit is also taken into account in

---

[97] Premm, „Dogmatic Theology for the Laity", 434. In: ibid. p. 103.
[98] Summa Theologica by Thomas Aquin (1225-1274). In: ibid. p. 104.

Chapter III: The Eucharistic Cosmic Christ and the Sacraments

purgatory. Therefore, according to this demonic tenet, purgatory is the last chance to gain justification before God through works!

The Catholic 'salvation' involves a long process which begins with the sacrament of baptism. By adhering faithfully to all other sacraments and doing good deeds, the soul continues on the way to salvation and becomes more and more justified. Hence, Roman salvation is based on the idea that the soul becomes good and righteous through it's good deeds. It does so with the help of the sanctifying powers contained in the sacraments! It then receives the last polish in 'purgatory'. In this demonic teaching, the soul essentially redeems itself. With time, it becomes agreeable to God. The chances are that God will approvingly accept it in the end and save it for eternity. In other words, the soul must become good in order to be saved. That is part of Catholic doctrine which cannot be renounced!

Our readers should not make the erroneous assumption that 'purgatory' belongs to the theological history of medieval Catholicism.

Image 3:
S. Rita da Cascia

The doctrine regarding purgatory continues to be a binding factor in the Catholic way to salvation. At the II Vatican Council from 1962-1965, this dogma was confirmed as an integral part of the Roman plan of redemption. The new catechism of the Catholic Church uses the term 'fire of purification', which means the same thing.

As we have already seen in this chapter, the Catholic who seriously practices his faith in sacraments is transformed into a so-called "new creation." This occurs imperceptibly at first. The spiritual cosmic rays out of the invisible world strike him and split off pieces of his spiritual life, which has become fragmented due to idol worship. These fragments or splits disappear into Hades, the realm of the dead in the invisible fallen cosmos. There,

Chapter III: The Eucharistic Cosmic Christ and the Sacraments

they are transformed by the symbiotic union of the human spirit with demonic spirits. These sinister "new creations" in the realm of the dead use their destructive influence to affect especially those Catholics who strongly believe in the sacraments. As mentioned before, these enslaved spirits are at work in and around Catholic churches. They surround statues, crosses, altars, graves, etc. An important part of their slave labour consists of fascinating living people "with the peace of death" and seducing faithful Catholics to practice hypostatic worship. The worshippers are then struck by spiritual, cosmic streams and filled with demonic powers of death. Many of the pictures in Catholic churches show this process very clearly, except that such transformations are described as holy.

In order to understand the cosmic system we live in, we must consult the Bible. It tells us that the cosmos consists of a visible and an invisible world. Before Adam's fall into sin, another fall had already occurred in the invisible world when a certain number of angels became demons (Isa.14: 12-14). They populate the invisible side of this world, our fallen cosmos. But for the sake of our redemption, these demons are under the control of angels employed by God to act as helpers of our salvation and keep the demons in check (Heb.1: 14; Ps.34: 7; Ps.91: 11+12).

Wherever visible idol worship takes place, the invisible world of the demons expands, unseen by the human eye. For this reason, Israel was supposed to destroy the pictures and monuments of idolatry (2 Kings 23) in ancient times. Today, after the law was fulfilled in Jesus, we no longer destroy material cult objects. Instead, we must destroy the **invisible** spiritual power behind the idolatry through faith. **Spiritual annihilation replaces the destruction of material objects!**

How does all of this relate to the subject of "purgatory"?

The human spirits, trapped and transformed in the cosmos, survive the material bodies they have in the visible world. Even the sacrament of the "last anointment" creates spiritual splits. A lot of these splits then land in "purgatory", supposedly to pay off their sins against God. However, they are tormented by demons. **"Purgatory" or the "fire of purification" was not set up by God. Instead it is a gruesome place of captivity, a jail, just as** the realm of the dead is described in 1 Peter 3: 19. These spirits are "purified" more and more from their humanity

Chapter III: The Eucharistic Cosmic Christ and the Sacraments

in order to be completely consumed by the demonic cosmos. The doctrine about "purgatory" is a cruel deception. But unfortunately, it is also a terrible reality in the form of the invisible cosmic place known as the realm of the dead. Once again, this exposes the esoteric roots of the Roman Catholic church in addition to its antichristian spirit.

In conclusion, I would like to illustrate this subject using an anonymous example out of my experience with practical redeemership. It concerns the circumstances of a consecration carried out by a living person. This person was very familiar with Catholic mysticism. Hungry for adventure and power, he wanted to come into contact with what he called "the greatest power." But instead, his "pilgrimage" led him to Lucifer, the greatest force in the fallen cosmos, and caused him to mutate completely into a spiritual being. After intensive battles in prayer, I was able to free this person. As a pastoral warning, I would like to add that it was a time of great misery for him. However, it must also be said that Jesus Christ gave this person an abundance of grace to liberate him from the transformation of purgatory. All honour and glory be to Jesus Christ alone!

"*... to the only God our Saviour, through Jesus Christ our Lord, be glory, majesty, power and authority, before all time and now and forever. Amen*" (Jude 25).

"Pilgrimage into Purgatory"

This is an account of real experiences and suffering in the realm of the invisible fallen cosmos. It concerns a spiritual split of a living person, created by the worship of relic idols.

(P stands for priest; C for candidate)

"P: What do you want?
C: I want to become clean.
P: Why do want to become clean?
C: In order to reign and to gain victory in the name of God.
P: Then let us bow our knees.
P: Is your soul ready for a pilgrimage into the purification?
C: Yes.

P: Close your eyes. Come with me on the pilgrimage. Free your soul. It clings too much to material, earthly things. Break every rope that still holds it in your body. Tell me the ropes and with the help of God I will break them and help you. (The candidate tells the priest what still holds him back.)

P: Now you are free. Your soul, bound to my soul, is penetrating the darkness. A darkness that seems endless. Fire, despair, and fear take over. Overcome these feelings. That is the only way you will penetrate this night.

Are these feelings gone? (The priest waits until the candidate says "Yes.")

P: We are penetrating further into the darkness. A bright light shines toward us and blinds us. You feel joy, pleasure and delight. Overcome these feelings. Do not let them rule your soul. Instead, govern them. Are these feelings gone? Don't let feelings move your soul anymore! (The priest waits until the candidate says "Yes.")

P: Let us climb down into purgatory. You feel heat, pain in your eyes, your mouth, your throat, your lungs, your stomach, your intestines, and your limbs. You go up in flames. You have only one wish: to die so that these torments finally end. But remember, they will never end. Therefore, endure them. Endure them. Endure them! (The priest waits until the candidate no longer shows any sign of pain.)

Peace comes, resurrection is near. Your soul [the split] is purified. You are clean.

Slowly, your soul returns to your body. Purified and clean for the glory of God. Open your eyes slowly. You are tired and need to rest." (End of the pilgrimage)

This is nothing but spiritual murder, wrongly called holy! The soul is brought into a state of indifference towards life, an expression of spiritual death.

12. The Sacrament of Orders

We now come to the last two Catholic sacraments of orders and marriage. It would go beyond the scope of this book to deal thoroughly with the priesthood and the whole hierarchy as well as their authority.[99] The sacrament of orders refers to the sacramental Catholic ordination through which "men are accepted as bishops into the episcopate, as priests into the presbytery or as deacons into the deaconate. These are the three steps of Roman Catholic

---

99 NB: The author McCarthy goes into detail about the authority of priests in his book „The Gospel According to Rome" see part 4 onwards.

ordination."[100] Upon receiving the "holy consecration", they have the authority "to shepherd the church through the word and grace of God."[101] A priest is given the title "Father" or "Pater" in Latin. There are 407,262 (as of 2008)[102] ordained, celibate priests in the entire church, who administer and mediate the power of the sacraments, and 815,237 people who live in orders.

"But you are not to be called rabbi, for you have one teacher, and you are all students. And call no one your father on earth, for you have one Father—the one in heaven. Nor are you to be called instructors, for you have one instructor, the Messiah. The greatest among you will be your servant." (Mt.23: 8-11)

13. Marriage

The sacrament of marriage is instituted by the Catholic wedding ceremony. **The power of the sacrament** sanctifies the marital relationship. "The couple receives a special grace as aid for their married life."[103] The Christian Catholic reason given is that "the Christian spouses signify and partake of the mystery of that unity and fruitful love which exists between Christ and his church. **Through the power of the sacrament of marriage**, they help each other attain holiness in their married life as well as in the rearing and education of their children and, therefore, have their own grace among the people of God in their position and their order."[104]

14. The "Gospel" According to Rome; The Faith in Sacraments

The hypostatic encounter[105] with Christ in the sacraments is seen as a "gift of grace through faith." This gift allegedly enables the Catholic to seek salvation in Christ. For practical purposes,

---

100 McCarthy, "The Gospel according to Rome" 1995, Appendix B.
101 Fischer-Wollpert, „Wissen Sie Bescheid?"(=Do you have wide-ranging knowledge?) 1982, S. 497.
102 Wikipedia International 2008.
103 Ibid. p.370.
104 II Vatican Council, Ki.11. In: Fischer-Wollpert, "Wissen Sie Bescheid?", 1985, p. 497 (=Do you have wide-ranging knowledge?).
105 See Chapter II.

there are only six sacraments available to each person. Their use is supposed to create a personal, or rather hypostatic, relationship to Christ. In the Catholic way to salvation through the sacraments, "God turns to man in order to give himself to man and offer him salvation."[106] Now it is the duty of the Catholic to believe in and accept the salvation offered by the sacraments as a gift of grace. The Catholic professes his faith by receiving these sacraments! In turn, the so-called faith of the Catholic is strengthened by the spiritual power at work in them. That is how the Roman church mediates the grace of Christ and hypostatically brings it to bear through the sacraments. According to Roman understanding, only the Catholic church possesses all mediums of grace. Therefore, only those belonging to the Catholic church can receive the divine grace. After all, Christ "has entrusted the [sacramental] mediation of his work of salvation to the church."[107] The spiritual way of life of the Catholic is characterized by receiving the sacraments and leading a "moral life." These characteristics also distinguish him as a "pilgrim on the road to salvation." Because the Catholic Church believes itself to be the mystical body of Christ, it automatically represents the "mother of all sacraments."[108] The sacramental nature of the church then unfolds itself in the individual sacraments.[109] They are understood to be the power source of grace in the "new covenant" which nourishes the believers. According to the II Vatican Council (1962-1965)[110], the sacraments of the "new covenant" help create a new heaven and a new earth.

15. The Sacramentaries

Based on Roman theology, the sacramentaries were instituted by the Catholic church, not Jesus Christ. They are alleged to be signs of the invisible workings of the spirit and are intended to prepare

---

106 Fischer-Wollpert, "Wissen Sie Bescheid?", 1982, p. 497. (=Do you have wide-ranging knowledge?).
107 Fischer-Wollpert, "Wissen Sie Bescheid?", 1982, p. 497. (=Do you have wide-ranging knowledge?).
108 Ibid. p. 601.
109 Ibid. p. 498.
110 I Vatican Council, Ki.35. In Fischer-Wollpert, "Wissen Sie Bescheid?", 1982, p. 498 (=Do you have wide-ranging knowledge?).

Chapter III: The Eucharistic Cosmic Christ and the Sacraments

the Catholics "to receive the actual effect of the sacrament. At the same time, such signs sanctify the different circumstances of life."[111] These so-called "holy signs" are understood to be a kind of imitation of the sacraments' effects. Just as for the sacraments, they include:
1. the outward action and
2. the inner effect.[112]

The sponsors of the sacraments are priests as well as deacons. Since the II Vatican Council, lay people can also be appointed as sponsors by the bishop in charge.

Through the sacramentaries, the Catholic church intercedes on behalf of different people:
- the office holder in the ordination of an abbot, for example
- for those who are legitimately commissioned to use an object consecrated for liturgical purposes, such as the consecration of a house, the blessing of a car or exorcisms.[113]

The intercession of the Roman church occurs by means of rituals and is a an act of blessing. The consecrated aids, or sacramentaries, like crosses, candles, etc. give off powers similar to those of the sacraments. As mediums of grace, they allegedly strengthen and promote faith. The acts of blessing, carried out with consecrated objects, or sacramentaries, involve ritual signs and procedures. Through the accompanying and supporting powers out of the cosmos, they are supposed to strengthen the faith in various phases of life and are understood to be "symbols of salvation." Faith in the salvation-bringing sign is necessary for the cosmic, eucharistic christ of the sacraments to do his work of salvation in the Catholic sense. Finally, we would like to list several of the well-known, officially recognized sacramentaries of the Roman church, including different ritual acts and consecrated objects:
"stations of the cross, crucifixes, scapulars,[114] miracle-working medals, genuflection, lighting candles, pictures and figures of saints, the

---

111 II Vatican Council, Lit. 60. In: Ibid. p. 499.
112 See Chapter II.
113 See Fischer-Wollpert, "Wissen Sie Bescheid?", 1982, p. 500. (=Do you have wide-ranging knowledge?).
114 Scapulars are a type of shoulder dress. They are worn to show the spiritual association with a certain order and, furthermore, the participation in the graces and merits of that order. Donning a scapular is rewarded with indulgences. See Fischer-Wollpert, "Wissen Sie Bescheid?", 1982, p.524 (=Do you have wide-ranging knowledge?).

sign of the cross, ointments with holy oil, holy water, putting ash on one's forehead, bell ringing, observing holy holidays, consecrated palm branches, the consecration of a new car, the blessing of the respiratory tract, and exorcism."[115]

What are the blessings promised to the Catholic who diligently uses these sacramentaries?

The Roman church specifies the following blessings:

"the reception of helping grace
- material blessings such as good health or protection
- an increased love for God
- remorse with respect to sin
- reduction of earthly punishment for sins
- forgiveness of venial sins
- protection from the devil."[116]

Obviously, the Roman Catholic faith in sacraments has nothing to do with the biblical Jesus Christ. It is the exact opposite of true faith. The principles of faith began to change in the 9th century. As the term "faith" was changed and emptied of meaning, a falsified Jesus Christ developed out of the antichristian spirit. In Greek, the Antichrist is literally called the "instead of-Christ."

With the development of the eucharistic "instead of-Christ", the Catholic church became more and more antichristian. As a result, the true, biblical Jesus Christ left this emerging Anti-church. **The eucharistic, cosmic christ took over the reign. This spirit out of the darkness saves people from life and not from death!** The fruit is the perversion of a religion based on faith into a faith based on sacraments.

"But even if we or an angel from heaven should proclaim to you a gospel contrary to what we proclaimed to you, let that one be accursed! As we have said before, so now I repeat, if anyone proclaims to you a gospel contrary to what you received, let that one be accursed!"
Gal.1: 8+9

---

115 See McCarthy, "„The Gospel According to Rome", 1995, part 1, Ch.3.
116 Ibid. p.65.

16. The "Charta Oecumenica"

Due to its timeliness, I have added this subject to the section about the cosmic-sacramental christ.

The "Charta Oecumenica," reflects this universal, cosmic christ. It was signed by the president of the Conference of European Churches, Metropolit Jéremie, and the president of the Council of European Episcopal Conferences, Cardinal Vlk, on April 22, 2001. The Charta is understood to be the "guideline for a growing cooperation among the churches of Europe."[117]

The first point of this Charta states unequivocally: We believe in "the One Holy, Catholic and Apostolic Church."

Jesuit dialectic makes use of Protestant terms, but fills them with a completely different meaning. In the specific declarations of commitment, for example, it sounds like this:

"jointly called to union in faith"
- "jointly preach the gospel"
- "move towards each other"
- "We commit ourselves to co-operation in Christian upbringing, in theological training and continuing education …"

Therefore, the Charta recommends ecumenical friendships, marriages, etc. On the international as well as the national level, the co-operation among the different church bodies is supposed to be increased, especially between the Conference of European Churches and the Council of European Episcopal Conferences. One of the main duties of Ecumenism is the reconciliation between nations and cultures, in addition to the preservation and protection of all creation.

From June 25 to July 2, 2003, the "Assembly of the Conference of European Churches" took place. Because a so-called reconciliation requires a reconciler, the Protestant state and free churches received a theological paper in advance, to help prepare them for the assembly. For better understanding, I would like to add that the Orthodox, Anglican and Old Catholic churches as well as almost all Protestant state and free churches belong to this conference. In

---

117 cec.kek.org/Deutsch/ChartafinG.htm.

Chapter III: The Eucharistic Cosmic Christ and the Sacraments

this preparatory document, the cosmic christ is introduced as: "Jesus Christ heals and reconciles ...". The duty of this ecumenical christ consists of "healing and reconciling through his power." Alleged Protestants also express regret that they are not yet allowed to celebrate the Eucharist with the Catholics "although we all believe that this is the central expression of the service of reconciliation." Furthermore, the theological paper points out that Jesus is the "crucified **healer**."[118]

All of the above are justified by the gospels where Jesus "healed many of the shunned people of his time." "He shared the healing power that belongs to the Kingdom of God with those who were robbed of every power."[119]

Now let us look at the reason for the sacrificial death of Jesus in our place from the perspective of satanic cosmology: "Sympathy brought Jesus to the cross: He took the worst upon himself in order to give us something better." Consequently, Jesus did not die for the sins of the world, but "as a benefactor for all of humanity." "His wounds on the cross" became " the source of healing for all human weakness." As I have already established earlier (see Chapter II), the Catholic theology of the cross also consists of sympathy for the dying Jesus. He supposedly died for the suffering of all people, i.e. humans as victims. In contrast, the New Testament says that He died for the sins of humanity because humans are perpetrators! But unfortunately, the Saviour for sinners has become a benefactor and healer of humanity, even in Protestant theology! This ensures applause from the Roman church as well as all religions, shaman sects and the satanic New-Age movement. According to this ecumenical Protestant theology, Jesus Christ heals **the world** through his death and resurrection and reconciles it with God.[120]

The healing reconciler, Jesus Christ, "is not just the redeemer for humanity, but also the saviour for the **whole cosmos** because he restores the original union of the cosmos and brings all people back together."[121] This cosmocrator or cosmic christ, who allegedly saved the whole cosmos, "restores the old harmony with nature." Thus,

---

118 cec.kek.org/Deutsch/A12ThemePaper-print.htm.
119 Ibid.
120 Ibid.
121 Ibid.

"**humans** are unified with God forever. Through the incarnation, humankind became part of a unity with the Divine."[122]

In summary, the "Charta Oecumenica" uses the old Catholic heresies and also adapts them to all other religious systems, paving the way to a religious union. This union is an important prerequisite for the coming of the Antichrist, the Intead-of-christ.

"Let no one deceive you in any way; for that day will not come unless the rebellion comes first and the lawless one is revealed, the son of destruction." (2.Thess. 2: 3)

17. The Rosary and its Significance for the Catholic Soul Today – The Chain of God's children that binds them to God

There is another way, or rather, another method of meditative, contemplative unification with the Catholic Trinity. This method consists of the prayer formula of the Rosary. When used according to the correct ritual, it creates enormous amplification of spiritual powers through the arousal of innate forces of death within one's own microcosmic environment. As a result of this cosmic-demonic awakening, the transcendent, mystical effects of the sacraments, the sacramental helpers and the sacramentaries are greatly increased. In this respect, John Paul II was one of the most important role models for devout Catholics. He prayed the Rosary at the relics or statues of Catholic saints in order to call on and worship them hypostatically, as is often done with Marian statues.

To understand this method of power amplification, we will take a detailed look at the Rosary, also called Rosarium Virginis Mariae. On Jan. 31, 2003, the official Vatican press published a documentation entitled "Rosarium Virginis Mariae" in the L'Osservatore Romano, starting on page 8. It was compiled by Barile, Professor at the Theological Faculty of the Dominicans in Bologna, on behalf of the Pope. No one in the Vatican, not even a future Pope, can go back on these "thoughts." They are binding. To ensure that no one misunderstands them as the personal opinion or mere recommendation of a professor, John Paul II issued a 45-page booklet with papal authority on Oct. 16, 2002, with the title: "Announcements of the

---
122 Ibid.

Chapter III: The Eucharistic Cosmic Christ and the Sacraments

Apostolic Chair – Apostolic Letter Rosarium Virginis Mariae, His Holiness Pope John Paul II to the Bishops, the Clergy, the Members of Orders and the Believers about the Rosary." In the following discussion, we will be referring to this booklet and its reprint in the L'Osservatore Romano, the documentation from Oct. 18, 2002, as well as the article already mentioned from Jan. 31, 2003.

The precise information about citations is very important to make people realize that these practices were not confined to the Middle Ages, but are still relevant today. Let us now look more closely at the Apostolic Letter, which begins with historical considerations.

The Historical Development of the Rosary

The Pope traced the "origin and development of the basic motives" from the obligatory Catholic perspective. First, we will quote the article in the January issue. It is supposed to yield a "synthesis of purpose and a method of prayer."

The Development into a Method:

1. **The prayer was compressed into a short form, understood to be the repetition of a formula. The well-known repetition in Psalm 69: 2 was cited as an example. In the Catholic translation, it reads: "Save me God, for the waters have reached my neck." With every repetition, the Catholic supposedly "always" breathes "Christ." This led to the development of the "hesychasm," a prayer technique of inhaling and exhaling, filled with the words: "Lord Jesus, Son of God, have mercy on me!" This technique stems from the 14th century mysticism of the Eastern church and is still practiced on Mount Athos.**
2. This repetition to "continually breathe Christ" needed to be numbered. The prayers were counted. According to the Pope's reasoning, "repetition and indefinite waiting periods create anxiety" while counting brings the release of completion.
3. "After all, counting in prayer underlines the meaning of the number," in allusion to the wellknown magic of numbers. The believers are supposed to pray the numbers of the Psalms, i.e. 150 prayer formulae! This gives the Rosary a connection to the book of Psalms.

Chapter III: The Eucharistic Cosmic Christ and the Sacraments

4. After some time of development, "the Psalms were replaced by a certain number of short forms." Allegedly, the petitions had increased so much that the content of the Psalms no longer covered them. One may accuse me of prejudice, but I presume the real explanation to be that Mary is not mentioned in the Psalms as the queen of heaven. Otherwise, the believers in the Old Testament would have had to pray to the queen of heaven, called Babylon, the great whore, in the New Testament. "As a result, the Psalms were **replaced** by the 150 formulae; and a varying number of Pater noster and Ave Maria for every hour of prayer took the place of the fixed-hour prayer." From then on, the Psalms increasingly lost significance and interest in favour of the prayerful devotion to the Catholic Mary.
5. The counting also promoted the prayer "for the mysteries of Christ." According to the Pope, the reason for this was the worship of the cross on Good Friday and the heartfelt sympathy with the death of Christ. At that point, the participation of the Catholic Mary in the suffering of Christ asserted itself. The believer was supposed to feel sympathy and love for her as well. In addition to the meditations on the life of Christ in the New Testament, the Marian psalms were created as a counterpart.
6. The Marian psalms originated in the Cistercian monasteries of the 12th century, a century characterized by mysticism. It became customary "to add a liturgical Marian antiphony to the Psalms." Later, the 150 Psalms were remodelled into 150 rhythmic Marian psalms. In practice, only one verse from a Psalm was used in order to create 150 liturgical Marian antiphonies. This gave rise to the meditations on the "Joys of the Blessed Virgin." Stephan of Sallay, who died 1252, developed the Marian "prayer exercise consisting of the 15 joys of Mary." The shift of focus from Christ to Mary had no significance in the eyes of the Pope. He insisted that the spirit of the Rosary still concentrated on the meditation of "vitae Christi." As proof, he mentioned that "the meditations about the public life of Jesus begin with His baptism and end with the Last Supper, whereby special attention is paid to the presence of Mary." Jesus supposedly even asked Mary to bless his public activity! Since the Scripture does not grant Mary any special status, a wide variety of myths continue

to flourish, like daisies in spring. According to the Pope, Christ first explained His upcoming Passion to Mary alone. Or, to cite another example, Christ is said to have greeted His mother with "Salve sancta parens" which means, "Greetings, Holy Mother." The formula prayers of the Rosary reflected this shift. The meditations for the worship of the Queen and Virgin Mary, also called Virginis Mariae, increasingly supplanted the meditations about the life of Christ, or "Meditationes vitae Christi."

7. "The formulae changed as well." At the beginning of the fundamental changes, "the Lord's Prayer was most often used ... as an instrument of counting the prayer formulae." Later, around 1200, the Marian greeting of "Ave Maria" predominated.
8. "Hence, a Rosarium consisting of 50 Ave Maria and a psalter of 150 Ave Maria crystallized." The process of development was completed in the 13th century.
9. Under the influence of the occupying Islamic Moors, the prayer chain established itself in Spain. For Muslims, it serves to visualize the 99 names of Allah.
10. A single method of prayer linked all of these factors and harmonized them.
    From 1408 onwards, the 150 Ave Maria psalms were organized into 15 groups of ten with an "Our Father" preceding every ten psalms.
    The 50 Ave Maria of the Rosary were combined with 50 meditations on the name of Jesus, creating a total of 100 clauses around 1460.
11. Circa 1465, a Dominican first used the Rosary "as a pastoral instrument." The "Brotherhood of the Rosary" was founded by the Dominicans around 1470. In the course of one year, the alleged 5475(!) wounds of the suffering of the Lord were supposed to be worshipped, i.e. 365 days a year multiplied by 15.
    50 formula prayers to honour Christ
    - 50 formula prayers to praise the crucified Lord
    - 50 formula prayers to praise the resurrection

This formed the basis for the Psalter of the Virgin with 150 Ave Maria which also belonged to the formula prayers. From roughly 1488 to the present, the same "mysteries" are prayed. The Rosary was now expected to provide magical acquisitions of power for the subsequent Counter-Reformation initiated by the Dominicans as well as the possibility of indulgences from the temporal consequences of sin. In 1569, the time of the Reformation, the Rosary became an instrument of power-laden magical prayer under Pope Pius V. He said: "The Rosary, or Psalter of the Blessed Virgin, is a type of prayer through which Mary is worshipped by repeating the greeting of the angel 150 times, corresponding to the Psalms of David. And after every 10 Ave Maria, the Lord's Prayer is added along with meditations to visualize the entire life of our Lord Jesus Christ."

Mary, the Mediatrix of "Grace" in the Formula Prayer of the Rosary

In his Apostolic Statement[123], published as a booklet and documentation on Oct. 16, 2002, the Pope insisted that the Rosary "developed gradually in the 2nd century under the inspiration of the Holy Spirit." It allegedly became a popular prayer among many saints and, therefore, "the Rosary remains a prayer of great significance in the 3rd millennium which has just begun and is destined to bring forth fruits of holiness." Consequently, the Rosary is supposed to be a medium to make Christ accessible to the world again. This thought paradigm stands in stark contrast to all teachings of the New Testament. As already redeemed children of God, we are taught to bring forth fruits of the Spirit, or fruits of holiness, through believing, studying, labouring, battling, and every other form of effort. Only under these conditions will a true believer be able to proclaim to the world the grace of God he has received with spiritual power. Beyond just believing in the facts of salvation, a real Christian is also led by the Spirit to live in and through them. See Eph.4-6. Only a learning Christian, also called a disciple, becomes an active Christian, or imitator of Christ, who produces fruits of holiness. On the other hand, a person who is merely religious will generate fruits of magical powers through invocatory repetition, as done in all esoteric, shamanistic religious systems. The more monotonous repetition, the more demonic transcendent power is freed. The same thing occurs with Hindu and Buddhist mantras (see Isaiah 8: 19).

---

123 Announcement from the apostlic chair, Oct. 16, 2002 and „L'Osservatore Romano", No. 42, Oct. 18, 2002, p. 9-16.

Chapter III: The Eucharistic Cosmic Christ and the Sacraments

The prayer formula brings those who practice it under the influence of spirits of death. These spirits give them powers out of the realm of death, which Rome falsely calls "fruits of holiness."

According to John Paul II, the Rosary leads those who pray it to the beginning of salvation, i.e. Mary! After all, the process of redemption is said to have begun when Christ became flesh in Mary's womb. This is always the reason cited for praising Mary virtually as co-redeemer. The Rosary thus starts out with "the prayer of Mary, her unceasing Magnificat." As a result, it initially creates contact with the Mary, the so-called queen of heaven, a cosmic spirit from the court of Babylon, the whore (see Jer.7: 16-20).

John Paul II continued: "Through the Rosary, Christian people attend the school of Mary where they are initiated into the meditation on [hypostatic visualization of] the beauty of the face of Christ and the depth of his love." Catholic salvation appears to lie in the arousal of mystical-erotic feelings! This is called "fullness of grace." Those who pray the Rosary "actually receive it from the hands of the mother of the Redeemer, herself."

In summary: Mary alone is the medium of grace that conveys the Roman gospel. She mediates grace in the form of spiritual powers from Hades, the realm of death. The words of Jesus in John 14: 6, "I am the way, and the truth, and the life. No one comes to the Father except through me," are twisted and detoured by Rome. Mary acts as mediator on the way to Jesus and the Father. According to the Catholic church, no one comes to Jesus except through Mary! It should have become very clear that the "Jesus" who can only be reached through Mary has nothing to do with the biblical Christ. Rather, it is Lucifer misappropriating the name of Jesus.

In the documentation, John Paul II professed to have "prayed" the Rosary since his childhood, as part of the "school of Mary." It allegedly gave him spiritual strength in times of joy and trial. At the beginning of his pontificate in 1978, John Paul II pointed out that, "in a sense, the Rosary is a commentary of prayer on the last chapter of the Constitution Lumen Gentium compiled by the Second Vatican Council, the chapter that deals with the wonderful presence of the mother of God in the mystery of Christ and the church."

As co-redeemer, as mediatrix of forces that Rome deems holy, and, in effect, as the incarnation of the Holy Spirit, Mary has the necessary powers to bring about the unity of all true and alleged Christians. She was the centre of the II Vatican Council from 1962-1965 where they decided to unify all Christians and, in the end, all people. Mary is the mistress of Ecumenism. In addition, the Rosary with its prayer formulae plays an important role in arousing the powers of magic to help reach the goals set by Rome, just like the sacraments, sacramentaries, statues and shrines. The forces connected with the Rosary are not produced by dead statues and pictures, spiritually animated by hypostatic contemplation. Instead, these powers are created by living people repeating mantra formulae to awaken the deeper layers of their microcosmos. The unification of the micro- and macrocosmos then takes place. Consequently, the position of the person praying also changes. A relatively passive worshipper of hypostatic statues becomes a relatively active worshipper, or rather conjuror, through the Rosary. Therefore, the Rosary does not serve as a religious alternative to the macrocosmic places of worship, but rather, a magical counterpart. It is used against the enemies of Rome in the same way, for defensive and offensive purposes. Mary, herself, receives the broken pieces of soul from the worshippers. These splits are subsequently transformed into demonic Marian power. Hence, a person who prays the Rosary becomes more and more susceptible to the control of Lucifer and his mistress from the house of Babylon. The "Ave Maria" opens his mystical eyes, allowing the events of Jesus' life to pass by hypostatically. These events make up "the joyful, painful and glorious Rosary", and give the Catholic "a living connection to Jesus through the heart of his mother." Personal, clerical and national events can also be included in the prayer formulae. An ex-Catholic told me that she was always beset by demonic Roman forces and mentally pressed to return to the bosom of the church, i.e. Mary, whenever her family prayed the Rosary at a Catholic shrine. Offensive spiritual battle was necessary until the soul of this believer had completely healed and could no longer be reached by such demonic attacks.

After the powers of the Catholic shrines began to recede, John Paul II rediscovered the often neglected formula prayers of the magical Marian Rosary for the church. This was another tactic of a Pope fighting for the whore of Babylon. He wanted to reanimate the Rosary and use the resulting forces of death against the enemies of Rome as well as for the promotion of Ecumenism. In the battle against the Reformation, the Dominicans had also used the Rosary "to protect the church from the spreading heresies." Because of the opposition to himself, John Paul II proclaimed the year of the Rosary for Rome, which started in October 2002 and ended in October 2003. It was supposed to be a "Marian coronation, in order to encourage the meditation on the countenance of Christ in the fellowship and school of the most Blessed Mother." The goal was to see Jesus through the eyes of Mary! Those praying the Rosary will indeed see what the false Catholic Mary sees, namely Lucifer! In his "Apostolic Statement," the Pope wished and called for the Rosary to be "presented and valued" in all Christian communities during the year of the Rosary. He saw it as a fruitful pedagogical opportunity "for neoevangelism," or rather re-Catholicisation. With respect to the other Christian denominations, he commented: "When the Mother is honoured, the Son is also recognized, loved and glorified in the right way." Thus, the Rosary was supposed to help promote Ecumenism. Interestingly, the Roman church and the German Bishops' Conference, together with the German Protestant state church, the Orthodox church, various Christian organizations, and the German Protestant Alliance, decided to proclaim 2003 as the year of the Bible, exactly the same year as that of the Rosary. That can hardly be a mere coincidence! Rome's participation in the year of the Bible and the reactivation of the Rosary in the same year had many negative effects. Surely, a lot of naïve Protestants began to understand the Bible through the eyes of Mary and discovered a different Jesus as well as a different gospel. Moreover, the Ecumenical contemplation of the Bible was undermined by the multitude of fanatical fundamentalists praying the Rosary. Many Protestants fulfilled the words of the Pope, honouring the Mother and seeing the Son in a totally different way ...

They did not want to recognize that the Roman-Babylonian system stems from the spirit of the Antichrist. This disobedience will bring about the curse of God.

"For the time has come for judgment to begin with the household of God" (1 Peter 4: 17).

Chapter III: The Eucharistic Cosmic Christ and the Sacraments

What other themes and subjects does Rome find fitting for the Rosary?

- World peace – in connection with the formula prayer to Mary, asking her for the gift of peace.
- Family – as a powerful prayer to maintain the institution of the family and as an act of submission to the maternal care of Mary, manifested especially in Lourdes and Fatima.
- Remembrance of the saints – those saints are mentioned who have "discovered an authentic way of sanctification" in the prayers of the Rosary, e.g. Louis-Marie Grignion de Montfort, Padre Pio, and Bartolo Longo. The latter allegedly made the following statement, which was sanctioned by the Pope: "Whoever spreads the Rosary, is saved."

Mary as the Basis for Christ-Centred Meditation

As we have already cited, the people praying the Rosary are supposed to contemplate Christ through Mary. That leads to Catholic sanctification and salvation. The goal of Catholic meditative contemplation is to become "enchanted with the beauty of the Saviour," just like the disciples. Meditation transforms Christ's painful Way of the Cross into splendour and glory. **For those praying the Rosary, salvation from all human suffering takes place through their sympathy for the suffering of Christ!**

Image 4: Rosary

They are "opened" in order to "receive the life of the Trinity within ourselves [i.e. themselves, the author]." In reality, this means that they become more and more open to the mystical, spiritual forces of death who are seeking to unite with them. That is called "seeing God."

"The contemplation of Christ has its incomparable model in Mary. The countenance of the Son belongs to her in a special way." Thus, the Rosary promotes

Catholic salvation through the mystical, erotic meditation on the beauty of Mary as the prototype of Christ's beauty. The corny erotic language and the focus on all types of feelings come from Babylon, the great whore. Contemplating Mary and her Christ supposedly "brings forth redeeming powers" and is seen as the key to freeing up spiritual cosmic streams. This meditation is not merely a recollection or reminiscence, but entails conjuring up the historical past and bringing it into the present transcendently. It leads to the development of transcendent demonic forces, programmed for historical, or rather, mystical memories. They demonstrate their power through hypostatic apparitions (see Chapter 2). Likewise, the liturgy in a Mass is more than just a mystical or historical recollection. It aims to conjure the object of contemplation into the present. The liturgy is "the climax [of the Mass , the author], which all the activities of the church are working towards. It is also **the source from which all its power flows.**" According to the Pope, the liturgy constituted "a work of salvation par excellence" and "the Rosary, as a meditation about Christ and Mary, a contemplation of salvation." The Rosary connects the faithful Catholic with Mary, who has taken on the duty of education. As John Paul II put it, Mary protects, preserves and educates to make the Catholic more like Christ. She "portrays the sanctuary of the Holy Spirit." In fact, she becomes an imitation of the Holy Spirit. Once again, it shows that the Catholic Mary is the hidden incarnation of the Catholic holy spirit. In the eyes of John Paul II, the worship of Mary was the form of piety that "makes a soul more like our Lord and devoted to God ... The more devoted a soul is to Mary, the more it is devoted to Jesus Christ, himself. Nowhere else does the way of Christ and of Mary seem so deeply united than in the Rosary." According to Catholic doctrine, Mary is Christ and Christ is Mary in the Holy Spirit. That amounts to a perverse imitation of the divine relationship of the Holy Spirit to Jesus (John 14: 15-17,26; 16: 8,13-15). Christ and Mary are synonymous and hold the synergistic powers of the Trinity. "Mary lives completely in Christ and in the functions of Christ." Furthermore, the constant repetitions of the Ave Maria in the Rosary form "the fundamental basis for the meditation on the mysteries to unfold." What is meant by these mysteries?

Chapter III: The Eucharistic Cosmic Christ and the Sacraments

- A "short version of the gospel" on the basis of the Ave Maria.

"The joyful mysteries."
- are rooted "in the event of Christ becoming human," but focus on Mary, to whom was said: "Greetings to you, Mary." "As far as she is concerned [through her], all of humanity is enclosed in the Fiat [affirmation] with which Mary immediately accepts the will of God."

The luminous mysteries
- deal with Jesus' public activities. "First, his baptism in the Jordan, secondly, his self-revelation at the wedding in Cana, thirdly, his preaching about the kingdom of God with the call to repent, fourthly, his transfiguration and last, fifthly, the institution of the **Eucharist**, the sacramental expression of the Easter mystery."
- These are said to be the mysteries of the light. A service "of mercy which he continues to exercise until the end of the world, especially through the sacrament of reconciliation [confession and penance] that he has entrusted to the church." The final climax of the luminous mystery "is the institution of the Eucharist. In Cana, Mary received her duty which accompanied Jesus to the end: Do whatever he tells you (John 2: 5)!"

The sorrowful mysteries:
- "The Rosary selects several moments of the Passion ... the sorrowful mysteries lead the believer to **relive the death of Christ by standing under the cross beside Mary, in order to penetrate the depth of God's love for humanity with her and experience the whole revitalizing power through this.**"

The glorious mysteries:
- "The contemplation of Christ's countenance can not stop at the picture of the crucified Lord. He is risen." In addition, the glory of Mary is equated with this: "... she was also exalted and gained the extraordinary privilege of **being allowed to take in advance** the destination intended for all righteous persons in the resurrection of the flesh. Finally, she was crowned with glory ... and shines as the queen of the angels and the saints as the

preview and climax of the eschatological reality of the church and in anticipation of it."

The mystery of Mary's path
- "A model path of the virgin of Nazareth, the woman of faith, of silence and of listening ... A path of Marian piety that is animated by the inseparable relationship that connects Christ to his mother."

"The mysteries of Christ are, in a sense, the mysteries of his mother as well."

The mystery of Christ is the mystery of man.
- Allegedly, the mystery of man can only be explained by the mystery of the Word becoming flesh. This realization, gained in contemplation, allows faithful users of the prayer formulae to grasp the "truth about mankind."

"The rhythm of human life pulsates in the Rosary, in order to harmonize it with the rhythm of divine life in the joyful fellowship of the holiest Trinity, which is the destiny and yearning of our existence." In other words, Mary is supposed to show those praying the Rosary who they are and also who and what God is. One day, these people will understand that they have not served the biblical Mary —if it were possible—, but Babylon. They will realize that they obeyed the **forces of death** in place of the crucified Lord, Lucifer instead of the risen Lord, and Babylon, the mediatrix of all powers of death, in lieu of the divine person of the Holy Spirit. But unfortunately, most will not realize this until it is too late.

John Paul II pointed out efficacious methods to help the forces of death unfold their effectiveness through the formula prayers of the Rosary. Here, the liturgy plays an important role as well as the embedded sacraments and sacramentaries, structured by a sequence of rituals. Moreover, John Paul II recommended the practice of Eastern breathing techniques. He admitted, "that there is a new need for contemplation in the Western world today, which **sometimes takes on very attractive forms in other religions."** The formula prayers of mystical Sufistic Islam and Lamaistic Buddhism fascinated him. Further, he said: "The Rosary fits in well with this picture of widespread global religious phenomena." Nevertheless, he wanted to maintain the unique characteristics of the Rosary, since it

Chapter III: The Eucharistic Cosmic Christ and the Sacraments

contained the Catholic theology that gives the Catholic users their religious identity. Yet, he did aim to create so-called improvements, or amplifications of power, through the integration of foreign religious elements. His friend, the Dalai Lama, saw it the same way. His Lamaistic Buddhism is supposed to strengthen Catholicism via the integration of Buddhist elements, without a mixing of religions or syncretism occurring. We must ask: How can they prevent that? Or do they even want to prevent it? One area this Pope specialized in was the seduction of all Protestants. The monopolization of Protestants began with the II Vatican Council in the 1960's, using every form of fraud. In his thoughts on the documentation[124], the constantly moralizing Pope was not afraid to lie shamelessly: "It should not be forgotten that the Ave Maria is, in itself, an Ecumenical prayer. After all, the theology of the Reformation never rejected calling on Mary so that she may pray for us and provide intercession."

However, the theology of the Reformation cited by the Pope did indeed say the exact opposite. Luther, for example, turned decisively against the pilgrimages which were used "to make money."[125] This included "the miraculous signs for which the Rosary is praised."[126] Luther called all such things "legends of lies." He held the view that, initially, there were numerous Catholics who remembered the saints in their prayers with good intentions. But, "soon afterwards, the invocation of the [deceased] saints followed. And soon after the invocation, strange pagan abominations and abuses spread one upon the other, such that the pictures [of the saints] were thought to have their own secret powers, just like the magicians and sorcerers …"[127] Further, Luther wrote that calling on the saints or expecting help from them has no basis in Scripture. The best act of worship is to call on Jesus Christ alone in all difficulties, since He is the **only intercessor**.[128] Of course, one should honour the living saints [i.e. true Christians leading a credible life]. Yet, this does not mean

---

124 L'Osservatore Romano", No. 10, March 7, 2003, p. 9, 10.
125 Die Bekenntnisschriften der Evangelisch-Lutherischen Kirche", 1979, p. 325. (The Confession Statements of the Protestant Lutheran Church).
126 Ibid. p. 325.
127 Ibid. p. 324.
128 Ibid. p. 83b, 83c.

that "that one should and must call on the dead saints."[129] Luther continued: "Therefore, we want to prove that they [Rome, the author] not only make intercessors out of the saints, but also *mediatore redemptiones* [mediating saviours, the author].[130] As a logical consequence, Luther also turned against the Catholic Mary. Rome claims that she:

- prays for the church
- overcame death
- protects Christians from Satan
- "came in place of Christ"
- "wanted to reconcile Christ."

Luther remarked that although the biblical Mary "is worthy of highest praise, she does not want to be equated with Christ." In summary, all biblical and post-biblical saints who were and are true Christians should be honoured for their acts of faith and named as role models. Yet, "we can neither commend nor accept their opinion and habit regarding the worship or invocation of the saints. One should not hope to become righteous before God through the merits of Mary."[131]

Thus, we can see how John Paul II, against his better knowledge; obviously lied when he cited the fathers of the Reformation and characterized the Rosary as an Ecumenical prayer with universal significance. In the already mentioned article from Mar. 7, 2003, the Pope expressed his thoughts and recommendations regarding the inter-confessional and inter-religious use of the Rosary. Then, he quickly inserted the "legends of lies" described above, aiming to promote antichristian Ecumenism and hoping that no one would bother to verify his statements. In our case, however, he was wrong!

Now, let us continue in our critical consideration of the Rosary. The Pope focussed especially on the contents of its contemplative, meditative prayers, whereby the Marian Rosary "is, in truth, only one method of contemplation." In this case, the method consists of a precise ritual order. When followed meticulously, it leads to a cosmic unfurling of power through the hypostatic contemplation of mythological Catholic history. Moreover, an amplification of the

---

129 Ibid. p. 317.
130 Ibid. p. 319.
131 Ibid. p. 323.

Chapter III: The Eucharistic Cosmic Christ and the Sacraments

cosmic-demonic spiritual powers occurs if foreign religious myths complement the Catholic mythology. The Rosary is slowly becoming a universal, multi-religious method with multi-religious contents that are supposed to help pave the way for religious unity. The aim of the Pope in promoting the Rosary was more than just to have Catholics remember the biblical stories and Marian myths. Cosmic power only develops when history is transcendently conjured into the present through hypostatic meditation. In reality, this method or ritual of transcendence amounts to sorcery. The method applied here is the same as in the Eucharist, the contemplative viewing of sacred statues and pictures, and meditative absorption in the liturgy. As the climax of their experience, those praying the Rosary strive to come to the Roman Jesus through the Catholic Mary. Therefore, the part of the Rosary with the tenfold invocation, "Greetings to you, Mary," is the most expansive. The Marian section supposedly emphasizes and underlines the Christologic part. "The midpoint of the 'Greetings to you, Mary,' the hinge between the first and the second part, so to speak, is the name of Jesus."[132] The Catholic Mary, who is really Babylon, the whore, leads to the Catholic Jesus, who is actually Lucifer, or the realm of death. This results in the doxology, i.e. glorification, of the Catholic Trinity through the Roman Mary over the so-called Jesus to the alleged Father – Satan, himself. The chain of pearls acts as the aid for the Rosary of the Virgin Mary, or Rosarium Virgines Mariae, to help count the sequential "Ave Maria." According to the Vatican, this chain of pearls is "a chain that binds us to God ... It is the chain of adoption that brings us into harmony with Mary, the servant of the Lord and, in the end, connects us to Christ, himself."[133] Whoever prays the Rosary "in unison with the intentions of the whole church," can receive an indulgence for the punishment of sins. Mary plays the role of "mother, leader and teacher" in the Rosary. Those who use it, "experience the motherliness of Mary so intimately that they feel an urge **to indulge in the praise of the Holy Virgin** at the end of the prayer." John Paul II concluded his statement, which is binding for the church and all Catholic believers, with an appeal to rediscover the treasure of the Rosary. "This appeal must not go unheard! ... I confidently lay this

---

132 Announcement of the Apostolic Chair, Oct. 16, 2002, p.35.
133 Ibid. p.37.

Apostolic Statement into the wise hands of Mary."[134] He described how he threw himself down before the Marian altar built by the blessed Longo, the apostle of the Rosary, and ended with the invocatory prayer of Longo: "O Rosary, blessed by Mary, sweet chain that binds us to God. Band of love, that unites us with angels, tower of salvation against the attacks of hell, safe haven in the general shipwreck, we will never let go of you again. You, our strength in the hour of death. The last kiss of our life is yours, when we die. May the last greeting of our lips be your lovely name, O Queen of the Rosary of Pompeii. O good Mother, you shelter for sinners, sublime comforter of the distressed, may you be praised everywhere, today and always, in heaven and on earth."[135]

On Oct. 7th, 1571, the Catholics defeated the Ottoman fleet in the naval battle near Lepanto in the strait of Corinth. Over 40 000 people were killed. The victory was attributed to "Our Lady of Victory," since Pope Pius V had called on a prayer assault with the Rosary.[136] Yet, it took until 1891 for a cathedral to be built in honour of the "Queen of the Rosary" by the blessed Bartolo Longo in Pompeii, Italy. While people back then thanked her for the victory in battle, she is considered to be the Rosary-Queen of peace today. Ironically, the cathedral stands in a place of death which was totally destroyed by the eruption of Mt. Vesuvius in 79 A.D. In modern times, Pompeii has become "the centre for the spirituality of the Rosary."

On Oct. 7th, 2003, the anniversary of the sea battle near Lepanto, the Pope flew to Pompeii for the celebration of "Our Lady of the Rosary." It was supposed to be the crowning conclusion of the year of the Rosary. Wojtyla had first visited Pompeii in 1979 to thank his spiritual queen for his election as Pope. Obviously, the Madonna commanded him to expand the already existing cycles. That explains why John Paul II added the "luminous cycles" by decree afterwards. During the last trip, 24 years later, the Pope added even more so-called mysteries, such as "the glittering of the Jordan, the flower-filled green of the Galilean hills, the light of Tabor Mountain, and the glow of Mount Zion in Jerusalem."[137] The newspaper,

---

134 Ibid. p.44.
135 Announcement of the apostolic chair, Oct. 16,2002; p.44, 45.
136 „Die Welt", Oct. 8,2003, p.10. (Newspaper).
137 Ibid. p. 10.

"Die Welt," commented onhis activities with the remark "that no Pontifex had risked such an intervention since Pius V in the 16th century."[138]

If a great magician loses his spiritual power, he has no choice but to take a lot of risks. On his second trip, the Pope thanked the spiritual Madonna that the year of the Rosary "had led to a remarkable revival of this simple, yet deep prayer."[139]

At the end of this section, I would like to summarize the development of the Rosary in a chronological outline.[140]

The Chronological Development of the Rosary

In the 5th century, Eastern Byzantine monks began to call on the name of Jesus in prayer formulae. They were striving "to overcome temptation and unite their whole being in the effort to achieve fellowship with God through the salvation-bringing name. Invocation and meditation melted together." During their vows, each novice received a Rosary as a so-called "spiritual sword." Later, these formulae were also repeated as short fervent prayers in times of difficulty, "with a stammering, shaky voice and quick as a javelin."

In the 11/12th centuries, mystical Islamic Sufism developed the form of prayer using a chain of pearls, or dhikr, to call on the 99 names of Allah. When the Moors occupied Spain, they brought this chain with them. Therefore, it seems likely that Islamic influences introduced the prayer chain to Western Europe. Muslims needs 99 pearls for the 99 names of Allah. The Islamic Rosary is called "sebhaa."

In the 12th century, Cistercian monks replaced the 150 prayer formulae based on the Psalter by 150 Marian psalms.

During the 13th century in 1252, Stephan of Sallay developed the prayer exercises called "15 joys of Mary."

In the 14th century, the Oriental prayer technique with ritual inhalation and exhalation was added. It developed as mystical contemplation or hesychasm in connection with the formula and stammering prayers practiced by the monks on Mount Athos, the forerunners of the Orthodox church.

---

138 Ibid. p. 10.
139 „L'Osservatore Romano", No. 41, Oct. 10, 2003, p. 6.
140 „L'Osservatore Romano", No. 10, March 7, 2003, p. 10-11 by Enzo Bianchi, Prior Kloster von Bose, Magnano.

Chapter III: The Eucharistic Cosmic Christ and the Sacraments

In the 15th century, the 50 Ave Maria meditations were combined with 50 mediations on the names of Jesus. The Dominicans, the main carriers of the Counter-Reformation, used the Rosary as "a pastoral instrument." The alleged 5475 wounds of Jesus were also worshipped. Since this time, the "mysteries" have formed part of the Rosary prayer.

In the 16th century, Pope Pius V made the Rosary into a powerful instrument of magic against all enemies of Rome.

Islam has influenced Roman Catholicism both culturally and religiously, especially in Spain and Portugal. At the same time, the chain of pearls also developed in other religions.

In Hinduism, "the mantra, a mystical formula to quickly call upon a deity, is repeated many times a day with the help of a pearl chain and sometimes in connection with psychosomatic techniques,(ajapamantra)."[141]

In the 10th century, this also became customary in Chinese Buddhism and, two centuries later, in Japanese Buddhism as well. Buddha's name is repeatedly called upon.

Consequently, it is not surprising that modern-day Lamaistic Buddhist monks wear the "Buddhist Rosary," or mala on their left wrist.

Even the Jewish Chassidic religion makes use of repetitive prayer formulae in contemplative meditation, whether with or without a chain of pearls is unknown to the author.

In light of all this, it is easy to understand why John Paul II increasingly wanted to employ the power of the Rosary for Ecumenism, by pointing out the common traditions of many different religions.

The Word of God stands in irreconcilable opposition to this idol worship. The Bible clearly states what the Antichrist, together with the ten rulers, will do in the end because he is jealous of Babylon's power and glory (Rev. 17: 10+): *"they and the beast will hate the whore [here: the church of Rome, the Vatican with the Mother of the church]; they will make her desolate and naked; they will devour her flesh and burn her up with fire. For God has put it into their hearts to carry out his purpose by agreeing to give their kingdom to the beast, until the words of God will be fulfilled. The woman you saw is the great city that rules over the kings of the earth"* (Rev. 17: 16b-18).

---

141 Ibid. p. 9.

Chapter IV
Mary, the Mediatrix of all Cosmic Powers

1. The Queen of Heaven

Driving from Meschede to Paderborn, one passes by an unusual place to worship the Roman Mary near the village of Aalen. A tiny Catholic chapel stands beside a cliff. It is usually closed to the public. A huge oak towers above, its roots clinging to the rock. In the midst of the roots, there is a small grotto in the cliff. Upon closer inspection, one recognizes the figure of a woman in it. She is dressed in the old Germanic style and looks down very sternly. All of these attributes show that she is none other than Freya, the Germanic goddess of fertility. In June of 1996, a high-ranking visitor came to see her. It was Pope John Paul II. During his visit to Germany, he interrupted his public appearances to worship here in private. The Pope was always eager to unite all powers under the Marian banner. He has to be counted as one of the most devout worshippers of the so-called mother of God.

At the beginning of the 3rd millennium, no one in the Protestant churches seems to have noticed that a goddess has assumed a position of power. Without her, there appears to be no further movement towards the unification of religions. In their efforts to avoid any disruption of the Ecumenical process and "remain in dialogue with the Vatican," many Protestant politicians try to turn a blind eye to these disturbing developments. They do not want to recognize that the Roman Mary has received unprecedented attention and power in the Catholic church since the II Vatican Council. The spirit behind the Catholic Mary has obviously been chosen to lead the unification of all religions against the true Christ. Therefore, it is very important for all believers to be aware of the history and current significance of this Mary.

Like all spiritual forces, the Marian spirit draws its power from the history of idol worship, primarily that in Europe. The longer and the more idol worship spreads, the more it gains power in the kingdom of darkness and influence over people. In this chapter, we will look at the development of Mariology: how the reverence for the mother of Jesus later turned into the worship of the queen of heaven (see Jer.7: 18; 44: 15-19) and the mediatrix of all graces. A goddess is created to combat the true Christ and keep people from accepting the eternal salvation in Him.

This chapter is vital for all of those who love Catholic people and want to learn more about Catholicism in order to help them recognize Jesus as their only Saviour. It will give us a better understanding of what kinds of demonic fortresses we are dealing with. In the life of a Catholic, every biblical notion, every longing for truth and every attempt to come into contact with the real God of the Trinity is thwarted by the Marian spirit. On the wall of the chief US Catholic church in Washington, DC, the Basilica of the National Shrine of the Immaculate Conception, it is written clearly: "To Jesus only through Mary." We should struggle to help Catholics gain eternal salvation, which is found solely in Jesus Christ, the only mediator.

This conviction urges us to fight so that all believers will be able to offer resistance to the demonic power of the Marian spirit, carry out the commission of Christ effectively, and lead as many people as possible to true salvation.

The Initial Historical Development of the Dogma on "the Sinlessness of Mary"

As early as the 2nd century, the "eternal virginity of Mary" is described in the Apocryphal "protogospel of James." Even the famous church leader Augustine (354-430) insisted that Mary had made a vow of "eternal virginity." After the death of Augustine, the Synod of Ephesus confirmed the doctrine that Mary "bore God" in the actual, divine sense. The reason cited was that Jesus, the Word of God, came from Mary according to the flesh. Whoever confessed anything else, should be excluded from the church. We have already clarified the meaning of Jesus coming into the flesh and the maternal role of the biblical Mary. In the Roman church, there was no uniformity on the nature and position of Mary until well into the Middle Ages.

2. The Theological Preparations and the Dogmatisation of the "Immaculate Conception"

The influential Catholic teacher Thomas Aquinas (1226-1274) set the binding theological course in his time and it is still being followed today, with increasing intensity. Thomas Aquinas spoke about Mary's two stages of purification:
1. She was freed from sin before her birth.
2. She was completely freed from all inherited sin before the conception of Jesus.

The concepts of "virginity" and "Immaculate Conception" melted with the ideas of premarital sexual purity and the purification from the inherited as well as every personal sin. We will discuss these terms in detail later. For 1200 years, the dogma of the "Immaculate Conception" had been part of the theological mindset and practice in the Catholic church. In addition, Rome continued to gain exclusive political and religious power over the Occident in the next 600 years. Both of these factors inevitably led to the dogmatisation of the "Immaculate Conception" in 1854. Four years later, the acting Pope apparently received divine confirmation for his dogma. On March 25, 1858, the "lady from heaven" appeared to Bernadette Soubirous for the 16th time in Lourdes, France, and introduced herself as: "I am the Immaculate Conception." When Bernadette "asked in surprise if she were not the mother of God," the apparition was gone. When the local pastor asked Bernadette if it "had not been the most blessed Virgin", Bernadette answered: "I don't think so, it is the Immaculate Conception."[142] The pastor was now sure that the apparition had been "Mary," sent to provide divine confirmation of the 1854 dogma of the "Immaculate Conception." Since as early as 836 in Toulouse, there had been three previous visions of the "Immaculate Conception" in different European places. After Lourdes in 1858, five more such apparitions occurred following World War

---

142 Hierzenberger/Nedomansky, "Erscheinungen und Botschaften der Gottesmutter Maria," 1996, p. 213, 214. (=Appearances and messages of Mary, the mother of God).

Chapter IV: Mary, the Mediatrix of all Cosmic Powers

II. Similar spectres with self-given names like "Immaculately Conceived" and "Immaculate Virgin" also appeared four times in various European locations throughout the 20th century. Only the apparition of 1917 in Fatima carried the special title "Immaculate Heart of Mary," which we will come back to later.[143] It is easy to see that the cosmicdemonic breakthrough for the "Immaculate Conception" did not come until after the dogmatisation in 1854. In the course of Rome's history, one can observe how the initial well-founded recognition of the biblical Mary and her exemplary faith turned into overexaltation through worship. It had gone far beyond the required level of deep respect among brothers and sisters in Christ. Thus, the more divine characteristics were attributed to the Catholic Mary, the more Western faith in Jesus Christ continued to degenerate. It inevitably followed that the "Immaculate Conception," who had been identified as Mary, was deemed to be immaculate and free of every sin from her birth. However, it is only possible for angels to be completely pure, more precisely, those angels who did not participate in Lucifer's fall into sin. In other words, Rome promoted the Catholic Mary to the rank of a transcendent angelic being at the top of the angel hierarchy. She continued to rise to the level of a goddess into whom the Holy Spirit incarnated. This will be discussed again later.

The increasing false faith in Mary as mediatrix is an expression of deepening unbelief in the biblical Jesus Christ.

After the main apparition and confirmation of 1858 in Lourdes, it follows logically that the Roman Mary was also dogmatically affirmed as a goddess. This was declared on Oct. 31, 1950 by Pope Pius XII, who had become known for his collaboration with Nazi Germany. How and why did this occur? The Vatican determined the date of Mary's death to be August 13th. As stated in the Apostles' Creed: "On the third day he [Christ] rose again." Similarly, Rome alleges that the Catholic Mary experienced a bodily resurrection on August 15th and ascended to heaven to be reunited with her son Jesus. The papacy had put itself on the same level as God when the dogma of the "infallibility of the Pope" was passed in 1870. Therefore, Rome's Mary is also bound to her divinity until the end of the Catholic church, described prophetically in Revelation 18. The

---
143 Ibid. p. 551.

Chapter IV: Mary, the Mediatrix of all Cosmic Powers

Pope, as the incarnation of the cosmic-eucharistic Christ, maintains complete unity with the Catholic Mary, the mediatrix of all graces.

3. Heathen Roots of the Marian Cult

The origin of the Roman church lies in Babylon. Since it continues to draw on its Babylonian roots, now even more so than before, the Roman church can be equated with Babylon and vice versa. The book of Revelation portrays Babylon as a woman, clothed in purple and gold and adorned with diamonds and pearls. She is characterized as a great whore seated on many waters (Rev. 17: 1), meaning that she is a product of the many different cultures which existed even before Abraham's time (see Rev.17: 15).

Image 5: Europe

To this day, she continues to influence all religious systems and the resulting cultures with her antichristian spirit. Obviously, all have collaborated with her and taken part in her abominable sins. The Apostle John reveals a secret to us: *"The great Babylon, mother of whores and of earth's abominations"* (Rev.17: 5). She is further described as drunk with the blood of the saints and riding on a scarlet beast.

European culture stems from Greece. In Greek mythology, Jupiter transformed himself into a bull and had sex with the goddess Europa. Jupiter, the greatest of all Greek gods, can only be a disguise for Satan, himself! He seduced Europa, kidnapped her, and transported her to a foreign land. This land is now called Europe as a sign of unity with the goddess. Hence, the goddess Europa can be decoded as "Mary."[144] One of the symbols of the European Union is Europa on the bull. In biblical terms, she represents the so-called "Madonna Mary" riding the beast, i.e. Satan or the Antichrist (Rev.17: 1-18). The deepest roots of Rome reach back as far as Babel which was founded by Nimrod, the first king, a great hunter, and rebel against God (Gen.10: 8+9). Nimrod

---

144 See Schmitt-Lieb, "Europa – Trilogie, Madonna und Europa,"1995, p.1-171.

had a wife named Semiramis. According to mythology, Nimrod's dead body "was cut to pieces, burned and sent to different regions." The citizens of Babylon deeply mourned his death. His wife Semiramis insisted that he was now the sun-god. When she later gave birth to a son called Tammuz, she claimed this son to be the reborn Nimrod, the hero of the nation: "... she insisted that her son had been conceived supernaturally and that he was the promised seed, the saviour."[145] From then on, mother and child were worshipped. Tammuz became the son of the sun-god Baal. Thus, we find the primordial cell of worldwide idolatry in Babel. By uniting with Babel and taking up all powers from other religious systems, the Catholic church, itself, became Babylon. Babel can be found everywhere in the world: "who is seated on many waters" (Rev.17: 1). In China, for example, they have a mother goddess called Shingmoo. The ancient Germans had the virgin Hertha. The Romans worshipped Venus or Fortuna, and the Egyptians revered their Isis. The mother goddess was always a virginal queen of heaven and wife of Baal, the god of fertility.[146] Even Israel worshipped the queen of heaven when it turned away from true faith (Jer.7: 18; 44: 15-19). Acts 19: 27 tells us that the mother goddess Artemis, or in Latin Diana, was idolized in Asia. All of these goddesses were virgins and carried a supernaturally conceived son on their arms. Clearly, the Marian-Madonna cult in the Catholic Occident is nothing new except that the Roman church took up and integrated all other religions and mother cults into their own religious system. This makes Rome the strongest and most perfected religious cult of the mother goddess. Therefore, the so-called "Immaculate Conception" can only represent Babylon, the great whore.

4. Observations of an Ex-Priest in the Pastoral Care of Marian Believers

The former Catholic priest Gregor Dalliard informed his past parish about the circumstances of his excommunication. In his book,

---

145 Woodrow, "Die Römische Kirche – Mysterienreligion aus Babylon," 1992, Ch. 1 (English title: Babylon Mystery Religion – Ancient and Modern, 1981). See also Hislop, Alexander, "The Two Babylons".
146 See ibid. p.19-26.

he wrote about his experiences with the Roman church. "They [the parish, the author] knew that I was striving for a church along biblical lines. They knew that I rejected sacramentalism and was trying hard to take open action against Roman occultism and spiritism in all its forms. It is peculiar that the same symptom keeps occurring in people who do not honour Mary, the mother of the Lord, but instead, worship a mother of God, a queen of heaven. In many cases, these people find no peace in their faith. Despite being strictly religious, they often indulge in sexual excesses and are bound to a powerful woman. These people like to indulge in lewdness, but continue to be dependent on this woman. Frequently, they are also addicted to alcohol and have severe depressive disorders. These people are often greatly afraid of Jesus and very resistant to the gospel as well as the Holy Scriptures because they are enslaved to this mighty demonic woman."[147] As pastoral carers, we experience the same things. This does not come as a shock or surprise. After all, the Catholic Mary as the "Immaculate Conception" is only a disguise for the whore of Babylon.

5. The Meaning of the "Immaculate Conception" for Pope John Paul II

John Paul II saw the Roman calendar's "Trinity Sunday" as the pilgrimage path of faith for the people of God, "led by Mary, the mother of the church." "Once and for all, Christ completed the perfect and final offering of love on the cross, *which is renewed daily in the Eucharist*. And Mary's life was a total following of the divine grace that became flesh in Jesus. She, the Immaculate Conception by the grace of God, who was protected from every blemish of sin through the divine grace, is the sign of secure hope for all people who need sanctification and justification."[148] We can tell how the Roman Mary and the eucharistic Christ belong together. Whoever believes in the Catholic Mary, the "Immaculate Conception," believes in Jesus because he came from the immaculate body of Mary. Jesus, therefore, received life through the allegedly sinless flesh of

---

147 See Dalliard, "Ich durfte nicht mehr Priester sein." In: „Zeit-Ruf" No.3/1996, p. 9. (= I was no longer allowed to remain a priest).
148 "L'Osservatore Romano", No.27, July 5,1996, p. 4.

his mother. As a result, she is the "sign of secure hope" for salvation and healing. The Roman Mary thus became the mediatrix of salvation for all people. According to Rome, the immaculacy of the Catholic Mary allowed Christ to perform "the final sacrifice of love" which must be repeated daily through the Mass! Without the so-called "mother of God," the Christ propagated by John Paul II is really a nobody. As reported in the L'Osservatore Romano, he preached a sermon in the Vatican gardens on June 9, 1996, during a celebration of the Eucharist there. John Paul II chose to speak from the grotto of the "Immaculate Conception." This grotto in the Vatican gardens is a reproduction of the original in Lourdes. It stands for the papacy's immutable devotion to Mariology, another thing all Protestant supporters of Ecumenism should consider. In the aforementioned newsletter article, John Paul II maintained that "Mary is the perfection of Abraham's faith. She became a maid with the servant, a queen with the king. She became the mother of all believers, the queen of the world." He ended his sermon with the wish: "May the heavenly mother of God, the seat of wisdom, awaken full knowledge of the Lord in your spirit and a perfect, faithful love for her in your heart ..."[149]

6. Rome's Theological Reasoning for the Mediatrix of all Graces

In another article of the L'Osservatore Romano, John Paul II talked about Mary being made full of grace. As God's chosen one, she received this grace as a gift. "Mary receives the fullness of grace (according to Paul's letter to the Ephesians) as the first fruit of salvation."[150] This fullness of grace is supposed to "explain the hidden spiritual riches found in Mary."[151] Through these feats of Roman theological acrobatics, Mary is transformed into "the mother of all believers." No Catholic who wants to believe in Christ can get around her. John Paul II also reminded the readers of the Council with the following words: "... the fathers of the church hinted at this truth [about being freed from every sin because of the fullness

---

149 Ibid. p. 4.
150 "L'Osservatore Romano," No.20, May 17,1996, p. 2.
151 Ibid. p. 2.

Chapter IV: Mary, the Mediatrix of all Cosmic Powers

of grace] and described her as completely holy while at the same time confirming that she was shaped *by the Holy Spirit, so to speak, and made into a new creation."* We can recognize that John Paul II's theological development began with the reverence of Mary, progressed to worship due to her fullness of grace, and was to reach perfection in the planned dogmatisation of the so-called "mother of God" as co-redemptrix. Theologically speaking, the fullness of grace was transferred from Jesus Christ to the Roman Mary. However, in the Bible we read: *"For in Him* [Jesus Christ, the author] *the whole fullness of the deity dwells bodily, and you have come to fullness in Him, who is the head of every ruler and authority"* (Col.2: 9+10). This whole fullness of grace comes only from and out of Jesus Christ, our Lord. *"From his fullness we have all received, grace upon grace ... grace and truth came through Jesus Christ"* (John 1: 16+17b). Mary, on the other hand, found mercy in the eyes of God as a fallen human being, just like you and me. *"For there is no distinction, since all have sinned ..."* (Rom.3: 22b+23a). *"They are now justified by his grace as a gift, through the redemption that is in Christ Jesus"* (Rom.3: 24). In other words, Christ Jesus alone is the carrier of the whole fullness of the deity, and therefore, He alone is the gift of grace from the Father, the fullness of God's grace, and the mediator of all graces which came through Him. Besides Him, there is neither a divine being, nor an angel, nor a human who could help carry the fullness of grace to the people. "All have sinned ..." In order to eradicate this fact, Rome gave its Mary "a completely immaculate origin."[152] The Catholic mediatrix of all graces mediates the "sanctifying grace," or rather, acts as a broker for it. The complete sanctification allegedly experienced by the Roman Mary amounts to a theological mutation. She was transformed from a human into a divine being which channels the grace of Christ to the people. Hence, she turned into a co-source of God's grace and a co-source of salvation, according to Roman understanding. Being filled with the "sanctifying grace", she became a carrier and mediator of it. As already mentioned, the "sanctifying grace" in the sacrament of baptism lifts the Catholic into the state of purification from inherited sin. He or she, now automatically saved and born again, becomes a member of the body of

---

152 "L'Osservatore Romano," No.21/22, May 24,1996, p. 2.

Christ.[153] The grace of justification through Christ is handed over by the Catholic Mary as mediatrix. With her birth, a new creation began. Essentially, she mutated into a new Eve. The other half of salvation is left with Jesus Christ, the new Adam. "The pure and immaculate conception of Mary thus appears as the beginning of a new creation."[154] "The holiness of Mary from her very origin onwards is the insurmountable example of the gift and the outpouring of Christ's grace in this world."[155] This means that there is no justification through Christ in Roman theology, without the mediation of God's grace through the Catholic Mary.

7. The Continuing Development of the "Immaculate Conception" by Rome

In Gen.3: 15, we read that the offspring of the woman will crush the head of the snake. This offspring is Jesus Christ. As evidence for the theology of Rome, the old Latin version of the so-called Protogospel is cited, where it says: She will crush your head. But, this translation proves to be untenable because it does not reflect the Hebrew text. Rome knows that too. John Paul II was, however, well-versed in the dialectic methods of the Jesuits and wrote: "This [Hebrew, the author] text does not accredit the victory over Satan to Mary, but to her son. Because biblical understanding assumes a deep agreement between the parents and their offspring, the portrayal of the Immaculata, who crushes the snake through the grace of her son, not through her own power, corresponds to the original meaning of this verse in Scripture."[156] But according to Gen. 3: 15, it is obvious that Jesus, Himself, will crush the head of the snake without delegating the task to anyone else. Nevertheless, Rome cites the enmity between the woman and the snake as well as the enmity between the offspring of the snake, the Antichrist, and the offspring of the woman, Jesus Christ, as proof for the "holiness of the Virgin" with respect to the "Immaculate Conception." The diabolical Vatican logic draws the following conclusion: in order to be a

---

153 See Chapter III.
154 "L'Osservatore Romano," No.21/22, May 24,1996, p. 2.
155 Ibid. p. 2.
156 "L'Osservatore Romano," No.23, June 7,1996, p. 2.

victorious, irreconcilable enemy of the snake, Mary must be free of sin "and that from the first moments of her existence onwards."[157] "The absolute enmity placed between the woman and evil by God presumes the 'Immaculate Conception' of Mary, i.e. a total absence of sin from the first moment of her life. The son of Mary ultimately conquered Satan and let his mother share in this victory in advance by protecting her from sin. *Consequently, the son gave her the power to resist evil and thus achieved the greatest effect of his work of salvation in the mystery of the 'Immaculate Conception'.*"[158] Further, John Paul II insisted that she is the beginning of a new order in the unique privilege of her grace! This new order is allegedly the fruit of friendship with God.[159]

8. The Historical Development of the "Immaculate Conception" and her Enthronement through the Marian Apparitions

It took 1500 years of theological development for the Catholic Mary to gain the crowned, absolute reign of the Roman church. Today, in the age of Ecumenism, she stands as the undisputed "mediatrix of all graces," the supreme, divine mistress of Rome and the whole earth. The English term "Ecumenism" stems from the Greek word "oikoumene¯" which refers to the entire inhabited world. As the so-called "queen of peace," the Roman Mary dominates the quest for religious peace through inter-religious dialogue aimed at establishing one unified world church.

Let us come back to the Catholic Mary's development into the "Immaculate Conception" within the last 1500 years of church history. In the first centuries, there was great resistance against the attempt to establish the complete sinlessness of Mary as theological doctrine. During this time, most people still took the Word of God seriously. Paul wrote very clearly and in detail on this subject, for example in Rom.3: 10: "There is no one righteous, not even one."

However, as early as the 2nd century, the fathers of the Catholic church began to deal with Mary in an unbiblical, anti-Paulinian

---
157 Ibid. p. 2.
158 Ibid. p. 2.
159 Ibid. p. 2.

way. The following examples will illustrate the most important aspects of this evolution.

Justin, the Martyr (executed around 165)

He was a Greek philosopher. In his "Dialogi cum Tryphone Judaeo II.,"[160] Justin wrote: "When Eve accepted the word of the snake, bearing disobedience and death, **she was a virgin** and intact. Likewise, **Mary was a virgin**. She, on the other hand, received trust and joy when she heard the proclamation of the angel Gabriel, to which she answered: Let it be with me according to your word. Thus, she became the mother to the one through whom God crushed the head of the snake and brought about liberation from death for all those *who give up their bad habits* and believe in him."

If only these heretical tendencies had been nipped in the bud! The exaltation of Mary in the above passage is still relatively minor. But, the mystical asceticism of antique Greece obviously influenced Justin when he made the unbiblical observation that Eve was a virgin, i.e. vaginally intact.. He then applied this mystical viewpoint to Mary as well, the new "pure" Eve who even remained intact during her marriage with Joseph. Justin laid the erroneous foundation for all further blasphemies and heresies. The Vatican interpretation turned the vaginal intactness, or virginity, of Mary and the Fiat of faith to her motherhood, "Let it be," into "a co-source of salvation for all of humanity."[161] These thoughts were later taken up by Irenaeus and developed further.

Irenaeus of Lyon (died 202/203 as a martyr)

Irenaeus was Greek and became the bishop of Lyon. He wrote an extensive literary work called "Against the Heresies," where he fought against the upcoming Gnosis. So far, so good. At the same time, he also expanded the erroneous assumptions of Justin. According to Irenaeus, God gave Eve to Adam as a helper, but she seduced him to commit sin.

The works of Irenaeus contain high-quality apologetics, at least in part. With a sharp mind, he battled against those who

---

160 See Sigl; „Die Frau aller Völker, Amsterdam – Rom", 1989, p. 37. (=The woman of all people).
161 Ibid. p.37.

Chapter IV: Mary, the Mediatrix of all Cosmic Powers

insisted that the Lord was conceived through the seed of Joseph. By means of the Old Testament, he proved that a virgin bore Jesus as our Saviour, without the natural participation of a man but solely through the Holy Spirit. Irenaeus professed this fact and opposed the heresy that Jesus is not true man as well as true God."[162] We thank God for the hard battle he fought against the Gnosis. But unfortunately, it also aroused his unbending and obstinate character. Because the Gnostics wanted to include Josef in the process of salvation as the biological father, Irenaeus made the mistake of going to the other extreme. He exaggerated the role of the virgin Mary. Her affirmation, i.e. the acceptance of the divine secret about to unfold in her life, was a typical act of faith. It was not a religious step, since she had no tradition or model to follow in her religious Jewish community. With her consent, Mary proved the quality of her faith. This was the faith that the God of her fathers first nurtured in Abraham and still seeks to this day. Jesus Christ represented the perfect fulfillment of this faith. Thus, Mary belongs to the heroines of faith because she accepted the mysterious, transcendent sign according to Isa.7: 10+14, which happened to her through the divine overshadowing (Luke 1: 35). She consented to the real, material pregnancy against all human experience by putting her trust in the God of Abraham, Isaac and Jacob.

But, with all due respect for the achievements of certain fathers of the church, it can not be overlooked that even Irenaeus succumbed to the great danger of falling into the other extreme. Instead of a natural conception and birth, he promoted the supernatural significance of Mary in his often fanatical battle. She began to play a role which wandered far away from God's purpose for her. When a divine sign occurs out of the realm of Godly transcendence, the miracle associated with it should remain focussed on God alone. Irenaeus fixated himself on the merits of Mary instead of giving all credit to God where it belongs.

---

162 See Irenaeus: "Des heiligen Irenaeus fünf Bücher gegen alle Häresien der Entlarvung und Widerlegung der falschen Gnosis," 1872, Volume II, Book III, p.31-52 (The five books of the holy Irenaeus against all heresies of the exposure and refutation of the false Gnosis).

"But she affirmed and testified to the fruit of the womb for the birth of the one who should come from the virgin ..."[163]

"... so that Josef had no part in this, instead Mary alone participated in the order of salvation."[164]

"Christ assumed true flesh through Mary. Therefore, all are mistaken who say that he received nothing from the virgin ... Because if he did not accept the substance of the flesh from a human, he became neither human nor son of man."[165]

In the eyes of Irenaeus, the acceptance of Jesus as true man occurs only through Mary. Even he, the great thinker, reduced the "mysterious sign" to a random banality in natural, material understanding. However, we are dealing with God's mysterious activity in the life of Mary which can not be fully deciphered. Mary, herself, is not important in this sense! God did not derive the humanness of Christ from her. As so often, the snare of wanting more led into sin and bore new heresies. In all mysteries of revelation, the focus of the believing person should be on God. Irenaeus was deeply influenced by the spirit of typical Greek asceticism and based his assessment of the Gnostics on this. If such damage of sin is not redressed and healed, it can only lead to sinful, i.e. incorrect, statements like the following:

"For she [Eve] had Adam as husband, but was **still a virgin**, both were naked in Paradise and were not ashamed of it, because having just been created, they did not yet know about procreation, since they first had to grow in order to multiply ..."[166]

Irenaeus then reasoned correctly that death came upon humanity as the consequence of their disobedience. Another biblical falsehood brought up by Irenaeus' speculation, and later the Roman church, was that Eve supposedly had no loving sexual relationship with Adam in Paradise. Yet God, the Creator, made them with the potential of having sexually erotic feelings to contribute to their enjoyment of life and also their spiritual health. Eve was not given to Adam as a permanent virgin. Furthermore, Adam and Eve were not created as children, according to the Bible. They immediately

---

163 Ibid. p. 44.
164 Ibid. p. 46.
165 Ibid. p. 48, 49.
166 Ibid. p. 51.

Chapter IV: Mary, the Mediatrix of all Cosmic Powers

received their purpose as an adult man and woman, bonded wholly together by love in body, soul and spirit. The conclusion that they had to have been children because they were naked also resulted from the influence of sexual sins and marital asceticism. In the Roman church, this inevitably led to celibate life and the idealization of the so-called "Holy Family" where the "sanctified sexuality" of man and woman should only be used to generate children. Therefore, it is not surprising that Irenaeus pointed the rod of his bent truth at Mary. His analysis looked like this: "So Mary, who also had a predestined husband and was still a virgin, became the **source of salvation** for herself and the entire human race."[167]

Image 6:
Woman for all People

Adam and Eve were the first of the dying while Mary, as the source of salvation, was the first of living. In subsequent times, this view gained more and more support among the fathers of the church. Mary allegedly had to continue to live with Joseph in celibacy, even after the birth of Jesus, so that "the loops of the knot could be looped back, the connections could be dissolved through the second [pair of humans], the second could free the first."[168]

Mary functioned as the redemptrix for Eve and, consequently, turned more and more into the new Eve. Irenaeus summarized the thoughts on co-salvation as follows: "Through the obedience of Mary, Eve's knot of disobedience came to be dissolved. What the virgin Eve tied together through disobedience, the virgin Mary dissolved through faith."[169]

Not surprisingly, the falsehood of Mary's permanent virginity led to the, in itself, logical theory that Mary dissolved the sin of Eve primarily through her virginity. Among other things, this laid the groundwork for the double salvation of Jesus, as the new Adam, and

---

167 Ibid. p. 51.
168 Ibid. p. 51.
169 Ibid. p. 52.

Mary, as the new Eve, which came up later. Irenaeus also attacked "all as heretics who do not understand the full work of salvation [of Jesus and Mary]."[170] Sadly, he, himself, became more and more of a heretic even though he wanted to be the apologetic defender against heresies. "And the human race became subject to death through a virgin, therefore it is saved by a virgin ... The cunning of the snake was defeated by the simplicity of the **dove**; the bonds which held us as captives of death were dissolved."[171] The II Vatican Council from 1962-1965 confirmed this role as co-redemptrix: "... just as a woman contributed to death, a woman was also to contribute to life."[172] Today, Rome argues: "If Christ, the source of our salvation, rightly bears the title of redeemer, why should the **co-source** of our salvation not rightly bear the title of co-redemptrix."[173]

Tertullian (†220)

Tertullian was Latin. In his work "De Carne Christi", he explained that God created man in his image for a second time. "What fell into ruin in this way through a woman, was also to be brought back to salvation through a woman. Eve had believed the snake; Mary believed Gabriel; what the former committed by [lack of] faith, the latter redeemed by faith."[174] All the so-called fathers of the subsequent church history are said to have fallen back on these fundamental statements.

Ephraim, the Syrian (†373)

For him, Jesus and Mary were a single principle of salvation and life. "United with her son, the king, Mary pulled Adam out of the abyss into which he had fallen through Eve and the snake. Thus, Adam received life through Jesus and Mary, **through both together**."[175]

---

170 Ibid. p. 299.
171 Ibid. p. 300.
172 Ibid. p. 38.
173 Ibid. p. 38.
174 Ibid. p. 38.
175 Ibid. p. 38.

Augustine (354-430)

Augustine expressed that "the holiness of Mary was an extraordinary gift of grace." In the controversy with his opponents, he passionately defended the following view: "Apart from the holy virgin Mary, with respect to whom I want no questions to be asked in regards to sin: Do we not know why she received a higher grace with respect to the complete overcoming of sin — she, who **deserved** to conceive and bear the one who was evidently without sin?"[176] In Augustine's view, Mary had such a worth and dignity that God could only choose her as mother. Thus, she deserved to be showered with graces by God, allowing her to overcome all remaining sin in herself. We can see how the influence of a man like Augustine prepared the church to think and act in a Catholic manner later. The Roman Mary was appointed to mediate and organize sacramental, spiritual powers. These could be nothing but powers out of the fallen cosmos, i.e. demonic forces. We don't think that the church teacher Augustine would have wanted this development. But by making more of Mary than a sinful human who needed salvation through Christ's sacrificial death, he paved the way for the spirit "Mary" as the so-called "Mother of God." Mary's holiness, in the sense of sinlessness and perfection, is taken for granted here. Even before Adam's fall, the danger of wanting more led some of the angels into sin (Isa. 14: 12+13). It ultimately results in apostasy from faith in God because greed, i.e. wanting to have more, is a root of all evil (see 1.Tim.6: 10). Augustine's doctrine of the "Immaculate Conception of Mary," as it was later called, greatly promoted the apostasy from true faith. In the course of history, it turned the church into an anti-church out of the Babylonian, antichristian spirit. Nevertheless, we want to give Augustine the benefit of the doubt. He may have had qualms of conscience when he saw that the complete absence of sin in Mary's life, which he professed, was inconsistent with Scripture. The Bible clearly states that all people have sinned and need salvation. However, the theologians who subsequently developed the Catholic doctrine no longer had these twinges of conscience. They became more and more convinced that "Mary received the benefit of the redeeming grace from the moment of her conception."[177] "In the 9th

---

176 „De natura et gratia", In: „L'Osservatore Romano", No.24, June 14, 1996, p. 2.
177 "L'Osservatore Romano," No.24, June 14, 1996, p.2.

century, the feast of Mary's Immaculate Conception was introduced in the Occident."[178] It was also the century of Charlemagne, the Grail, the Eucharist and the first church buildings as the mystical, hypostatic body of Christ. This century gave rise to the anti-church in Europe, born out the antichristian spirit. The apostasy from faith was complete.

Hieronymus (†420)

Anastasius I (†599)

Among others, these two teachers of the church repeated the thought that death came through Eve and, therefore, it was necessary for salvation and life to come through Mary.[179]

Modestus of Jerusalem (†630)

He went one step further into apostasy and insisted that "Mary is the one **through whom we have received the forgiveness of sins** and through whom we have been redeemed from the tyranny of the demon. She is the one through whom we have been created anew in a mystical way and have become the temple of the Holy Spirit."[180] In Heb. 5:9, Scripture clearly states that Jesus became the source of salvation.

Germanus of Constantinople (†733) and
Alkuin (†804)

Both claimed Mary to be the origin of salvation and said that the whole world had been saved through her.[181] For these last two heretics, Mary was not **only** the co-redemptrix, but the **redeemer**.

Milone of Amando (9th century)

He went so far as to insist that Mary sacrificed her son Jesus. Because of her active sacrifice, she participated in our salvation as co-redemptrix.[182]

---

178 Ibid. p.2.
179 See Sigl: "Die Frau aller Völker, Amsterdam–Rome," 1989, p.39 (=The woman of all people).
180 Ibid. p.39.
181 See ibid. p.39.
182 See ibid. p.39.

John the Geometer (10th century)

John expressed his thoughts about Mary's role as co-redemptrix by thanking Christ "that, in addition to yourself, you also gave us your mother as ransom, since she **sacrifices herself every moment**. You sacrificed yourself for us once and for all times, she sacrificed herself, with a burning heart, thousands of times in her will."[183]

In summary: The beginning of Rome as the anti-church out of the antichristian spirit dates back to the 9th century. Consequently, it is not surprising that Mary was even worshipped as redeemer in the 10th century. The reasoning was that she stood under the cross of Jesus and suffered the spiritual sacrifice through the "sword," as prophesied by Simeon. The theologians of the Middle Ages continued in the same tradition and expanded the arguments for Mary's participation in salvation:

Eadmer (died around 1141)

Arnold of Chartres (†1165)

Anselm of Canterbury (†1109)

Bonaventura (†1274)

John Tauler (†1361)

Bernhardin of Siena (†1444)

These men of the Middle Ages fortified Mary's role as co-redemptrix so that this title was in common usage. In other words, Mary became Jesus' helper or partner resembling him. Christ sacrificed the blood of his body. Mary sacrificed the blood of her soul. Mary became the mistress for the restoration of all things. Together, Mary and Christ offer themselves like a living Eucharistic host for the salvation of all.

Nevertheless, influential theologians battled the assertion that Mary had been completely sinless again and again. As the centuries passed, there was some successful opposition to the Babylonian doctrine. Even in the 13th century, certain apologetics felt the same twinges of conscience as Augustine.

---

183 Ibid. p.39.

Chapter IV: Mary, the Mediatrix of all Cosmic Powers

They had intellectual problems reconciling the teaching of the church with the statements in Romans 3.

Their main argument was that Mary would not have been redeemed if she had not been afflicted by inherited sin. As a human, she had to have been a sinner right from the beginning. This theological resistance rallied the sliest Marian dialectics of Rome. They countered that Christ, as the perfect mediator, had "performed the utmost act of mediation in Mary by protecting her from inherited sin."[184] These Marian theologians were only able to offer wishful assertions, not evidence, to say nothing of biblical proof. They coined the terms "pre-protective and pre-active salvation." Diabolical lies were heaped upon lies: Instead of being redeemed from sin in a miraculous way, Mary had now been protected from every sin! The role she allegedly played became more and more removed from her position as a human who shares in the fate of fallen mankind. At the beginning of the 14th century, the Marian doctrines were taken up by Franciscan theologians. When Pope Pius Sixtus IV carried out the approbation of the "Mass of the Immaculate Conception," crucial theological schools accepted the doctrine of the so-called "perfect holiness of Mary." Now there was no turning back. All opponents were persecuted. Mary had irrevocably become the "Mother of God." We see a clear escalation from the sinlessness at the point of Christ's conception all the way to the Mother of God who "had to be perfectly holy from the first moment of her existence."[185] In theology, it was now routinely accepted that the salvation of Christ not only freed from sin, but also protected from it beforehand. They insisted that the protection had been absolute in Mary's case, allowing her to be born and remain free of sin. Let us hear what John Paul II had to say to this subject:

"In Mary, Christians see the first person to be redeemed by Christ, who had the privilege of not being subjected to the power of evil and sin for a single moment, the perfect original image and the icon of that holiness (see LG65) which she was to achieve in her life according to her calling through the helping grace of the Lord."[186] The Council of Trient from 1545 to 1563 set the course for the Counter-

---

184 Ibid. p. 39.
185 Ibid. p. 39.
186 Ibid. p. 2.

Reformation and reaffirmed Mary's role of mediation in addition to her new nature between God and man as the queen of angels. With its demonic spiritual power, the inquisition was carried out against all people committed to the gospel. Ironically, the "Immaculate Conception" sullied herself with blood of true saints and revealed herself as the whore Babylon: "Babylon the great, mother of whores and of earth's abominations" (Rev.17: 5b). At the so-called "Written Council" in the 19th century, Pope Pius IX demanded a comment on the subject of the "Immaculate Conception of Mary" from all theologians and bishops. The majority was now in favour of a final dogmatic definition to express the true belief of Rome. The beliefs of the people were taken into account as well. Over the centuries, a cult had developed out of the relationship with the Catholic Mary. What had been practiced for centuries was finally supposed to be confirmed as theological dogma. In addition, the appearances of the Roman Mary increased rapidly with each century along with the rise of Babylonian faith among the people of the church. This forced the Vatican to act dogmatically.

Until the 11th century, only 30 Marian apparitions were reported worldwide. From the 11th to 15th century, the number jumped to 150. Between the 16th to 20th century, the power of the "Immaculate Conception" exploded and she revealed herself 731 times in various different places. The frontrunner is the 20th century with 427 appearances. All figures are taken from Rome's own statements.[187] These Marian apparitions gave rise to many Marian places of pilgrimage which possess great cosmic-demonic spiritual powers. They are used to maintain and expand the power of the Catholic Mary and, hence, that of Rome. The alleged appearances of Mary have also helped her become the true mistress, or Domina, within the Roman Catholic church.

The Marian Apparitions in the History of the Church

Let us take another look at the number of Marian apparitions in the different continents and countries from the first century onwards. Europe, the core continent of the satanic, antichristian empire of

---

[187] Hierzenberger/nedomansky, „Erscheinungen und Botschaften der Gottesmutter Maria", 1996, p. 553. (=Appearances and messages of Mary, the mother of God).

Rome, tops the list with 774 transcendent, revelatory apparitions out of 918 reported worldwide. Among the European nations, the frontrunners with respect to transcendent Marian revelations include:

1. Italy with 199.
2. France with 171.
3. Germany with 112.
4. Austria with 72.

This number is the sum of all Marian apparitions in countries associated with the Habsburg empire in its 400-year-old history, such as Hungary, the Czech Republic, parts of Poland, Slovakia and the former Yugoslavia.

5. Spain with 52.
6. Belgium with 51.

In comparison to the figures mentioned above, the relatively low number of apparitions in modern day Catholic countries like Poland (23) and Ireland (10) may be surprising at first. The assessment is further complicated by the occupations of Poland. For a long time, it was divided and did not exist as an independent nation. The numbers still make sense if we consider the role the first six countries played in Western Christianity. They, or rather, their historical political leadership, were the prime carriers of the spirit of Rome. In its first empire which lasted over 1000 years from 800-1815, the "Holy Roman Empire of German Nation", Germany became the chief European upholder of the Roman spirit. The German emperors dominated the Vatican, and the Vatican controlled the German emperors. It should be remembered that Italy did not exist as a sovereign nation at this time and was dependent on the goodwill of the Germans. The Austrians also felt affiliated with this spirit and wore the crown of the German emperors for a long time. By taking the history of Western Europe into consideration, one starts to understand that the first six nations are the primary carriers of Marian power as well as the Roman-Babylonian spirit, the spirit of the "whore Babylon" described in the book of Revelation.

The Reformation in the 16th century was a special masterpiece of our beloved Lord Jesus Christ. For one, He allowed it to occur in Germany, a relatively large country. With the Reformation, the Marian power in Germany decreased abruptly to only 2 apparitions

Chapter IV: Mary, the Mediatrix of all Cosmic Powers

in the 16th century. However, as the Protestant faith was weakened by rationalism and humanism in the 17th century, the number of appearances exploded, increasing tenfold. In the time of spiritual renewal in the 19th century, they rapidly diminished again. Due to the apostasy from Reformational Protestant faith, our 20th century shows an unparalleled 50-fold jump in Marian apparitions. During the same century, the First and Second World Wars proceeded from Germany, in addition to the war of the SS against the Jews. Switzerland, the second country of the Reformation, had a decrease in Marian apparitions after the Reformation of Calvin and others too. Shortly before, they had increased markedly. But now, the appearances are on the rise again there too. It should not come as a surprise to us. In this small country, the blessings of the Reformation fathers are also turning into a curse through massive unbelief. In England, the Reformation of Central Europe led to more spiritual revival than in any other Western nation. The greatest Reformational preachers and missionaries came from England. More blessings of the Reformational fathers likely spread to the whole world from there than anywhere else. North America is still profiting from this today. During the time of revival, there were no Marian apparitions in England at all. However, it must also be mentioned that they already had fewer appearances in comparison to Germany beforehand. Today, apparitions even occur in places where such phenomena where previously unknown. The Netherlands also belong to the countries of the Reformation. Marian appearances were practically unheard of there, but are now becoming more and more common. In Europe, we are dealing with the bundled power of the whore Babylon, who has appeared in 774 places. On the other four continents, the Catholic Mary has only revealed herself a total of 144 times. The hundreds of Marian shrines are primarily located in Europe. They make cosmic-demonic spiritual powers available in order to break the last bastions of true believers in the Reformational sense and transform the faith in God's gift of grace, Jesus Christ, into a sacramental, Ecumenical and syncretistic substitute. Therefore, we are experiencing a Marian awakening of incredible proportions, especially on the Continent. Every year, many millions of people make pilgrimages to the Marian shrines. They receive spiritual powers from the "Immaculate Conception" who acts as mediatrix for forces out of the cosmos, the earth and the realm of death. Unimaginable demonic powers have been revived in the last decades of the 20th century and released on the people. This includes thousands of Roman churches which contain copies of shrines. These copies are fed by the spiritual forces of the original shrines. The method of seduction preferred by these spirits is the estrangement from the mindset of the Reformational fathers. The Catholic Mary constantly shoots her cosmic powers at people and tempts them into ecumenical or charismatic ways of thinking. Through dialectic Jesuit exegesis, the Bible is used to veil the truth. The goal is re-catholicisation by means of re-intregration into the mystical Roman "Body of Christ." In the meantime, the "Immaculate Conception" has procured more than 179 titles on the occasion of her transcendent self-portrayals. They range from "advent mother of God", "lady of all nations", "queen of heaven", "empress of heaven and earth", "queen of the apostles and angels", "queen of peace", "co-redemptrix", "mediatrix of all graces", "mediatrix between heaven and earth", "mother of all people", "mother of the Eucharist, of love, of the church, of the universe and of the refuge for sinners", "Notre dame", "snake-crusher", "tabernacle of the most high", "door to Jesus", "Immaculate Conception or Heart", "our dear lady of ...", "reconciler of sinners and all nations", "representative of my Son before the Father", all the way to "refuge for sinners."[188]

We can see that Marian spiritual powers are undergoing a revolutionary explosion due to the abandonment of our Reformational roots and biblical faith. Rome has conjured up overwhelming forces of darkness through the cults around saints and relics, sacramentalism, and the worship of Mary. In view of this apocalyptic situation, one may feel that there is no way out. We hope we have shown convincingly that only a return to our biblical and Reformational roots can help us against this Marian revival leading into the great apostasy. We must finally take up the spiritual battle of faith. It is not enough just to complain about the errors of Rome. We must employ the spiritual weapons (Eph. 6;10-18) everywhere in the world. These weapons are already being used in the decisive battle

---

188 Ibid. p. 548–552.

by several courageous groups worldwide. However, these men and women do not suffice. While they are sacrificing much for their beloved Lord Jesus Christ, most believers are occupied with their well-being on this fallen earth ...

9. The Dogma of the "Immaculate Conception"

In the 19th century, there were so many Marian apparitions und transcendent experiences with the "Immaculate Conception" among the people that Pope Pius IX finally proclaimed the dogma of the "Immaculate Conception" in 1854. "The doctrine that the most blessed virgin Mary was completely protected from every blemish of inherited sin in the very first moment of her [own, the author] conception through the unique grace and preference of the almighty God with respect to the merits of Christ Jesus, the Saviour of the human race, *has been revealed by God and should therefore be firmly and steadfastly believed by all faithful people.*"[189] This dogma of the "Immaculata" brought the centuries old theological quarrel within the Roman church to a close, so to speak. In his bull of 1661, Pope Alexander VII had stated that Mary's soul was protected from sin when it was created and poured into her body. The majority of theologians in the Middle Ages shared this view. But, 200 years later, the apostasy had progressed so far that Pius IX omitted all elastic and unclear explanations about Mary's protection and the time when her soul was poured into her body. He laid down firmly: Mary was protected from inherited sin in the first moment of her conception, i.e. born free of sin. She was now considered to be an angelic being, the queen of angels, and the crowned saint of all saints. After this dogmatisation, the number of Marian apparitions exploded, especially in France and Italy. The climax of this explosion was reached in Lourdes, France, in 1858. Even today, Lourdes is the most significant place of pilgrimage along with Fatima in Portugal. The Vatican saw the apparitions in Lourdes as divine confirmation for its proclaimed dogma of 1854. However, for the most part, even Pius IX referred only to the freedom from inherited sin. The freedom from lustful desire in Mary's earthly life was still ignored for the time being. Yet in the course of the next decades, theologians increas-

---

189 "L'Osservatore Romano," No.25, June 21, 1996, p. 2.

ingly presumed that, having been protected from all inherited sin, she remained free of lust-related sins as well. This also shows how Rome keeps attempting to push its Mary into a position equalling that of Christ: true human and true God. As far as we know, they have never made such a theological statement, but in practice, it occurs nonetheless. For example, the Catholic Mary's theological equality is demonstrated when Pius XII said that she "had a unique privilege that was never granted to any other person."[190] Mary's husband, Joseph, was canonized on Dec. 31, 1870, and proclaimed to be the patron saint of the whole church. Yet to this day, he has not received this "undeserved divine privilege" of being protected from every sin. He is not a divine person. He remains an outstanding human, a Catholic saint. According to Rome, Mary did not have to be redeemed directly, further underlining her unique privilege. Pius XII put this special feature in the following words: "She was bought free in the most sublime way."[191] Therefore, the 1962 Vatican Council under John XXIII praised Mary as the "most sublime fruit of salvation."[192] In order to approach equality with Jesus Christ, they said that Christ redeemed his mother in the most perfect way from the very first moment of her life. Just like Pius XII in the 1930's, John Paul II also repeated the "doctrine revealed by God" under Pius IX in 1854: "This doctrine should be believed because it comes from God. Whoever does not believe it, or even fights it, falls away from the union of the church and his faith suffers shipwreck."[193] Pope John Paul II expressed his irrevocable agreement with this dogmatised teaching of the "Immaculate Conception" and the deification of the Roman Mary: "… my honourable predecessor was aware that he was acting in the authority of infallible doctrine as the universal shepherd of the church, which was solemnly defined during the I Vatican Council several years later. Thus he put his infallible teaching duty into the service of the faith of God's people."[194] It is very significant that the emphasis on this dogma was linked to the dogma of the "infallibility of the Pope," proclaimed in 1870. Pius IX's

---

190 Ibid. p. 2.
191 Ibid. p. 2.
192 Ibid. p. 2.
193 Ibid. p. 2.
194 Ibid. p. 2.

statement was a so called divine, and hence irrevocable, doctrine in the age of the European cultural struggle, a few decades before the worldwide Ecumenical movement began. Remarkably, the Pope did not use his alleged "divine teaching authority" to dogmatise biblical statements about the divinity of Jesus Christ. Instead, he blasphemously portrayed the whore Babylon as the mistress and co-redemptrix of the church, uniquely worthy of worship. Pope John Paul II fully supported the dogma of the deification of Mary with his authority of the "infallible teaching duty" and confirmed it by citing the 1870 dogma of the "infallibility of the Pope." He further strengthened this Roman doctrine by exalting Pius IX "to the honour of the altars," on Sept. 3. 2000, i.e. beatifying the Pope of the I Vatican Council (1869-1870), who had died in 1878. Ironically, John Paul II also addressed the Protestants as "separated brothers." One is surely forsaken by the Holy Spirit if one does not notice that John Paul II aimed at the same Marian revival that John XXIII had unsuccessfully striven for. Both wanted to lead all "separated brothers" to the "Immaculate Conception." No one would then be able to reach Jesus Christ. Rather, everyone would end up under the influence of the counterfeit cosmic-eucharistic Christ who lives out of the Roman, Babylonian and antichristian spirit. Furthermore, I would like to add that the late Pope John XXIII was exalted to the "honour of the altars" on the same day as Pius IX. This Pope, who died on June 3, 1963, had called the II Vatican Council (1962-1965) and planned to lead the Marian revival to full victory through the Ecumenical movement. Both Popes shared the same understanding: only to Jesus via Mary. Sadly, the outwitted Protestant negotiators in the Ecumenical movement have nothing to say about this unbelievable deception and simply remain silent.

Let us briefly summarize the main developments with respect to the Council and the deification of the Catholic Mary:

The Council of Chalcedon in 451 made the binding statement that Christ "was born out of Mary, the virgin and divine God-bearer."
- The III Council of Constantinople in 861 talked about Jesus Christ being "conceived by the Holy Spirit and Mary, the virgin, the actual and true God-bearer."

- "Other Ecumenical councils, like the II Council of Constantinople, the IV Lateran Council, and the II Council of Lyon, described Mary as the everlasting virgin and underlined her permanent virginity."[195]
- In addition to these statements by the different councils, there are those made by various Popes on the basis of the papal teaching duty and the "infallibility of the Pope" since 1870.
- After the dogma of the "Immaculate Conception," these include the doctrine about the "most blessed Virgin Mary" and the bodily ascension of Mary into heaven. In 1950, Pope Pius XII determined the day of Mary's death to have been August 13th by the authority of his "divine teaching duty." According to Pius XII, her resurrection occurred exactly 3 days later, on August 15th! It has been celebrated as day of the "bodily assumption of the immaculate God-bearer and permanent virgin Mary into heaven"[196] ever since.
- Again, we can recognize the theological attempts to dogmatise the Roman Mary as co-redemptrix. The whore Babylon is indeed the redeemer of the human race, not from death, but from life! Thus, the "Immaculate Conception" developed more and more into the all-encompassing mistress of the church.

10. The Everlasting Virginity of the Roman Mary

Vatican theology has turned its Mary into a deified saint, the "Immaculate Conception." They cite the verses in Isa. 7: 14 and Mt. 1: 23 where it says that a virgin shall conceive and bear a son, and shall name him Immanuel. This is, of course, quoted correctly. The biblical Mary had abstained from natural sexual intercourse out of free will and obedience to God because she was not yet married to Joseph. Therefore, she asked the angel Gabriel, "How can this be, since I am a virgin?" (Lk.1: 34), when he foretold the birth of Jesus. Here, the spirit of the whore Babylon entered the scene of Catholic theology. Mary's premarital abstinence is interpreted such that her voluntary abstinence, her vaginal intactness, laid the groundwork for her intactness with respect to sin. This Babylonian theology in-

---
195 „L'Osservatore Romano", No. 29, July 19, 1996, p. 2.
196 Ibid. p. 2.

evitably leads to a link between holiness and virginity as a principle of faith, so to speak. The erring theologians maintain that Mary had promised God to remain a virgin for the rest of her life, "because she was filled with the wish to give her whole heart to God."[197] Her virginity is "closely linked to her motherhood of God and perfect holiness."[198] As a result, celibate life became the symbol of Catholic holiness and those who take part in it are true saints. Though not said outright, this does infer that the sexual relationship of a married couple is sinful and unholy. According to this demonic doctrine, all pleasure of love must die, leaving only the wish to conceive and bear children. Otherwise, marital sex is sinful. The Roman Mary is portrayed as the divine, spiritual model of the everlasting virgin. Whoever follows her example of abstinence must lead a celibate life or, if married, only sleep together in order to conceive children. This is the way to "sacrifice oneself for God" and attain holiness! Here lie some of the reasons why the Roman church opposes every kind of family planning. In the thinking of Rome, outer vaginal intactness and inner spiritual intactness from sin belong together, and even become interchangeable. The loss of intactness can only be justified if it occurs for the sole purpose of having children. Let us recall what was said about the two levels in the hypostatic worship of pictures. The transcendent, in this case demonic, level reflects the immanent, material world and vice versa. Esoterics and disciples of the so-called New-Age movement say: The microcosmos is in the macrocosmos, and the macrocosmos is in the microcosmos. With this logic, spiritual sinlessness lies in vaginal intactness and being sexually untouched is the prerequisite and foundation for holiness.

Yet, Vatican doctrine goes one step further and insists that the Roman Mary remained a virgin forever! The virginal motherhood of Mary gains significance for Catholic salvation. "The conception of Jesus is the fruit of her generous cooperation with the work of the spirit of love, the source of all fertility."[199] Consequently, the Catholic Mary acts as co-worker, co-designer and co-redemptrix in Jesus' work of salvation. She becomes the new creation, the new Eve, because she cooperated with Jesus, the new Adam, through

---

197 Ibid. p. 2.
198 Ibid. p. 2.
199 "L'Osservatore Romano", Nr. 32/33, August 9, 1996, p.2.

her consent to motherhood in her sinlessness. Therefore, all faithful Catholics are born out of the same source as Jesus: Mary! In other words, Catholic believers receive new life through Mary in order to attain salvation in Christ. Since Jesus died for all people, the motherhood of Mary also encompasses everyone, according to Rome. She allegedly continues to cooperate in salvation through her motherly love. Only through virginal conception and motherly influence, can people be made into adopted children of God in the Son of the virgin and God."[200] In light of these assumptions, it is not surprising that virginity, as such, was more and more equated with holiness. Even the church teacher Augustine must have projected his Babylon-inspired mother complexes into the biblical text Lk.1;46ff. He pronounced that Mary had made a voluntary vow to remain a virgin permanently. This thought was further expanded in the next centuries. According to Augustine, the Roman Mary could be used as a "role model for all holy virgins in the whole history of the church. She dedicated her virginity to God, even before she knew what she was to conceive."[201] John Paul II added that "the angel did not tell Mary to remain a virgin. Mary, herself, reveals her voluntary decision for virginity."[202] He argued that this decision to stay a virgin forever made her a role model for the church which is fully devoted to the Lord too. From Augustine onwards, Rome equated virginal selfdedication, brought about by the inspiration of the Holy Spirit, with holiness. John Paul II said: "From the testimony of the gospels, it follows that Mary made the personal decision to remain a virgin."[203] Consequently, the Catholic Mary is transformed into the true bride of Christ, the daughter Zion and the new Eve. According to John Paul II's assertions, God accepted her sacrifice, the willingness to stay a virgin even in her future marriage with Joseph, as proof of her special holiness and worthiness. That also made the perfect unification with God possible and allowed her to be deified. Ultimately, the perfect form of marriage is the virginal form in the eyes of Rome. They claim virginity to be "the source of spiritual

---

200 Ibid. p. 2.
201 Ibid. p.2.
202 Ibid. p. 2.
203 Ibid. p. 2.

fertility, the source of motherhood in the holy spirit."[204] Thus, the deification of Mary, her development into the so-called mother of God, is rooted in her everlasting virginity as well as her immaculate conception. These are the two levels to be looked at hypostatically. The Roman church developed Mary into a virgin "before the birth, during the birth and after the birth."[205] The II. Vatican Council from 1962-65 emphasized that "the firstborn of Mary did not lessen her virginal intactness, but instead sanctified it."[206] Based on Rome's portrayal, Mary bore no other children after the birth of Jesus. However, Mt.13: 55 and Mk.6: 3 state that Jesus had four brothers and several sisters out of the marriage between Mary and Joseph. As others before him, John Paul II met these biblical objections with the childish indication that the words for brother and sister could have a very broad meaning in Hebrew and Aramaic, including cousin. He also proposed that these passages may refer to a different Mary who was a follower of Jesus. In any case, the people mentioned were close relatives of Jesus.[207] At the end, John Paul II remained obstinate: "the holy Mary is **consequently** the everlasting virgin."[208]

What implications did this virginity have on the marriage of Mary and Joseph, according to Vatican understanding?

1. Before the wedding, Mary and Joseph agreed to live together as virgins, even in their future marriage.

2. In a dream, Joseph received confirmation that he was to participate in God's plan of salvation through virginal fellowship. This supposedly led both into a higher form of spirituality.

3. Through the free choice of Mary and the obedience of Joseph, both received the charisma of "marriage in virginity." For this very reason, it was a true marriage!

4. Joseph was inwardly perfect and, therefore, able to "carry on a marital relationship with Mary in virginal love."[209] Thus, Joseph's participation involved the voluntary acceptance of his role as father.

---

204 Ibid. p. 2.
205 „L'Osservatore Romano", No. 36, September 6, 1996, p. 2.
206 Ibid. p. 2.
207 See ibid. p. 2.
208 Ibid. p. 2.
209 See ibid. p. 2.

These demonic fallacies in Catholicism have led to a wide variety of undesirable developments, ranging from the spiritual misery of frigidity and impotence as well as other dysfunctions to the worship of the so-called "Holy Family" and Joseph as the protector of the saviour. In 1870, Pius IX delegated the patronage over the whole church to Joseph, as mentioned earlier.

11. Mary – the Representative and Redemptrix of Humanity

The "new Eve, the true daughter of Zion"

Image 7
Jesus-Mary Medal

More and more, Mary became the all-encompassing divine mediatrix of Jesus' work of salvation. A total unity in voluntary dependence on each other was theologically constructed between Jesus and Mary. That reminds us of the divinely inspired biblical statements regarding God, the Father, and Jesus, the Son. The gospel of John, in particular, tells us about their voluntary unity. But according to Catholic doctrine, Jesus was dependent on Mary because she contributed to his work of salvation with her "yes." Catholic theology attributes 51% of the work of redemption to Jesus, and 49% to Mary, so to speak. This Roman dialectic gives Jesus the mathematically greater share. However, Jesus is nothing without Mary.

We will examine this blasphemous thinking and what is behind it in more detail later. The II Vatican Council from 1962-65 used Mary's "yes" to justify her contribution to the work of salvation, as already mentioned. Her willingness was interpreted "such that in the same way as one woman contributed to death, another woman may also contribute to life."[210] The Vatican cites Irenaeus, insisting that Eve's disobedience made Mary's obedience, her consent, necessary. This allowed Mary to become "the advocate of the virgin

---

210 LG 56. In: „L'Osservatore Romano", No. 39, September 27, 1996, p. 2.

Eve." Her "yes" further became the "yes" of all humanity. Through her "yes," Mary was made "completely free before God."²¹¹ By Roman thinking, the future of humanity depended on her consent. God supposedly laid the fate of humanity in the loving hands of Mary. "Mary's 'yes' was the prerequisite for the realization of God's plan of salvation for the world."²¹² Just as all of humanity "became subject to death through a virgin [Eve, the author], it [humanity, the author] is also saved by a virgin. The disobedience of the virgin was counterbalanced by the obedience of the virgin ..."²¹³ These statements very clearly emphasize the role of Mary as co-redemptrix from inherited sin, especially the sins of our ancestor Eve. Through this alleged co-salvation, Rome made her into the "new Eve," the mother of all the living! Vatican II saw Mary as the first and perfect follower of her son and praises her for her complete devotion to Jesus and his work of salvation. Therefore, she was elected to be the "new Eve," having "served the mystery of salvation under him and with him in the grace of the almighty God."²¹⁴ Although John Paul II said that Mary served under Jesus, she served with him at the same time and completed the work of redemption together with Jesus. John Paul II cited Irenaeus, who had expressed what the II Vatican Council underlined, i.e. "that she [Mary] became a source of salvation for herself and the whole human race through her obedience."²¹⁵

Thus, to this day, Mary is praised as a participant in Christ's work of redemption by Rome, "as the true mother of all the living." "Her motherhood, freely accepted in obedience to the divine plan, becomes the fountain of life for all of humankind."²¹⁶ Though said to be very evangelical and ecumenical, the Council called Mary the fulfillment of prophecy in Zech. 9: 9+10: "Rejoice greatly, O daughter of Zion ..." "With Mary, as the noble daughter of Zion, the time is finally fulfilled after a long period of awaiting the promise and a new economy of salvation began when the Son of God accepted

---

211 „L'Osservatore Romano", No. 39, September 27, 1996, p. 2.
212 Ibid. p. 2.
213 Ibid. p. 2.
214 LG 56. In: „L'Osservatore Romano", ibid. p. 2.
215 „L'Osservatore Romano", No. 39, September 27, 1996, p. 2.
216 Ibid. p. 2.

human nature through her, in order to free people from sin by the mysteries of his flesh."[217] The Word of God clearly stands against this theology. For example, Paul's letter to the Hebrews tells us that Jesus learned the obedience of faith through his suffering.

"And having been made perfect, He became the source of eternal salvation for all who obey Him" (Heb.5: 9).

12. Mary – the Prototype of the Roman Church

Rome calls Mary "the new Eve, the first of all believers and the first of those raised."[218] "Because she is full of grace, she ascended into heaven,"[219] according to Catholic theology. The Roman Mary fully participated in her son's work of salvation. She is said to be "the new woman at the side of the redeemer as his helper, who was supposed to share in his passion and spiritually give birth to children of God."[220] The popular belief about seven swords piercing Mary's heart stems from the assumption that she suffered for the redemption of the world, just like Jesus. In other words, she was included in the suffering of Christ as the daughter of Zion and, thus identifies herself with the Roman church. Jesus allegedly included his mother in his suffering and, therefore, she, too, became a sign that is opposed (Lk. 2: 34). Consequently, whoever opposes her, opposes Jesus. Due to the temporal priority of Mary's suffering in comparison to Jesus, she is spoken of as the source of salvation!

Image 8:
Mary as co-redeemer

Dialectically, they say that Jesus has the primacy. However, other statements, especially those of the Pope, as well as the practice of the sacraments indicate a relationship of 49% to 51%, i.e. practical equality. Rome claims that the role of the woman in

---

217 LG 55. In: "L'Osservatore Romano," No.19, May 10, 1996, p.2.
218 See "L'Osservatore Romano," No.35, Aug. 30, 1996, p.8.
219 Ibid. p.8.
220 "L'Osservatore Romano," No.3, Jan. 17, 1997, p.2.

the redemption of humanity is irreplaceable! Through her suffering, she is insolubly linked to the suffering of Christ's salvation. Essentially, Rome has transformed Jesus, the Christ, into a Jesus/Mary, the Christ! This is the blasphemous demonic theology that makes the Catholic church into the whore Babylon. According to Rome, Mary is "the radiant queen sitting at the right hand of the king to reign with him for eternity!"[221]

Moreover, the Roman Mary became the prototype of the church in the Babylonian spirit for another reason. She portrays the second side of Christ, who transforms himself into a "sun-cake" on a daily basis during the Eucharist. As a matter of fact, there are wafers stamped with "Mary", the queen of heaven. Through "Mary", the church is connected with this second side of the Catholic Christ in his suffering and in the resurrection. "Ascended from the earth, she draws everyone close to herself, day after day, preparing our passage from this world to the Father."[222] Mary's complete unification with her son forms the basis for her de facto equal participation in the cross and the resurrection of Christ. Consequently, she is the source that brought forth Christ, the life. The Roman Mary thus represents the hope of the church. Through her participation in redemption, she has the right to influence her son, Jesus. Catholics pray to her as the "queen of angels, queen of the saints, queen of the prophets and apostles, or co-regent of Christ." They believe that these prayers bring them salvation since she, as the mother, can refer to her merits in the work of co-redemption. Then Christ, the son, can not turn down any of her petitions. As a result, the Roman Mary has become the real mediator for the Catholic believers. She has developed into the hope of the church and all of humanity.[223] Vatican II from 1962-65 confirmed her as the "mother of the church, not just the mother of the saviour, but also, in a unique way, as his generous companion."[224]

To recap:

---

221 See Angelo Cardinal Sodano. In: "L'Osservatore Romano," No.35, Aug.30, 1996, p.8.
222 Ibid. p. 8.
223 See "L'Osservatore Romano," No.15, April 11, 1997, p. 2.
224 "L'Osservatore Romano," No.16, April 18, 1997. p. 2.

Chapter IV: Mary, the Mediatrix of all Cosmic Powers

According to Catholic theology, Jesus Christ is the new Adam and Mary, the new Eve. The mother turns into her son's companion!? This is another perverse picture created by the vulgar theology of Rome. The so-called "new Eve" laid the foundation for the universal motherhood: "Therefore, she is the mother for us in the order of grace."[225]

Image 9:
Picture of grace
of Jasna Gora

In his message at the Marian Congress in Czestochowa, John Paul II referred to a Polish pilgrimage song which includes the verse: "Greetings to you, Jesus, Mary's son, true God, present in the holy host."[226] We think that it has become very clear how Rome sees Mary: she is living in complete spiritual unity with the Catholic Christ and is present with him in all the sacraments. The same applies to the sacrament of the Eucharist. When the priest celebrates the praise "to the Christ present in the mystery of the Eucharist,"[227] he also thinks of the second side of salvation: Mary. "Through her son's legacy of love,"[228] she was most closely joined to the Saviour in his life and suffering. Her motherhood was extended to all people by her becoming a mediatrix between them and the result of Christ's death, i.e. the rebirth into a new life. These alleged privileges made Mary into the divine symbol for the mystical body of Christ, the Catholic church. Consequently, the Roman Mary always participates in the Eucharist! One does not only remember the death of Jesus Christ, but also her role in salvation, "how she unified herself lovingly with her suffering son, **agreed with** his sacrifice, and offered the Father her own pain. That means, when one celebrates the Eucharist, the memory of Christ's **Easter**, the remembrance of his mother's suffering becomes not only alive but is carried into the present time ... Through the spiritual association with the

---

225 Ibid. p. 2.
226 "L'Osservatore Romano," No.40, Oct. 4, 1996, p. 12.
227 Ibid. p. 12.
228 Ibid. p. 12.

Chapter IV: Mary, the Mediatrix of all Cosmic Powers

pain-filled mother of God, they [the believers] take special part in the Easter mystery and become open for the extraordinary activity of the Holy Spirit." According to Rome, Mary stood at the beginning of Jesus' mission and, therefore, at the source of the Eucharist as well. **"Mary is the origin of the Eucharist, which unites the believers with the presence of Christ, because she leads them there."**[229]

Image 10:
Mary with Cone of Rays

In the Catholic celebration of Christ's sacrificial death, the sacrament of the Eucharist, Mary's co-salvation is obviously remembered just as much and she is hypostatically materialized too!

We have also recognized that the Roman Mary mediates the powers of the sacraments, including the Eucharist, due to her participation in her son's work of salvation. Therefore, what John Paul II said does not surprise us: "... In the mystery of the incarnation, this power [the Holy Spirit], which is love in the Trinitarian life of God, was revealed in the highest measure, since she [Mary] had the duty of giving the world the incarnation of the Word."[230]

This statement only shows what Bible-believing Christians have already recognized as heresy: Based on Roman theology, Mary is the personification and incarnation of the Holy Spirit, **"who represents divine energy, in accordance with the Old Testament."**[231] Thus, the Catholic Mary is the mediatrix of all spiritual powers associated with the sacraments. Since she suffered with him, she redeemed humanity under Christ and with Christ. As the sign of her resurrection and glory, she has the powers of the Holy Spirit at her disposal. This Holy Spirit is merely a form of energy, according to the Roman church. All sacramental pictures of Mary depict rays emerging from her, symbolizing this blasphemous theology. The so-called "holy spirit" incarnated into the Catholic Mary and she personifies

---

229 See ibid. p. 12.
230 "L'Osservatore Romano," No.32/33, August 9, 1996, p. 2.
231 Ibid. p. 2.

him! Therefore, whoever sees Mary, sees the holy spirit. According to Rome, the holy spirit was only "divine energy" in the Old Testament. Then, in the New Testament, it manifested itself in Mary, the "new Eve"! This view is also depicted in the dove, symbolizing Mary, that sends its rays of divine energy down on Christ. In other words, the Catholic Mary mediates all the powers of grace of the Holy Spirit and all Jesus' merits of grace! According to Rome, she is the mediatrix of redemption because, in chapters 14 and 16 of the gospel of John, the Holy Spirit takes grace from Jesus' work of salvation and entrusts it to the believers. The Catholic trinity consists of:

God – the father
God – the son
God – the holy spirit = Mary, the Immaculate Conception

This trinity worshipped by Catholics stems from the realm of darkness. The spiritual powers mediated by the Roman Mary come from the fallen cosmos. They can be traced back to the first fall, that of the angels which became demons and the second fall, that of the humans, as well as all cultural and individual sins. Enormous demonic powers are freed up through the Roman church in the Babylonian spirit and include those from:

1. the cosmos or the universe
2. the earth
3. the realm of death

These threefold synergistic demonic forces are the basis for the so-called "Holy Trinity" of Rome. The Marian spirit mediates these energies of death to the Catholic believers and slowly frees them from their life, so to say. The true Christ revealed Himself as the only mediator of the new covenant (Heb.9: 15) in the New Testament through His cross and His resurrection. Whoever does not want the new life in and out of Him, ends up under the influence of the mediatrix of death and its energies. Rome's great deception is deadly. Let us consider the most important passages of the prayer that John Paul II spoke at the Marian pillar on the Spanish Square in Rome on Dec. 8, 2001:

"Immaculate Mother, on this festive day, enlightened by the shine of Your virginal conception, we gather to your feet again on this historic square in the heart of Christian Rome. As every year, we came here to renew the traditional presentation of the flowers on Dec. 8th.

Chapter IV: Mary, the Mediatrix of all Cosmic Powers

With this gesture, we want to express the childlike love of the city which has so many signs of Your motherly presence. We have come in humble pilgrimage, and on behalf of all believers, we call to you full of confidence:

1. "Monstra Te esse matrem ...
Show that you are the mother of all of us,
Present our prayer;
May Christ accept it benevolently,
He; who became your son
2. "Monstra Te esse matrem!"
Show that you are the mother of all of us !
Here before your famous portrait, we say thanks to the
Lord for your Immaculate Conception with joyful hearts.
You are the completely beautiful one, whom the Most
High has clothed with his power. You are the completely
holy one, whom God has chosen for the unblemished
residence of his glory. Greetings to you, mysterious
temple of God, greetings to you, full of grace, intercede for us!
3. "Monstra Te esse matrem!"

We ask you to bring our prayer before him who clothed you with grace and protected you from every blemish of sin. Dark clouds are gathering on the horizon of the world. The human race, which greeted the third millennium filled with hope, now feels threatened by new, shocking conflicts. Peace on earth is in danger. Therefore, we come to you, Immaculate Virgin, and ask you, as an understanding and strong mother, to cause the hearts of humans – freed from the intoxication of hatred – to become open for mutual forgiveness, for constructive solidarity and for peace.

4. "Monstra Te esse matrem!"

Protect, O Mary, the great family of the church so that all believers, as true disciples of your son, may proceed forward in the light of his presence.

5. "Monstra Te esse matrem!"

You star of the new evangelism, encourage and accompany us on the steps of indefatigable, missionary pastoral work through a unique and decisive program: preaching Christ, the Saviour of the world. May mission become the everyday testimony of every believer, corresponding to the respective circumstances of his life, may the Christian face of Rome be renewed through them, making it become clearly visible to all that faithfulness to Christ transforms the personal existence and creates a future of peace, a better future for all.

6. "Monstra Te esse matrem!"

Be a firm rock of courage and faithfulness for us, you humble girl of Nazareth, you glorious queen of the world. Present our prayer to the divine Word: When he became your son, he made himself into our brother. Through your mighty intercession, may all the people of God and especially the beloved church of Rome 'drive forth' to every holiness that is of decisive significance for every fruit-bringing apostolate. Mother of mercy and mother of peace, immaculate mother of God, pray for us!"[232]

In contrast, the Word of God tells us:

"For this reason he is the mediator of a new covenant, so that those who are called may receive the promised eternal inheritance, because a death has occurred that redeems them from the transgressions under the first covenant" (Heb.9: 15).

"For Christ did not enter a sanctuary made by human hands, a mere copy of the true one, but he entered into heaven itself, now to appear in the presence of God on our behalf. Nor was it to offer himself again and again, as the high priest enters the Holy Place year after year with blood that is not his own; for then he would have had to suffer again and again since the foundation of the world. But as it is, he has appeared once for all at the end of the age to remove sin by the sacrifice of himself. And just as it is appointed for mortals to die **once**, *and after that the judgment, so Christ, having been offered* **once** *to bear the sins of many, will appear a second time, not to deal with sin, but to* **save those** *who are eagerly waiting for him"* (Heb.9: 24-28).

"But when Christ had offered for all time a single sacrifice for sins, 'he sat down at the right hand of God,' and since then has been waiting 'until his enemies would be made a footstool for his feet.' **For by a single offering he has perfected for all time those who are sanctified**"(Heb.10: 12-14).

---

232 "L'Osservatore Romano," No.50, December 14, 2001, p. 7.

"For if we wilfully persist in sin after having received the knowledge of the truth, there no longer remains a sacrifice for sins, but a fearful prospect of judgment, and a fury of fire that will consume the adversaries.

How much worse punishment do you think will be deserved by those who have spurned the Son of God, profaned the blood of the covenant by which they were sanctified, and outraged the Spirit of grace? For we know the one who said (Deut.32: 35+36), *'Vengeance is mine, I will repay.' And again, 'The Lord will judge his people.'*

It is a fearful thing to fall into the hands of the living God"
(Heb.10: 26,27,29-31).

We can not help but say that the Roman 'Mary' is the whore Babylon in European-occidental cultural form. **Through her, the Roman Catholic church became an anti-church out of the Babylonian-antichristian spirit.**

13. Mary and the Significance of her Places of Worship

On a trip, we discovered the Catholic church of America, as such, on the outskirts of Washington, DC, USA. In contrast to Europe, America has a short history and, therefore, cannot compete with the many places of pilgrimage there. However, Rome did not want to leave the so-called "new world" without the cosmic spiritual power of the Immaculate Conception. The original, consecrated Marian places of power were located primarily in Europe and could not easily be transported to the "new world" for worship. Yet, Rome knew what to do. In the 1920's the "Basilica of the National Shrine of the Immaculate Conception" was built in the city of Washington. This unique church displays copies of almost all Madonnas approved by the Vatican which have significant places of pilgrimage. In the two-story building, 26 Marian places of worship were set up, centred around the copies of statues or icons. This is Rome's magical attempt to bring North America under the influence of its Mary. In Santo Domingo, in the Dominican Republic, I also discovered a gigantic mausoleum in honour of Columbus, Faro de Colon. It displays copies of all the Middle and South American Madonnas. They represent the power-laden proof that this continent belongs to the Roman Mary ever since it was discovered by Columbus. As we have already said, there are more than 179 Marian self-descriptions and titles of honour. Like many family names, they almost always indicate her characteristics or occupations. These Marian Madonnas have very different cosmic-demonic spiritual powers and are highly specialized in the way the power is mediated. The term "Madonna" is the most comprehensive, encompassing all Marian figures. The Italian word literally means "my mistress" and stems from the Latin term "domina" or mistress. In French as well as English, the version "madame" was used to address noblewomen. In German, we have the word "Dame" or "Frau," leading to the name "Unsere liebe Frau …" or "Our dear Lady …" The strongest expression of this so-called mistress manifested itself in the "Immaculate Conception." Therefore, the Immaculate Conception's place of pilgrimage in Lourdes, France, is the prime of its kind. In addition, the copy of Lourdes is practically the centre of the National Shrine in Washington and, incidentally, of the Vatican Gardens in Rome too.

Let us come back to the Marian or Madonna copies. A copy is always dependent on the original and must be recognized as such. Everything else would be a forgery. Similarly, the Madonna copies depend on the cosmic-demonic spiritual force of the originals in their original places. The 26 Marian copies in the US National Shrine as well as those in the Dominican Republic serve to establish a worldwide network of cosmic-demonic spiritual power, stretching from the original places to the copies. These cosmic energies supply power for the replicas. The invisible, spiritual forces captivate the visitors and seduce them to worship the copies. Through the abominable sin of revering this "queen of heaven," forces of death are produced in horrendous amounts. By means of the worldwide network, these steadily increasing cosmic-demonic spiritual powers amplify the energies at the point of origin, e.g. the major places of pilgrimage. They can be sent from the original to the replica and back, so to speak. For example, the National Shrine in Washington acts as a distributor for the demonic-cosmic spiritual forces from the countries of origin, primarily in Europe. As a result, Protestant America is becoming more and more infiltrated by the Marian-Babylonian spirit. It was reported to us that even many non-Catholic members of government or Congress go to the Immaculata Basilica to pray. Naturally, what has been said about the Marian network also applies to each Catholic church with consecrated Marian statues or images.

Every Bible-believing Christian should know about these connections and understand how to deal with them. Out of faithfulness to Jesus Christ, we can not tolerate such centres of Marian power spiritually. On the contrary, they should be battled with spiritual weapons on a broad front. As we have seen, the whole Marian faith leads to a faith in sacraments and in the Eucharistic-cosmic Christ, stemming from the spirit of the Antichrist.

14. The Marian place of pilgrimage in Lourdes, France – the basis for the "Queen of Peace"

In 1858, Bernadette Soubirous, a 14-year-old girl, had eighteen Marian apparitions. Post revolutionary France had just successfully completed the secularization ordered by Napoleon. The omnipotence of the Roman church was broken. At the time, Emperor Napoleon III reigned. The famous French author Emilé Zola took up the subject in his novel "Lourdes" and dealt with it from a critical, philosophically enlightened perspective. For these reasons, Lourdes stagnated until 1905, when the late Pope Pius X became involved. He ordered a medical examination of the healing miracles that had occurred after the Marian apparitions to little Bernadette. However, the secular French world, including the French medical profession, attacked Lourdes so severely that the first medical records were not handed over to the church officials until 1946. Yet, most of these records, kept since 1905, had suddenly disappeared. In the literature circulating on this subject, an attentive reader will notice the dubious nature of these alleged miracles, even as a medical layman. So-called medically proven cases are very rare and usually consist of laughable and naïve claims. It is similar to the spectacle of the "Toronto blessing" in the 20th century. We must recognize this. On the other hand, we should never forget that a demonic force exists in Lourdes which continues to spread and poison the souls of many, not just the pilgrims. It is even spreading to the Protestant world through the Ecumenical movement. The fact that we do not need to take most of the alleged miracles seriously should not lead us to the wrong conclusion. The Marian power is more than just hot air, so to speak. Based on our worldwide experience with centres of spiritual cosmic-demonic power, we must also warn people about the

Chapter IV: Mary, the Mediatrix of all Cosmic Powers

Image 11
Madonna of Lourdes

other extreme of enlightenment. This critical perspective of miracles can quickly prove to be a deception. It stems from one's own rationalistic thinking that still needs to be battled and discarded.

According to Läpple, only 65 healing miracles were recognized by the church from the first miracle in 1858 to the end of 1976. Ten of these occurred between 1858 and the end of the 19th century. The other 55 took place in the 20th century.[233] Still, "many believe that the miracles in Lourdes set new records year after year and have already reached a dizzying height."[234] If this is the case, one might ask why the Vatican acknowledges so few as true miracles. However, it would go beyond the scope of the book to examine the issue further. Interestingly, Lourdes attracts over 5 million pilgrims per year on a regular basis. But, only 70.000 of these are sick or disabled. Those seeking to be healed make up a relatively small proportion of the total number of pilgrims.

Lourdes as well as Czestochowa in Poland with 5 million and Fatima in Portugal with 4.5 million pilgrims yearly belong to the strongest places of spiritual power in Europe, although the latter two have a completely different emphasis in the form of their demonic seduction. Yet, the number of pilgrims can not be correlated directly with the demonic force. If there were a direct relationship, Guadeloupe in Mexico City would be the most powerful Marian place of pilgrimage with its alleged 20 million visitors a year. However, this is not the case. I can make the assessment with confidence because I have checked this location personally as well.

Let us now deal specifically with the Catholic Mary of Lourdes, the "Immaculate Conception," as the basis for all strong Marian places. We will then understand why Lourdes has a lot to do with the apocalyptical situation, i.e. the religious and political Babylon. As already shown, the Madonna of the "Immaculate Conception" in Lourdes is the conclusion of a development in Vatican theology

---

233 Läpple, „Die Wunder von Lourdes", 1995, p. 209. (The miracles of Lourdes).
234 Ibid. p. 17.

Chapter IV: Mary, the Mediatrix of all Cosmic Powers

which began roughly 1500 years ago. Here, the Roman Mary reached the highest level of her Catholic development. She mutated from the biblical believer into a goddess and became the true mistress or Madonna of the whole Roman church with her mediation of all cosmic spiritual powers. Lourdes represents the fundamental Catholic forces of the "mother of God." In 1917, 59 years after the first miracle at Lourdes these forces gave rise to the "queen of peace" in Fatima, Portugal. They put her mediation powers into the worldwide service of the global Marian revival. Since the "queen of peace" is such an extensive subject and also closely linked to parts of the European Union's philosophy, we will take a closer look at Fatima later. However, it should be mentioned here that Pius XII already called Mary of Fatima a "bringer of peace" back in 1942, claiming that she was paving the way for the kingdom of Christ. According to the Vatican, the so-called "Marian era" began in 1917. The "Immaculate Conception" of Lourdes with its branches in Altoetting and Werl (Germany), Einsiedeln (Switzerland), Mariazell and Mariataferl (Austria), Tschentochau and Annaberg (Poland) as well as Banneux (Belgium) form the basis and the unifying European political band for Fatima's "queen of peace" with her most recent branch in Medjugorje (Bosnia-Herzegovina) since the 1990's.[235] This basis ensures sufficient power for the continuing development of the queen of peace. Let us now examine more closely the 18 apparitions in Lourdes to Bernadette Soubirous. They began on Feb. 2, 1858, in the Grotto of Massabielle and ended on July 16, 1858. The first transcendent appearances consisted of the order to pray the Rosary, the command to appear in the grotto every 14 days and the announcement that Bernadette would soon be made happy in the "other world." Bernadette was instructed in the prayer of personal protection and brought many people with her to the apparitional meetings. Three further appearances involved the request to "pray for the sinners and the sick world," to call for repentance and to have a chapel of worship built. At another five appearances, the apparition asked Bernadette to drink from the small spring, wash herself, and then eat some of the herbs growing there. After several days, the spring expanded to its present capacity with an output of

---

235 See Fonseca, „Maria spricht zur Welt", 1988, p. 480. (Maria speaks to the world).

122 400 litres a day. It has supposedly stayed the same ever since, never more and never less. Bernadette was ordered to climb up the hill to the spring on her knees and kiss the ground repeatedly as an act of penitence for the sinners. The apparition also renewed its demand for a place of pilgrimage. On the occasion of the last five appearances, Bernadette gathered 20,000 people and the first healing miracles occurred. For the first time, the apparition introduced herself as the "Immaculate Conception." However, there was a lot of negative pressure from the anticlerical French state under Napoleon III, leading to the closure of the grotto. Only after Napoleon's own son was healed by the consecrated Marian herbs near the spring, did he allow the grotto to be reopened to the public.[236] The penitence demanded on behalf of the sinners in the sick [irreligious] world consisted of praying the Rosary and sacrificing oneself so that the world may be healed of the atheistic illness. It was supposed to bring about a revival of Marian religiosity in the face of secularization through philosophical enlightenment and rationalism. The miracles and apparitions were to convince people that the so-called religion, i.e. the transcendent world, represented the actual reality as opposed to the secular, material world. Interestingly, the "Immaculate Conception" and her mysticism took so much out of Bernadette that she died as a nun at the age of only 36. Her undecomposed body can allegedly still be viewed in Nevers, France, today. When I visited Nevers, I saw a doll, not a real, intact body. It is nothing but another typically cheap Catholic deception, exploiting the stupidity of public faith. In 1933, Bernadette Soubirous was canonized. According to the pilgrimage offices, 5000 people are supposed to have been healed. But under the pressure of the secular public, only 65 healing miracles have been scientifically acknowledged.

Knowing the origin of the miraculous power, the impudence of the Roman church is astonishing. A Catholic physician described it as follows: "The healing miracles in Lourdes occur according to a prescribed ceremony, strangely similar to the ceremonies enacted in the temples of Äskulap [Asclepius]. Day and night, processions pass by the multitude of the sick. During all processions, the religious

---

236 See Hierzenberger/Nedomansky, „Erscheinungen und Botschaften der Gottesmutter Maria", 1996, p. 210–215. (= Appearances and messages of Mary. the mother of God).

Chapter IV: Mary, the Mediatrix of all Cosmic Powers

masses recite prayers and are increasingly seized by emotionality. At this point, seriously ill people suddenly rise from their stretchers at the request of the priests and declare themselves healed. Others throw away their crutches and walk."[237] We attended such a procession twice and saw only wheelchair patients who were disappointed and unhappy because they had been deceived. Moreover, we noticed how these sacramental processions led to the demonization of the participating people. It is conceivable that many will become psychologically ill as a result. The ancient Romans had adopted the Greek Asclepius and renamed him Äskulap. Asclepius was the son of Apollo and Coronis. He served as a healer in the Greek world of the gods. His greatest skill was his ability to perform healing miracles on the dead. Asclepius had Chiron as a teacher, the inventor of the healing art in Greek mythology. This Asclepius had undergone a development similar to Mary. In the writings of Homer, Asclepius does not yet appear as a god. Homer described him to be mortal. He is portrayed as a man who possessed a lot of infallible medical knowledge. In subsequent myths, Asclepius has taken on the nature of a demigod, born of a mortal mother and fathered by the god Apollo. Note the astonishing similarity to the mortal mother Mary and the conception through the holy spirit as Catholics understand it. With time, Asclepius was promoted from a demigod to a god because of his deep faith. Again, we can see a surprising resemblance to the hierarchical development of the Roman Mary.[238] To symbolize his healing power, this Asclepius had a magic wand with a snake coiling around it. In modern times, his magic wand has become a symbol for the healing art of humanistic physicians. I visited Epidauros, the ancient Greek place of pilgrimage, primarily in order to study and evaluate it critically. Everywhere, I could see the general international efforts to revive and rebuild this old demonic location of the snake. The most famous sacred shrine besides Epidauros stood in Pergamon. This fact also speaks clearly for the Satanic background of Asclepius, who let himself be worshipped as "soter," the Greek word for saviour.

---

237 Läpple, „Die Wunder von Lourdes", 1995, p. 22. (The miracles of Lourdes).
238 See Lurker, „Lexikon der Götter und Dämonen", 1984 (Encyclopedia of gods and demons) and Irmscher, „Lexikon der Antike", 1990. (Encyclopedia of antiquity).

Chapter IV: Mary, the Mediatrix of all Cosmic Powers

This makes the position of Lourdes even more obvious! Most healing miracles happen after the patients drink from the Marian spring or wash themselves with its water. Here, the mediation service of the Catholic Mary takes place. Afterwards, processions pass by the sick with the holiest sacrament of the altar, the crucified Roman Christ. This saviour, however, is the Greek idol of healing Asclepius or Äskulap. The worship of the eucharistic Christ in Lourdes is really the worship of Asclepius. Even though the double demonic source can be recognized so clearly, more and more people make pilgrimages there, supposedly to worship God. The so-called graces mediated by the "Immaculate Conception" in Lourdes stem from the demonic source of the third ancient antichristian world empire of Greece. The remarkable characteristic of this place of pilgrimage involves the teamwork of the Catholic mediator "Mary-Jesus," and is in full agreement with the Vatican/papal theology: "There is healing flair in Lourdes as well as outside of Lourdes."[239] It has been reported that healing miracles have occurred in the "holy district" of Lourdes as well as places of pilgrimage hundreds of kilometres away. The water of the spring is the "sign of the dignity of the creation."[240] Through the water of Lourdes, the pilgrims are supposed to be brought back to the God of creation. From the Catholic perspective, this means that they are freed from agnosticism and immersed in religiosity. As the co-redemptrix and goddess of the earth, the "Immaculate Conception" mediates the demonic magical forces of the earth and the water, combining them with sacramental Roman Christ's power of death. Hence, the allegedly healed, as well as the healthy, are led to the "Saviour-God," as they call it. All of this occurs through the mediation of the Catholic Mary. The "Creator and Saviour God" of Lourdes is none other than the god of this world!

In 1958, the late Pope Pius XII published an encyclical on the occasion of the 100th anniversary of Lourdes. With strong words, he stated: **"The whole Christian world is a Marian world**, and there are no people bought by the blood of Christ who do not willingly recognize Mary as his mother and patron."[241] He continued

---

239 Läpple, "Die Wunder von Lourdes," 1995, (The miracles of Lourdes p.208).
240 Ibid. p.211.
241 Ibid. p. 237.

Chapter IV: Mary, the Mediatrix of all Cosmic Powers

"that France became a model through its Middle Age mystics and its Marian faith. Therefore, it has so many Marian shrines, headed by Lourdes. Through the fullness of power, Mary is still the 'guardian of our salvation' today."[242] *The Pope repeated "that it is part of the Catholic faith that Mary was exempted from sin from the beginning, as the virgin herself began to perform her miracles in Lourdes."*[243]

15. Lourdes – the Basis for a Religious Babylon

From the Vatican perspective, the real fame of Lourdes lies in the fact "that all nations [from all religions, the author] are led to the worship of *Jesus Christ in the Holiest Sacrament* by Mary, such that this sacred shrine is the hub of the Marian cult as well as the throne of the Eucharistic mystery at the same time, whereby it likely surpasses all other shrines of the Catholic world."[244]

The case is clear for every true Christian. In the strength of the cosmic spirit, the Roman saviours Mary and Jesus have the whole power of the Catholic trinity at their disposal at Lourdes. This can not be said of most other Marian locations. Here lurks the danger for true Christianity. The entire demonic spiritual power, combined with the network of all Marian places worldwide, form the basis for the universal "queen of peace." They are made available to her for her duty of bringing the Antichrist, a product of the cosmic Christ, to power. She will only succeed if she can also convince other religions and esoteric systems to accept her power "of all graces." This is already happening in Fatima and, to a lesser extent, in Medjugorje. Lourdes plays a decisive preparatory role. "In Mary's school," all nations and cultures are supposed to "learn to live for the sole purpose of giving Christ [really the Antichrist] to this world,"[245] according to Pius XII. At the end of his encyclical, he cited Bernard of Clairvaux, the greatest French mystic of the Middle Ages, saying: "In dangers, in difficulties, in doubts, think of Mary, call on Mary ... if you follow her, you can not go wrong. If you ask her, you will not despair. If you think of her, you will not err. If she holds you, you will not

---

242 Ibid. p. 237.
243 Ibid. p. 237.
244 Papst Pius XII. In: ibid. p. 237, 238.
245 Ibid. p. 243.

fall."²⁴⁶ Even the late Pope John Paul II did not get tired of confirming this position, mindset and perspective again and again. Therefore, the spirit of Lourdes is of vital significance for the Ecumenism of the world religions. In Lourdes, "a dialogue takes place between God and man."²⁴⁷ For this reason, all people of all cultures and religions should enter into a dialogue with each other. Further, it is said that all people who pray experience the philanthropic God, not just those of the "biblical religions." He allegedly heals in all other religions too, since we are always dealing with the same Creator-God, or so they say. The Catholic Lourdes should be understood as a prelude to the unification with all world religions. Therefore, Fatima is only a logical continuation and the endpoint of the Roman Mary's development with respect to her political message. Lourdes offers the religion of universal salvation as the prerequisite for this apocalyptic antichristian plan. The Catholic Mary, in the form of the "Immaculate Conception," wants to be the mediatrix for the cosmic-demonic spiritual powers out of all cultures and religions. She also appears under another label as the mediatrix of esoteric, sectarian forces. Consequently, Mary becomes the mediatrix of the religious and political Babylon. In the last phase, she will produce the Antichrist out of the Roman spirit.

Hence, we are calling on every believer to engage in spiritual battle!

Stand up, stand up for Jesus, ye soldiers of the cross; lift high His royal banner, it must not suffer loss. From victory unto victory His army shall He lead, till every foe is vanquished, and Christ is Lord indeed.

Stand up, stand up for Jesus, the trumpet call obey; forth to the mighty conflict, in this His glorious day. Ye that are brave now serve Him against unnumbered foes; let courage rise with danger, and strength to strength oppose.

Stand up, stand up for Jesus, stand in His strength alone; the arm of flesh will fail you, ye dare not trust your own. Put on the Gospel armour, each piece put on with prayer; where duty calls or danger, be never wanting there.

Words: G. Duffield

---

246 Ibid. p. 245.
247 Ibid. p. 212.

Chapter V

The Development of the European Union and the Significance of Fatima's Madonna

1. Introduction

I have no wish to write a chapter about why we are for or against a political union of Europe. First, we will deal with the realities that will become crucial for all Christians and try to determine whether or not the ability to live together peacefully still exists. These realities consist of the emotional conditions of the people in modern Europe. People make up the raw material, so to speak, for a political as well as a religious Europe. Will this political union immediately be called "United States of Europe" where the differently developed cultures are integrated into a new form of the "Holy Roman Empire of European Nations"? Or will there be a transition phase with a federation of European states and the renaissance of the Roman empire? We can only wait and see.

We as pastoral care workers and analysts of this apocalyptic age and its spirit are mainly interested in the psycho-social condition of the European people. That knowledge makes it possible to estimate how the mostly antichristian European politicians will be able to use their human resources. We will clearly show what philosophical and religious sources these EU politicians draw on and what their fundamental goals are. Furthermore, we will look at what the religious Babylon, i.e. the Roman church, contributes to the unification process. For Rome, the "Immaculate Conception" of Mary plays an indispensable role in all of this. I have already explained our view in a booklet called "Vereinigung,"[248] which means unification and was published in 1990. Before the countdown to an antichristian state, a single world government, and/or a federation of ten states begins, a renaissance of nationalisms must occur. A unified Europe will be included in this development. In other words, a universalistic European Union will only materialize after a national-cultural, or rather, ethnic reawakening has taken place. In the aforementioned

---

248 See „Unification", "News", special edition October 1990.

booklet, I have listed numerous spiritual reasons for this paradox and do not think it is necessary to repeat myself here. I would simply like to point out that ethnic battles and ethnic cleansing have indeed occurred on a regular basis since 1990. In Europe as well as other continents, this led to the formation of new states.

2. The Spiritual Condition of EU Citizens at the Turn of the Century

An Impulse-driven Society

Politicians, pastors, and even the Pope, the representative of the religious Babylon, all face the same problem: people moulded and formed by the spirit of the age! Since the 1960's, a major fruit of this spirit is the refusal to grow up. These people then act based on the lowest primal instincts. We are repeatedly confronted by the unwillingness to mature of those in our pastoral care. Without this refusal, many of those seeking help could grow into a social and independent life considerably faster. It is true that spiritual health depends on the ability to assume responsibility. Yet, our world is increasingly comprised of half-adults who have cultivated their morbid infantilism and declared it to be the societal norm. Should a pastoral care worker, pastor, or other active member of a Protestant church be interested in this observation? It is conspicuous that the churches with the greatest numerical growth consist of people who never fully mature. For the most part, they belong to the charismatic side of the theological spectrum. Here, the people can live it up with fun, games, and drive-oriented activities. Events offering emotional experiences are the most attractive. The goal is no longer to learn to live according to the standards of God's Word, which would be a sign of maturity. In the so-called "society of fun," the pastor must mutate into an entertainer to secure the loyalty of his congregation. All alleged modern revival movements are tailored to these infantile half-adults, or stem from them. All western societies are affected, and hence, most Protestant churches too. Living by impulses and drives is a characteristic of post-modern society.

3. The Infantile Half-Adult as the Product of an Altered Consciousness

These half-adults constantly need television, radio and cell phone to keep in touch with their world. They all wear the same brand of jeans, speak the same universal computer language, and listen to the same music. Throughout the Western countries, you can observe the same uniformity and monotony. There are few people with a mind of their own. I have seen the same childish face without individual expression on the 30-year-old skateboarder near the Cathedral of Cologne as well as in Los Angeles. Another common characteristic is that they all amuse themselves for hours on workdays, when one should be working. I have noticed the same impulse-driven attitude and equalization at the meetings of charismatic churches. Some time ago, several co-workers and I attended the Taizé youth meeting as critical observers among over 7,000 participants. The youths coming from Western countries all conspicuously had the same standardized faces and a blank stare looking off into the distance. As we walked through the hall with young people from the former Eastern European Communist countries, especially Poland, we were somewhat surprised at the difference. These youths from Eastern Europe stood out from the rest through their seriousness. They looked more grown up and showed it too. Even though all had been influenced by Catholicism, the young people from Eastern Europe appeared to be far less standardized than those from Western countries. We experienced the same thing as critical observers at the Pope's 1997 World Youth Day in Paris with its alleged one million visitors. A shocking lack of individuality presented itself to us among the Western youth. Even the Vatican acknowledged this infantile personality type by calling 35-year-old men and women "young people," instead of adults. We made the same observation as before: the 30-year-olds from Eastern Europe appeared more earnest and grown up. Unfortunately however, this did not keep them from believing the seductive words of the Pope along with all the others. Numerous thoughtful contemporaries have said that authentic life, a life with spiritual identity, is only possible with a vertical orientation, i.e. a religious conviction of purpose and values. In our opinion, they are right. The misery of infantilism indeed arose as an evil fruit of an absolute horizontal, materialistic world view. Our Western societies are now being governed by people who have never past the childish stage, or have fled back into spiritual childhood as adults. They represent classical examples of infantilism. In such a pathologically childish society, there is little left that could protect people from demoralization, spiritual atrophy, and a primitive fascist lifestyle. The award-winning American author and poet Robert Bly claims to have discovered two tendencies in Western civilizations: infantile regression, i.e. adults developing backwards into spiritual childhood and a regression to the early period of humanity.[249] He uses these concepts to help explain why many adults, who ought to live responsibly, act in such a decidedly primitive and childish way. If Christians take into consideration what crimes are committed by adults, they understand such worldly trains of thought especially well. We need only think of crimes against children such as child prostitution and pornography, the offences of youths who refuse to grow up, or the primitive violent crimes that occur. "A profound change is the cause of this primitivism ... The mass movement swallows the individual and makes him uniform with itself. As a result, the individual is thrown back into an early childhood stage ... Children are primitive being. They gullibly join a mob."[250] Bly also presents the second argument that time is necessary for a person's maturation. Yet, no one wants to give up their restless leisure activity and quest for fun. Instead of a mature spiritual identity, a cultural primitivism develops. We can only confirm these perceptions from our own pastoral care experience. After this introduction, let us now take a closer look at the so-called youth who attended the Taizé meeting and the World Youth Day in Paris. Most were around the age of 30. One would expect the young adults to listen carefully to what the older adults tell them, especially since these elders had attracted them like magnets. However, their attitude and behaviour were completely different:

Some waited for a transcendent experience, often with outstretched hands, that would suddenly come over them and solve all problems immediately, in this case the lack of global peace. Others

---

249 See Bly, "Die kindliche Gesellschaft," 1997, p. 40 (English title: "The Sibling Society").
250 See ibid. p. 9.

Chapter V: The Development of the European Union

simply continued to chatter in a shallow, childish manner without listening to the speeches. Both matadors, Roger Schutz of Taizé and Pope John Paul II indeed made allowances for these drive impulses by showering the event-hungry youth with cosmic-demonic power, camouflaged as effects of the Holy Spirit.

In our day and age, what is said does not matter to the older as well as younger half-adults. They do not want to hear life-changing truth. All they want is an interesting or exciting experience. Nothing else matters!

Charismatics and similar pseudo-Protestant groups attract the same visitors with an infantile, half-mature mentality. We are dealing with a faceless, uniform mass of people who have come to experience the effects of a spirit passively. I do not mean to be arrogant by making this observation. We felt great sympathy for the mass of adventure-hungry people who looked like cloned sheep without a loyal shepherd. Their pseudo-shepherds even turned out to be wolves.

To summarize, this type of infantile half-adult can be found everywhere throughout Western societies: in all age groups, from 20 to 65, in politics, in all esoteric sects, in all churches, and in many Protestant congregations too. Whether Christians or non-Christians, they have the common characteristic of wanting to experience something interesting or exciting. They do not want to bear responsibility, let alone endure difficulties. Even many believers do not want to hear the Word of God in order to learn to live accountably, but rather to experience what they think is God. They live by the maxim that everything creating pleasant experiences is good; and everything demanding responsible actions is bad.

The Christian churches have to deal with the new species of people just as much as the secular society and its institutions. In reality, this so-called "new human" is the desired result of demonically inspired spiritual transformations into a being with "a more expanded or higher level of consciousness." Let us recall what was already said: "Children are primitive beings ... [They] gullibly follow a leader and like to join a mob." For some readers, that may explain why such pseudo-spiritual movements can mobilize so many people. In Taizé, Paris, Toronto, or elsewhere, there is and was no substance worth taking seriously. But to us, these meetings seemed to be dress rehearsals for the appearance of the Antichrist. They looked like experiments in transforming people for D-day. One is learning how to capture people in mass movements and manipulate them with the help of cosmic-demonic forces. Since the 1930's, the European people of our time are being prepared for this. The development continued with the cultural revolution of 1968 and has reached a certain kind of climax with the 'golf generation' at the beginning of the 21st century.

The extent to which a western person denies accountable actions and refuses to accept responsibility shows how much he is already demonically transformed.

4. The Patriarchy – A Solution for a Feministic, Fatherless Society?

We are living in a fatherless society. It came about by the sweeping rejection of all fathers, even in cultural history, which was shaped by male elders. Feminism, the perverted form of justified societal emancipation, has taken the place of a paternal society. The mothers have been abandoned by the fathers and are left alone in raising the children. However, they cannot fill the vacuum. The fathers are often undergoing an identity crisis because they were not allowed to act as fathers. Instead, they are expected to be a sort of pal. Another consequence is that the sons become more and more feminine, stopping their spiritual development and keeping them at a childish level. They have next to no genuine, credible fathers as mentors who feel comfortable with their mature manhood. And if such men do exist, they are defamed as "oriental patriarchs." There is little hope that real grown-ups will ever again shape the world, or even Bible-believing churches. We need true fathers, but the problem appears insolvable. Daughters have just as much trouble maturing, although their situation is somewhat different. It would be too easy to blame everything on feminism. Even though extreme feminism thrives on the hatred of God and fathers in general, the whole movement is too multi-faceted and heterogeneous to allow for sweeping criticism. Three religious men, in particular, took and are taking advantage of this Western cultural calamity: the former Pope John Paul II, the late Roger Schutz, the leader of the mystical Ecumenical youth movement of Taizé who was murdered by some of his own young followers some years ago, and the Buddhist Dalai Lama. All three have portrayed themselves as fathers of all half-adults in order to redeem them from their identity crisis. They played on the fatherly longing of immature people, only to seduce them once again. Real fatherhood has to do with helping young people become responsible adults. But, this was not offered. Instead, these men exploited the yearning of the youths by leaving them immature and promising them so-called "power of heaven" if they were prepared to give their lives to the church, or the Buddhist system. And it was meant literally! The young people are supposed to turn their spiritual life over to the realm of death. In its stead, they receive forces of death which are called holy. Although John Paul II and the others could and would not offer true fatherhood, they let themselves be addressed as "Holy Father," or "His Holiness." But then, what did they have to offer the half-adults? They wanted to go back to a patriarchy based on androcentrism, or a modified androgen centrism, and called it fatherhood! This also applied to Roger Schutz, even though he passed himself off as very moderate and liberal on the outside. However, this type of fatherhood results in permanent immaturity and only represents a change from one oppressive regime to another. It does not lead the half-adults to freedom and responsibility, helping them become mature. In the "Letters of Taizé" from 1997, Roger Schutz described his approach as follows: "If we allow ourselves to be clothed in forgiveness like a robe, we sense how something in us is transfigured ..." That is their message to half-adults! Reconcile yourselves so that there is peace. Upon closer inspection, an adult discovers that they have no interest in talking about the causes, i.e. sins, in order to receive forgiveness from other people and God. On the contrary, the youths are supposed to remain silent while they are being showered by the spirit and forget all memories of sin! God does not even figure in this Benedictine-Buddhist concept! They talk deceptively about forgiving, when they actually mean forgetting! I think the reader will agree with me that the acceptance of such a message requires an infantile, childish mindset. All the messages of the Ecumenical movement are set up in a similar way, cut out for people who have not reached adulthood! With this attitude, the Pope confirmed continually the patriarchal, papal infallibility doctrine of 1870. The abuse of fatherhood can also be found in the debate around abortion and contraception. At the II Vatican Council in the 1960's, abortion was strictly forbidden from the point of conception onwards for the first time. Yet, they did not talk about abortion and contraception in the same breath. These are indeed two different subjects which need to be assessed individually. John Paul II, on the other hand, was able to talk about murder with respect to abortion and we can only agree. But, whenever he said this, he was also referring to contraception. He alleged that this amounts to killing too, since the creation of a new human is being prevented. All of this is only possible because of our infantile society. Bishop G. Eder was allowed to put it into these provocative words on behalf of the Vatican: "The line can be drawn from Euthanasia back to abortion and, from there, back to contraception."[251] Most people do not even notice how two, or rather, three subjects are contracted into one, although the Pope expressed it often enough. Even some Protestants cling to this so-called "moral Dad" like children. In my view, this is another typical sign of infantilism. The belligerent feminists, on the other hand, and the political liberals usually catch this dishonest intellectual bundling of two different subjects. Thus, Rome's position provokes an unnecessary cultural battle against the extremes of the abortion front. Only the widespread infantilism on all sides allows the papacy to abuse its androcentric patriarchy like an oriental despot. It is true that children can not be expected to notice such subtleties. But, are they really subtleties? These manipulations are only successful in a world of half-adults. The same tactic, tailored to the extensive infantilism, can be found in the whole Ecumenical movement as well as in politics. From our perspective, the modern patriarchal behaviour is a perversion of true fatherhood because it keeps the natural young adults from growing into their responsibility. Patriarchal androcentrism depends on stultification to maintain its power and, therefore, promotes spiritual infantilism. Although the Vatican rallies millions of half-adults around itself, it is not a moral alternative to the feministic or androgenic infantilism of our time. This should be a warning to all Protestants who are moving closer and closer to Rome for alleged moral reasons. Enslavement of thinking always leads to dictatorial subjugation.

---

251 „L'Osservatore Romano", No. 28, July 13, 2001, p. 11.

We can tell that all of this extends into the apocalyptic phase we are living in. Infantilism is wanted and controlled by all antichristian rulers. It was intentional, not an accident, that we were estranged from true fathers. Only real fathers and real mothers can restrain the antichristian spirit by raising their children to become true adults. It is important for fathers to renounce dictatorial, patriarchal behaviour. Mothers must refrain from raising their children to become uniform, feminine persons, where boys and girls are interchangeable, or even androgynous. It would go beyond the scope of this book to delve deeper into the subjects of patriarchy as androcentrism and feminism as gynocentrism, i.e. abuse of female leadership. In any case, the papal path with its established patriarchy is definitely not the way for any Bible believing Christian to overcome infantilism. After all, the dictatorial patriarchy gave rise to the feminist movement by stultifying and suppressing people, especially women. Feminism, in turn, has now created the eternal half-adult in feminine, or rather, androgynous form.

5. The Structure and Goal of the European Union

A View from the Outside

After looking at the spiritual condition of the average EU citizen and the religious efforts to influence him, we will consider the direct plans of the European Union. Between 1997 and 2008, several co-workers and I visited the three cities where EU institutions are situated, namely Strasbourg, Brussels, and Luxembourg. The pillars of these institutions are the European Commission, the Council of the European Union, the European Parliament, the European Court of Justice, and the European Court of Auditors. There are offices for brochures in Brussels which are free of charge. Otherwise the institutions are closed for individual visitors. In Strasbourg, a group tour is possible if booked months in advance. The European authorities disseminate an air of bureaucratic pomposity and secrecy. In an EU booklet, one can read the following: "Although the EU is in a process of integration, it has also committed itself to the protection of the cultural and linguistic diversity of its nations and regions."[252]

---

252 „Luxemburg in der Europaeischen Union," (Luxemburg in the European Union) 1995, p.8).

However, the only language that every civil servant speaks is French. There are 20 official languages, as of 2007, at all the three places of work, but the commission in Brussels restricts itself internally only to English, French, and German. The self-commitment to linguistic diversity obviously applies solely to the countries themselves. In 2007, the entire EU bureaucracy consumed more than 120 billion Euros. The 27 commissioners of the European commission, including the president, hold the rank of ministers and represent 27 member states with 455 million citizens. You also ask yourself why these commissioners claim to be the legislative as well as executive body in one, even though the Council is the most important decision-making organ? Each member state appoints respectively one commissioner, which adds up to 27 commissioners. But these commissioners are completely independent of their national governments. They govern in Brussels. One should note: The parliament in Straßbourg is supposed to represent all citizens of the EU, but they have little power in comparison to the Brussels-commission. It has one president and 14 vice-presidents. It consists of 8 fractions with 785 seats, as of 2006. 20 parliamentary committees are operating. 25 000 civil servants are needed to assist the commissioners (as of 2007) although in 1996 there were only 15,000 co-workers. That amounts to roughly 1,000 employees per commissioner, not counting the president! As in all authoritarian systems, criticism is met by anger. Meanwhile, two European parliamentarians were fired who had dared to expose corruption. The president at that time resigned, but only as a sort of pacifier. Up to this day, little has actually changed! Nevertheless, these public authorities claim to "give all EU citizens a feeling of common identity."[253] There is no attempt to establish one universal European language which would be absolutely essential for a European identity. In the mid 90's they employed 3,500 translators for nine official languages. Since 2007 there are 20 official languages. How many translators does that require?

All three European cities have another thing in common. They are building, expanding, and creating the infrastructure for a super state. In Brussels, whole street blocks with mostly well-kept houses were demolished in the year 2.000 to make room for more bureaucratic buildings. All protests were useless. Due to our experience in pastoral

---

253 The Household of the EU in 2007.

Chapter V: The Development of the European Union

Image 12:
Complex of buildings of the European parliament in Strassburg

care and spiritual battle, we could not shake the deepening sensation that the infrastructure for a future dictator was being built here in all three cities at once. Who will he be? One can at least speculate! Based on our observations from the outside, we can only describe the EU bureaucracy as sinister and secretive. This raises the question of what really happens behind closed doors. The former EU lawyer Hubert Dessloch, who is now the general secretary of the International Academy for Philosophy in Liechtenstein, puts it like this: "The national parliaments have been practically stripped of their power. More and more, their activity consists merely of converting EU guidelines into national law. The heads of state receive papers at such short notice that they barely have time to study the contents before the flight to the summits. There, the heads of government just have a brief, 5-minute opportunity to express their opinion on the documents. This procedure shows a totalitarian structure where every pretension of democracy has been abandoned." Further, Dessloch says, "that the EU-dictatorship is an answer to the cultural revolution of the 1968 generation which shook and destroyed the structures and hierarchies in society, thus encouraging a development toward lawlessness."[254]

In June 2009 the Federal Constitutional Court in Germany (Bundesverfassungsgericht) made an extraordinary judgement. The reason for this was because a complaint had been made regarding the EU Treaty of Lisbon (initially known as the Reform Treaty). This contract had replaced the EU constitution which had been rejected by the citizens of France, Netherlands and the Republic of Ireland. According to the 'Spiegel' magazine 28/2009, the highest German court of con-

---

254 Topic No. 1, January 2003, 5. In: „Zeit-Fragen", December 16, 2002.

stitution made the following declaration: "the German Lower House had been careless because it gave away important rights of control to Brussels. In so doing, the people it represented were unconstitutionally exposed to an insufficient legitimized bureaucracy.

That is the "end of a politics of growing integration". The court has decidedly put on the brakes of the EU politics in use so far.
For the future, the judges demand a competent examination, so that the "unimpeachable core of the constitutional identity of the basic law is upheld". With this decision the court lays claim to determine the "limits of the European integration". The court stated further that not only Germany but all member states remain "masters of the contracts". The national legislator and the Federal Constition Court carry the responsibility of integration. The highest court of constitution puts itself above the European Court of Justice because it protects national constitution.
In the Treaty of Lisbon it is stated that the EU Parliament works on the basis of representative democracy. The Federal Constitutional Court decided however, that the EU Parlament was not "a representative organ of a sovereign people". There is no equality of vote, i.e. "one man, one vote"; the members of parliament are voted according to "national quota". The following example shows this undemocratic example: Malta, with its 67,000 citizens, is the smallest member state and has one Member of Parliament. Germany, with its eighty-two million citizens has the biggest population but has only one Member of Parliament per 857,000 people.
The court followed from this, that the EU is not a state but a unity of sovereign states. For this reason the national democratic state must have substantial more rights.
The court declared that "the EU-Parliament is incurably undemocratic according to the conception of constitutional law of a representative democracy. For this reason the national state must be given more possibilities when applying legal rights. National politics has the responsibility of safeguarding the interests of
- national politics
- commerce
- culture
- social security

Chapter V: The Development of the European Union

Fundamental rights such as those of tradition and peculiarities of language, civil and military power monopoly of the national state, the organization of family and educational rules and conditions, the association with religious confessions (ideological) and different world-outlooks (philosophy), are also part of these responsibilities.

The judgement was that cultural identity must rank higher than integration. As the European Union is an alliance of declared solidarity of sovereign states it comes only of secondary importance. The Federal Constitutional Court in Germany (Bundesverfassungsgericht) said in its ultimate statement, that under the authority of the basic law there will be no "European State".

When the author wrote some years ago, that the EU organization was developing into a dictatorship, many people considered this over-exaggerated. Now this personal judgement, made years ago, has been confirmed by the Federal Constitutional Court in Germany.

After an investigation, the support for further expansion has receded. In Germany, for instance, two thirds of the population are against further expansion. Support for an EU constitution is, on the whole, on the recline.

The hidden goals

A "Trilogy of Europe" was commissioned and published by the EU. The first volume alone, called "Madonna and Europe," has 1136 pages. In this volume, one can find some of the goals hidden from the general public and they do not deal with the respected "consumers of a market of 455 million." It is about the awareness and declaration of the "historical cultural heritage of Europe."

It is surprising how the philosophical architects of Europe attribute spiritual, philosophic meaning to certain data. In the view of pragmatic technocrats, these numbers were created by chance or compromise. Some examples include:

According to the sources listed, the EU had nine parliamentary languages up to 2006. The so-called "fathers of Europe" see an intention of fate in the number nine. The world of numerical magic suggests the following interpretation: "The number nine is regarded as the symbol of harmony ... It also expresses the completed hierarchical structure of the world ... Somehow, it belongs to the spiritual side of human life."[255] Moreover, other significant cultural groups like the Arabs or the Chinese look at nine as a spiritual number as well. Therefore, this numerical magic must receive its spiritual meaning for the developing Europe too. While the infantile society of Western Europeans amuses itself, the real designers of Europe are trying to catch up with the spiritual world of Eurasia. In the eyes of pragmatists, everything happens by chance. Yet, macrocosmic paradigms are gaining significance for the philosophical thinkers of Europe. Even the three capital cities of the EU are becoming more and more important in terms of numerical magic. "The threesome: A development of the one person to perceptibility."[256] Here, C.G. Jung endeavours to explain that the opposing tension (of two) is resolved through a third person and thus the lost single person can emerge again."[257] One can also apply this to the three-fold truth. The ancient Greeks understood it as the level of the gods made up of the realm of death, the Earth and the cosmos, or heaven. The Catholics' three-fold view of God is then zealously combined and unified with the numerical magic of antiquity, the Jewish Cabbala sect, and the freemasons. The twelve stars, the circle, and the blue colour all have their occult meaning as well. According to the terminology of the EU designers, this is spiritual symbolism. Using "the circle of twelve stars," the author describes the structure of Europe as "unity in a sequence of steps." All of this is well-known to the freemasons and other religious-esoteric groups. Europe is being connected with the twelve Greek gods of Mount Olympus as well as the astrologic religion of ancient Oriental cultures. They are even making esoteric attempts to establish a connection that goes all way back to Babylon, which should not surprise us anymore. The "circle of twelve stars" symbolizes a philosophical holism that first began with Aristotle. In modern times, the antichristian New Age movement favours this philosophy because it teaches that "cosmic energies and forces", i.e. cosmic-demonic spiritual powers, belong to the entirety of a human

---

255 Willy Schmitt-Lieb, „Europa Triologie", 1995, p. 156.
256 Ibid. p. 486.
257 See ibid. p. 486.

being. Hence, it does not come as a surprise to read how the former German President of the Bundestag, Suessmuth, tried to bundle the cultural diversity of Europe in the greeting section of the book. She wrote about the diversity being characterized "by the Arabic Islamic world, Judaism, as well the ancient world and the Christian tradition of the Occident ..."[258] All of these are supposed to be revived as the 'roots of European culture' and fuse into one: unity in a series of steps! Strangely, the great cultural civilization that grew out of the Reformation has been forgotten, but not due to ignorance! After all, our modern age would be unthinkable without the Reformation! The former Bavarian Minister President Stoiber showed great enthusiasm in his greeting: "Who would not recognize it, Mary's circle of stars, und who would not know about her identification with the star-filled dome of the sky."[259] Please look up Jeremiah 44: 17-19 on the subject of the queen of heaven. Stoiber continued: "Bavaria is culturally and historically a Marian land ... It is good to live under this constellation."[260] The magical signs are clear. The flag of Europe is the flag of Mary. At the same time, feminists accept her as a goddess, the Olympic queen of heaven. Nothing here has occurred by chance. As already mentioned earlier, symbols are more than just signs or allusions. They have the characteristic ability to reach from the demonic world into this immanent world with their hidden powers.[261] Even the colours of the European flag with its blue background and golden stars are meant to express "human fellowship in the circle of like-minded people" and the mobility of the spirit. Blue is the colour of the sky

Image 13:
Europa with Bull

258 Ibid. p. XII.
259 Ibid. p. XV.
260 Ibid. p. XV.
261 See Chapter II.

and the divine, while gold represents the earthly reflection of the divine."[262] The seekers of Europe's philosophical roots also point out that the European course of development runs from the Orient to the Occident. For them, this is much more than just a philosophical observation. They are hoping for a unification with the spirituality of the East. In fact, for them Europe does not even exist geographically. "It is an edge of the central continent of Asia. Europe is a product of our imagination. It is unique through history and culture, through faith and orientation. Europe is also the partially self-produced foundation of life based on the Christian-Occidental civilization ..."[263]

Now let us look at the bull that the goddess Europa sits on. As we have already explained in Chapter IV,[264] Revelation 17: 5 tells us that the whore Babylon rides the Antichrist. He is the beast who will receive all his power from Satan. Here, the goddess Europa represents the whore Babylon. The Roman Mary makes up the Catholic part of the whore Babylon, the cosmic goddess of the air and queen of heaven. The flag blowing in the wind symbolizes her. These are the roots and the goal of a unified Europe. No one should look at European symbols superficially. I think I have made it clear that they all have a spiritual meaning. As critical visitors, we were able to notice that they radiated cosmic power too. The statue of Europa with the bull, or beast, is located on the left side of the old main entrance of the parliament building in Strasbourg. There is also a wall painting of it inside. When we visited the EU city Strasbourg, we saw two sculptures in close vicinity to the EU building. One of them showed a couple whose bodies were intertwined. It was created by Ludmila Tcherina and has since been replaced. The bodies looked the same, i.e. gender-neutral, and were most likely supposed to depict the androgynous human demanded by the Yin-Yang principle of the New Age movement. They were designed to "embody Europe in the harmony of a human couple with one single heart." The inscription under the sculpture read: Through their "loving embrace they reflect the circle of stars of the European flag." There will probably be no place for Reformational Christians in this Europe with the so-

---

262 Ibid. 20.
263 Haack, "Europas neue Religion," 1993, p. 8. (Europe's new religion).
264 Chapter V (image No. 12).

Chapter V: The Development of the European Union

called "one heart." Another sculpture in front of the EU building several hundred meters away, pictured a boy sitting on the hand of a woman situated above a globe. One is inevitably reminded of Mary with her child. On the earth under the woman and her boy, there is a scene of war, death and misery with men in battle. The eyes of the dying men are fixed on the woman as if seeking her redeeming help. The following message was written underneath:

"The European wind is blowing from the old continent, which is the guardian of a culture that is over one thousand years old and which is being shaken by new ideologies and problems like environmental pollution and national independence movements[265]. It is spreading a spiritual message which is aimed at overcoming the reigning philosophical and practical materialism in every form and overcoming the existing gap between people and nations. More and more firmly, a new portrait of the family is emerging, strong and steady enough to give history and the daily existence of all nations new vitality and hope for the future. In the fall of materialism [only dogmatic materialism and its carrier, communism, are on the decline], Europe of today denounces the modern consumer society and shows the weakness of every social project that is not rooted in the family. In its bare simplicity, as a symbol of being undefiled by social and moral vices, the family stands for values like unity and solidarity and is also the nucleus thereof. A sitting child stretching upward, is emerging from oppressive cloud of torturous suffering that every person is burdened by. A hymn to life that glows in new hope under the mighty wind of Europe."

One can easily recognize the Vatican trademark here. This is what morally impresses many Protestants and blinds them. At any rate, the interpretation does not seem to come from the esoteric, feministic side. They are the ones who have destroyed and are still destroying the European families. In the lay-out of Europe, two decisive nuclei have crystallized out more and more: The Roman church, the alleged only representative of Christianity, and esoteric feminism. For the time being, they are still battling each other. Rome claims to be the only guardian of the family! Thus, the Roman church sees itself as the successor of the antique Roman empire and the Pope as the Roman Pontifex Maximus. Over the years, there will suddenly

---

265 See also Chapter V.

be a reconciliation between the two adversaries. To date, the things they have in common include:
Protection of the environment
- Anti-Materialism
- Religiosity
- The green feminist movement is increasingly joining forces with a gentle spiritual to form an organized esoteric system.

The same battle for supremacy is already being waged within the Catholic church. Names like the Pope and his opponent Eugen Drevermann stand for this battle. What still seemed impossible fifty years ago, has long become reality today, e.g. the already completed reconciliation of Rome with freemasonry! Likewise, there will also be a reconciliation between the Catholic church and dogmatic feminism by means of unification. After all, feminism characterizes post-modern society and is dominating the infantile modern European person more and more. The Buddhist system of the Dalai Lama gives it additional power. The Dalai Lama is monopolizing and integrating the Western feminists with growing success by absorbing them. He conquers and overcomes them spiritually. The apparent adaptation of Rome is occurring via post-modern esotericism. It receives its magical power from Lamaistic androcentrism, i.e. the abuse of male leadership.

The Mainstay of the Religions and their Systems. The Illusions of Greek and Roman Culture

The Ecumenical movement in Europe had planned to achieve the unification of the Protestants, who were influenced by Greek philosophy, and the Catholics, shaped by Roman culture. Moreover, they wanted the union to be complemented by cultural elements from Judaism and Islam. The former German Chancellor Kohl, one of the most important political proponents of such cultural unity, also expressed this in the presence of the late pope, John Paul II, on June 22, 1996, in Berlin. It was significant that the representatives of the infantile post-modern society reacted to this statement with loud protest. These older Europeans had the illusion that the European future in a union of European states could only be shaped by Catholics, Jews, and Muslims. As we can see today, the Protestant church plays a decisive role in promoting the adaptation to the post-modern spirit of the age in the German-speaking countries and elsewhere too. It acts as the avant-garde of unification by integrating cultural elements of esoteric feminism and Buddhism. The Protestant churches, in particular, provide a trusting leadership basis for the Dalai Lama. This includes many regular church members and not just the feminists among them. Furthermore, the Protestants are gaining influence in the Roman church all the way up to the bishops' level with their Buddhist spiritual power of magic, among other things. As we all know, Pope John Paul II and the Dalai Lama got along with each other excellently. On one side, the conservative Catholic youth were being monopolized by magic and, on the other side, the irreligious post-modern people under the driving force of feminism are overcome by the power of black magic. That is the transcendent demonic form of so-called reconciliation. Therefore, the Pope has deprived the Roman bishops of their power more and more. In an on-line information service of the Vatican, I read that John Paul II appointed another 30 cardinals in October 2003 and even asked them to "remain faithful to the church all the way to the point of bloodshed." At the beginning of John Paul II's pontificate in 1978, 111 cardinals were eligible to vote. As of Oct. 21, 2003, the number had climbed to 135 cardinals who were under 80 years of age and therefore eligible to vote. Another 59 cardinals were over eighty years old. 130 cardinals were appointed by John Paul II and followed his theological line.[266] It was from their own ranks that the new Pope, Benedict XVI, the closest confident of John Paul II, was elected as his successor. Benedict XVI, formerly known as Cardinal Ratzinger, had been the head of the faith congregation, formerly the office of inquisition, for 25 years. Next to the pope, he was the highest ranking theologian of Rome with interpretation powers. Although John Paul II had put his house in order and taken steps to ensure that his confidant would become his successor, even Pope Benedict XVI, the former Cardinal Ratzinger will not be able to stop the modern spiritual trend. John Paul II, himself, made many compromises with the esoteric fraction during his pontificate. How else could the 1986 meeting in Assisi and other subsequent meetings, even with shamanistic magicians, have materialized? To the typical European citizen, dependent, socialistically-minded and ori-

266 See www.ZENIT.org, October 21, 2003.

Chapter V: The Development of the European Union

ented toward the welfare state, both extreme movements are convenient. The dirty and seductive art consists of manipulating these thoroughly infantile types of people so that they weakly submit to those fighting for power in Europe. We can already see the Catholic-Marian spirit swinging round and adapting to the new situation. The Roman Mary's new seduction is aimed at Muslims, Western Buddhists, Esoterics, and Feminists. In addition, it reaches well beyond Fatima, Lourdes, and Medjugorje. On the previous pages, I have already made a couple of remarks about the role of the Dalai Lama as the incarnation of the antichristian spirit of the "Maitreya Christ."[267] Now, I would like to report on our practical, spiritual resistance to the Dalai Lama. For this purpose, we drove to Graz in October 2002. Over the course of 12 days, initiation rituals took place for aspiring Western Buddhists in the exhibition hall. A mass event was planned on the last day, where the so-called "Kalachakra for world peace" was celebrated by the Dalai Lama and the most important leaders of the other Buddhist schools. To give the readers an understanding of what is meant by "Kalachakra," we would like to quote the "Journal spezial" No.13, February 2000, pages 29-30: "The spirit of Buddha lives in the female sex organs, in the womb of the diamond lady." Tantrism stems from Tantra. A Tantra transforms the natural sexual power of a person into spiritual power through transcendence by means of rituals. The spiritual power, in turn, is supposed to lead to political power. By the 10th century, this transcendent sexual ritual had developed into its present form. Experts and supporters of the modern scene also call this type of religion "Kalachakra-Tantra," or time-tantra. "Kala" denotes time with respect to the male. He sets up demonic centres of power through ritual sexual practices. They become destructively creative through the turning sun-wheel, or Chakra. He

Image 14:
Mandala

---

267 For further study, we recommend our series "Journal spezial," No.9 / Feb 1999 and No.13 / Feb 2000.

then uses these centres of power to dominate the woman who is called "Kali" in Indian/Hindu culture.

Consequently, we are dealing with a destructive, sexually perverse, and magical secret doctrine in the "Kalachakra" initiation. It is utilized as a means of conquering the Western cultures spiritually. The world peace they are striving for signifies the end of the previous culture and its people by successful spiritual infiltration. One of the reasons why Pope John Paul II supported the Dalai Lama was that he, himself, no longer had the power to act as the unifying organizer for all religions. The Dalai Lama has thus become an interim leader for the future universal world religion out of the antichristian spirit. At the conference in Graz, he tirelessly assured the 8,000 visitors that he was not interested in proselytizing. He only wanted to complement and enrich the existing Occidental religions. As usual for such conferences, the audience consisted mainly of the 25 to 45-year-old generation. Members of a late hippie movement were conspicuous. Using spiritual weapons, we turned against the "Mandala" that was set up behind the stage and charged with power. Before it could be scattered as planned on the last day, we were able to render the spiritual forces harmless. It was supposed to be a symbol of the Buddhist power freed up over the region. Fifty monks representing the four schools of Buddhism assisted the Dalai Lama. They brought amplification and were an expression of the Dalai Lama's success in uniting with all Buddhist schools, or denominations. He, himself, led the rituals as the alleged "god-king," rocking sideways like a hospitalized child.

No one, except us, was interested in the truth. On the contrary, the infantile masses allowed their own death to be aroused inside themselves, strengthened by the demonic spiritual power of tantric Lamaism. The buxom Buddhist "Tara," a counterpart of the Catholic Mary, would become the female leader of the possessed people. As a result, the death-hungry mass of the initiated ended up under the reign of the whore Babylon.

Image 15: Dalai Lama

Another thing worth thinking about: The conference of this demonic spectacle for European half-adults cost 3.2 million Euros, according to their own information. Public funding, by either Austria or the EU, contributed a third of that sum!

The New Occult Faith

Reformational, biblical values have crumbled, and those who once stood for them are mainly responsible for their decay. Now, the Christian, Catholic, and Occidental values are breaking down more and more. Sectarian groups, who often gain their sympathizers in a greedy, antidemocratic, and aggressive manner, are increasingly dominating European society. In our pastoral care work, we have noticed a steady increase of such influence. Through our international activity against sects and cults, we have also found that this trend predominates in the entire Western world. Our work is so successful, especially against esoteric sects, because we still stand up for the truth and are not afraid to expose lies and destructiveness. We understand the gospel to be an offer that either provokes acceptance or rejection. Most of the old European churches have a totally different view. F.W. Haack expresses it like this: "It appears to me as if there were ideologists of organized piety at the helm of the leadership [of the Protestant state church, the author] in some places, for whom mediocrity is a goal and the avoidance of tensions a matter of faith. The offensiveness of the gospel turns into a guiding principle of widespread pacification and the creation of conflict-free and easily administrable circumstances. Sometimes, it seems to me that the biblical verse: let your word be yes, yes or no, no is translated into: let your word be yes as well as no."[268] In fact, the ecclesiastical trend of avoiding every conflict unintentionally promotes destructive sects. In our opinion, there is only one way to cope with the evil of the 'new religions' stemming from the New-Age spirit. We need truthful and objective sharpness as well as biblical fairness, provided that we are willing to defend the fundamental, indispensable truths of the gospel. If we believe what the Bible tells us as the Word of God, we must also be prepared to fight for it in spiritual armour. According to Gal. 5,16ff, spiritual warfare is part of spiritual conduct. We should not shy away from conflicts about vitally important truths of life and

---

268 Haack, „Europas neue Religion", 1993, p.8. (Europe's new religion).

faith. Therefore, the conflict-avoidance strategy of church dialogue can not be appropriate and is doomed to failure. It destroys the life-giving truth of the gospel. In addition, we must distance ourselves from all other so called "-isms," including all authoritarian, fundamentalist fanatics. This one single aspect exemplifies why the state churches can not be successful against the individualistic sects of the spirit of the age. While they are carrying on their religious, conflict-avoiding dialogues, destructive cults are gaining more and more control over the formerly irreligious European person and the religious scene of the entire continent. In the majority of people, the level of consciousness has long been altered along New-Age lines. We agree with F. W. Haack's interpretation that our religious European spectrum is an imperialism of Western Hinduism. He writes: "... we are becoming witnesses of the emergence of a new religion, a kind of Western Hinduism, which is based on a view of humankind that is contrary to Christian faith as well as our inherited Greek-Latin cultural roots. On one hand, the person puts himself in an autonomous position, takes the place of a God outside of himself, and glorifies himself. On the other hand, he has no respect for his equals and ruthlessly asserts himself against poorer, weaker, and less fortunate people. This religion will not be tangible or concrete, but instead be composed of innumerable religious trends and religiosities.[269] Almost all current therapies that claim to cure the human soul are furnished with hackneyed Hindu ideas. This Hinduism has already penetrated Catholic and Protestant seminaries as well as infiltrated the churchgoers. I do not know of any sect that is not decisively based on Hindu, Buddhist or Taoist elements. The religious feeling of people in Europe and the whole Western world has become a solely private affair anyway, subject only to personal taste. As a result, it is slipping more and more out of ecclesiastical and state control in the Occident. At the beginning of the 20th century, similar circumstances prevailed. Religious racism, the occultism of theosophical, anthropological cults and the emerging dialectic materialism of Marx/Engels contributed significantly to the destruction of the so-called "Christian Occident." The subsequent world wars in the first half of the 20th century with the national socialist and Marxist ideologies as well as the cultural revolution of the 1960's

---

269 Ibid. p. 10.

dealt the Occident severe blows. It has been lying in the throes of death ever since. Furthermore, the 1960's also brought us the sects stemming from the antichristian New-Age movement. For better understanding, I would like to add another short quotation from Haack: "The term 'Occident' should be used as the proper term to describe the European cultural environment once dominated by Christianity. This cultural environment has spread colonially, so that especially North America is included in the Occident."[270]

We are not interested in defending the Occident, mainly because the chief carrier is the Catholic church. Rome's religious imperialism does not tolerate anyone beside itself. We are convinced that the classical Occident with its Catholic Christian religion is irretrievably gone. In the future, it will simply become a part of the religious basis for the universal world religion, albeit an important one. The Roman church is using its 1,500-year-old experience and abilities to integrate all anti-Roman, New-Age esoteric movements into the church. It is also trying to subjugate and utilize the cosmic spiritual powers for its own purposes. But this time, the resistance of the post-modern people who cherish their religious privacy is greater than 100 years ago. In addition, the Roman Mary has constantly lost mediating power through active spiritual resistance in the last 20 years. Therefore, a renewal of the Catholic church's absolute power over Europe has become less and less likely. On the horizon, a synthesis of all religions is taking shape. Europe and the world are inevitably developing in this direction. Rome's absolute power belongs to the past, despite the almost thirty year renaissance period during the papacy of John Paul II. The EU with its fusion of all religions will play an important role in the antichristian confederation of ten described in Daniel 7: 23. It would go beyond the scope of this book to look at special features of the non-Christian religions and cults. My aim is to make it clear that the traditional Christian churches of the former Occident will no longer hold absolute power in the EU. At the beginning of the third millennium most Europeans have a hostile attitude towards the Christian view of God and humankind. This fact is not changed by the wide variety of pseudo-Christian religious activity. For example, the public appearances of the Pope take place with tremendous propaganda

---
270 Ibid. p. 14.

campaigns and attract hundreds of thousands of people. Europe is supposed to be newly evangelized. There are Ecumenical marches for Jesus as well as miracle and healing conferences with a Christian veneer. Furthermore, many Toronto-congregations have sprung up. This mock Christian spectacle will collapse like a house of cards in the course of the next years anyway. First of all, it did not originate from the Holy Spirit and, therefore, lacks God's blessing. Secondly, there is overwhelming competition from the entire antichristian, anti-Occidental spirit of the New-Age movements. For quite some time, the XIV Dalai Lama, the main representative of Kalachakra Buddhism, has taken over at the top of the non-Christian New-Age spectrum. He is trying to fill the gap and stop the drainage of power caused by the weakening of the late John Paul II and to offer it to Benedict XVI.[271] However, the pope keeps his distance. As we already know, representatives of the Catholic Christian Occident are just as devoid of the Holy Spirit as the sacramental Christian traditions they follow. Therefore, we need not shed tears or lose heart in the face of these developments. Let us now take a closer look at what the majority of people believe and how they define their faith. The rationalistic German magazine "Der Spiegel" does not do justice to the transcendent subjects of cults and sects because of its arrogant and ignorant interpretation. Nevertheless, I would like to quote some statistics published by this magazine with respect to the German-speaking population:

"200 years of enlightenment could not prevent it: every third German now believes that the future can be foretold, every seventh person trusts in magic and sorcery: 50% of Germans profess to believe in extraterrestrial beings, every third person thinks that UFOs exist, two thirds are afraid of the destructive influence of earth rays on sleep. Around 20% are convinced that it is possible to make contact with the next world. Germans are really crazy about astrology: every second person believes in the power of the stars ..."[272]

In the same article, the magazine also lists the reasons for occult beliefs, which often lead into the sects: "broken families, few friends, a confused quest for values, a diffuse religious neediness."[273] Other

---

271 See „Journal spezial" No. 13/2, 2000.
272 „Der Spiegel", January 12, 1998, p. 171. (magazine).
273 Ibid. p. 174.

sources confirm these numbers. In the rest of the EU, the results are similar, or even more negative. For example, the German federal state of Lower Saxony is pioneering the introduction of occultism into kindergarten programs: "... children should learn to put themselves into a mild form of trance, leave their bodies in order to make contact with beings from the next world."[274] The Protestant Christian newsletter "Topic" also reported about North German schools where students are introduced to esoteric and magical themes in class and have to memorize witch songs, witch dances and magic formulae."[275]

Even though the papacy considers itself to be a royal regency, the representative of Christ on Earth, Europeans are increasingly evading the Roman church's claim to power. Statistically, the Catholic church has the greatest share of members in the EU with 270 million Catholics. Since 1958, a European Madonna stands 20 meters high in the region of Milan. The inscription reads: Our Dear Lady and Mistress of Europe.[276] Nevertheless, many cultural Catholics and Protestants in the EU also believe in private esoteric systems. According to a scientific religious-sociological study, the majority of young Germans no longer believe in a personal God. They want nothing to do with sin, redemption, and salvation. Almost everyone under the age of 40 believes in an afterlife along esoteric lines, with cosmic powers to help them overcome deficits in their life, battle depression and compensate for their inability to cultivate satisfying social relationships. It is their belief that they can make use of these powers. The European standard has been reduced to a desire-orientated religion, or rather, a system that no longer wants to have anything to do with a holy, righteous, gracious, and merciful God.[277] It would go beyond the scope of this book to discuss deeper insights into the scientific results presented by Joerns. His book is well worth reading. Yet, I think I was able to cover the most important aspects of this subject. The generation of Germans under 40 have started to influence and represent the German society. Incidentally, 22% of the EU citizens were Germans as of 2003. Apart from this, the religious attitude is very similar throughout the EU. The membership

---

274 „Topic", No. 1/98, p. 6.
275 Ibid. p. 6.
276 Ibid. p. 2.
277 See Jörns, „Die neuen Gesichter Gottes", 1997, p. 24.(The new faces of God).

Chapter V: The Development of the European Union

statistics of compulsorily baptized Catholics does not make any difference. The majority of them no longer believe in the Roman doctrine. This is a fact that the old European state churches will have to face in the future. One asks oneself: What role will the religions and/or esoteric systems play in the future EU?

The Bible's Apocalyptic Prophecies about Rome

We have already detailed the last, apocalyptic events listed in the Bible: the universal world government as the third phase of Rome (Dan.7: 23), the federation of ten states in the fourth phase (Dan.7: 24), and the autocratic reign of the Antichrist as the fifth Roman phase (Dan.7: 24+25). Parallel to the primarily political ruler out of the antichristian spirit, Revelation chapters 17-19 tells us that the whore Babylon can be found in all cultures as the mother goddess (Rev.17: 15). She is in symbiosis with the beast. Rev.17: 3 portrays this in the woman, i.e. the whore Babylon, sitting on the scarlet beast. Verse 8 informs us that the beast represents the Antichrist. He wants to become the sole religious leader and be worshipped as god. Together with the regional presidents of the ten states, he will fight and destroy the spirit and its incarnation, the whore Babylon (verse 16). Only then, will he be able to assume universal and absolute political as well as religious power for a very limited number of years. The Revelation provides a valuable complement to the book of Daniel. After seizing all religious and political power, the Antichrist and his fifth phase of the Roman Empire will be swept away forever by the judgment of Jesus (2 Thess.2: 8 and Rev.19: 19+20). To summarize, all religious and esoteric systems are combined under the whore Babylon. The so-called "queen of peace," who will help everyone gain wealth and power, is an especially strong expression of this whore Babylon: "I sit as queen ..." (Rev.18: 7). The Roman church represents the incarnation of the whore Babylon. It was given the biblical name "Mary" after the strongest cultural Madonna spirit who "sits on many waters [cultures, the author]" (Rev.17: 1+9+15; Isa.47). The Vatican must make great compromises by freeing up space for all esoteric systems favoured by Western European nations. Nevertheless, the Roman church will continue to be the main carrier of the whore Babylon. The woman on the beast is even one of the symbols of the European Union. In preparation for the final divine judgment, the integration of all esoteric, religious, pseudo-religious, and philosophical systems into the great melting pot of the whore Babylon will succeed. What is taking place in politics will repeat itself with the religious systems. First, fragmentation into small national cultural elements will occur in order to revive old cosmic cultural powers. Then, these forces will be given to the Antichrist as a sacrificial offering for a powerful unification. We will see the same thing happening on a religious level. Today, they are still fighting each other. But soon, in the height of their revival, they will be integrated into a single system. Even many of the former Protestant churches in the EU are already standing in line for the integration into the religious system of Rome. There is a general feeling of bankruptcy and demolition in the Protestant churches. The esoteric immorality is driving especially Protestant free churches into the arms of the Catholic (im)morality. Yet, none of those saved through Jesus Christ should let themselves be discouraged in any way.

"Because you have kept My command to persevere, I also will keep you from the hour of trial which shall come upon the whole world [oikoumene⁻ in Greek], to test those who dwell on the earth. 'Behold, I am coming quickly! Hold fast what you have, that no one may take your crown.'"
Revelation 3: 10+11

6. The Significance of a Madonna or Domina in a Post-Modern, Esoteric Europe

The Madonna of Fatima as Co-Redemptrix

Because of the importance of this subject, I will first give a short summary of the main points:

The Vatican officially says that Mary, the "Immaculate Conception", is the prototype of the Roman church. She supposedly took part in the suffering of Christ through the "seven swords that pierced her heart." According to the Vatican, this allows her to share fully in the salvation of her son. Even if Mary has not yet been dogmatised as co-redemptrix, or goddess, de jure, she has long been recognized as such de facto. Since 1854, the Pope declared her to be the "Immaculate Conception." That gave her divine attributes. In 1950,

Chapter V: The Development of the European Union

they were amplified and rounded off when Pope Pius XII claimed ex cathedra that Maria ascended into heaven bodily. Her position as co-redemptrix includes more than just the assumption that she was free of sin from the very beginning. Her suffering and death occurred for the sins of the world too. Therefore, she was also raised on the third day in accordance with her de facto deification. This Pope declared August 13th to be the day of her death and August 15th to be the day of her resurrection. This third day was also associated with her ascension. In addition, Pope John XXIII called Mary "the mother of the church" at the II Vaticanum (1962-1965), which was said to be so liberal. We do not need more proof that the Catholic Mary has long become a redeeming goddess, analogous to Jesus Christ, true man and true God. We have already dealt in detail with the subject of Mary as the mediatrix of all cosmic powers. Hence, these explanations are only meant to be a reminder of what is especially important with regards to Europe. As mentioned earlier, the place of pilgrimage in Lourdes represents a sort of conclusion to the Marian deification development through 1,500 years of church history. The traditional Roman church thrives on the fundamental Catholic powers of all Madonnas which reached their peak in Lourdes. Lourdes stands for a kind of border crossing point between the traditional Catholic world and the world of universalism, an expression of the spirit of the universal world church. The Madonna of Fatima is now transforming the Roman world church into the universal world church. In it, the Roman spirit provides the crucial basis, especially with respect to the apocalyptic events portrayed in the Bible. The old cultural continent of Europe is essential in all of this.

The Madonna of Fatima:
Mother and Queen of Peace for the Whole World?

Rome sees Fatima as a mystery with a mission of historical, international significance. In a book about Mary of Fatima, published with the permission of the church, this mission of salvation for the whole world is described as follows: "The Holy Father [Pius XII, 1942], himself, fully recognized the truly unique mission of Fatima for the future fate of humanity and, according to the wish of the Mother of God, consecrated the church and humanity to the "Immaculate

Chapter V: The Development of the European Union

Heart" of Mary, so that they can find refuge and salvation from the dreadful catastrophes that have befallen the world in the bosom of the purest virgin."[278] The "Immaculate Heart" is synonymous to the "Immaculate Conception." Both express the deification of Mary. In Fatima, the deified Mary speaks to the whole world, i.e. all cultures and religions, while she primarily addressed the Catholic world in Lourdes and similar places. Yet, the cross-border Madonna of Lourdes already showed strong signs of universalism. The demonic spiritual powers of the Roman Madonnas formed a militant bulwark for Catholicism against Protestantism, especially since the 30-year European war in the 17th century. For better understanding, we will study the history of the place of pilgrimage in Fatima, Portugal.

The village of Fatima was named by the Arabs who occupied Portugal in the 12th century. Fatima was the favourite daughter of Mohammed in the 7th century. This family founded a famous dynasty and their successors were called Fatimides. Fatima was also the name of a young female descendent of this dynasty who lived in a region 190km north of Lisbon when the Saraceni tribes occupied Portugal in the 12th century. She was taken captive by Portuguese knights along with other royal Arabs. After forcing the Saraceni princess into Catholicism, the Portuguese crusader Don Hermingues arranged her marriage to a victorious knight.

Image 16: Fatima

She was worshipped as mistress, or Madonna, and following her early death, a chapel and a convent were built in her honour. The village received the Arabic name of "Fatima," even though she had been given a Portuguese name with her compulsory baptism.

Now, we will take a great historical leap into the 20th century. On May 13, 1917, three shepherd children, seven, nine, and ten years old, were grazing their herds as usual. Just like every day, they prayed to Mary in an olive grove at noon, using the Rosary. Suddenly, in the bright sunlight, they saw a ray of lightning several times, which was more brilliant than the sun. "A few steps in front

---

278 Fonseca, „Maria spricht zur Welt", 1988, p. 5. (Mary speaks to the world).

Chapter V: The Development of the European Union

of them, a beautiful woman hovered above a small holm oak in a brilliance that shone brighter than the sun."[279] She was supposed to have been between 15 and 18 years old. "She had black eyes. Her dress was white as snow ... A rosary with white pearls and a small silver cross hung from her folded hands. Bright light beamed around the face; but, the pure, infinitely tender features appeared to be overshadowed by sadness."[280] The luminous figure called on the children to come to the meeting place every month at the same time until Oct. 13th, a total of six times. The Madonna would appear to them and tell them who she was and what she wanted. During these announcements, the children were irradiated by a "flood of light." They received the warning that they would have to endure very great suffering because of the atheistic world! They were told that they would have to suffer much on behalf of all people "as atonement for the many sins which offend the divine majesty, to achieve the conversion of sinners and to make amends for the curses and all other offences against the Immaculate Heart of Mary."[281] The three children chosen by Madonna, were punished like sacrificial lambs for certain sins of the world and also imagined or supposed sins. They also had to sacrifice themselves for all alleged sins of the Protestants who saw the deification of the Roman Mary as blasphemy and had thus offended her. Lonely and forsaken, two of the children died a terrible death through the so-called light of the Madonna after prolonged suffering. "From the hands, a flood of light radiated out over them [the two children who had been sentenced to death], in which they saw themselves in God."[282] On May 13th, 2000, John Paul II beatified these two children in Fatima. I can testify to this, since I witnessed the act as a critical observer. The eldest of the seer-children lived in a Carmelite convent until her natural death at an old age in 2005. She was available to Pope John Paul II as an advisor on matters concerning Fatima until her death. When New-Age sects physically and spiritually murder their children through their alleged light effects, they may be prosecuted judicially and punished. Should not the same principles be applied to the Catholic church?

---

279 Ibid. p. 20.
280 Ibid. p. 20-21.
281 Ibid. p. 24.
282 Ibid. p. 35.

Chapter V: The Development of the European Union

The Madonna told Lucia, the girl who was later to become a nun: "Jesus wants to use you so that the people get to know and love me. *He wants to establish the worship of my Immaculate Heart in the world; I promise salvation to everyone who practices it*; these souls that I bring before his throne are favoured by God like bees."[283] In other words, not only Catholics, but all cultures and religions are supposed to recognize and honour this Marian Madonna as the deified redemptrix! She even promises salvation! Should not people who still know about the holy and righteous God spiritually curse this blasphemous Madonna and bring the judgement of God upon her more than ever before? On July 13th, 1917, the Madonna assured the children that she alone was be able to ensure a quick end to the First World War. There are reports of the so-called three mysteries of this Fatima-Madonna. The first consists of the "vision of hell." After she repeatedly called on the children to sacrifice and deaden their souls, she opened her hands. "The bundle of rays radiating from them appeared to penetrate the earth, and we saw something like a great ocean of fire, and sunken into it, black, burned creatures, devils and souls in human form that looked like transparent, glowing coals."[284] It is another typical example of how this inhuman religion first uses the fear of God and hell in order to make people more amenable to the second mystery. What follows is the appeal to the world to recognize the Madonna as the deified woman, so that souls would be saved and there would be peace.[285] Furthermore, she predicted the outbreak of the Second World War as "a punishment from God." Fortune-telling is always a demonic affair, even if it turns out to be true, as was the case here. The recognition of the "Immaculate Heart of Mary" as well as the papal consecration of Russia to the "Immaculate Heart" were supposed to prevent World War II. When the Madonna made this demand, the Bolsheviks had not fully conquered Russia and the Soviet Union did not exist. Initially, she just seemed to be aiming at the emerging atheism and the morally bankrupt orthodoxy. Hence, she did not predict the victory of communism! The fruit of this consecration was supposed to be the conversion of all of Russia. This could only mean that the orthodoxy

---
283 Ibid. p. 35.
284 Ibid. p. 44.
285 See ibid. p. 44.

Chapter V: The Development of the European Union

would bow to Roman Catholicism, i.e. the unification of Eastern and Western Rome. Then, only a few months later, the Bolshevistic October Revolution occurred, creating the Soviet Union and making the demanded consecration even more urgent. Our legitimate questions:
- Why did Pope Pius XI not obey this Marian demand in any way?

He was busy establishing the worship of the Jesuit "Heart of Jesus," which he successfully completed in 1928. In general, the Vatican saw the consecration to the "Immaculate Heart of Mary" as a necessary supplement to the worship of the "Heart of Jesus." From 1928 onwards, the papal path to the deification of Mary was open. However, this went against the will of the Fatima-Mary, who wanted to have the consecration to her "Immaculate Heart" carried out promptly. The church and the whole human race was not consecrated to the "Immaculate Heart of Mary" until Oct.31, 1942 by Pope Pius XII. On Dec.8, 1942, he consecrated the world to Mary again.
- Why did the successor of Pius XI, the Nazi-collaborator Pius XII, wait so long with the consecration?
- Was he counting on the victory of the German Third Reich, especially over Soviet communism?

When he finally carried out the consecrations Mary had asked for, Germany could no longer win the war. Rommel's army was already conquered in North Africa and the defeat of the 6th army near Stalingrad was looming on the horizon. The consecration of Russia did not take place until July 7th, 1952, 7 years after World War II.
- On Oct.31st, 1950, Pope Pius XII proclaimed the deification dogma of "the bodily ascension of Mary into heaven." Was he trying to make up for his Marian disobedience?
- Why did the war pope remain silent for so long in the face of Nazi atrocities?

In searching for the truth, the initially open outcome of the war against the Soviet Union provides an interesting perspective. He never made a secret of his sympathy for Nazi-Germany.

In any, case Pius XII consecrated the whole world, the 'oikoumene', to the Fatima-Madonna at the end of 1942. But at this point, he had not consecrated the Soviet Union, including orthodox Russia! Pius XII: "The kingdom of Christ comes through the kingdom of Mary, after the worldwide dissemination of the 'true worship' and the conversion of Russia."[286] **So, according to seductive Catholic thinking, Jesus will return after the world wide, universal acknowledgment of Fatima, the victory over the Soviet Union and the conversion of orthodox Russia to the Vatican, uniting the old Eastern Rome with Western Rome. That is Vatican Ecumenism!** The 1942 consecration of the world marked the beginning of the Marian age through the heavenly queen of Fatima, who was identified as the queen of peace. Through this belated consecration to the Fatima-Madonna, the apocalyptic Fatima cult really got started at the end of 1942. For Catholics, the acknowledgement of the deified "Immaculate Conception" had already begun with Lourdes in 1854. Pius XII now became a glowing zealot for the worship of the Fatima queen of peace.

In 1943, he ordered all bishops to consecrate their dioceses to the Fatima-Mary.

- By a decree of this Pope in 1944, the celebration of the "Immaculate Heart" of Mary was supposed to take place in all churches on Aug 22nd.
- The Fatima-Madonna's statue of grace is crowned as the queen of peace in 1946.
- In 1948, Pius XII justified the global consecration to Mary with the atrocities of the Second World War and his responsibility for the world since "we essentially represent the family of humanity redeemed by God ..."[287]
- On May 1, 1948, the Pope emphatically pointed out that the consecration must be carried out in all diocese of the world to combat the increasing Catholic opposition.
- As a Marian reward, Pius XII experienced four apparitions of light in the Vatican on Oct.30th + 31st, and Nov.1st + 11th, 1950. They were described as a "miracle of the sun", similar to 1917.
- 1951 was celebrated as the "Holy Year" in Fatima.
- On July 7, 1952, the consecration of Russia finally took place.
- In 1954, Pius XII proclaimed the monarchy of Mary.
- All true Catholics are supposed to consecrate themselves to the Fatima-Madonna. As early as November 1942, the Roman

---
286 Ibid. p. 192.
287 Ibid. p. 471.

church promised all Catholics who recited the prayer formulated by the Vatican "an indulgence of three years; those who pray it daily, a complete indulgence once a month ..." The prayer of consecration begins like this:

"Queen of the Rosary, aid of all Christians, *refuge of the human race, victor in all the battles of God! We throw ourselves down before your throne, begging ...*" At the end of the prayer, where the "Queen of Peace" is also asked to transform the hearts of people through her "power of graces," it reads: "... and so we consecrate ourselves in the same way to you forever, to your Immaculate Heart, you, our mother and *queen of the world.*"[288] In a radio message on the occasion of the entire human race's consecration to the Fatima-Mary, the Pope repeated the following confession in unison with Portuguese Catholics: "Our dear lady of Fatima, it's in your hands now! *Tell your divine Son only one single word and the world will be saved* ..."[289] As always, the Roman Mary, the alleged great mother, claims to have the last word over Jesus! The worship of the "Immaculate Heart" consists of three main redemptory parts:

- Praying the Rosary daily
- Receiving the Communion of reparation on the first Saturday, together with bringing sacrifices and making amends
- Performing a religious exercise on the first five Saturdays of each month from June to October, which includes contemplating the mysteries of the Rosary with the intention of honouring the "Immaculate Heart" of Mary

The Marian promise of grace for all those who observe these prayers is the mediation of the great graces in the hour of death, that are supposed to be absolutely necessary for eternal salvation.

With events like:
1917: apparition of Mary as the universal queen of peace
1928: the Jesuit worship of the "Heart of Jesus"
1942: consecration of the world to the "Immaculate Heart" of Mary
1950: bodily ascencion of Mary into heaven
1952: consecration of Russia,

---

288 Ibid. p. 458-460.
289 Ibid. p. 451-452.

Chapter V: The Development of the European Union

the Roman church has undergone a dark development in the past century. This shows, clearer than ever before, that the mistress (Madonna) of the Catholic church is indeed the whore Babylon described in Revelation, chapters 17-19.

The worship of the "Heart of Jesus" and the "Immaculate Heart" of Mary makes Rome the representative of the whore Babylon and guarantees the Catholic church the decisive role in the coming of the Antichrist. As Pius XII said: "The kingdom of Christ comes through the kingdom of Mary!" The following Roman blasphemy will hopefully wake up all Protestants who are already blinded by Ecumenism: *"There, one calls to that woman who is the victor over sin and hell, who wears the lily wreath of purity, who is queen in heaven and on earth, who has crushed the head of the snake and killed all heresies of the whole world alone."*[290]

The Marian spirit wants to use Fatima to "conquer the whole world."[291] Those who worship the crowned queen of peace "are registered as crusaders in the conquest or re-conquest of her kingdom, which is the kingdom of God, itself ..."[292] Through Fatima, "the re-Christianisation [or rather, re-Catholicisation, the author] of Europe is supposed to begin."[293] This Ecumenical goal of Roman Catholicism is called new-evangelization. Every sect with such aggressive intentions would run into political and legal trouble in Europe. Why does this not apply to the Roman church as well? On May 13th, 1917, the Fatima apparitions began, and on Oct.13th, 1917, the last official appearance to the children occurred, in connection with two "miracles of the sun." Interestingly, the Fatima-Madonna had chosen the late Pope John Paul II to witness a recurrence of that miracle. The whore Babylon wanted to use this to validate him as the authorized religious leader for all religions. It has to do with the third mystery, published by the Vatican Congregation for the Doctrine of the Faith in the L'Osservatore Romano on June 30th, 2000. Cardinal Ratzinger, the head of the Congregation, received the honor of becoming pope after the death of John Paul II on April 2nd, 2005. In order to veil the obvious spiritual powerlessness of Pope

---

290 Ibid. p. 249.
291 Ibid. p. 334.
292 Ibid. p. 234.
293 Ibid. p. 234.

John Paul II which became apparent as early as in the year 2000, mind-dulling banalities were published as the so-called third mystery. I will go into more detail about this later. First, let us return to the beginning of the Fatima appearances. The chief editor of a Portuguese newspaper reported on the "sun-miracle" of October 13th+15th, 1917:

He compared the supernatural "sun" with a disc of rather dull silver, but not similar to the moon. He continued: "It looked like a shining wheel that appeared to have been taken from the silver cover of a shell."[294] This "sun-disc" could be clearly seen and "stood out distinctly from its background and surroundings."[295] Remarkably, this disc, described as a shining sun-wheel, was in a state of racing motion. "It revolved around its own axis with enormous speed."[296] At the end, it turned blood-red, approached the Earth and "threatened to crash onto the ground."[297] Interestingly, the "sun-disc" did not have the usual shine. One could look into it with the naked eye. There were reports that all objects beamed in all colours of the rainbow during the appearance, which lasted only minutes. Now, let us take a leap back to John Paul II, the successor of the last Marian Popes Pius XII, John XXIII, and Paul VI. He was mentioned as the addressee of the third mystery since he succeeded in reviving all Marian places of pilgrimage worldwide, filling them with triumphalism and spiritual power. These core forces of Catholicism provide the necessary cosmic power supplies for the universal Fatima and the planned future world power of the Roman church over all religions and systems.

In the third mystery, the Madonna also said that the Pope would go through much suffering. This is cited as a reason for the election of John Paul II One refers to the injuries he received during the assassination attempt on May 13, 1981 and the many other ailments in the course of his pontificate. John Paul II, in particular, advocated the line of the II Vatican Council, which said the following about the Catholic Mary: "Her spiritual motherhood surpasses all boundaries of time and place and spreads to include the entire history of

---

294 Ibid. p. 98.
295 Ibid. p. 99.
296 Ibid. p. 99.
297 Ibid. see p. 100.

the church, yes, even the history of the salvation of humanity."[298] The Vatican sees the Madonna of Fatima as the apocalyptic "sign of God" described in Revelation 12: 1.[299] To underline this position of the Vatican, John Paul II travelled to Fatima on May 13, 1982, one year after the assassination attempt and his partial recovery. He thanked the Madonna for her protection and sought guidance for future steps towards the realization of one universal world religion under the leadership of Rome. Since that day, one of the bullets that almost killed John Paul II rests in the crown of the Madonna. In the end, this Pope failed. Many true Christians fought him with spiritual weapons, but most importantly, Jesus the Christ alone is the one who determines the time and the names connected with the end of all time. John Paul II finished off his visit of thanks to Fatima on May 13th, 1982, with a renewed consecration of the world to the Fatima-Mary. There, he underlined that his pontificate was inseparably bound to the Mary of Fatima! "World peace comes from Fatima," became the new salvation-bringing slogan for this Pope. John Paul II expressed the significance of Fatima for our day and age as follows: "What Lourdes was for the past century, Fatima has become for the 20th century under different circumstances."[300] The Madonna of Fatima personifies the II Vatican Council's new dimension of the Marian doctrine with respect to the so-called "mother of the church." Through the "Immaculate Heart" of Fatima, all of humanity is supposed to be saved! That really amounts to something new compared to the Marian claim of Lourdes. In addition, the Vatican sees only Fatima as the great sign before the Second Coming of Christ. This apocalyptic Madonna is made to stand out from all other Madonnas of the world and touted to be the forerunner of the coming Christ. Especially the Popes Paul VI, the successor of the 33-day-Pope who died under mysterious circumstances in 1978, and John Paul II both gave Fatima this apocalyptic hallmark and linked her inseparably to the II Vatican Council. This Council, which ended in 1965, made Ecumenism with the Protestants irrevocable. For the Ecumenical movement, Fatima represents the demonic, cosmic-Catholic spiritual power which reaches beyond

---

298 ibid. p. 44.
299 ibid. p. 44.
300 ibid. p. 86.

the Ecumenical union of the Christian churches. It is supposed to bring about the unification of all religions and religious systems in the spirit of the whore Babylon. The continuity of this apocalyptic Madonna began with Pius XII, the Pontifex marianus, continued under Paul VI, and reached it's absolute climax under the greatest papal reviver of all national Marian spiritual powers, Pope John Paul II. No future Pope will be able get around these Marian dogmas and statements issued with papal authority. With Fatima, "a new spiritual atmosphere is supposed to be created everywhere, *which seizes the souls and takes possession of them*. Through prayer and repentance, the new Christian human is formed ... We want to work for the kingdom of God and proclaim Fatima."[301]

In an attempt to achieve inter-religious, end time recognition for the Madonna of Fatima, a conference under the patronage of the World Conference of Religion and Peace (WCRP), a branch of the UN for the United Religions Organization (URO), was organized. This took place at the end of 2003 in the cultural city of Fatima under the appropriately titled theme "The Future of God". High-ranking representatives of the religions and esoteric sects met in the ritual place of worship, including Michail Gorbachev, who is affiliated with the New-Age movement. The director of Fatima, Luciano Guerra, told all those present that Fatima must become a place where all religions can worship their gods. "The future of Fatima, or rather the worship of God and his mother at this holy shrine must grow into a shrine where different religions can intermingle. This is the will of the blessed virgin Mary."[302]

One of the main speakers at the congress, the Jesuit theologian Jacques Dupuis, demanded that all religions must unite. His statement: "The religion of the future will be a general flowing-together of religions in a universal Christ who will satisfy everyone."[303]

The Hindu representative added the remark that millions of Hindus feel "positive energies" when visiting Marian shrines, without their Hindu faith being endangered.

---

301 Ibid. p. 482.
302 See „Topic", No. 1, 2004, p. 2, 3.
303 See ibid. p. 2, 3.

Chapter V: The Development of the European Union

The Unification of Europe and the world through the powers of the Fatima-Madonna

Before the religious world unites under the spirit of Rome, the unification of Europe must occur, not just politically, but also religiously. Why does Europe play a key role? The old spiritual continent is one of the most important regions of the world to be united in the coming antichristian "federation of ten" mentioned in Daniel 7: 24. The antichristian kingdom described in the Bible refers to Rome and, for Rome the core continent is Europe. According to a press release in "L'Osservatore Romano", even the former German president Herzog declared in 1997, in 20-30 years he expects this political unification of the world into 10 regions as the solution for the upcoming problems.[304] Rome for instance will by the use of cosmic power, strongly manipulate the former communist countries of Eastern Europe in order to make them super Catholic countries again, thus ensuring that both the political and religious power structure falls under the control of Catholicism.

In order to manipulate politically with demonic spirit forces, a replica of the statue of the Fatima Madonna was brought into the densely populated Polish region of Upper Selesia in November of 1995. It is hard to believe, but I assure you that the following events are authentic; I was an eye witness. The Madonna of Fatima was brought into every town and church. The priests, who were standing under the "eschatological protection" of Fatima, conducted a massive campaign; even with pictures of the Marian candidate Walesa. The Madonna manipulated the people through the aura of her cosmic powers to make them vote for Walesa. From day to day and step by step, the Marian candidate moved to the front line defeating his socialist rival Kwasniewsky. Many Protestant believers united with us in prayer to the true Redeemer Jesus Christ. We all entered into spiritual warfare in Upper Selisia, in order to pray against the harlot spirit of Babylon. The Lord Jesus answered our prayers, and we witnessed how the Marian candidate lost his point advantage two days before the election and lost the election with around 2% less votes. Since then Poland has not had a Catholic-Marian president. The militant Marian influence of Rome, that overshadowed the whole

---

304 "L'Osservatore Romano", No. 24, June 13, 1997, p. 1.

country, has now been receding in Poland from year to year. Today, Marianism in Poland is no longer the great danger for Europe as it cannot tip the balance of power in Rome's favour. In 2003 we were rather faced with a neo-Renaissance of Polish nationalism.

Another example of enhancing Marian power is the "Blue Army of Mary". It was founded by a Marian, named Colgan, close to New York in 1947. And, as fitting for a right-wing American, he wanted to fight: "We are a Blue Army fighting the Red Army of Moscow!"[305]. The founders included many cardinals and bishops. Through their devotion to the "Immaculate Heart"of the Fatima Madonna, they hoped "to contribute to the conversion of Russia"[306] in order to achieve world peace. In a private audience, Colgan received from Pius XII the papal blessing: "A leader in the struggle against godless communism."[307] There is a report about the first German chancellor of postwar Germany, Adenauer, that he prayed in front of the statue of Fatima. After this, the German prisoners of war were released out of Russian captivity. Adenauer was a founding member of the "Blue Army". As well as in other places of pilgrimage, there is still one in the Black Forest where "prayers" are offered – 24 hours a day – to the Fatima for world peace. Also, the founding fathers of the present European Union were convinced Marians, devoted to the doctrine of Fatima. In the early 1960's a universal decision was made by the members of the 'Blue Army' to make and consecrate a copy of Fatima to be taken on pilgrimages. So up to the present day, the Madonna travels at regular intervals throug out the whole world spreading the Marian Catholic peace. White doves, which are supposedly not trained, accompany the Madonna on her journeys as "guard of honor"; therefore we have the report of a dove miracle. However, we did not see any doves at the Marian election campaign trip in 1995 in Poland. By now, there are reports of over 20 million people worldwide "praying" in 110 countries who support the "Blue Army" of Fatima. When I visited the headquarters of the "Blue Army" in 2000, which is directly behind the "Holy Grounds of Fatima", I understood a little bit more about the dangerous nature of this militant "Order of Knights". The worldwide devotion of

---

305 Fonseca, "Maria spricht zur Welt" (Mary Speaks to the World) 1988, p. 130.
306 Ibid. p. 131.
307 Ibid. p. 134.

Fatima is understood "as a unifying cord that wraps around the people of Europe, because the **'mother of God' of Fatima is behind the pictures** and is really identical with the 'mother of God' of...".[308] And then the most important Madonnas of the European nations are listed here – including Lourdes as the European highlight. The phrase "behind the pictures" signifies,

1. that all national Madonnas have also received an additional universal Catholic commission with the set goal of a future dominion of Rome over all world religions.

2. that in order to achieve this objective, the European national Madonnas have received the cosmic-universal antichristian spirit powers of Fatima. Fatima herself is the expression of the Roman deception of this antichristian "spirit of the age" ("Zeitgeist") with the name of "world peace". This helps us to understand the pronouncement of the bishop of Leiria (in the region of Fatima): "We know it is the power of the blessed Virgin, the mother of the church *and of all mankind, who gathers and unites her children in one world* ...".[309] What we know already about the Madonna of Lourdes, this national Marian bridgehead to the whole world – the world Ecumenical Movement – is perfectly personified in the "Peace Queen of Fatima". "Therefore, Fatima is only the consequential continuation and the last phase in the development of Mary with a political message."[310] Furthermore she claims to be the "queen of the Apostles and the queen of missions". The spirit of Fatima travels everywhere in the world disguised in a beautiful physical statue. "So she is joyfully waited upon, called upon in all needs, and received by the people with praise, *even by those who are not Christians (...) She is ready to save the world that is in the struggle with death.*"[311] Therefore, it is no longer a surprise that Fatima receives great enthusiastic welcome on her pilgrim journeys in typically Islamic countries. Some time ago, I read in the press that a Persian delegation of mullahs made a trip to the Fatima in Portugal. We do not even need to ask why (...). In the Koran, Sura 19 is addressed to Mary which has the name of Miriam

---

308 Ibid. p. 480.
309 Ibid. p. 481.
310 See Chapter IV.
311 Ibid. p.342.

there. She is a virgin according to Moslem tradition and a virgin chosen by God without sin!

The struggle for a newly demanded dogmatizing of Amsterdam's "Woman of all People"

Some alert readers might ask: Why do they still wrestle in the Vatican about the firm inscription of the Co-redemptrix although Mary has already held this position in practice for a long time, and Pope John Paul II had confirmed the statement of the church fathers when they said, "Christ sacrificed his flesh, Mary her soul"?

According to Sigl, Pope John Paul II avoided the title "Co-redemptrix" most of the time, but not the title of "Mediator" and "Intercessor", in order to prevent irritations for Ecumenical reasons. Furthermore he explains that John Paul II officially designated Mary six times as 'spiritual mother of the whole human race" and as "Co-redemptrix" between 1982 and 1991. In his speech to sick pilgrims in Rome on 24th Mar.1990, the pope said the following, "May the most holy Virgin Mary, Co-redemptrix of the human race at the side of her Son, always grant you courage and trust ..."[312] Sigl expands on this and determines, "Merely what John Paul II said about Mary during his pontificate will suffice completely to justify the new, last, and greatest Marian dogma. Therefore, years of theological preparation are no longer necessary for the proclamation of the dogma of Mary: Co-redemtrix, mediator, and intercessor, because basically everything has been said."[313]

One wonders if the pope delayed again and again the dogmatizing – the inscription with universal application, as church law and binding – only out of Ecumenical considerations? By 1998, according to their collections of signatures, over 4,7 million Catholics, including many dignitaries, had expected the dogmatizing by the Pope. Why was this, seeing as the Pope had long ago acknowledged Mary as Co-redemptrix by calling upon her and by designating her as such? Among the dignitaries are the following popes of the past: Pius XII, John XXIII (the Council Pope) Paul VI, John Paul I, the 33 day pope, who lost his life in a mysterious way. Also, among the

---

312 Sigl; „Die Frau aller Völker, Amsterdam – Rom", 1989, p. 70-71.(The woman of all people).
313 Ibid. p. 71.

supporters was the late Pope John Paul II. So all the late popes since World War II spoke for dogmatizing, as did the following cardinals: Glemp, Warsaw; Lustiger, Paris; O'Connor, New York; Ribeiro, Lisbon; Schoenborn, Vienna.[314] Some of them have died by now.

"Mary herself gives the reasons: She commanded as long ago as 1954, "Work for it and request this dogma. You shall implore the Holy Father for this dogma."[315] Why again does the pope not obey right away – as was also the case at Fatima? In the year of 1957, the "Woman" of the seer of Amsterdam commanded, "Go to the Holy Father and tell him that I have said: The time has come to proclaim the dogma. I will come back for the church and the priests privately at the time the Lord will determine. Tell him also that *the state of celibacy is threatened from within.*"[316]

The Babylon Harlot (Rev. 17 and 19) the woman of all nations, demands during the apparitions to the seer Ida Peerdeman, a prayer with the concluding remarks: "… May the woman of all people, *who once was Mary*, be the intercessor of us all!"[317] This was just as much a surprise for the seer as for any catholic.

The Babylon Harlot subsequently insists that the addition: "Who once was Mary", shall not be left out! The reason: "Many people knew Mary as Mary. However, now in this new time period I want to be the woman *of all* people. Everyone understands this."[318]

Really, does every Catholic believer understand this? Consider this: World War II was over just 9 years previously when the vision of the "Woman of all People" appeared. By this time the Vatican had already decided on the concept of the Fatima-Madonna.

Image 17: Woman of all People

---

314 See ibid. p. 85-86.
315 Ibid. p. 86.
316 Ibid. p. 118.
317 Ibid. p. 164.
318 Ibid. p. 166.

In Revelation 17: 1-2, we read: *"One of the seven angels who had the seven bowls came and said to me, "Come, I will show you the punishment of the great prostitute, who sits on many waters. With her the kings of the earth committed adultery and the inhabitants of the earth were intoxicated with the wine of her adulteries".*

The many "waters", on which the Babylon Harlot sits, are perceived as the dominion of this Domina (mistress) over many cultures, people, or ethnic groups, nations. The name "Mary", however, stands only for the Catholic people of the Western World. However, from the beginning at Fatima (1917) the Babylon Harlot made a universal claim, first of all for the Catholic world. Now, since the fifties of the 20th century she wants to be even honoured and worshiped by means of the apparitions of Amsterdam with all the names of the goddesses from all cultures as, e.g., Miriam (Islam) or Maya, respectively Tara (Buddhism) etc. This sounds, at first, like a competitive appearance of the Catholic "Mary" with the "Woman of all People". With the title: Mother, or Woman of all People, she emphasizes her claim to rule over all cultures and religions. As Lucifer works at the doctrine that all religions have the same God in our age, so does the female demonic equivalent, the Babylon Harlot, work at the title, which is acceptable to all worshippers: The Woman of all People! This is saying 'good bye' to the exclusively Catholic picture of the Babylon Harlot, which once was just "Mary".

As we have seen, one reason behind the desire for this dogmatizing is to establish the dominion of "the Woman" over all cultures and religions. Similarly, the so-called mercy picture of 1951 is an expression of the universal claim of the Babylon Harlot as co-redeemer, mediator, intercessor. "For on the picture of mercy, we do not see Mary as the Immaculata – therefore it is not at the beginning of her calling [Lourdes 1858, the author] – and similarly, not as the juvenile mother of the divine child [Biblical Mary, the author]. Rather, Mary shows herself at Amsterdam in the most glorious display of her calling as co-redeeming mother for us, as mediator of *all* grace for us, as universal intercessor for us. Her co-redeemer position is visually depicted in a threefold way: She stands in front of the cross of her son [the son no longer hangs as a corpus on the cross, the author] with the loin cloth of the redeemer around her middle and with transfigured wounds on her hands (...). Later on, this picture will be used for the co-redeemer."[319] A little while later the 'woman' supplements this claim with: "I am standing in front of the cross of the Redeemer. My head, my hands, my feet *are as those of the Son of Man*. The body as from the Spirit. I have put my feet firmly on the globe, because the Father and the Son wanted to bring me into this world as co-redeemer, co-mediator, and intercessor at this time (…). I stand on the globe, because this concerns the whole world."[320]

It is very obvious that this attempt is intended to substitute the crucified Jesus with "the Woman". The substitutionary death of Jesus is and remains an annoyance for all religions (1 Cor. 1: 18). Furthermore, the Babylon Harlot presumes to maintain that she is the only one who "will bring back the scattered sheep" into one fold. On her "picture of mercy", one can see in both hands the scars of a crucifixion. Out of each scar, three rays of light shine forth which are directed toward the sheep on the globe. "These are three rays, the rays of mercy, redemption, and peace …"[321] "The Woman" provides reasons that she is also the "mediator of all graces". "At first the suffering of the co-redeemer, [she is crucified, the author] then the joys of handing out grace."[322] In this way, the Babylon Harlot is going to be fashioned in the shape of the "Woman of all People" as the perfect woman who sits "on many waters". Therefore, Guadeloupe, a suburb of Mexico City (1531), Lourdes (1858) and Fatima (1917) *are only a few out of the many examples of her mission*".[323]

This "Woman of all People", however, had not yet become reality in a dogma. Now we may be able to understand the struggle in the Vatican. Whilst the Babylon Harlot has not yet been unveiled, we can perceive how Satan, in conjunction with her, has started the assault on all humanity. We should remind ourselves of the image of the animal with the woman sitting on it … (Rev. 17: 3).

If the pope endorses the dogma, then the Babylon Harlot will have her way, according to chapter 17 of Revelation, to establish

---

319 Ibid. p. 173.
320 Ibid. p. 173.
321 Ibid. p. 175.
322 Ibid. p. 175.
323 Ibid. p. 175.

the Satanic rule as "mediator of all grace", i.e., as mediator of all sinful spirit-death-powers together with the Antichrist.

Why then is the dogma necessary? First of all, the "woman of all people" is regarded as the capstone of Marian development. The Catholic "Mary" will be replaced by the universal woman, in order to be recognized by all religions. "The new and *last* dogma in Marian history will be: The dogma of co-redeemer, mediator, and intercessor."[324]

I feel that the hypocritical humility this woman adopts is incredibly insulting and arrogant. She assumes to be commissioned "to return" the scattered sheep "into one flock", although Jesus the Christ has said that he knows his sheep and they know him, and *"no one can pluck them out of the Father's hand. I and the Father are one."* (John 10: 29-30). Only the son has the divine commission for the protection and unity of the redeemed. Jesus alone is *"the radiance of God's glory and the exact representation of his being, sustaining all things by his powerful word. After he had provided purification for sins, he sat down at the right hand of the Majesty in heaven. So he became as much superior to the angels as the name he has inherited is superior to theirs."* (Hebrew 1: 3-4).

Jesus alone is the redeemer, mediator, and intercessor with the Father. No one stands beside him, only below him. No one else is put over the universe but Jesus alone. No one else has accomplished redemption from sin and death, but He only. No one could or needed to help him in this. He alone "became as much superior to the angels as the name he has inherited is superior to theirs." (Hebrews 1: 4). He alone is the only high priest who atoned for our sins (Hebrews 2: 17; 4: 15; 7: 16. 25. 26; 9: 14. 24). Nowhere in the Bible is a divine woman mentioned who participated in the plan of redemption in the sense of co-redeemer, co-mediator, or co-intercessor. "... because by *one* sacrifice he [Jesus, the author] has made perfect *forever* those who are being made holy. (...) And where these have been forgiven, there is no longer any sacrifice for sin." (Hebrews 10: 14. 18).

Therefore, the "woman" belongs to the devil and his death. The Babylon Harlot is the mediator of all powers of death. She co-redeems people from their life and leads them to death, and she is as

---

324 Ibid. p. 185+.

intercessor the entrance gate to the "cosmic Christ" as the occidental culture prince of Satan. "The woman" appears in the most different shades and is a strong seductress in our last, end-time dispensation. "I saw that the woman was drunk with the blood of the saints, the blood of those who bore testimony to Jesus. When I saw her, I was greatly astonished. Then the angel said to me, "The waters you saw, where the prostitute sits, are peoples, multitudes, nations and languages." (Revelation 17: 6. 15). The "great city", Babylon, which she had also ruled and which had a bad reputation in the biblical story, shall be judged for the sake of believers. The reason: "Your merchants were the world's great men. By your magic spell [mediatrix, the author] all the nations were led astray ..." (Rev. 18: 23). Jesus has condemned the great Harlot (woman of all people) because she has ruined the earth with her harlotry of deception and idol worship. Jesus has avenged the blood of his servants on her. The "great city" and the Harlot Babylon are synonymous. They are also symbiotically connected with each other – inescapable for judgment. It is very easy to identify the "great city" and the 'great harlot", as the synonym "Babylon", with the historic, political, and religious reality. The antichristian spirit had started with Babylon. Since then Babylon is used as a cipher for the Antichrist. The Medo-Persian empire has sucked up this spirit and carried it over to Greece. From there, the flame of the Olympus was carried to Rome, the first phase of antiquity (Daniel 7: 7) and then into the second phase which was the separation of West and East Rome (since 1053 A. D.). We still live today in this phase of separation. All efforts of the spirit of Babylon, i.e. Rome, aim at establishing the unity of Rome (from the Atlantic to the Ural Mountains) which signifies the immersion into the third phase of Rome (Dan. 7: 23ff). All Ecumenical efforts and deceptions of the Babylonian spirit are orientated towards the political as well as the religious unity (comp. Dan. 7). After two more phases the Antichrist (false Christ) will appear at the completion of human cultural history in the spirit of Babylon and then be judged by the Lord of human history, Jesus the Christ, who is the perfecter of God's salvation and redemption history.

"... and then the lawless one will be revealed, whom the Lord Jesus will overthrow with the breath of his mouth and destroy by the splendor of his coming. The coming of the lawless one will be in accordance with

the work of Satan displayed in all kinds of counterfeit miracles, signs and wonders, and in every sort of evil that deceives those who are perishing. They perish because they refused to love the truth and so be saved." (2 Thess.2: 8-10). "But the beast was captured, and with him the false prophet who had performed the miraculous signs on his behalf. With these signs he had deluded those who had received the mark of the beast and worshiped his image. The two of them were thrown alive into the fiery lake of burning sulphur." (Rev. 19: 20).

According to allegedly cosmic tactics of the Vatican, the desired – but not yet accomplished – dogma of the divine Marian upgrading had seven dogmatized forerunners. We recognize the Babylon Harlot in the initiation name Mary which infiltrated church history, and how she gained importance as the demonic mediator of all spirit – death powers. Caused by the weakening of Lourdes and Fatima since 1997, they reasserted the forgotten and unheeded visions of the 1950's of "the woman of all people". They had thought they could do without her, because Fatima was the favourite for the preparation of the Antichrist. All popes of the postwar era were betting on the universal, yet still Catholic Mary of Fatima – from the "immaculate conception" of the Lourdes Madonna to the "immaculate heart" of the Fatima Madonna. After the demonic spirit power losses, they call now for the Madonna "which once was Mary". Now the Babylon Harlot has to do it herself with one of her all-religion Madonnas which stands before the empty cross with signs of wounds on her hands. The blasphemies become more explicit. The deception becomes more obvious. The Babylon Harlot wants to enforce now the unity of religions, because she does not have much time left. She loses in the process her Christian facade. So she introduces a Madonna to mankind which, although coming from a Catholic tradition, can now be accepted by all religions, because the despised man of the cross is gone! Why now another dogma? With each dogmatizing in the sense of a deepened redeemer divinity of Mary, a gigantic cosmic spirit death force came onto the people who worshipped her. We have dealt with this already. Precisely because demonic spirit forces are lacking since the decline of Fatima, new death forces have to be magically produced by the deputy of the "cosmic Christ", the pope. How does this woman herself view her mission and her objective? "When the last dogma in Marian history has been proclaimed, then the woman of all nations will give peace to the world, the true peace (...) With this title, it will be granted to me to redeem the world from a great worldwide catastrophe."[325] Even Fatima had promised this once. Yet the pope hesitates to dogmatize this claim; for this "woman of all people" causes the Roman church to drift more and more into dependance on other religions. The Catholic Church would lose more and more her face, even her identity. The critics in her own ranks increase. This pope, however, will not be able to create "The Woman of all People" through dogmatizing and to make it binding for the Catholics. The plans will disappear in the drawers for now. At the opportune time they will be taken out again – but only when the Biblical God wants this for judgment. He alone determines time and mode of the last phase of history for his judgment over all contempt of God and people.

The Secular World on a Quest for a Madonna?

Also the non-Christian, post-modernistic world of the half-grown is on a quest for a madonna. After the Reformation in the 16th century and the Enlightenment in the 17th/18th century all of Roman Catholicism entered into an identity crisis, because worship and appearances of Mary declined abruptly. Now the Roman Church increased their efforts to stimulated faith in Mary in order to give back to the unsettled Catholics the lost religious cultural identity by means of the subsequent demarcation from the Protestants. Even our post-modernistic time, the time of transition from dogmatic materialism and atheism to the esotericism of neo-romanticism, is searching for transcendental image guides on the way to still very diffuse cults and religious systems. One example of many is the "Mona Lisa" which feminism venerates as a madonna.

We are also reminded of the accidentally killed British Diana who thousands now invoke as a non-Catholic madonna, as mediator to the "world of angels", as spirit. Here as well, the deficient identity of a world of half-grown-ups seems to be the basis of the infantile nonsense.

The late Pope John Paul II failed in his Marian faith since many true believers united in spiritual warfare to break the Marian cosmic spirit forces. This arrogant queen of heaven is an abomination for

---
325 Ibid. p. 205.

the Lord Jesus Christ, because she originates from the spirit of the Babylon Harlot. By the will of the Lord, the mediating of cosmic spiritual powers and integrating them into a unified future world religion will be reduced out of mercy for true Christianity and to enable the genuine conversion of Catholics to the biblical Jesus Christ. John Paul II gambled with idol worship on an extremely high level. His failure became a heavy burden for his successor Benedict XVI. Even now some Mariologists blow the horn for a decent retreat after 20 years of Mary revival, i.e., a Marian renaissance by the "Totus tuus – Pope" (all yours, Mary). The new trend of retreat looks like this:

The Vatican sends a Mariologist by the name of Perella from the papal Marian faculty in Rome as a spokesman for the retreat. In an interview, which he gave to the German news magazine "Focus", he said, "We have to find our way back to the Mary as she was, to the historical Mary, to the woman of Nazareth, to the woman of Faith and not to the Mary of our needs".[326] This sounds good only if we did not know the pronouncements of the popes since the 40's which are binding for Catholicism and which no pope can recind. Either a soon to be dismissed outsider is talking here, or these tactics are part of the retreat manoeuvre because of Marian power loss. This pronouncement can also be a political move of appeasement to the other Christian churches of the Ecumenical Movement. The following statement would confirm with this: "The Madonna image was a hindrance for the dialogue with the other churches."[327] This applies particularly to the "Woman of all People". In any case, it is outrageous hypocrisy when the same Perella refers to the church leadership of the Vatican that supposedly said, that Mary as a redeemed person cannot be Redeemer.[328] As the readers of this book have learned from the many pronouncements of the Vatican, which are binding for all Catholics, the importance of Mary is inscribed so firmly that there is no way back. Therefore, a statement like this, that she, as a redeemed person, cannot be Redeemer, is the individual, unbinding opinion of an outsider from which the Vatican can and will distance itself at an opportune time. In the meantime

---

326 "Focus", No. 52, 1997, p. 90. (German magazine).
327 Ibid. p. 90.
328 See ibid. p. 90.

the outsider is "ditched". This opinion, however, is intended to pull wool over all people's eyes who do not look into this topic closely, especially the Protestants. For some years now this author has read the official paper of Rome, "L'Osservatore Romano". On the second page of every edition Pope John Paul II offered a theological exegesis as proof of Mary's "Immaculate Conception". Whether this is the opportunistic trumpet call of the minority liberal Catholic forces of the Vatican, or the tactics of the beginning popish power struggle; there has been a slight retreat from the Marian belligerence. For some time now much fewer Marian articles appear on the second page of a "L'Osservatore Romano" edition.

Feminist theology has been interested in "Mary" for some time now. The deceased German protestant "theologian" Dorothee Soelle (God-is-dead-theology) had discovered for herself the demonic transcendence through the esoteric for quite a while, and in addition an interest in a feminist "Mary". She defended the Catholic dogma of Mary's ascension with the argument, that through the reception into heaven, "her female body was liberated from the degradations of the Judeo-Christian culture. To live independently now means liberation".[329] This seems to be pathological. Mary as liberator – thus, nevertheless the redeemer – from male oppression? Since April 2003 it can be said: Soelle is dead, but God lives eternally. Not just Roman theology, but also the post-modernistic Protestant theologies, which are very open for the esoteric, also choose a Madonna from the Apocryphal books. While Rome finds its "Mary" in the Sophia (wisdom) the respective Protestant theologians, who come from the Greek tradition, pick the Sophia Madonna in the Apocryphal book of Wisdom. In this book, chapter 7 from verse 22, it says, that she is hidden in creation and she rules the cosmos. We read that Sophia is the divine wisdom, logos, and spirit at the same time. Unfortunately, even among some Ecumenical groups, this reference is related to "Mary" and not to Jesus, the Christ, as the New Testament testifies (Colossians 2: 3). They search for a goddess even in circles which are not yet Catholic. Which name will she get in our feministic era? The search is on for a mother goddess which pleases and is acceptable to all Europeans whether they are Catholic or not. However, Rome will continue to specify the decisive sound in the antichristian spectrum of

---
329 Ibid. p. 86.

Chapter V: The Development of the European Union

the Babylonian spirit in spite of the Marian power crisis. In the above mentioned Europe Trilogy, Mary is seen in the picture of the woman. "The picture of the feminine is reflected in the primeval mother Eve – in the circle of the gods of antiquity – and reaches its peak in the 'mother of God' Mary."[330] For the formation of the future Europe, the Roman church is important as well as the Greek pantheon, the esoteric grail as well as the freemasonry. Europe is seeking a common religion. The commonality which joins together all religious systems will be a "great mother". In our age of feminism it should not be difficult to create within a few decades a "great mother" acceptable for all; for redemption, protection, for unity towards "world peace", and out of this spirit, the Antichrist. This is then the revealed Babylon Harlot of the last times, the mediator of all cosmic-demonic spirit forces from all cultures. Whether she is then called Mary or Mona Lisa, Sophia, Diana, Hera, Artemis, Aphrodite, Miriam (Islam) Maya or Tara (Buddhism) or Demeter, is almost irrelevant and it does not change anything about the basic facts. The unity of Europe, followed by the unity of the world will be achieved by a woman with transcendental powers. Without this woman, which the Bible calls the "Babylon Harlot", the Antichrist will not gain his power which God has enacted for judgment. Never before in modern times, has an important, but unheeded appearance succeeded that far: the whole Western world has degenerated so much by means of the "Zeitgeist" (spirit of the age) through infantilism, that man no longer perceives his social responsibility. It is easy now to seduce Western European man through manipulation. A humanity of reckless, egocentrically spoiled half-growns has no mental power to resist the coming evil power of the female mediator of all demonic spirit forces from all cultures (Rev. 17: 9, 15). Unfortunately, this condition affects many Christians as well. Europe no longer has people who are fitted for a good social unity.

The majority are not even able to maintain a relationship of two over a longer period of time, never mind living together in a larger national socio-cultural unity in democracy. Soon the infantile Western Europeans will become ungovernable! Among the half-grown men in Europe, an unruly rage, an unruly disgust, and a dislike of people emerges. Even more and more women harbor this disgust. This is the almost brutal analysis of the empty and worn out complaint about

---
330 Schmitt-Lieb, "Europa Trilogie", 1995, p. 119.

the general indifference. Only a thin cover restrains the all destroying, blindly raging force. The disgust of people makes headway not only in the abortion issue, in euthanasia, in fundamentalism, and in terrorism, but it has gripped all levels of society. The human being without any sense of responsibility is the material that will invite the strong man, the strong dictator which the Bible calls Antichrist.

7. Summary: The antichristian preparation for the coming of the Antichrist

As we have demonstrated in-depth, with Lourdes, the outset of the Catholic sacramental Trinity was put into motion by means of the power mediating "Immaculate Conception". With this Marian bridgehead in place, the unification of all religions is ready. What then, is Fatima?

As "Queen of Heaven", she assumes the power to bring peace onto the earth. She shall prepare the returning "Christ". So the Madonna of Fatima is the almost undisguised Babylon Harlot who transcends by far her role as Catholic Co-Redeemer. Her eschatological political message is: " and it will be peace if one fulfills my request ". The " woman of all people " is obviously a "perfect" program the enemy of God has revealed carelessly. It would have been her turn only after the fulfillment of the Catholic Madonna with a universal political message, as Fatima had claimed. Or did the tremendous power loss of Fatima trigger the exposing revelation of the Babylon Harlot? Whatever the case may be, the Babylon Harlot has also entered into a symbiotic relationship of reason with Lucifer in the "intellectual" (demonic) interest of Europe. For this symbiosis, the Luciferian-male "Santiago de Compostela" in the northwest corner of Spain stands beside Fatima (female) who integrates all cultures. A part of the advertising for this important European place of pilgrimage is the reference that the former president of the EU, the Italian Prodi, made a pilgrimage to this place once every year. So a coexistence according to reason exists between the Catholic Europe (Santiago) and the all globalizing Fatima. The extremely numerous Marys in Santiago are all pure expressions of the Babylon Harlot. What is obvious, however, is the hatred of these Madonnas for men. So we find this male/female rivalry also among the spirits; quasi the original of the immanent worldly reality. The powerful male symbol of the dragon, or the bull with the woman sitting on it, belongs to this symbiosis! So I found on our visits to Santiago de Compostela and Fatima the "hypostatical" windows to the described power filled places of the spirit demonic construction of Europe. Furthermore, I found the globalizing power of the religious political world unity out of the antichristian spirit. Apparently, only since World War II has the papacy, through Pope Pius XII, bound himself to the Fatima Madonna as the intercultural Babylon Harlot (Rev. 17). With it, since the 1940's, the Roman church has become culturally-religiously globalized. Under the retention of the exoterically (male) visible rulership of the papacy, the Vatican was now ruled in reality gynocentrically (female) in an esoterically hidden way. That was the price for the global power of Rome. However, this was the prerequisite for the abundance of power of the late Pope John Paul II that never existed previously. He was extremely loyal to the Babylon Harlot who wanted to be worshipped through the hypostatic window of Fatima and from whence she ruled. This loyalty necessitated that John Paul II had to consecrate anew and revive all Catholic culture Madonnas (Mary) in all countries in order to submit them to the universal Fatima. This was the logical outcome of a series of developments which started in 1854 at Lourdes, progressed into the papal dogma of infallibility of 1870 and continued into the Marian dogma of ascension in 1950. The unimaginable absolute power of the gynocentric Babylon Harlot over Rome in the hypostatic window of Fatima expresses itself also in the fact that only in Fatima, nuns hand out the host-Christ at the Eucharist and drink with the priest of the wine. People who know the Roman scene only theoretically may question this female/male ritual cooperation. However, we were eye witnesses in front of the Fatima Basilica on May 13, 2000, and saw this indication of the symbiotic unification celebrated by Pope John Paul II.

8. The publication of the "Third Mystery" of Fatima as an admission of Marian power loss

Now we come to important details of the documentation "The Message of Fatima", which are to be regarded as binding. This was published by the "Congregation for the Teaching of Faith", formerly

"The Holy Authority of Inquisition", respectively "Holy Offizium", and which is supposed to be a publication of the revelation of the third mystery, which had not previously been published.[331] The head of this congregation was Cardinal Ratzinger who became Pope Benedict XVI after the death of Pope John Paul II in April 2005. Because of political relevance, we will focus on some already known statements. In the introduction of the document, it is stated, that Pope John Paul II had determined to make public the third part of the "Secret of Fatima" on the threshold of the second to the third millennium.

Accordingly, this "Third Mystery" was supposedly written down by the still living witness Lucia on Jan. 3rd 1944, but handed over to the "Holy Offizium" only on 04. April 1957. However, what kind of weight does a testimony have that was written down in detail 27 years later? According to the Faith Congregation, the crux of this document consists of "the crucial events in human history, in the bloody attack against the mild Christ on earth." Pope John Paul II publicly represents Christ!

The popes John XIII and Paul VI decided not to publicize these "secrets". After the attack on Pope John Paul II on the 13. May 1981, he requested the envelope containing the "Third Secret" in order to read it. One result was that the pope consecrated the world once again "to the Immaculate Heart of Mary" (Fatima). The prayer of consecration contains the salutation, "Oh, Mother of mankind and of peoples". Fatima is invoked to take "the whole human family" under her protection, in order that times of peace, of freedom, of truth, of righteousness, and of hope may begin. On the 13. May 1982 the pope performs this "act of confidence" at Fatima and repeats it on Peter's Square in Rome with all of the bishops of the world on 25. March, 1984.

Then the first and second part of the secret was summarized and explained on a whole page of a newspaper. The tenor is: The world can only be saved from the coming catastrophe if "the devotion to my [Fatima, the author] Immaculate Heart" is established. For this purpose, all the world consecrations of the past were necessary. I have already reported them.

---

331 "L' Osservatore Romano", No. 26, June 30, 2000, p. 18+.

It is even stranger and more hectic with the Third Secret. Although Lucia received this "revelation" of Fatima on the 13. July, 1917 she had the "premonition" at that time, that the bishop shown in the vision and dressed in white was the "Holy Father". Lucia had in mind the pope who was shot at in 1981! Now, the vision describes that the "Holy Father" ascends a steep mountain with other bishops, priests, and members of holy orders to the cross on the top of a mountain. Before that, the pope went "through a big city, half of which was destroyed, and with shivering and shaking step, depressed from pain and sorrow, he prayed for the souls of the corpses he met on his way. Having come to the mountain, he knelt at the foot of the big cross. There he was killed by a group of soldiers who shot at him with guns and arrows. In the same way, the bishops died one after the other (…). Under the arms of the cross were two angels, each of them had a watering can in his hand which was made out of crystal. They gathered the blood of the martyrs in them, and they gave this to drink to the souls of those who drew close to God."

According to this document, Pope John Paul II wrote a letter to Lucia on 19. April 2000, to announce a visit to the town of Fatima by Msgr. Bertone of the Faith Congregation and by the officiating bishop of Leiria, Portugal. These gentlemen were to "submit some questions for the interpretation of the third secret" to Lucia in the name of the pope. One is surprised that in May 1981 (after the attack) Pope John Paul II is, supposedly for the first time, in possession of the "Third Secret". Nineteen years later he asks Lucia to interpretate the third secret "openly and honestly" to the papal messengers.

The shepherd children of Fatima realized in 1917 that the person they saw "fatally wounded falling on the ground" was Pope John Paul II who started his pontificate in 1978. The "fatally wounded" was changed, because "a motherly hand guided the course of the bullet, and the pope who struggled with death remained on the threshold of death". The attack on the pope in 1981, however, had a completely different background. On three whole pages, the theological problem of the "Immaculate Conception", i.e., the divinity of Mary is relativized and reinterpreted with Jesuit dialectics. The "Immaculate Heart" is interpreted as "an organ that exists in an inner unity with God and therefore sees God". "My Immaculate Heart will triumph" means now, that the heart open to God has become pure and is now stronger "than guns and weapons of any kind". The mountain and the city in the vision "symbolize now the places of human history (…) the places of danger and of uttermost threat". The cross on the mountain now symbolizes "goal and point of orientation in history". The killed and dressed in white man is now "the pope who obviously walks ahead of the others, shivering and suffering because of all the horrors that surround him". The path through the corpses becomes the future way of suffering for the church, i.e., the way of the cross. Then again, Jesuit dialectics become the way of exegesis. The envisioned blood of the martyrs flows together with the blood of Christ. Therefore, "their martyrdom is one with the suffering of Christ, it has become one with it". According to this theology out of an antichristian spirit, the martyrs supplement the sacrificial death of Christ, and only this makes it complete! So, this life of martyrdom became "Eucharist itself" and therefore comprises the second side of Christ's work of redemption. "… as out of the death of Christ, *out of his open side* the church sprang forth, so the death of the witness is fruitful for the ongoing life of the church". This is true: The church originates in the death and not in the life of Christ. "Out of the suffering of the witnesses comes a power of purification and renewal, because it is making present Christ's own suffering and his healing power extends into the present", by means of the hypostatic paradigm.[332] It was Pope Benedict XVI, earlier known as Cardinal Ratzinger, the dialectic Jesuit, who brought about this new interpretation.

We conclude: the Catholic Mary out of the spirit of the Babylon Harlot has failed in the age of our 'spirit of the times' ('Zeitgeist'). She was not able to mediate and channel the demonic-cosmic spirit powers to the desired extent. Will a new 'Zeitgeist' now provoke the death of many people, which they will then call martyrs, so that "the future life of the church can be fruitful"?

Furthermore, we maintain this:

Christ Jesus died once (once and for all) for all sins of all mankind (Hebr. 9: 12-28).

Even genuine martyrs die because of the sins committed against them and even they were sinners who needed redemption through

---

332 See Chapter II.

Chapter V: The Development of the European Union

the blood of Christ. The work of Christ's redemption never came about by additional blood of martyrs!

As a consequence of the declining Marian importance and page after page of reinterpretations of the "Third Secret" – which turned out to be no secret at all – it became necessary

for the Vatican to concentrate on other matters.

These are:
- Martyrs (Therefore, the innumerable beatifications and canonizations during the years 2000-2003).
- A "Jesus" who is universal and who promises compassion to all people if he is honoured. What then does the new Jesus look like?

9. A new star in the cosmic heavens: The "Jesus" of Compassion

We should not come to the short sighted conclusion, because of what was said above, that Fatima and the Marian powers are finished. The pope still consecrated the whole world to Mary on the 8. Oct. 2000.

Image 18:
The Compassionate Jesus

For this purpose the original statue of Fatima was brought to him in Rome.[333] At the present time the Babylon Harlot has been greatly weakened in the Western Marian culture by the grace of the true Christ. The impairment shows itself as it did in Santiago de Compostela. The exclusive Marian powers of the Babylon Harlot have to be shared with Lucifer, under the disguise of "Jesus of Compassion". The goddesses out of the Babylon Harlot's spirit have lost much power; therefore, they have to hand over authority to the male gods out of the spirit of Satan. This is a cunning deception. A "Jesus", who is in reality Lucifer, (2 Cor. 11: 14) is now placed beside the Madonna for worship and admiration. This has been the case especially

---

[333] "L'Osservatore Romano", No. 41, Oct. 13, 2000, p. 7.

Chapter V: The Development of the European Union

in Poland in Marian power centers since the autumn of 1999. As a picture of "Jesus of Compassion" with the slogan: "Jesus, I trust in you", Lucifer was on the verge of entering visibly the end time world stage in 2000 as another deceiver. Shortly before the printing of the first edition of this book in the middle of January 2004 a message of a credible and responsible sister in the faith reached me. She reported that the Protestant Alliance in Cologne, Germany, had advertised at the premises of the main railway station with this "Jesus of Compassion" for the annual Alliance week of prayer. This naivety in falling away from faith is unpardonable. Applause now only comes now only from the antichristian pope church. The Fatima Madonna had already declared in 1999, that "my appearances in the world, as they happen at the moment, will come to an end soon".[334] She perceives herself as the summary and also as the fulfillment of all Madonnas. But now this new "Jesus" appears with a church wide campaign and speaks through mediums (human speech channels of spirits) in places of pilgrimage! (Oct. 1999): "I look at Lourdes, Fatima now as if I would return. These are only two places I mention. *I had sent my mother – now I come myself* as I also have come to other places and I still come".[335]

Image 19:
Faustyna and the Compassionate Jesus

For tactical reasons the Vatican did not acknowledge Marpingen, an unimportant place of pilgrimage, since 1876. It was upgraded by the pope after the canonization of the former polish nun Faustyna (1905-1938).

Faustyna had received the order from "Jesus" in 1931 in Krakow to paint him and to publish his picture. It was not until the year of power loss 1999/2000 however, that this message and this order from "Jesus" were remembered. Now after the canonization of Faustyna, this "Jesus" receives a new evaluation by the pope. He even decreed a liturgical innovation for honouring this "Compassionate Jesus". "The second Sunday during

---

334 See "Kurzbericht Marpingen", No. 9, p. 3. (short account of Marpingen).
335 "Kurzbericht Marpingen", No. 8, p. 8.(short account of Marpingen).

Easter time, which will be called "Compassion Sunday" in the whole church from now on ...".[336]

This "Jesus" responds to this with: "I desire that the celebration of compassion becomes a refuge and shelter for all souls, especially for the poor sinners. Whoever comes to the fountain of life on this day experiences a complete remission of his guilt and penalty".[337]

On this Sunday "the priests shall tell the souls of my unfathomable compassion".[338]

The cannonization of Faustyna, the acceptance by the Vatican, the order to make public and worship the new image, and the obligatory liturgical innovation are an expression of a very belated "divinely" demanded obedience.[339]

The construction of the new church in Krakow, Poland for the "Jesus of Compassion" was almost completed in 2004/2005. There seemed to be financial problems then. Important additional work was not completed. After the canonization of the nun Faustyna in 2000, the number of pilgrims exploded to over one million visitors. Redemption is promised if one worships daily. If the worshipper exposes himself to the red beams which emanate from the heart (see picture) then he receives power for living "from the blood of life". When one commits oneself to the white rays life power is released out of the "water of life". These are the most important gifts of the "Compassion". With this, the historical sacrificial death of Jesus is made null and void without saying it, for the worshipper receives compassion for eternal life even in the last hour of death. In Europe, the icon of "Jesus" is increasingly placed beside the icon of "Mary". The Babylon Harlot has to share her declining power and authority with Lucifer. He no longer leaves his Mary from the court of the Babylonian Harlot to gather all the death powers out of the abominable idol worship of people.

This "Jesus" identifies himself with the "Jesus" in the tabernacle. He laments the lack of attention from Catholics with the words:

"Follow My petition and do not forsake me. Not even in the tabernacle where I am present in the form of the small holy wafer. Visit

---

[336] "L' Osservatore Romano", No. 19, May 12, 2000, p. 7.
[337] "Kurzbericht Marpingen", No. 8, p. 1. (short account of Marpingen).
[338] Ibid. p. 1.
[339] See "L' Osservatorre Romano", May 12, 2000, p. 7.

me in the church often, *pray in front of my prison* where I endure out of love for you".³⁴⁰

Then the repetition of "Mary's" speeches from 5. Sept. 1999 follows: "Visit my son in the church! Receive the sacraments! Be faithful to the pope! Confess your sins! I implore you all today. I do not ask you, I implore you today: Help me! Help me, it is time now! I am in a hurry, *I have no time left! It is so late*".³⁴¹ In these messages, "Mary" and her "Jesus" now appear frequently together, and not only on the altars as hypostases. "Mary's" threats, that "Jesus" will send his judgment on "his children", follow. This can be "diminished, postponed, and withheld" through Rosary prayers.³⁴² Then this "Jesus" announces himself again very sweetly — in deceptive "compassion" with the following words:

"My judgment consists in the fact that you see that you have not loved the love enough."³⁴³

"My mother leads all people to Me. Only through her Immaculate Heart [Comp. Fatima, the author] can you reach Me".³⁴⁴ With this Catholic, antichristian doctrine, this "Jesus" misleads furthermore by demanding, "The worship of My Heart is a way to Me. Another way is the worship of the Immaculate Heart of My Mother" [Comp. Fatima, the author]. "At the same time, I want the triumph, My triumph to be celebrated in the Holy Eucharist".³⁴⁵ One asks oneself, why a "double-admiration" of the "divine Immaculate Heart of Mary" and the "Heart of Jesus" has to occur? The Babylon Harlot does not accomplish the preparation for the appearance of the Antichrist alone anymore. Lucifer works now with his powers of death — primarily with the male sin powers — symbiotically together with the Queen of Heaven in our days. The self proclaimed "Queen of Peace" mediates the powers of sin for the coming Antichrist together with the "Redeemer for Death", Lucifer, who has disguised himself as "Jesus". The message out of the antichristian spirit is: "Before there can be peace in the world, peace has to come to individual

---

340 "Kurzbericht Marpingen", No. 9, p. 2. (short account of Marpingen).
341 Ibid. p. 2.
342 Ibid. p. 2.
343 Ibid. p. 2.
344 Ibid. p. 2.
345 Ibid. p. 2.

countries first, and this peace comes with the triumph of my Immaculate Heart [Comp. Fatima, the author]".[346]

We experience worldwide: attempts to revive old ethnicities, in order to force with violence a pseudo-peace via national ethnocentrism. This separation, or apartheid, is an ethnocentric spirit segregation (Holy Earth). The objective is to arouse and revive a singular mind in order to present the ethnicities to the god of this world in their original strength. Every strengthened and revived ethnicity will be presented then like a sacrificial gift to the coming Antichrist as a power and death resource.

Image 20:
Medjugorje

The preparations of ethnic cleansing have their place here. Examples are the Balkans, the Basque region, Ireland, etc. Therefore, "Mary" has been troubled constantly in these ethnic regions. We remind ourselves of the Madonna of Medjugorje in Herzegovina (the Balkans). She was active as the "assistant" of Fatima in order to "reconcile" the ethnic groups of Catholic Croatians, Orthodox Serbians, and Islamic Bosnians – after ethnic revival had happened. The Madonna wanted to become the mistress of all three religions in this part of Europe. This pilot project collapsed finally in the year 2002, so that the universal world peace which was supposed to begin failed to materialize. This necessitated the multiple "world consecrations" to the "Immaculate Heart" of Mary by Pope John Paul II, who called himself the deputy of God and has even received the "divine" title of "The mild Christ on earth".

When the same old monthly admonitions were repeated again and again during appearances and when the appearances finally ceased altogether, most of the congregations in Medjugorge broke up. Then, when the cosmic powers failed to appear, even Benedict XVI thought it opportune to question the authenticity of this Madonna. See chapter VI.

---

346 Ibid. p. 2.

10. The eschatological-antichristian character of the pope and the finished role of the past president of the former USSR, Gorbachev

This deceptive Catholic autocrat out of the spirit of the Antichrist, who served devotedly the Babylon Harlot, was the most blasphemous and aggressive pope of modern times. Accordingly, at the beginning of 2001 Pope John Paul II used his absolute authority, to which divine claims were attached, to make himself untouchable like an absolute medieval sovereign by establishing "The new constitution of the Vatican State". This "constitution" came from the area of responsibility of the present Pope Benedict XVI. The "L'Osservatore Romano", No. 8, 23rd. Feb. 2001, introduces this with the words: "... the Pope has promulgated the following law out of his own initiative and with certainty of knowledge in full possession of His highest authority." It is hard for us Christians and also for people of our time to believe what is stated straight away in article 1,1: "The Pope possesses as the supreme head of the Vatican State the fulness of the legislative, executive, and judicial power."

This absolutism, that this pope confirmed and manifested, is the mirror image of the Marian authority over the Roman Church, and a foretaste of the absolute dictatorship of the coming Antichrist which Rome will also influence. Whoever encountered this pope exposed himself to the demonic – transcendental power of Lucifer and of the Babylon Harlot. Martin Luther would say that one has met the Antichrist.

"*I saw a woman* [Babylon Harlot, the author] *sitting on a scarlet beast* [Satan incarnate in the Antichrist, the author] *that was covered with blasphemous names* ..."(Rev. 17: 3).

As the multi collector of all spirit-sin powers from all religions and esoteric cults, the pope was able to incarnate with the eschatological Roman antichristian spirit in the former Soviet president Gorbachev. So he spoke in a new "consciousness" – or in trance like an automaton? – as the voice of the Lord, for the pope. One can see how this Ecumenical collector pope overcame his former anti-religious enemies with demonic manipulatable power in order to create a European Union in the spirit of the Babylon Harlot and of Lucifer. Gorbachev did not want to abolish communism, but he wanted to revive the spirit of Leninism, as he expressed in his books in the mid 1980's. Through the Leninist "spirit-revival, communism, which had been suffering from a lack of efficiency, was supposed to be revived. He viewed himself as a reformer of Soviet communism and not as it's conqueror. What was new was the openness in which people talked about socialist freedom or non-freedom. This was related to the Russian terms 'glasnost' and 'perestroika'. No other politics, like anti-socialist, or anti-Soviet, were intended, to put a democratic parliamentary democracy in its place. The goal was, that paralyzed Soviet communism rethought its "spiritual" mind roots. In essence it meant this: Gorbachev wanted to move the spirit of Leninism to new, i. e., spiritual power through the practice of occult magic methods. He was obsessed by the demonically inspired Ecumenical idea, that all religions and other philosophical movements have the same roots. "Being different" consisted of the insight, that atheistic communism, which denies the transcendent, should acknowledge its transcendental − esoteric roots again. Because this had been forgotten in Soviet socialism, the demonic death forces were not "nourished" sufficiently, so that the whole Soviet edifice was paralyzed and powerless. Gorbachev had relatively few followers in the Kremlin. He was fascinated, how Pope John Paul II, who had been in office since 1978, played the esoteric spiritual card, and how he brought the paralyzed roots of the Roman Church to new vitality through consecrations, i. e., ritualistic witchcraft, which precipitated especially in Mariology. The concerted ecumenical-spiritual understanding was that Gorbachev wanted to learn from the pope without, however, being dominated by him. But the pope used this spiritual deficit skillfully and overpowered not only Gorbachev, but the whole of Soviet communism through the Marian power of the Babylon Harlot. Now both of them had the same global objective: "The building of the European house", the unification of West and East Rome, in order to get to the third phase of unification according to Daniel 7: 23. So the eschatological kingdom of the Antichrist would become a reality via the next step of the unified world government. If the God of the Bible in Jesus Christ had permitted that this time table be taken out of His hand, then Gorbachev would have been elected as president of a world government, even by the European West, in these years after "Assisi"(1986). And the pope?

He would have been the most important religious power component as the incognito forgery of John the Baptist, as forerunner, collector, and coordinator of all death -forces for the prepared Antichrist. But the Lord Jesus is the LORD of world history. He puts up and he puts down. Among the nations, Germany played a special role – yet again – for the antichristian spirit. The political reunification of Germany was supposed to be a symbol for the unification of west and east. Gorbachev's and the pope's failure did not occur through the mistakes they had made, because the political-religious deception was diabolically ingenious. But God in Jesus Christ will determine the countdown, i. e., the point of time when the world government (Dan. 7: 23), the union of the ten (Dan 7: 24) and the absolute dictatorship of the Antichrist (Dan. 7: 25) come as a judgment over humanity. Christ will also determine this man which the Bible characteristically calls the BEAST.

Thus it is also not surprising, that after more than ten years of political failure, Gorbachev gave an interview to the Vatican, in which he, as a conquered one, like a slave, gives honour to the pope through his confessing statements. The pope also needs these honours at the end of his failed journey. Neither his Mary could (was permitted to) confirm him by extraordinary signs and miracles as a precursor of the (Anti) Christ, nor did he accomplish the unification of religions as a precondition of political union.

We will now turn to this interview of July 12, 2000.[347] Gorbachev: "There would not be any "Perestroika" without the spiritual Christian dimension [he means the Catholic dimension, the author]".

Gorbachev mentions that Pope John Paul II had an important influence on his life and his decisions. He stated that he had become closer to the pope step by step. The path toward this seems to have been unification and the targeted world government. Gorbachev was very impressed by the example which the pope used. "Europe", John Paul II said during the time of the Cold War, "has to breath again with both sides of the lung – the eastern and the western parts. This epoch-making intuition has given important affairs a decisive turn. Even to my life. It was a spiritual intuition, but spirituality is really true politics in the highest sense of the word". He mentioned the fall of the Berlin Wall: "... and I also believe that everything, beginning

---

347 "L'Osservatore Romano", No. 30, July 28, 2000, p. 6.

with the fall of the wall, would not have been possible without the enormous spiritual power of Christianity (...). The problem of man exists in man himself, and one can find the solution for this only in the heart of man. This is, as it appears to me, John Paul II's great lesson. He testifies that God is in the heart of man". This shows first of all, that this statement originates in the spirit of the mysticism of all cultures. The god, who lives in the hearts of all unredeemed people, is Lucifer, the god of this world. In this respect, all the antichristian spirits of our day and age agree. Therefore, Gorbachev can even say, "This message speaks to non believers as well."

So the Christian (Catholic) ideas of Gorbachev are always present in his work. However, he never refers to the doctrine of the Roman Church, nor does he give any Biblical references. He refers only, and exclusively to the statements and the "testimony" of the pope. In dealing with the theme "House of Europe", Gorbachev opines, "You can't simply ignore Christianity" [Roman Church, the author].

Then Gorbachev again displays a devout attitude, "There is no voice which reminds us more strongly and more authoritatively than that of the pope (...) Europe – I repeat the words of the pope – has to breath with both sides of the lung again. It has to rediscover the testimony of its great personality, whose action was inspired by faith."

He desires a Europe that is truly "free" without giving an explanation. Free of what – and free for whom? Then he speaks like the government spokesman of the Vatican, "Politics in Europe without a relationship to the culture and ethics can not have success ...".

However, Catholic culture and Catholic ethics have brought more bondage and persecution in European history (e.g. of Jews and of Protestants) than freedom and human dignity. Only someone who has never read a book about European history, who was forced by the Catholic spirit to offer praise, or who perhaps was bought with money, could be as ignorant as Gorbachev.

Finally this "interview" ends with his statement, that there are people, who think deeper than others. "John Paul II also belonged to these people".

Chapter VI

The Pontificate of Pope Benedict XVI.

What kind of person then is Pope Benedict XVI as a successor of the most successful pope of modern times, John Paul II? With what kind of tactics and politics does he rule the world church since April of 2005? Before we grapple with him and his office, we have to say this in advance:

The present pope cannot go back behind the basic statements of his predecessors.

And this pope does not even want to. By orders of John Paul II, Cardinal Ratzinger, now Pope Benedict XVI, had framed in unity with his predecessor most of the binding policies anyway and published them for all Catholics in the "L'Osservatore Romano". Benedict XVI expresses this unity beyond death in the "L'Osservatore Romano" of May, 21-26, 2006, No. 21, p. 1 by adding a request to the greetings addressed to the pilgrims of Poland, "to pray with the whole church of Poland, so that we strengthen each other with the help of the grace of God in testifying for the faith. The servant of God, John Paul II, accompanies us." Benedict XVI needs the spiritual guidance of his deceased predecessor and counts on it. In order to discern the continuity of spirit with his predecessor, we relate two events, that Benedict XVI held and which demonstrate that he is actually the immanent arm of the deceased pope. A change of emphasis to different points can only occur because of the enormous loss of spiritual power. Government can then no longer continue as before. We will say more about this later. The first two happenings with large scale events under the rule of Benedict XVI were:
- The World Youth Event of August 2005 in Cologne, Germany
- The visit to Poland in May of 2006.

1. World Youth Event with Pope Benedict XVI in Cologne in August of 2005.

The pope tried to stir the youth to engage in a worldwide Catholic revival, just as his predecessor had done successfully. However,

Chapter VI: The Pontificate of Pope Benedict XVI

Benedict XVI did not succeed in effecting new impulses. He was holding intellectual but dry speeches like a man who has to administer the inheritance of his deceased predecessor. He lacked the mental power for a new breakthrough characteristic of him. Therefore, at least 1,000 young pilgrims with their national flags left the lawns of the "Plains of Mary" close to Cologne before the celebration of the mass. If one listened to the reports of the media, Benedict XVI's appearance was a great success. The German media are only interested in one thing: this man managed, just like his predecessor, to attract 1 million visitors to the main event. This was success for the secular world. We wrote a journal about the events and the observations we made as spectators right on the spot during the whole world youth event. It reads like this: "The pope appears to be a powerful teacher during his preaching, who stands up for his theology. He lectured like a professor in an auditorium. He looked however, powerless as a Pontifex Maximus, who supposedly is in control of an unimaginable army of transcendent spirit forces. Also what was missing was the booster effect of emotional eruption. Therefore, unlike his predecessor, he could not ignite the spiritual kick that the youths were waiting for."

The difference to his predecessor could also be seen in the fact that Benedict XVI did not emphasize primarily the power of Mary for a Catholic revival, but the spirit power of the Eucharistic Christ. Instead of the former Marian articles in the "L'Osservatore Romano", now articles about the new center of Catholic faith appeared exclusively: The Eucharist. He wants to liberate the administration of the Eucharist "from the shadow of the fellowship experience with the pastor." So he explained that he had come to the youths, "in order to kneel with you in front of the white consecrated (deified) host, to realize with the eyes of faith the real presence of the Redeemer of the world."

World change, as he wants it, would only be realized through continuous participation in the Eucharist, which is the adequate source of power for world change. The Eucharist is meant to be the Catholic source of life. It is because of the loss of power of the Catholic mediatrix of cosmic forces, Mary, that this pope reverts back to the original Catholic element of the Counter Reformation, the Eucharist. So his goal was primarily to motivate the visitors to participate regularly in taking the Eucharist. Whereas his predecessor activated the Marian death forces during his pontificate until his defeat, Benedict XVI banks on the "life force" of the cosmic Eucharistic Christ. In this way, many protestants will be deceived to believe, that this pope is more "protestant" than his predecessor. He will blur the irreconcilable differences between the Eucharist and the Lord's Supper. Most of the Protestant churches, desire fellowship at the Lord's Supper with Catholics. The pope, however, does not want fellowship at the Lord's Supper, but eucharistic fellowship. This pre-supposes Catholic faith in the consecration (deification) of the host and the wine. As long as the Protestants do not confess this faith, there cannot be fellowship among Catholics and Protestants. In this respect this pope is more Catholic and more anti-ecumenical than his predecessor. Unification with the Catholic Church, according to Benedict XVI, will only materialize via unification with the Eucharistic Christ through the eucharistic sacrifice. This demand is nothing less than betrayal of the gospel and of Jesus Christ.

So Benedict XVI uses seductively and increasingly terms of the New Testament. Nobody in the Protestant camp seems to test the source, although the Catholic source for understanding the New Testament is the main sacrament of all sacraments, the Eucharist. Consequently, words from the Bible are transformed into magical faithfulness to the Bible. Many protestants are satisfied with energetic action which originates in Biblical morals, in order to recognize the pope as one of their own. However, he says so many obviously wrong things. He did so in the sermon at the WYE too, e.g.: "Jesus came to restore the order of the world."

Jesus as a religious fundamentalist with a program for a new world order? Basically it sounds like this: "The faith is not completed, until one encounters him, who has the power to establish that universal kingdom of righteousness and peace that people strive for, but are never able to achieve on their own."

People strive for peace in a universal kingdom without Christ. So they will meet him, who has the power to realize their sinful wishes: the Antichrist.

The pilgrims were furthermore provoked and deceived with the pronouncement that "they should seek out someone, who is not deceived himself and can not deceive, and who is then able to offer a security, that is so unshakable that one can live by it, and eventually even be able to die for it." Who is that someone? Does the pope refer to himself, the cosmic Christ, or the expected teacher of the world, whom the Bible calls Antichrist?

Another deception happened in his sermon: "Christ does not take anything away from the beauty and greatness you have in yourself".

What is beautiful and great in an unredeemed man, who has trouble finding his own identity? The young Catholics shall devote themselves "unreservedly to serving Christ, no matter what it costs", because of the relativization of Catholic morals. For this purpose, according to the pope, they shall devote themselves to the relics of the Three Holy Kings (the shrine is in the Cologne Cathedral). "These relics lead you to God." This is, presumedly, the god of this world and his death which the pilgrims then absorb when they carry out this command.

And furthermore: "Only from the relics of the saints, only from God comes the revolution, the radical change of the world." About the worth of the relics of the Three Holy Kings he says, "Do not forget, that these bones belong to people, who were permeated by the transcendent power of God. The relics of the saints are traces of that invisible but real presence, which lightens up the darkness, which makes the kingdom of God that is in us visible." We can recognize the emphases of Benedict XVI:

- The revival for the Eucharist to unite the believers with the Cosmic Christ and to change them (transform) as well as to unite them with each other through networking.
- Veneration of saints via statues and icons and their relics because "this veneration leads to God."
- "Love for Holy Scriptures."

At first one is amazed. Then the lie becomes obvious: One only discovers the truth of the Scriptures "via the catechism of the Catholic church and the compendium of the catechism." In both of these basic books it is explained how to understand the Bible. With this the Roman Church controls Holy Scriptures.

In conclusion, we report an interview, which cardinal Meisner gave to the news magazine "Der Spiegel". Only those passages will be reported which show how Rome is connected with spiritism. This cardinal said that he was devastated when Pope John Paul II died. However, he was comforted in front of the laid out body, when the deceased pope suddenly spoke to him. He said "You should actually know this. When saints are in heaven, they participate in the unlimited possibilities of God." According to Meisner's intuition Ratzinger would be voted the new pope at the next election as he regarded Ratzinger as a symbiosis to the late pope. He then appealed to the deceased Pope with the words, "Papa Woityla, do something so that he becomes your successor." According to the report of the Spiegel magazine, Meisner also asked the spirit of the deceased, "Why do you want to have the World Youth Event in Germany?" The pope's spirit answered: "In the 20th century both world catastrophes originated in Germany. I want a positive movement to come out of Germany at the beginning of the 21st century." This spirit has a universal revival in mind. The US-American Cunningham and the Korean Dr. Cho had transmitted the demonically inspired privileges to the Protestants in the 1990's. The worldwide charismatic movement adopted this counterfeit prophecy and represented it demagogically. This came to a climax in the "Toronto-Revival". After God had used judgment against some of the major false charismatic prophets and exposed this movement through its demise as a demonically inspired movement, the Cosmic Christ now tries it with the Catholics. As critical observers of the WYE, we noticed, that this rally under the leadership of Benedict XVI did not reach its goal of a huge pseudo-spiritual revival. Many genuine believers had taken up spiritual warfare against this fraud, which was then confirmed by God in Jesus Christ. According to the expectations of the leadership of the WYE, this event was supposed to be ignited by the spirit-powers of both popes. At the beginning of the event Cardinal Meisner expressed this with the following words: "We celebrate this first WYE with two popes: With Pope John Paul II from Heaven, and with our Pope Benedict XVI from the earth." Since then one has been able to purchase pictures in Poland, on which both popes are portrayed: Benedict XVI on earth, and John Paul II in the air as a spirit represented by a dove.

2. Benedict XVI visit to Poland in May 2006

Benedict XVI wanted to use this visit to connect up with the late pope and his legacy in order to shape the Polish Catholics into the most active European Catholics. The conservative Catholics, militantly Marian, regard themselves as a messianic nation anyway, because of their historic sufferings. The Catholic people represent the suffering Christ through the late pope and should not be criticized, but have the right to be loved and honored. This perspective was transmitted primarily by the late pope to the Polish Marians. Even now these Catholics call him affectionately John Paul II the Great; they will not rest until this title has become official.

Catholic Poland as the vanguard of the anticipated Christian-Catholic Europe?

This fits in with the fact that the German Pope Benedict XVI during his visit to Warsaw also visited the Basilica of John. This was to win over Catholics who believe in symbols and myths. After the national constitution was ratified in Lublin, Poland in 1793, a thanksgiving mass to celebrate it took place in the Warsaw Basilica. This national constitution was the first democratic constitution in Europe after the French Revolution of 1789. It was compiled with much pride, because of the victory over the monarchic European nations. This constitution was far ahead of its time in Europe. The superpowers at the time, Prussia, which developed 77 years later into the 2nd German empire, Austria, and czarist Russia felt that their monarchies were threatened by revolution, and they started to break up Poland and divide it among themselves. This third division lasted till 1918. All European monarchies perceived this democratic way as a declaration of war against the monarchic state order. The bourgeois ideals of the French Revolution had to be destroyed according to their perception of things. Therefore, even until today this Cathedral of John is important for the new democratic Poland, which now belongs to the EU. It has always been part and parcel of Polish history, that politics are secured, even legitimized by the Catholic-Marian religion. Now Benedict XVI "prayed" in this church for "revival" of these transcendent historic powers. Was this meant to be a Catholic help for the rejected European constitution which sees itself closer to humanistic enlightenment than the ideals of the Catholic Church? The Catholics are grateful to Benedict XVI for the sensitivity that he showed as a pope from Germany for their historic symbolism, and they expected from him the corresponding papally authorized transcendent cosmic power. Benedict XVI also held a sermon on Pilsudski Square with a mass afterward. What the Catholics had not expected and were not used to from their former Polish pope was the following: with harsh words, Benedict XVI called on the Polish Catholics for a radical change, because "the un-Catholic life style of the Polish people reflects itself in the state of the church." He seems to have in mind the moral decadence of the Roman believers, who have faith only in their heads, and the Catholics who live worldly and according to the spirit of the day. The youth too, upon which the Polish pope had put his hope, is today far from being a vanguard of the planned Catholic Europe. However, the ones present did not want to hear any criticism. They were deeply disappointed because they had hoped that Benedict XVI would impart to them emotional sentiments and memories of John Paul II. It was surely a surprise that at the reception of Benedict XVI all the favourite songs of his predecessor were sung. Even the shouts were the same: "We love you; stay with us." The Polish magazine "Newsweek Polska" on June 4th 2006 commented: "One sensed the constant presence of John Paul II at all events and appearances of Benedict XVI." Even in speeches of government representatives it was reported, that Benedict XVI was a special guest "because he reminded us of John Paul II." Does the expectation of the Catholics consist only in this, that Benedict XVI has only his significance as a reincarnation of John Paul II? Indeed, according to a representative survey, 80% of Poles expect, that Benedict XVI speaks Polish as much as possible and that he refers in his speeches to John Paul II. If the German pope does not adopt this role to be just a mouthpiece of John Paul II, the veneration for him is finished. The question arises whether Benedict XVI, as an intellectual, will tolerate such humiliation to be merely the mouthpiece of the spirit of John Paul II? Should he accept this role as a "humble worker in God's vineyard" voluntarily, or compulsory, then John Paul II would not only be elevated to the position of saint, but to the position of

Chapter VI: The Pontificate of Pope Benedict XVI

Christ himself by the Polish Catholics. What was also remarkable about this speech on the Pilsudski Square, was that Benedict XVI. always received frenzied applause when he appealed to his predecessor. The name John Paul II alone ignited enthusiastic shouts.

In order to rid himself of this criticism by the Polish church in this emotional chaos, Benedict XVI strove for rational objectivity. He accused the church, of the bishops not having a transparent spiritual program. Their whole accomplishment consisted in their having prepared the meeting with the pope well. While the bishops were being accused of inactivity the priests especially, applauded. Right after the critical speech the priests rushed like juvenile fans to the podium of the pope. Everyone wanted to touch him, to get eye contact with him, and receive his blessing. Now Benedict XVI smiled and spoke gently to them.

The pope accepted an invitation from the Protestants in Warsaw for a dialogue in the Trinity Church. All Protestants, whether they belong to the traditional churches, or free churches, are all in the same discriminating situation. For it still counts to be both Polish and Catholic.

Basically, the Protestant Poles are badly treated like a foreign minority. They are referred to as the "Germans", because one presupposes, that Germany is a Protestant country. During the meeting in the church the Protestants reported to the pope cases where they were discriminated against by the Catholics. In rural areas for instance, Protestant children experience tremendous pressure to participate in the Catholic mass. The children as well as the adults complain that they are regarded "as something inferior". In mixed marriages, the engaged couple has to promise before marriage to submit their future children to Catholic baptism and Catholic upbringing. Or, under massive pressure, Catholic baptisms are forced upon non-Catholic spouses. The Protestants complain that through the Catholic populist government, which ruled till 2008, much hatred was planted. The government of these years was Marian based and therefore antisemitic and anti-protestant.

We do not know and we do not believe that the Protestants found an open ear, or that in the future they can count on more fairness. Of course, the pope travelled to the foundation of the Polish Catholic

Chapter VI: The Pontificate of Pope Benedict XVI

culture identity to Czestochowa, in order to worship the transcendent cosmic guardian of the Polish nation, the Black Madonna.

Then Benedict XVI flew from Warsaw into the old royal city of Krakow. There he challenged the approximately 600,000 young people: "Do not let those mislead you who oppose the Christ of the church." That was the hammer blow that is worrisome to all protestants. The Bible becomes acceptable when the Catholics have the Bible interpreted by the tradition of the church. Therefore, the order is first the church, then the Bible. The same thing happens with faith in Jesus Christ. The way to the savior leads through Mary to Christ. The Bible and the personified Word of God, Jesus Christ, have to tolerate, that the church and the "Mother of the Church", Mary control them. In this way no one can come to Jesus Christ and to his word. Another Christ, an antichristian spirit will rule with the misused name Jesus Christ. However, the truth is this: Jesus Christ controls through His Word the church and interprets the Bible to the church, the body of Christ. By so doing, His Word tells us how to receive life for eternity. Christ is the Lord, but not the church. So the old Roman lie becomes transparent through the new pope, i.e., that the tradition of the church and not the Word of God interprets the truth. According to the report of "Newsweek Polska", the pope did not conceal, that he only spoke to the "Catholics of deeper faith, out of which he will grow the vanguard of new evangelization for the European crusade. This should take Christianity back again to all Europeans and to all European institutions." Part of this Catholic Christianity is of course to remove decision making from the believer and to bring him under the control and manipulation of the Catholic Church. The world has learned this from all other totalitarian movements.

Benedict XVI visited the place of worship of the "Compassionate Jesus" in Krakow to renew the lost cosmic powers through ritual witchcraft, which is called "prayer". We have reported extensively about this important place of worship already. On the way to the birth place of his predecessor John Paul II, the Upper Silesian Wadowice, the pope also visited the Counter-Reformational bulwark of Kalvaria. We are still amazed that the responsible Protestants ignore the symbolic language of the pope. In Wadowice everything turned around John Paul II, the Great. Benedict XVI fulfilled the desire of the Catholics for the super elevated "greatness", divine greatness, of John Paul II. This idol worship was not only disgusting to us as critics of Roman Catholicism, but to others as well. The importance of the spirit guide through John Paul II remains unbroken even after his death. Will the successor Benedict XVI receive his very own significance from the church people? He makes an attempt with his first quasi-declaration of government, the encyclical with his signature, which has the name: "Deus Caritas Est". This encyclical was published, and therefore became binding, in the first year of his pontificate on 25.Dec. 2005.

3. The Encyclical "Deus Caritas Est" of PopeBenedict XVI.
(www.vatican.va/holy_father/BenedictXVI/encyclicals/document)

Eros vs. Agape

Benedict XVI sends this encyclical to the hierarchy of the Roman Church. It is a binding circulation letter of the pope for the hierarchy. It affects decisively the ecclesiastical, social, and political development of the Roman Church. Therefore, it is a decision about orientation accompanied by papal teaching authority through interpretation by the officiating pope. This writing is about the love of God and love of one's neighbor.

Benedict XVI writes, that the Greeks gave the name "eros" to the word love for the love between husband and wife. He is right in so far as saying, that in the New Testament (NT) the word "eros" does not even come up, but that the word "agape" is used for love. Furthermore, the word "philia" appears in the NT, which expresses the love of friendship, e.g., between Jesus and his disciples. It has been determined correctly, that "eros" as a term for love is not used in the NT, because "agape" as spiritual love — the love from the Spirit of God — is the new content of the Gospel of grace. In spite if this, Benedict XVI continues to use the word "eros". He wants to purify "eros". He gives a simple reason, "that "love" (he means "eros", by the author) is somehow connected to the divine. I have shown, that on the way of everyday life it is not easy to get to the greater thing, the eternal through the eros, because of it's overpowering strength. Purification and maturation are necessary, which also lead across the path of abstinence. This does not mean saying farewell to "eros", it is not its poisoning — as Friedrich Nietzsche has it — but it's healing to it's true greatness." Benedict XVI uses "eros" synonymously with "agape", as far as "eros" is purified from it's natural impulses.

Related to this, Huntemann says the following in his "Biblisches Ethos im Zeitalter der Moralrevolution" (Biblical Ethics in the Age of Moral Revolution) Haenssler Publ., 1999, p. 172+: "The original kerygma (proclamation) was changed by the so called church fathers from the 2nd century. This happened through separation from Judaism. In this way, the early church was virtually stripped of its topsoil. The Hellenistic foreign infiltration got into the early church through the separation from Judaism and the immersion into the pagan world with its terms and experiences. Instead of salvation and reconciliation through participation in the cross and resurrection of Christ, that really affects one's whole existence, a sacramental-mystical teaching of salvation takes the place of this existential process." Through participation in the "flesh substance" of the Eucharist, immortality would be magically transmitted so to speak.

Concerning this topic, Werner says in his book "Dogma", quoted by Huntemann: "Salvation according to Rome consists of being saved from the death of the flesh, because the flesh became mortal. Therefore the flesh should be revived again from it's mortality through redemption." Already the church father Tertullian (around 220) says that the flesh of man became spoiled, therefore the flesh of the savior had to be holy or spiritual (comp. ch. IV). According to Huntemann, Rome is propagating here a physical dogma of salvation. The Catholic believer becomes gradually "deified" by eating the sacramental flesh of Jesus. The dogma of salvation turns into a dogma of deification. The Roman system lives by this Hellenistic foreign infiltration, or better said alienation, with the pope at the top as the supreme bridge builder (Pontifex Maximus) between the earthly people and the Greek mountain of the gods, Olympus. Pontifex Maximus originally comes from the Babylon: bab-ilani, and is called there: Gate of the gods. So the pope judges from the Olympus.

He long ago abandoned the hill of Calvary on which the salvation of mankind was accomplished by Jesus Christ, because of man's fatal sin (missing the mark). Therefore, it is simple logic, that Benedict XVI has to stand for the dichotomy of man (duality). He says, that "the challenge of the eros has been met, when body and soul have returned to inner unity." Concerning this topic, it is historically remarkable, that under the early rule of Pope Nicholas I the Great, who ruled from 858-867, a dispute erupted about the emerging doubts concerning the trinity of God. During this Carolingian time the understanding of the relationship of the Holy Spirit to the Father and to the Son was the issue. However, this also influenced the understanding of the creation of man. In 869 at the Council of Constantinopel the trichotomy (trinity of man) was abolished. During this time, the patriarch of Constantinopel, Photios, was deposed by Nicholas I. In this way, the church of the west gained more power over the church of the east. So with the doubt about the Trinity of God, the creation of man as a trinity was also changed. This Biblical trinity of man means that man consists of body, spirit, and soul, and that each part with its particular gifts has to contribute to the wholeness of the image of God.

According to the church one was only allowed to believe that man consisted of a duality (dichotomy) of body and soul. Characteristics of the spirit, e.g., transcendent characteristics, were reinterpreted as psychological characteristics. How will the believer then worship God in spirit and in truth, as in John 4: 23, if the spirit of man does not exist? However, the NT states clearly, that we have been chosen, and our spirit was sanctified in the faith of the truth (2 Thess. 2: 13). The word of truth separates the soul from the spirit and from the body (Hebr. 4: 12). This presupposes a trinity (trichotomy). It is also presupposed, that the whole man is in darkness and needs further purification (sanctification) — even after his redemption (1 Thess. 4: 3). The NT demands separation of spirit and flesh. Even the soul belongs to the flesh according to Biblical understanding. This separation is necessary to make action possible that comes out of the redeemed spirit. Life out of the Spirit is called "spiritual".

Rome, however, wants to harmonize instead of separate, and to make "pious flesh" out of body and soul (comp. chapt. III.). Such a species of "God-man", of a 'transformed' man, will be open for "supernatural" powers, i.e., demonic spirits, which control the magical believer with incoming "perceptions". But precisely this is aimed against the NT, the Spirit of Jesus. "For if you are living according to the flesh, you must die; but if by the Spirit you are putting to death the deeds of the body, you will live." (Rom. 8: 13). The redeemed spirit of man (the inner man, also called new man) becomes a created tool of the Holy Spirit. "For the mind set on the flesh is death, but the mind set on the Spirit is life and peace, because the mind set on the flesh is hostile toward God; for it does not subject itself to the law of God (the law of the Spirit of life, Rom. 8: 2) for it is not even able to do so." (Rom. 8: 6-7).

Now Benedict XVI has to stand up for the dichotomy (dualism). He can so talk about the holiness of the flesh. He continues to say in his encyclical, that agape and eros (flesh) have to become a unity (harmonization). "Only in the actual unification of both, does man become totally himself. Only then can eros mature to its true greatness."

Spirit and soul/body are used by Benedict XVI synonymously after the accomplished piety of the flesh. He does not acknowledge "agape' as the only divine love! But it says in the NT according to 1 John 4: 7, 8: He who loves out of agape is born of God (born again, saved) and knows God! To get true agape love, however, man has to be born again, i.e., he has to have a resurrected spirit, which is also called new man, or inner man, in whom the Holy Spirit, the Spirit of Christ, dwells and works. (Rom. 8: 9, 14). These facts of the NT are blurred by the papally ordered decree of the human spirit being merged in the soul. Nicholas I initiated this in the first Holy Roman Empire in the year 869. But the NT wants first of all separation (Hebr. 4: 12) of soul (in which "eros' is active) and spirit, in order to purify them separately. This includes the redeemed human spirit (2 Thess. 2: 13) in which the Holy Spirit dwells and performs (Rom. 8: 15). The "sacramental-mystical salvation doctrine" (Huntemann) is based on the power of the flesh, and is therefore enmity against the salvation of Jesus from the power of sin of the flesh. In this way, Benedict XVI can harmonize "agape" and "eros". According to the pope, only the purification of the "eros" from the physical impulses is necessary. Benedict XVI: "Love (eros) is ecstasy, but not in the sense

Chapter VI: The Pontificate of Pope Benedict XVI

of the intoxicating moment, but ecstasy as a persistent way out of the self-imprisoned ego into the liberation of the ego to devotion and so to the finding of oneself, yes, the finding of God." According to Benedict XVI, this is the way up from the carnal motivated "eros" to a "deified pure" eros. In the same way, temple prostitution in Hellenism was handled as deification of eros because it was purified. The truth is, that through the unity of the sinning flesh, demonic forces of death were set free, which served the religious system as transcendental power sources. This holds also true for the celibacy. Abstention "from being overpowered by drive" is supposed to bring the "eros" into contact with God, because abstention is holy. Erotic, physical vitality is in reality drained from the celibates, transformed, and channeled into the system as a cultural power. Rome is interested in the exploitation of vitality, which is either generated by powers of sin, or through denial of life (comp. Rev. 18: 13). The first happens through Rome in secret, e. g., via the courtesans' army, the second as a Christian virtue of purity as a maneuver of deception for the public and secured in the sacrament of the priests. Also the "Mother of the Church", the Catholic Mary, perceives her power over the men of the church strengthened when they confirm faithfulness to their "Mother" primarily by celibacy. Coming to the point, it means: Rome demands of its cult servants that they free themselves from the huge amount of 'sexus', which is contained in the "eros". If they manage the change (transformation) then they are holy and serve the living "God" with this "eros". We recognize easily the rebellion against God in this. They want to make the flesh holy, so that it serves God. God tells us through the word of Holy Scriptures that the flesh is and remains sinful, and eventually it can be purified only through our inevitable death in the framework of the first resurrection (Phil. 3: 11; Rev. 20: 6). We can serve God only in our spirit (spiritual). The flesh has to be under the control of the Spirit through discipline (Hebr. 12: 1-11). Benedict XVI calls the "part" of love, which is based on faith, "agape", while "eros" is the representation of worldly love. It is comprehensive and not only giving like "agape". "Man cannot give all the time, he has to receive too." Therefore the giving and receiving love has turned into "eros".

Benedict XVI: "The fathers saw this indissoluble relationship of ascent and descent of the God seeking 'eros' and the passing on of 'agape' symbolically.

About the God of Israel Benedict XVI says, that he loves his people. "This his love one can surely call "eros", which is at the same time totally 'agape'."

Benedict XVI interprets the agape-love of God, which speaks of the passion for his people, as evidence of his erotic love. However, the "erotic" pictures of the love of man and woman are only parables, spoken into the social environment of the people, but not evidence for God's erotic sensations. According to the pope, the eros of God develops into agape, because God "gives and is forgiving love". So for Benedict XVI the expression of the passionate love "eros" is the forgiving love "agape". In "this way righteousness and love shall be reconciled with each other." He wants to improve "eros" through purification. So "eros" and "agape" melt together. He "reconciles" spirit with flesh, on which the NT puts a "curse" (punishment). For "he who unites himself with the Lord is one with him in spirit."(1 Cor. 6: 17). The Holy Spirit which lives in the redeemed wants to glorify Jesus, the Savior, through the deeds of faith, which will only last, if they originate in the new man, i. e., out of our spirit (1 Cor. 3: 10-16). The final goal of all Scripture-based teaching is love from a pure heart (1 Tim. 1: 5). This love is agape, and only this originates in the divine fountain. Nowhere in the Bible is love split up into giving and receiving love to turn it into eros and agape. The Bible warns against this mixture everywhere.

The old Israel failed at this point, and many believing Christians fail here as well. Benedict XVI takes even a further step out of an antichristian spirit. He says, "that Jesus had anticipated (taken beforehand) his death and resurrection through the Eucharist (although it was actually the Last Supper, the author) by giving himself to the disciples in bread and wine at that hour ..." Why then was the death on the cross necessary? When the Catholic participates in the Eucharist, "Jesus draws us into his act of giving. Through this eucharistic fellowship in receiving his body and blood, unification with Jesus happens." Man loses his life bit by bit, and becomes "divine" according to Catholic interpretation. However, this becoming divine is transcendent demonic in nature.

Chapter VI: The Pontificate of Pope Benedict XVI

Paul tells the Galations as well as us (Gal. 3: 3): "After beginning with the Spirit, do you want to finish now with the flesh?" And in Galatians 5: 17: "For the flesh desires what is contrary to the Spirit, and the Spirit what is contrary to the flesh. They are in conflict with each other, so that you do not do what you want." It is the understanding of the Vatican that the believer becomes united with the "Lord" in Communion (Eucharist) as well as with other Christians. He receives "an existence that is melted together with the others." God's love and neighborly love, agape and eros "now are truly united". Therefore it is understandable, that agape becomes a term for the Eucharist. "God's and neighborly love become indivisible." So far, so good. But to maintain, that through purification of the flesh eros – and not agape – is love in the fullest sense, can only be understood from the perspective of Jesuit dialectics. Benedict XVI harmonizes, i. e., he shifts spiritual matter into the flesh. So the Catholic spirits of error can unfold unrestrained their falsely devoted magic in the flesh of Catholic believers. Satan, the ruler of the cosmos, mixes up indispensable spiritual principles with lies. He assimilates the lie into the truth, so that the truth becomes so obscure through this mixture, that the light expires. A few examples shall illustrate this idea.

Benedict XVI harmonizes by absorption and unification:
- God's love into neighborly love
- agape into eros
- spirit into soul
- judgment into grace
- spiritual inner strength into "Heart Jesus" cult
- prayer into Eucharist
- man as image of God into true humanist
- righteousness into purified reason
- Christ into the sacrament and sacramentaries
- guidance of the Holy Spirit into guidance by Mary, the "Mirror of all Glory"
- death of Jesus on the cross into dedication, to give oneself away, "an act of turning against oneself" (With this, Jesus recants his curse that was on him for the sin of man, the author).

Now, after the analysis of the papal encyclical, we turn to the Lutheran theologian Anders Nygren and to his book "Eros and Agape" (1955, C. Bertelsmann). This professor of theology has "Calvary" as his foundation and rejects the Hellenistic estrangement by means of Biblical theology, just as professor Huntemann does. Nygren reasons in line with the NT, that only agape love is the basic ethical concept of the Christian faith. As a result, all Greek values were reassessed in the time of the NT. Agape love was and is at odds with the Platonic eros-love concept. Early Christianity accomplished this breaking away from the Hellenistic-Platonic eros concept for the first time; and the reformers of the 16th century the second time. According to "Religion in Geschichte und Gegenwart" (1929) (Religion in History and at the Present Time) this is said in theology about the subject of "love" up to the present day, "that it is self-love based on self-esteem, and that it is necessary for the development of a Christian character." According to Nygren, agape-love has been abolished, or it has been mixed so much with other contemporary spiritual values, that it has lost its core. Actually agape and eros have nothing in common. The more Christianity was shaped by the spirit of the Greeks with their gods of Olympus, the more love was filled with the Platonic eros. The other way around, the more the Christian faith was shaped by the Hebrews, i.e., by Calvary, the more the concept of agape-love got into theology and into the church communities. With the eros-concept, one lives according to the "flesh", in line with Romans 7, whereas Romans 8 points to the concept of the Spirit, which is a concept of life, and which has to be practiced by faith with agape-love. In the history of the Christian idea of love, we always meet the mixture of eros with agape, i. e., flesh with Spirit, according to Nygren. Regrettably, also the translation of the NT into the German language does not distinguish between eros-love and agape-love. The Word of God always uses the term agape, when it deals with the theme of "love". Eros and agape are basic attitudes with incompatible outlooks on life. They are so incompatible, that they cannot be harmonized, similarly to flesh and Spirit in the NT which cannot be united. Agape, therefore, is the basic concept of the NT faith of the Spirit. It is the driving force of the Holy Spirit who strives for change of character through the new man and who instructs in this respect. Jesus has reconciled the believer with the Father through his atoning death, so he can present us blameless through transformation as holy (Col. 1: 21-23). The eros-love stands in opposition to this as the driving force of carnal activities. In order to know what originates in the Spirit (agape), or in the flesh (eros), the motive of the one acting has to be explored. The carnal, out of the concept of eros, is always present, when Jesus the Savior is not the goal of all teaching and acting, but man. In this case, the apparent spiritual, beside humanistic mankind, consists of historic dates and Bible references, which are taken all out of context. Nygren names this spiritual atomization, and calls this carnal theology "historical-genetic research". So he wants to classify the two systems through motive research as analysis method. If the motives are compared, one can distinguish, whether Olympus or Calvary rules; so whether the carnal eros, or the NT- spiritual agape is in charge. For this reason, we preach in the whole context of the Bible with the pastoral objective of a deeper faith in Jesus the Savior. Without this goal in mind, proclamation of only particular historical elements of facts about salvation history remains sterile, and leads not to God, but to man, and with this to an idealized eros. In extreme charismatic churches, or mystical churches of other denominations, the carnal eros-concepts are rampant. Therefore, such churches are especially in danger of being assimilated by the Roman Church, because they are in many ways compatible with Rome. Differences of motives become equally visible in the area of "ethics" as well, according to Nygren. The eros ethics of antiquity is individualistic, but the ethics of the Bible is fellowship orientated. The fellowship is the starting point of ethical consideration. When the question about the good comes up, the Bible answers it with fellowship with God and with fellow men. Therefore, agape-love pushes for a "theo-centric faith" and away from an "egocentric faith", which has its roots in eros. Coming to the point, it means: The theo-centric faith asks for the will of God before it acts ethically. This is a sign of agape. However, the egocentric faith uses God for the desires of the ego. So agape is the basic motive and the answer for all faith related and ethical questions. Without agape-love, Biblical faith loses its character. The fellowship orientation is a fruit of the agape-love (Acts 2: 42; 1 Cor. 13).

The starting point of agape-love is God and fellowship with him. While in the Old Testament (OT) the commandment for love was exclusive, Jesus made this commandment a universal requirement. So the commandment of love was fulfilled through Jesus. "Universal" means without limits. People of all ethnicities are included (e.g. Luke 10: 25-37; Matth. 12: 49-50). Faith, which stands on the basis of agape, does not know racism, hatred of foreigners, rejection of the weak, of children, of women, etc. This fellowship of God is agape-love fellowship, and not legal community. We summarize the meaning of agape in four points:

Agape-love is "unmotivated" i. e., it is unconditional, free of ulterior motives. The one, beloved by agape does not produce a reason for being loved. The difference to the legal community consists exactly in this, that love depends on the worth of the object. That would be typical for "eros".

Agape-love is "indifferent to values". God loves the sinner (Rom. 3: 10-12, 23) not because of his sin, but in spite of his sin.

Agape-love is creative. "That, which does not have any worth in itself, receives it's value by becoming an object of divine love. Agape does not state values, but creates them." So the value is a result of agape love. It is a value generating principle.

Agape-love is creating fellowship. There is no way from man to God, but only a way from God to man. This way is agape (Rom. 3: 23; 2 Cor. 5: 18ff.). God himself meets man to offer him his fellowship. The fellowship generating agape prompts him, who has accepted God's agape, to apply the principles of agape in contact with his fellowmen (Mk. 12: 30-31).

Whoever believes this, wants to do the will of God completely. Faith, nourished out of agape, has lost the character of an achievement. The agape-love of one's neighbor has now the same root as the love for God. Therefore it is not motivated like eros. The two elements of love for God and love for one's neighbor shall not be separated. One is the cause for the other.

Eros-love, however, is self-love, and is rejected in the Bible by God, even fought against.

Therefore the Biblical term "sanctification" (purification) has to be devoid of self-love. So the judgment of God is the other side of agape-love. Eschatologically, the final war of the end times, is a total war against the selfish way of life and against the self-assertion of man, which did not want agape and fellowship with God. So we find in the letters of the apostle Paul to the Corinthians God's struggle with the church, which brought eros into the church via the gnosis (knowledge) and established it through a cultivated charismatic faith. The theology of the Roman Church is exactly like this. The result of this was that the Corinthians were mixing up eros with agape, which led the church into syncretism (the mixing up of religions). The syncretism with the gnostic Hellenism made the demarcation through the agape-precept necessary. So it says in the 1st letter to the Corinthians, that knowledge puffs up. This refers to the gnosis and its eros, but agape love is constructive and not puffed up. It is the most precious way to indestructible life (1 Cor. 12: 31).

So Benedict XVI carries on in his encyclical with a Luciferian syncretism. He is inspired by Hellenism and the mountain of the gods, Olympus. From whom then comes the idea, that agape has been overcome by eros – after absorption – so that it was harmonized?

The eros idea started with the Greek philosopher Plato (427-347 B.C.). Plato was first of all a political thinker. He was looking for a just form of government. Through disappointment he established a theocratic police state. He fought greed through overcoming private property. Then he sought the way out in the myth "of the superheavenly place of ideas". The world of myth is the world of the gods. He arrives at the realization, that "the soul is immortal and that death is the beginning of true life". From this starting point, neo-Platonic mysticism, the Roman Church, the Gnosis receive their intellectual tools. Plato's term for love (eros) is supposed to be the overcoming of the mere sensual (earthly). The eros shall develop into an affection of the soul free of lust, a striving for sensual beauty, for philosophical knowledge. He defines eros as "spiritual love free of sex of people of the same mind". Originating with Plato, eros became a world force (enlightenment, humanism, Roman Church, etc.). Plato fought for the liberation of the eros from the mere sensual (sexuality) to elevate it to the transcendent world. This is the

Chapter VI: The Pontificate of Pope Benedict XVI

constant antichristian attempt to manage the advancement of man without God. Eros ascends, according to Plato, through "spiritualization and sublimation up to the celestial eros". The Vatican did not have this Platonic recipe only since the pontificate of Benedict XVI. There is the danger of subversion for agape in Christian churches because both of them look "divine". However, the blending of both precepts leads to apostasy from the true faith which is grounded in Jesus Christ. So even the "celestial eros" is the archenemy of faith and agape. Idealized love is supposed to be lived by the "flesh". So man develops into a higher form of being good, e.g., "into Christian humanism". It is not only the present pope with his theology who perceives himself as the perfecter of humanism. Eros and caritas, this Platonic "celestial love" comprises in Catholic Christianity the divine, as well as neighborly love. Both have the same roots. their power comes from the Olympus and not from Calvary. Regrettably, the same eros-precept rules for the most part also in Protestant churches. Nygren says, that Dante and the esteemed church father Augustine share the same understanding of love concerning the "celestial eros". Also caritas (love for one's neighbor) is determined by the "heavenly" eros motive. Nygren says, that the fusion of the eros and agape motive was transmitted by Augustine to medieval scholasticism and mysticism. Under the primacy of the eros motive, the caritas doctrine of the Middle Ages came about. Further powers came through the medieval piety of love (Minne). So eros gushes into the Renaissance. Through Martin Luther and his Reformation around sixteen hundred, the agape motive erupts again. Nygren says, that Luther ranks as the Reformer of the "Christian idea of love". He is "the destroyer of the erotic idea of love of the Roman Church and the constructor of the pure agape love". Do Bible believing churches still practice self-condemnation of the carnal ego (1 Cor. 11: 31-32)?

Agape flows towards other people through love fellowship with God's agape (Gal. 2: 20). "To be in Christ" (2 Cor. 5: 15-18) means, that the believer does not receive life out of his own "flesh", but out of God's agape through the Holy Spirit (Rom. 14: 7-8; 1 Cor. 12: 13). It is the spirit that receives its motivation out of the power of the agape.

So Benedict XVI is exposed in his encyclical, for he understands "love" from the Greek-Roman spirit, which stands as a deadly enemy for the Word of God. Therefore, Catholic Christianity has brought to power the antichristian spirit by mixing the Hebrew agape with the Greek eros. The Apostle John tells us:

"Dear friends, let us love (agape) one another, for love comes from God. Everyone who loves has been born of God and knows God. Whoever does not love does not know God, because God is love (agape)." (1 John 4: 7-8).

The training objective of a church consist of practicing agape love.

"The goal of this command is love (agape) which comes from a pure heart and a good conscience and a sincere faith." (1 Tim. 1: 5).

4. The inappropriate reactions of Benedict XVI and his leading clerics as a reflection of the insecurity of the pope?

After the change of popes, it could be noticed, that the former cardinal of the "Congregation of Faith", formerly office of inquisition, Joseph Ratzinger, the stern guardian of the Grail of Catholic teaching changed apparently into a smiling, jovial world thinker after taking over office in April of 2005. The "Sueddeutsche Zeitung" (newspaper of Southern Germany) remarks in its edition of Oct. 20/21 2007, that the unenthused had to explain at the beginning of the pontificate, "why they refused themselves the papacy by not participating in its life of Catholicism with Baroque and church music, Latin, incense and values." In a short timespan the enthusiasm for the pope was gone just as fast. The hoped for encampment, even of the young people through the World Youth Events, did not materialize. Catholicism under Ratzinger, Pope Benedict XVI, withdrew back into its old traditions. Bishops and cardinals in Germany perceive it as their responsibility now to attack verbally the secular world from the standpoint of their Catholic values which did not happen to that extent under Pope John Paul II. A bishop in Augsburg criticized the German day care politics with the words, that the mothers are degraded to "birthing machines". The most fervent admirer of the late John Paul II, Cardinal Meisner of Cologne, told the non-Christian public that every culture degenerates if it is disconnected from the worship of God. Of course, he has in mind the worship of God in the Catholic sense. Furthermore, he compares the abortion pill "RU 486 with cyclone B. Another bishop, from Regensburg, covered up for a priest, who was previously convicted of child abuse, by assigning him to another church, which led again to sexual abuse. No remorse, no acceptance of responsibility on the part of the bishop, never mind on the part of the guilty priest. Pope Benedict XVI also preaches and publicizes against the "dictatorship of relativism" in the Western World and there is basically nothing wrong with that. The density of the attacks are the points of criticism which came about through a lack of differentiation. All of this happened during the first years of his pontificate.

This pope is a humanistic Greek throughout. He lives and judges out of the Olympic tradition and not from Calvary. Therefore, the Vatican is — and was — a pagan construct, out of which the Western World came into being. The pope mixes Greek philosophy with the theology of the cross as he did with the theme of agape and eros. Therefore only an imitation of the Biblical faith is the result. Benedict XVI, as an erudite German professor, has an excellent knowledge of Greek philosophy but takes little notice of the truth of Biblical theology of the NT. As pope he was a guest lecturer at the University of Regensburg in September of 2006. He was carried away intellectually, so that he apparently forgot his cause as mediator of the dialogue of cultures and religions. In his lecture, he quoted the Byzantine emperor Manuel II, who apparently discussed Christianity and Islam with a learned Persian in Ankara in 1391. The emperor supposedly said, "Show me then the new thing, that Mohammed has brought, and there you will find only bad things and inhumanity such as this: that he ordered that the faith that he preached be spread with the sword." Emperor Manuel II explained then, that it is contrary to the character of God to act unreasonably, because God has no pleasure in shedding blood. An outcry of hate after this lecture by the Islamic world against the Vatican and the Western World was the answer. Was this the vaunted rationality of the pope which he exerts again and again as a philosophical Greek thinker? According to the Cathol. Net. from 12. Sept. 06, p. 3, Benedict XVI says the following about this, "Manuel II really spoke out of the inner character of the Christian faith and at the same time out of the essence of Greek culture which fused together with the faith."

This is the theme of Benedict XVI. The logos — he has however the pure reason of Emanuel Kant in mind — is in accordance with God. Benedict XVI sees, as do Thomas Aquinas and others, reason as not being spoiled by sin. Therefore it is divine. Pagan Greek culture is not compatible with Hebrew thinking which validates Jesus Christ as the logos, as the personified Word of God (John 1). This Greek estrangement was the death of original Christianity, according to Huntemann. With this the Roman Catholic Church came into being as an imitation out of Greek antichristian spirit. As we have already heard, the Reformers liberated theology from Greek culture and from the Renaissance. Then about two hundred years later the coming enlightenment had yet again its foundations in both the Greek culture as well as in the Renaissance.

Faith and Greek thinking do not complement, but exclude each other (Prov. 3: 5). We recommend the booklet of the author "Life out of DEATH of the Autonomous Rationalism", May 1999, Publisher 7000, for further studies of the topic. Up to the year 2009 Pope Benedict XVI and his council scored more "own goals", which deservedly did much damage to the world church.

5. The identity crisis of the worldwide priesthood?

Another problem was that Benedict XVI had to deal with the identity crisis of his worldwide priesthood. In "Kreuz.net, katholische Nachrichten" (Catholic News) an article by bishop Bernard Fellay appeared in 2006. "The church has been in a crisis since the Second Vatican Council because they have robbed the priesthood of its power." Archbishop Lefebvre, who was excommunicated by the former pope, said exactly this in the 1980's, that the last Vatican Council from 1962-65 has led the priesthood into the greatest crisis in church history. In order to be open to Protestantism and to the world, an essential prerequisite is, that the mass is celebrated in the respective native language as a rule. Ultra conservative Catholics perceive this as a protestantization of Rome. Consequently Lefebvre founded the Priestly Brotherhood of St. Pius X. With this, the whole church should be renewed through the restoration of the conservative priesthood. Its highest bishop Fellay says according to kreuz.net: "In order to achieve this, the inner relationship between priest and Holy Mass, which has an unimaginable depth, has to be restored. The council fathers admitted openly that the priest is the great forgotten one of the Second Vaticanum." The council has obviously dealt with the common priesthood of the baptized Catholic believers intensively, at the cost of the consecrated official priesthood, so that the position of the priest is only vaguely discernible. The ultra conservatives interpreted this as disrespect for the spiritual power which came through sacramental consecration. Martin Luther won in this matter because his intention to turn the priest into a preacher materialized. The sacramental power is lost, because for the most part the sacrifice of Jesus which needs to be repeated constantly through the Eucharist, no longer belongs to the main objective, says Fellay. So it was unavoidable, that the priesthood underwent an identity crisis, which still continues. For church political reasons Pope John Paul II kept the priests under close control. This worked only as long as the cult places of Mary delivered the necessary spirit powers. When these became less and less, the present Pope Benedict XVI got into a dilemma. What should he do? The pope described in many articles the absolute necessity for the church to put the Eucharist back into the center of the religious happenings, in order to achieve "renewal of the church". Now the ultra-conservative power-seekers gained a hearing with the pope. "Priests who understand that their reason for existence is the sacrifice, for which they were consecrated, are needed for the mass sacrifice." Fellay says about this, that the "supernatural life, which manifests itself in the whole mystic body, is mediated through the mass sacrifice." So the supernatural power is the issue here. Rome's losses of power in the Catholic cosmos have to be urgently substituted now by the abomination of the Eucharist. Is the necessary supernatural power equally inherent in modern languages when the mass is celebrated? The conservatives say, no. Pope Benedict XVI now goes back another step. On 14. Sept. 2007 Benedict XVI allowed back the "Old Mass" again. The ultra-conservatives were jubilant. Now the complete faith seemed to be restored. The Latin language basically belongs to the "Old Mass", which brings the antique Roman power of idols into current cultish practices. The early pope, Holy Gregory the Great, is implicated in the history of the mass. He made sure that a symbiosis of power was established between the Catholic faith and the "accumulated cultural treasures of the ancient Romans. These powers were then bundled up and handed over to the young nations of Europe." This Gregory ruled, that "the Holy Liturgy – the mass sacrifice, as well as the Officium Divinum – shall be preserved." The "Motu Proprio" of Pope Benedict XVI states this according to kreuz.net on 07. July 2007. One should realize, that Pius V reformed the whole Latin Liturgy at the Counter Reformation Council of Trient (1545-63) which then became a transcendent offensive weapon against the Protestants. Since the Second Vaticanum (1962-65) the following has been valid:

-the orderly, regular mass in the respective cultural language, also called New Mass. Pope Paul VI (1963-78) licensed renewed liturgical books in 1970. Also John Paul II (1978-2005) continued reforming this mass book. In 1988 John Paul II requested the bishops to handle the wishes of individuals generously and to grant the old Latin mass in exceptional cases.

-The extraordinary form of the liturgy of the old Roman mass book was never abolished, but it lost its privileged, generally valid position. Since then the Old Mass is invalid for the "people". It can only be celebrated in an exceptional case with permission, "when the welfare of the soul warrants it."

6. The Priestly Brotherhood of St. Pius X

The name is derived from Pope Pius X, who was in office from 1903-1914. The Priestly Brotherhood celebrated the innovations of Pope Benedict XVI as one of their stages of victory. However they, as well as all of their worldwide activists, estimated at 500 priests and 600,000 followers, want more. This group consecrated priests illegitimately through their highest bishop Bernhard Fellay in Bavaria even up to 2009. The Vatican labeled these consecrations "illegitimate", but this had no consequences for the Brotherhood.

The Vatican wants to integrate the Brotherhood into the Catholic Church again. "sueddeutsche.de" of 29. June 2009 reports, that an Argentinian consecrated priest said in his sermon, "The Holy Mass is the basis of Christian civilization. However not just any holy mass, but solely the only one valid, namely the Tridentine Liturgy in the Latin language, as it was exclusively common until the Second Vatican Council." This Brotherhood recognizes the obvious responsiveness of the pope, but it is not enough for them. They want to have the old Roman Mass back as a rule. In order that this happens, and that this pope becomes convinced of the Fatima Madonna, the supporters are asked to pray the rosary in their project "Prayer Storm". 12 million rosaries shall be prayed. An English St. Pius brother, bishop Richard Williamson, caused another worldwide scandal in November 2008, on the occasion of an unauthorized consecration of deacons, and this happened again in Bavarian Zaitzkofen. There he denied in a sermon the existence of the Holocaust and of the gas chambers. Almost simultaneously Benedict XVI canceled the excommunication of 4 bishops of the Pius-Brotherhood, which had been imposed more than 20 years previously. This Williamson had been one of them. Only after worldwide protests, did Benedict XVI admit a "mistake", several weeks later. What was this mistake? Benedict XVI knew the resumées of these previously excommunicated bishops. Previously similar opinions of Williamson became public. In spite of this, Benedict XVI wants to include this ultra-reactionary Pius X Brotherhood into the Catholic Church again. As far as the responsible German prosecution is concerned, the case of the denial of the Holocaust has not been completed and they are still investigating according to criminal code. Because of Germany's history it is a criminal offence to deny the holocaust in Germany. Williamson defected precautiously to London, and supposedly "devoted himself completely to prayer".

7. The Trip of Benedict XVI to Israel

A further revelation of intellectual dishonesty manifested itself during the trip to Israel in May of 2009. Pope Benedict XVI visited the Holocaust memorial Yad Vashem. Here he would have had the opportunity, as a pope from Germany, to repeat the request for forgiveness, which his Polish predecessor had offered at the same place in June of 1979. According to justified public criticism, Benedict XVI only talked about "mistakes", which had happened. But it appears that such "mistakes" are further revelations of an attitude that Williamson holds. The German newspaper "Frankfurter Allgemeine Zeitung" summarizes the frustrations of his Israeli hosts in "FAZ. Net" of 15. May 2009: Many Israelites regard his statements as non binding. The speaker of the Knesset, Reuven Rivlin, expressed the climate of public opinion like this, "As a Jew, I waited in vain to hear an apology and a request for forgiveness by those, who caused our tragedy. The Germans and the church also have their share in this responsibility. He came and spoke to us as if he were a historian, but he belongs to this group. With all respect for the Holy See, we can not ignore the burden he carries, for as a young German, he entered the Hitlerjugend (Nazi youth organization) and as an adult, he joined Hitler's army." The chief-rabbi Meir Lau regretted that Benedict XVI did not mention the Germans and the Nazis who participated in the murders. Only vaguely did the pope speak about the millions of murdered Jews, instead of saying, that there were 6 million. Also Lau desired a word of regret. Was the Holocaust just an error, an accident, so that Benedict XVI talked about Jews being killed instead of Jews being murdered? Other critics mentioned that he talked like a "typical" professor without showing compassion. Another criticism came from the president of the "Central Council of the Jews in Germany", Charlotte Knobloch. She was surprised that the pope neither distanced himself in Yad Vashem, from the followers of the Pius-Brotherhood, "which still call us murderers of God, nor from the controversial Good Friday petition for the enlightenment of the Jews." No clear dissociation from the anti-Semitic Pius-Brotherhood or from the Williamson case was made. The general secretary of this Central Council, Stephan Kramer was also critical, that Benedict XVI "did n0t take stronger action against Williamson." Kramer accuses the pope of a "lack of credibility". "There is a huge gap between what he says and how he behaves in reality." We are of exactly the same opinion.

We do not regret the fact that Benedict XVI is destroying everything that his predecessor had built up with much deceptive skillfulness.

Chapter VI: The Pontificate of Pope Benedict XVI

8. The Community of Medjugorje and Pope Benedict XVI

A further irritation comes from the conduct of the Vatican concerning Medjugorje. The former Pope John Paul II and his then deputy and head of the Faith Congregation, Ratzinger, the present Pope Benedict XVI, listened to all criticisms of the bishop of Mostar about Medjugorje, which aimed at prohibiting this fellowship. However, the Vatican was silent and allowed the many processions of Catholics from all over the world to that place. They were even permitted to have their worldwide meeting in Lourdes with the blessing of the church. This author himself was in Lourdes at that time as a critical observer in 1997. After the apparitions with their monthly admonitions became more and more banal, and eventually stopped altogether, most of the communities of Medjugorje were dissolved. When the cosmic powers stopped even Pope Benedict XVI, according to "kreuz.net" of 07. July 2006, found it necessary to declare "that one was always wondering in the Faith Congregation how all these appearances can be considered valid for Catholic believers." It is a fact, however, that his predecessor received representatives of Medjugorje many times in private audiences. According to their reports, the pope encouraged them and supported them spiritually. This lasted as long as they had success. For only the successful magic faith of the people receives the recognition of the Roman Church in the end.

9. The "Woman of all Peoples" and Pope Benedict XVI

We present another example of the duplicity of the pope. His predecessor had barely died at the beginning of 2005, when Benedict XVI rejected the addition of "Woman of all Peoples, which once was Mary" to the title of Mary of Amsterdam, which had been acknowledged since 2002. As head of the Faith Congregation, Ratzinger had accepted this title **with** the addition under John Paul II. The Crucified, who is hated by the non-Christian religions, was no longer at the cross of this "Woman of all Peoples". In this way the "Woman of all Peoples" should become acceptable to all religions. Since the acceptance of the addition "which once was Mary" in

2002, the chief spirit of the Catholic Mary, named as the Babylon Harlot in Revelation ch. 17 and 18, has taken charge in order to force the unity of religions. The internal struggle of the church after this "authorization" was now about dogmatization of this additional heretical title. The reader will find the historical development of the planned final expansion for all peoples from the Western-Catholic Mary to the Madonna for all religious cultures.

So, Benedict XVI "paddles" back into secure Catholic waters. The present pope did not want to get burned by burdening the universal title with the not yet accepted but requested title of Co-Redemtrix, and dogmatizing it. Since 2005 the following title is now binding "Woman of all Peoples, the Blessed Virgin Mary". "Woman of all Peoples" goes even beyond what is Catholic. The Jesuit statement; "might is right", is in use here. The spirit-power diminished, therefore the Catholic truth is also changing. Incidentally, Pope Benedict XVI is acting contrary to the explicit command of this "Woman of all Peoples", just as the Popes Pius XI and XII did with the Madonna of Fatima.

10. Mary, the Co-Redemptrix as Dogma?

The Marian theologians persist. On 16. June 2008 an article appeared in the newspaper "Die Welt" in the feature section, p. 27, in which a group of bishops urged Benedict XVI again to finally declare "Mary" as Co-Redemptrix, i.e., to dogmatize this title by virtue of the papal teaching authority. His predecessor, John Paul II, had still refused to do this in the year 2000 for opportunistic reasons. He pronounced that it would not be advisable to define a new tension-creating dogma because of the Second Vaticanum and the condition of the Ecumenical Movement. The Orthodox Churches and the Protestants accused the Vatican frequently, that it expounded the last two Marian dogmas "unilaterally without consultation of the separated brothers".

These were the dogmas under Pope Pius IX in the year of 1854, the "Immaculate Conception" of the Immaculata and of Pope Pius XII when he established the last Marian dogma for the "bodily reception of the immaculate Mother of God and everlasting Virgin Mary in Heaven" in the year 1950.

The hypocrisy "without consultation of the separated brothers" is unbearable. After all, there was no theological need for consultations on the highest level during the time after Napoleon since 1815 and around 1870, the founding of the German empire and the denominational culture wars. There were also no "brotherly talks" about this before and after World War I, nor after World War II. The front lines between Catholics and Protestants were clearly marked. Pope John Paul II (1978–2005) declared that first of all a "certain convergence" concerning the question of unity had to be established, before it would be appropriate to declare the desired dogma. However, the Marian lobby has still not given up. Just as his predecessor Benedict XVI also received a list with signatures of distinguished bishops and cardinals under the leadership of the Indian cardinal Toppo to approve the proclamation of the dogma of Mary as Co-Redemptrix. He was petitioned to proclaim Mary "as the spiritual mother of mankind; as Co-Redemptrix with Jesus, the Redeemer; as mediator of grace with Jesus, the one mediator; and as intercessor with Jesus Christ for all of mankind." It is striking this time that the names of the advocates are all men from Hindu, Buddhist, Islamic, Shamanistic societies. Even in Fatima, the Hindus were involved. We have already reported that following visits of the representatives of the New-Age and also Hindu priests to the cult site Fatima in the year 2003, the director Guerra announced that Fatima should now become a place, where all religions can worship their gods. The C0-Redemptrix should finally turn into Mary. Jesus, the great annoyance would then be removed. They are not that far yet. Beside the title Co-Redemptrix, Cardinal Toppo wants to see dogmatization of Mary include the title "the spiritual mother of mankind". He also thinks that it would "be helpful for the inter religious dialogue with the Moslems, who are familiar with Mary through the Koran. Mary ranks in Islam as the greatest of all women without sin and virginal." According to the newspaper "Die Welt", the Marians stick close to Fiores, who clarified and restrictively said, "it is not about putting Mary on the same level with Jesus; the central character of the act of redemption of the Savior is something that goes without saying, and one regards the Mother of God as a participant in this salvation; equality is not the point in the work of redemption of Jesus Christ, but participation, a dependance in redemption, and that has to be clear." According to these words, Jesus the Savior depends upon Mary's participation in his work of redemption. Therefore, no redemption without Mary. To put Mary almost on the same level of salvation as Jesus would certainly be heretical. This is even the opinion of "Die Welt". There are also German Catholic theologians who distance themselves sharply from this proposition. Mary may be, as these theologians say, "interwoven in the work of salvation." But this would not be sufficient for co-redemption, and would also contradict Holy Scripture and would be a heresy. We gladly confirm that not all Catholic theologians are militant Marian heretics. But how does the papal universal church decide? Wherever the church community in the past called on Mary and worshipped her according to the so-called "religion of the people" with characteristics, which turned into titles, the Vatican followed suit most of the time. It was only a matter of time for its recognition. A hint for the topic is appropriate. At the Second Vatican Council (1962-65) more than 200 bishops, among them Karol Wojtyla, the later John Paul II, urged for Mary to be defined as Co-Redemptrix. This was rejected in controversially conducted debates, as was the title: "Mother of the Church". This again happened out of opportunism and ecumenical considerations. Pope Paul VI, in the last phase of his office, amazed everyone by simply overriding the majority vote of rejecting Mary as "Mother of the Church", and solemnly proclaimed Mary as "Mother of the Church" (Mater Ecclesiae) in November 1964. Since this date Mary is "Mother of the Church" against the will of the cardinals and bishops. However, this papal decision is binding for the church.

11. Surrendering the papal title: Patriarch of the Occident

Almost unnoticed by the public, at the beginning of 2006 Benedict XVI gave up one of his many titles, namely "Occidentis Patriarca", patriarch of the Western World. The "Patriarchal Basilicas" are now called "Papal Basilicas". According to "zenit.org/article" of 11. July 2007, Benedict XVI confirmed, "that the Peter's Office of the pope has to be distinguished from all other offices and authorities of the patriarch." The assignment that goes with the title of patriarch does not mean renunciation of property. He puts together the primacy of the Pontifex Maximus (as supreme bridge builder between immanence and transcendence, the author) with worldwide legal claim. So Benedict XVI says 'good-by' to the idea of a "Council-Ecumenism", which would have an influence on the task of the pope. Thus he exalts his office in respect of church law and grants it exclusive right (divine right) and therefore does not need any advisors at all. So he intensifies the papal primacy. Out of this position he wants to continue the ecumenical dialogue. He stands on the foundation "in the service of the truth". "The papacy is the truth". Furthermore it says, "The pope does not just stand for Peter, he is Peter. The mystical body of Christ would evaporate into nothing without his service of love. The pope, therefore, is not a patriarch, but he condenses in himself the essence of the church."

With this, Benedict XVI destroys any open dialogue with the Protestant Churches. But maybe the obsessed ecumenists of the dialogue did not even notice this intensified situation? His predecessor, John Paul II, had practised all of this before, but Benedict XVI, formerly Cardinal Ratzinger and the chief of the Faith Congregation (once the office of inquisition) was restrained by John Paul II again and again, when he wanted to intensify the primacy of the pope and make it church law. John Paul II was a player, who was willing to take chances but although he increased his stakes he did not achieve his goal. Benedict XVI wants to secure the Roman Church which has lost power along the way, and he wants to lead her back into the storm-proof haven of tradition. Anxiety about further losses circulates in the Vatican.

12. The Theory of Evolution and the Pope

John Paul II believed, that the theory of evolution did not contradict the Christian (Catholic) faith. According to Kreuz.net of 27. July 2007 Benedict XVI also says, "that there are decisive scientific proofs for the theory of evolution." Benedict XVI adds, or confuses the situation and says, "that reason, however, precedes everything, and that even man is an image of creative reason." The creator has added a new element, namely that "of a great cosmic harmony." It is not the task of this book to respond to the papal attempts of befriending the atheistic world, just as little as to deal with his favourite topic of Greek rationality. One is even more amazed, when Benedict XVI says in the encyclical "Caritas in Veritate" (which still needs to be discussed) of 07. July 2009, p. 41, "When nature, and man above all else is regarded as the fruit of chance, or of evolutionary determinism (causal predetermination, the author), the sense of responsibility in the consciences becomes weaker. However, the believer recognizes in nature the wonderful work of God's creative intervention, which man is allowed to use responsibly in order to satisfy his justified material and mental needs with respect to the inner balance of creation. When this concept wanes, man will in the end treat nature either as an untouchable taboo, or, on the contrary, exploit it. Neither approach corresponds to the Christian view of nature, which is the fruit of God's creation." He continues that nature precedes us because it is the plan of God of love and truth. "It (nature) talks to us about the creator (comp. Rom. 1: 20)." Anyone who reads the New Testament recognizes in the quoted reference of the Letter to the Romans that it is not nature that precedes but that God is acknowledged as creator. One may ask oneself what spirit drives the pope to make such contradictory statements, sometimes pro evolution, then pro creation. The vernacular says about this: Whoever lies has to have a good memory.

13. Ecumenism and Pope Benedict XVI

There had been much turmoil because the Vatican under the authority of the former prefect, Cardinal Ratzinger, had published "Dominus Jesus" in the year 2000. The author has already written about this. The reason for this commotion on behalf of the Protestant churches consisted primarily of the fact, that according to this papal document they are not valid churches. Therefore the Protestants are addressed only as "communities". In 2007 the Vatican under the leadership of Benedict XVI issued a Vatican paper of the Faith Congregation, that states again the position of understanding the church. The document refers to the Second Vatican Council where it was interpreted that "there can be no talk about church in the true sense of the word where the historical office of bishop in apostolic succession and the full Eucharistic mysteries are missing." Now Rome complains in its 2007 published Vatican paper about the present leading protestants who appeal "to their Reformation principles" and do not want to take seriously, that there is no agreement in "the sacramental life and in the question about the office of the church." This means, that this recognition and acceptance is the precondition for the visible unity in order to be "church in the true sense". The Eucharist is denied to Protestants because the acceptance and the recognition are not there. One asks oneself, whether the leading Protestants ever read the documents of the Vatican? Obviously, the Protestants ignore the fundamental difference between the Lord's Supper and the Eucharist. They constantly demand participation in the Last Supper, which Rome, however, has substituted with the magic Eucharist instead. The Vatican paper points out that the criticisms come especially from Germany, the land of the Reformation. The Lutherans in the USA, Methodists in England and USA, and the Anglicans in England do not have this negative criticism, and after these clear words from Rome look joyfully towards continuing the ecumenical dialogue, so the Anglo-American "dialogue-Protestants". The significance of the Vatican paper is to put inaccuracies straight. Rome is looking for "deepened theological efforts for the church concept and ecumenism." But the paper also determines, that even in the controversial questions "there is a deep layer of commonalities." The questions then are listed: Communion (Rome only recognizes the Eucharist), office problems, understanding of church, Mariology!, or even the pope issue.

The darkness gains more and more ground from the "deep layers" towards Western Catholic unity with the churches originating in the Western World. Basically, the dialogue of Ecumenism of the Christian churches consists of mostly cultivated exchange. The retired Catholic canonist, Prof. Georg May of Mainz, wrote a book arguing against the Ecumenical movement with the title: "The Trap of Ecumenism", Publisher Sarto Buch, 2007. The author states in this book that the "Protestant religious federations" are not at all interested in an organized unity. All they want from Rome are two things:

1. "The individual Protestant churches want to be recognized as fully valid Christian churches."

2. "They want to have complete Communion fellowship with Rome", which means again Eucharist fellowship. As already mentioned, the Ecumenical Protestants miss, or ignore the fact, that Rome rejects Communion as a meal of remembrance. At the Vaticanum (1962-65) the Eucharist of the Counter Reformation Council of Trient (1564) was again confirmed. It concludes with the sentence: "Whoever should say, do this in remembrance of me, shall be condemned." The readers may review the corresponding pages of this book, to realize the incompatibility of Communion and Eucharist.

Prof. May attacks Protestantism furthermore by writing that the Protestants adhere to a birth defect with their religion, namely to the Augustine monk Martin Luther, who defected from the priesthood. May perceives only pressure from the Protestants everywhere. They want to be recognized as having equal rights in all of their rituals like services, marriages, Communion, etc. The author May criticizes furiously, that this egoistic German Protestantism is insincere. Compared with this, the attitude of the American Southern Baptists is refreshingly honest. They concluded the dialogue with the Catholic Church with the short statement: We are not Ecumenists, we are evangelical. This position has to be respected by Rome, because of its honesty, according to May. Is May only an outsider? Our opinion is, that there are signs of fatigue in the management committees of the Christian Ecumenical movement. Especially the Protestant side tries to let the Ecumenical movement grow through the church people, because only little progress for unity can be expected from the "top".

14. Rome befriending Islam

However, internally and among themselves, the Catholic "dignitaries" are everything else, but an Apostolic church. Hans Kueng, Catholic theologian and former professor of the Catholic Theological Faculty at Tuebingen, speaks up once in a while. In the 1970's he adopted the program of the godless, Protestant, Bible critical, and libertarian "theology", feminism included. He adhered very closely to the program of the esoteric New Age, whereby his teaching license as a Catholic professor was withdrawn by the Vatican in 1979. Kueng never recanted. For some years now his interest is directed more and more to the world religions. According to various news reports he wants to "transform" the world religions with the goal of unification. Reports of the media have it, that there is one, but very typical, confession of his: "As a Christian I can have the conviction, if I have chosen Jesus as the Christ for my life and death, that I have also chosen his follower Mohammed as far as he refers to the one God and Jesus." Any comment on this is superfluous. But we should not assume that Kueng does not have any friends in the Vatican. They say that Cardinal Lehmann of Mainz has a good theological understanding with Kueng. Even Benedict XVI is on this point explicitly pro Islam. Whereas Kueng had his office revoked by Pope John Paul II, other church leaders say similar things, but without consequences. In 2005, at the occasion of a visit of the Jordanian King at the Catholic University of Washington D.C., the Cardinal and Archbishop Mc. Carrick gave a speech. We are here only interested in what belongs to our topic. Mc. Carrick told the Islamic King, that he had prayed for him to "Allah, the tender hearted and all compassionate Lord of the whole world to bless you and to help you turn your country into a bridge over which all nations can move in unity, friendship, and love." Mc. Carrick referred to Benedict XVI, who had met with Islamic representatives of religion shortly before on the occasion of the World Youth Conference.

Benedict XVI said, "I invite you all to eradicate together the feeling of hatred from the hearts, to abolish every form of intolerance, and to oppose every manifestation of violence."

Mc. Carrick could only talk so pro-Islamic, because he was in the context of papal politics. The readers can detect, that B, XVI practices opportunistic politics of religion, maybe in order to make the dialogue craving Ecumenical Protestants jealous. We are interested here in which attitude the Vatican had since the Vaticanum, and which one the present pope has today. He talks increasingly of a trialogue, instead of a dialogue with the other Christian churches. He is seeking, in spite of harsh criticism of Islam and Judaism, communication in order to connect the religions, where there is no longer any place left for the Protestants. Does he continue and intensify the politics of unification of religions which his predecessor expedited very energetically? This would be a change of his initial politics. The Catholic Church and Protestantism agreed on one point at the time of the Reformation and afterwards concerning the military conflicts with Islam that moved into the Western World: The God of the Bible is not identical with the God of Islam, Allah. Pope Benedict XVI proclaimed the opposite of that on his journey to Turkey at the end of November 2006, namely, that both religions worship the same God, albeit in different ways.

Benedict XVI even "prayed" in 2006 in the Blue Mosque in Istanbul towards Mecca. Already in the important Vatican Council documents of the 1960's "Nostra aetate" and "Lumen gentium", they had declared that Christians and Moslems worship the same God, and also venerate Mary together. In 1985 the papal predecessor John Paul II had professed in Marocco, that both sides believe in the same God. At the inter-religious prayer meetings in 1986, 1993, and on the 24. Jan. 2002 in Assisi, this attitude of John Paul II was also the prerequisite for the events, at least with the Islam. A short while after the last prayer meet in 2002 John Paul II "prayed" in front of the Al-Aksa Mosque in Jerusalem and at the Jewish Wailing Wall in order to establish a trialogue with the religions of "the same God". Also during the visit in the Omaijaden-Mosque in Damascus John Paul II kissed the book of the Koran. The "pope-disciple" and closest confidant of John Paul II, the present Pope Benedict XVI, formerly Cardinal Ratzinger, continues rigorously this recognition of Islam. One even forgets his hit and miss shots against Islam. One even forgets his objections against Islam. A debate with Islam about its pros and cons would go beyond the limits of this book. But a few things have to be recognized to get a clear picture of Benedict XVI and his politics of religions. He also knows that Islam pursues a new world order. According to Zeitjournal, 2/2007, publisher: AG fuer religioese Fragen (AG for religious issues) the radical Islamization in the previous century started with the founding of the Moslem Brotherhood in Egypt in 1928. It inspired many Islamic fundamentalist movements, and it refers to the Koran and the example of Mohammed. The Moslem Brotherhood is an imitation of European fascism. Until today adoration of Hitler is unbroken in these circles. According to Zeitjournal, there existed numerous Islamic SS-divisions in the second World War. Through the same spirit the Neo-nazis worldwide find more and more a common goal. In December of 2006 a conference for people who deny the Holocaust took place in Teheran. The common hatred of Jews by Moslems and non Islamic Neo-nazis was the common ground of this fascist conference. Among Islam experts for some time now, the title "Islamo-Fascism" circulates as the coming anti-Semitic superpower. A note in the newspaper "Die Welt" of the 21.Sept.2009 ended up in the hands of the author. It says there concerning our topic of ignorance about the dangers of Islamism: "During a speech at the University of Teheran, the highest ranking spiritual head of Iranian Islam, Ali Chamenai, talked about Israel as a deadly cancerous growth which is spreading in the region. The speech was accompanied by shouts of "death to Israel". The Iranian president Ahmadinedshad repeatedly denied the Holocaust and murdering of Jews by the millions, and he called this a myth and an excuse for the founding of Israel." Hatred of Jews is produced again and just ignored by the Vatican? The religious Vatican Roman principle of domination which has controlled the world order, was interrupted by the 30 Years War in the 17th century in Central Europe and then again at the beginning of the 19th century when Napoleon more or less brought it to an end. Then Napoleon, later Hitler and Stalin, erected a new world order with their secular movements. After the fall of Hitler's empire, the break up of the Soviet Union andthe visible signs of weakness of the USA as a superpower, radical Islam has tried to initiate a new world order with the spirit of fascism, nurtured by hatred of Jews and hatred against the Western way of life, as tries to become a superpower. It uses the same tools of intimidation as Hitler did. At that time they had tried to preserve world peace through continuous concessions to Hitler, but they achieved the opposite. Today the same mistake is repeated by constantly giving in, in order not to hurt "Islamic feelings". With these religious fascists, the end result will be just the opposite as well. According to our conviction, one man, however, knows for sure, what he is doing: Pope Benedict XVI.

He wants to regain the lost power of the Vatican through the power of the spirit of Islam. Even at the risk of losing Catholic identity, he wants, just like his predecessor, unification for a common world religion with Islam first, because it takes him too long to achieve it with the Protestants and Orthodox. After giving up the Christian-Reformation heritage, the West has too little power left to defend itself against religiously fanatical Islam, which fights with the spirit power of Allah.

More than 200 years ago the followers of the French Revolution declared in a ritual "The deposition of God" in Notre Dame, Paris. Instead of God, they enthroned a naked prostitute on the altar as the "Goddess of Reason". Since then she stands as the highest principle to be worshiped. The secular movements which followed in the 20th century especially the German fascism and the Soviet Marxist-Leninism acted according to their ideologies in the spirit of this "reason". The outcome of this "reason" was around 100 million dead people.

So, in this way God reject godless reason. History is a moving testimony for what this "reason" is worth. It is completely given over to caprice. It was also "reasonable" in the scope of the ideology to liquidate people who didn't want to, or were not supposed to, integrate into their new world order.

In the Proverbs of the Old Testament, it says admonishingly: "But whoever fails to find me (God) harms himself; all who hate me love death" (8: 36). "The fear (reverence) of the LORD is the beginning of wisdom, and knowledge of the Holy One (Jesus) is understanding" (9: 10). This Biblical knowledge which leads to life has become undesirable in our days. "But whoever finds me (Jesus) finds life" (Prov. 8: 35). These life foundations are broken off by "deposing God" which came about by arrogant ignorance. And finally, there is no power left to resist the murderous spirit of Islamism. The pope deals with this spirit and tries to agree with it, in order to receive transcendent demonic power from it. The newspaper "Die Welt" of 14. Sept. 2009 reports that a "forum of conservative German Catholics" recognized in a resolution the Moslems "as natural allies " in the struggle against a culture of death! They find their common ground on these issues: Rejection of birth control, of abortion and gender-ideology. "Christians and Moslems should face these challenges together, which a godless age poses for us." Then the danger of Islamism is relativized. "Not the strength of Islam is the dangerous threat for Europe, but the systematic displacement of the Christian (Catholic) faith from politics and public life …" All of this sounds very much like the Greek "reasoning" of the present pope. Two imitations of Biblical faith shake hands. One interprets the Bible through falsification of sacraments and worship of saints, the other labels the Bible as forgery and Mohammed instead of Jesus as the one sent by God.

Those who know the Vatican and have been defected insiders have reported for some time that Ecumenical pressure for unification also came from the Freemasons, who made sure that principles of Masonry entered into the documents of Vatican Council II. The dirty bank business of the 1970's by the Vatican Bank and the conspicuous peace making of the Vatican with the Freemasons are still in the memory of many contemporaries. There are many well-known Catholics who oppose this mendacity vehemently. It became public, that Pope John XXIII who opened Vatican Council II, and his successor Paul VI, belonged to a secret lodge as Freemasons. The same Catholic critics maintain that John Paul II was also a Freemason. The willingness for unification among religions is compulsory for Freemasons. Are we still amazed about the attempts of the last two popes to get close to the Moslems? "Christians and Moslems worship the same God" is the beginning of this collaboration.

15. The Christian-Ecumenical Immorality

Some information is still necessary, namely about the mendacity in respect of the topic of Catholic morals. On 07. May 08 the Catholic news "Kreuz.net" reported very critically about the porno-businesses of Catholic bishops.

"Whoever wants to buy films with sexual content does not need to go to erotic-shops. He can get these things at the Catholic publisher "Weltbild" as well. Then various "samples" are mentioned. We want to report only one that is typical. "A DVD for 16.99 Euro with the title: 444 sex positions" and this is available from 16 years of age upwards.

The author asks ironically: Why not put the number 666 straight away? The critical Catholic news comments that the revenue benefits German dioceses which are all from the Bavarian homeland of Pope Benedict XVI. Among them is that of Bishop Mueller from Regensburg, about whom we had reported, that he tolerated one of his priests, who had abused children sexually. This Catholic publisher "Weltbild" offers condoms free of charge through the Caritas (a Catholic relief organization). Under the authority of Cardinal Meisner of Cologne, this "caretaker" and militant defender of the pope, condoms are also offered to young people. "In the diocese of Speyer/Rhineland-Palatinate the Catholic Caritas collaborates, so that children and youths can get a so-called "condom driver's license." The catholically critical article concludes with the statement, "that at the German Catholic Events, condoms were distributed by Caritas, otherwise these events would have been too boring for the young people."

This present Pope Benedict XVI, who likes to be celebrated as the great moralist, who raises his finger admonishingly at the evil world of relativism, may go down in history as the pope of revealed fraud and of hypocritical pharisaism. Could the preference of eros over agape, which Benedict XVI granted in his encyclical "Deus Caritas Est", be an indication of how the church people practice this in life? We believe that he is a "great bridge builder" from eros to the Babylon Harlot (Revelation, ch. 17 and 18) and that he also wants the second side of the celibate Catholic Mary. The spirit of the Babylon Harlot hides behind his erudition.

In the Protestant Church of Germany, sexual immorality blossoms through this spirit as well. One year before, in 2007, there was a Protestant Church Convention in Cologne. Within this framework a church service took place with the title: "The event in the vineyard of love. Erotic church service." "Kreuz.net" of 11. June 2007 also reports about this very critically, but objectively correct. According to "Kreuz.net", Catholic News, one could hear in the church before the beginning of the event: "Ladies and gentlemen, please move a little bit closer together, after all, it is an erotic church service. A woman in a red shirt appeared and threw scented rose petals down from the balcony. Another woman talked about the delicateness of the leaves and pointed out the exuberance, sensuality, and eroticism of life". The pastor of the church greeted the congregation with the words: "Praise God with your passion, your lust, with your tenderness. Another woman in a red, short dress and skimpy underwear skipped over the rose leaves ..." The website of the Church Conference interprets: "Eroticism is red, feminine, and young". And further down on the web site: "The red female dancer presents herself one more time with an orgastical dance. The drummer shakes his body accordingly, as if he were on the verge of an orgasm." The pastor then has a spirited red light insight: "Prayer and sex are close together. Both want to be lived out, experienced, felt, and tried out."

One gets the impression, that the antique temple prostitution should also prevail among Protestant church people. The 400 spectators applauded loudly at this contribution from the red light district with religious undertones. The spirit of the Babylon Harlot has meanwhile many Christian churches in its grip.

In the Letter to the Galatians in the New Testament, chapter 6: 7-8a, is a warning: "Do not be deceived: God is not mocked, for whatever one sows, that will he also reap. For the one who sows to his own flesh from the flesh will reap destruction".

16. The Encyclical Caritas in Veritas, of Pope Benedict XVI

*About the holistic development of man
in love and in truth.*

In this encyclical we will recognize the spirit and the goal by which this papacy lives and in which this papacy wants to find its fulfillment in this 3rd millennium. We perceive deceiving fragments of truth for post modern man who has acceppted the idea of love coming out of eros. A preparatory aim is the ecumenical attempt to discriminate against those who believe in the true Christ and his Word by calling them fundamentalists. By so doing they will justify various types of persecution in the near future – even in the Western World. In the New Testament, in the 2nd Letter to the Thessalonians in chapter 2: 3-4, 6-7, it explains and warns: "Do not let anyone deceive you in any way. For that day will not come unless the rebellion comes first, and the man of lawlessness is revealed, the son of destruction, who opposes and exalts himself against every so-called God or object of worship, so that he takes his seat in the temple of God, proclaiming himself to be God ... And you know what is restraining him now so that he may be revealed in his time time. For the mystery of lawlessness is already at work. Only he who now retains it will do so until he is out of the way." The rebellion is understood as willfully turning away from Christ, which serves the cleansing of the church, in order to discern the original from the imitation of the faith. 'Man of lawlessness' refers to the Antichrist. 'The one who now holds it back' refers to the Spirit filled church, because it is purified, which, according to 1 Timothy 3: 15, shall live "in the house of God, which is the church of the living God, the pillar and the foundation of truth." The intention of the antichristian spirit of the Vatican is the elimination of New Testament truth, so that the spirit of lie from the eros can produce the Antichrist, whereas the Spirit of truth (John 16: 13, 14) is the personified truth in Jesus Christ. Jesus sent his Spirit, "the Spirit of truth, which will lead you into all the truth; for he will not speak on his own ... He will bring glory to me by taking from what is mine and making it known to you." Therefore Jesus asks his Father in the high priestly prayer (John 17: 17): "Sanctify them by your truth; your word is truth."

To put it in a nutshell, it means: Words of Holy Scripture, which were fulfilled in Jesus in the New Testament + Holy Spirit + agape love = this is the truth alone (Comp. also 1 Timothy 1: 5). A truth different to this, is perception out of the erotic spirit of the Babylon Harlot, and leads inevitably to the "man of lawlessness", the Antichrist, who lives out of the power of Satan.

This Encyclical is a documentation that the papacy is waiting for the "man of lawlessness" which it calls "political world authority" and it wants to enforce its peace agenda with the power of the eros love. This encyclical is a paper of instruction by Rome which presents itself as a bearer of antichristian Babylon. Benedict XVI begins his obligatory writing with the observation that "love – caritas – is an extraordinary power ..., which has its origin in God, who is eternal love and absolute truth." This statement is deceiving, because it draws from the spirit of eros, the spirit of Hellenism and not from the spirit of agape-love. The readers may compare the encyclical "Deus Caritas Est" on the previous pages with this topic.

As stated before, a correct statement reveals itself as truth only if the spirit from whence the statement has its source, agrees with the Spirit of truth in Jesus.

The word and the spirit have to be in unison with each other. The colloquial expression "in the spirit of the letter" is the meaning of this idea. The source of this encyclical "Love (eros) in Truth" is related to the "power of the flesh", which leads to omnipotence through the spirit of Babylon. Therefore, this false love does not lead to truth, but inevitably through the perception of pretended truth into lie and to the "father of lies".

"You belong to your father, the devil, and you want to carry out your father's desire. He was a murderer from the beginning, not holding to the truth, for there is no truth in him. When he lies, he speaks his native language, for he is a liar and the father of lies." (John 8: 44). Here the theological dispute with Rome has to be executed:

Agape-love out of the Spirit of Christ vs. eros-love out of the spirit of Babylon and Hellenism, which Huntemann calls "alienation of the Gospel". Benedict XVI says, "That love is the main road of ecclesiastical social teaching". Therefore, theologically speaking, the term "love" used by the Vatican and the resulting responsibility for the world, that springs from it, is the anti-, or the instead- way of man spoiled by sin. The natural, fallen man wants to assert himself before God, because he denies the guidance by the Holy Spirit. But only those people who are born again can receive by grace this Spirit of Christ. The natural man is called by the Bible the man of flesh, and is indwelt by sin. Jesus states his position in his answer to the question of a leader of the ancient Jewish people, Nicodemus: "How can a man be born when he is old?" All people pose the same question, because they come from the natural wealth of experiences of the "man of flesh". Jesus speaks out of the Spirit of truth, the Holy Spirit, when he says, "Unless a man is born again, he can not see the kingdom of God." A little further down he explains this: "Flesh gives birth to flesh (natural birth), but the Spirit gives birth to spirit." (John 3: 3-6). The Holy Spirit creates in the flesh of man in an ex-territorial area a new man, also called inner man. Only what comes out of this new, inner, or spiritual man in thinking, feeling, and actions is spiritual and has the exclusive right to be truth out of the Spirit of Christ.

The prerequisite is that the Holy Spirit works in a man and that man recognizes himself fundamentally as a sinner, which means in the Greek language, that he misses the purpose of life without Jesus. So the New Testament tells us in the Letter to the Romans, ch. 3: 10, 12, 23-25: "There is no one righteous (without sin), not even one." And furthermore: "All have turned away, they have together become worthless ... for all have sinned (missed the mark) and fall short of the glory (righteousness) of God, and are justified freely by his grace through the redemption that came by Christ Jesus. God presented him as a sacrifice of atonement, through faith in his blood." Faith refers here to the necessity of the substitutionary redeeming death of Jesus. Before the Holy Spirit works in man, he (man) has to:

- realize his fundamentally sinful nature;
- acknowledge it in himself, i.e., that he takes responsibility for it;
- ask God for forgiveness. That is Biblical repentance.
- God forgives in Jesus Christ if the petition was done in honesty and with regret before Jesus Christ.
- Jesus now justifies this person because of his pardon. He pronounces him righteous.
- Jesus sends his Holy Spirit in response, as a promise for the accomplished reconciliation with God.
- Now this man is called a "child of God". The Holy Spirit can now work spiritual deeds in him.
- Then the Holy Spirit will guide this believer "into all the truth step by step" through nurture and by breaking down more inherent sin.

The spiritual as well as emotional maturity is the objective of the discipline of Christ's Spirit. The person, justified by Jesus, lives by grace and by the Spirit. (Romans 3: 22-28, 31, and Romans chapter 8).

In contrast to this, Rome's objective is to believe and to live by the natural, sinful human nature (Romans 6: 2-5). So a grave, topsy-turvy situation is the result, because Rome is striving to turn agape-love into eros-love, and a spiritual responsibility with no political striving for power into responsibility for the world together with political power. Rome is therefore, the biggest religion of fundamentalism, because it relates religion/faith to political world domination. Rome has left the Biblical road of faith long ago. Its leaders work with the unredeemed man. In order to have enough power for the "flesh" of the followers, Rome makes people dependent on sacraments and sacramentals which finally lead to the "god of this world", Lucifer. This is the imitation of the Christian faith. Unsaved people who do not know Biblical repentance (turning around) also do not receive salvation through forgiveness. Therefore, they do not live in a reconciled relationship with God the Father.

"Therefore, brothers, we have an obligation— but it is not to the sinful nature, to live according to it. For if you live according to the sinful nature, you will die; but if by the Spirit you put to death the misdeeds of the body, you will live, because those who are led by the Spirit of God are sons of God." (Romans 8: 12-14).

With these principles of Holy Scripture we can now better understand the "work of the flesh" of the Encyclical. We must rate it as a stillbirth of a fundamentalistic world organization, which cannot stop putting its religious, sacramental stamp on world politics. Therefore, a "kingdom of peace" built on the old, sinful man is a dangerous illusion. The world lived through 1000 years (appr. 800-1806) of carnal fundamentalistic rule of Rome in the First Holy Roman Empire. After that, the Protestant-Freemason Second Empire (1870-1918) appeared. Then the undisguised satanic Third Reich (Empire) (1933 -1945) followed. The over 70 years of Soviet-communist rule should also not be forgotten. These were all attempts to create a dominion of peace out of the respective carnal spirit of the time which all failed because of the old, unredeemed Adam.

Jesus Christ will establish the longed for kingdom of peace with the new man "in which righteousness dwells" (Isaiah 32: 1) through the power of his Spirit once and for all.

The pope wants to make his "love" visible not only in human relationships but also in "the public realm". "Love only shines in the truth and can be lived by with credibility." Fine, but deceiving words, because beside his "love", "truth" mutated into a lie. Through eros-love the public sphere, including politics, is declared as the kingdom of God. A kingdom of God with unredeemed people, who are lacking the established foundation? With the eros-love and the "truth" that dwells in it, a kingdom of God should arise in which eternal peace reigns, consisting of the old Adam, who is spiritually totally unstable and defective and ruled by darkness?

We only need to look at world history. There are countless attempts to build a world of peace with the old, unredeemed Adam. This resulted in dictatorships, which tolerated only one synchronized opinion. This synchronizing turned people into machines, which just had to function. When this happened, people were in unison with the love and truth defined respectively. All these attempts failed because of the old, unredeemed Adam, regardless if they were done with gentle, or rude force, whether by religious Catholic, or non-religious regimes, like Hitler and Stalin in Europe. Also the newest attempts in our age to create peace and to preserve creation with the old Adam and his "sense of good will" are doomed to fail because of the old Adam, and they are conducive to push mankind into the greatest crisis of world history, from which there will be no escape for the old Adam.

Wherever agape-love rules through redeemed and therefore new people, the truth inherent in it will be recognized, which has the name: Christ Jesus. It is said about Him, that he is the true Word, bringer of life, which he passes on to those who are saved by Him (John 1: 1-4). This is life out of the Spirit of Jesus. Jesus says, "If you hold to my teaching, you are really my disciples. Then you will know the truth, and the truth will set you free." (John 8: 31-32). Eternal peace is at stake! The way leads from the Word of the Holy Scriptures to Jesus Christ, the personified Word, who is the life-giving truth (John 14: 6). Sin, understood as being far away from God and missing the mark, is defined as being dead for real life, "As for you, you were dead in your transgressions and sins, in which you used to live when you followed the ways of this world and of the ruler of the kingdom of the air, the spirit who is now at work in those who are disobedient. All of us also lived among them at one time, gratifying the cravings of our sinful nature and following its desires and thoughts ..." (Ephesians 2: 13a).

If peace is to be established, then the old Adam has to be removed. The basis is the new man, who shall be guided by the Spirit of Christ. This spiritually "revolutionary" process is agape-love. "Therefore, if anyone is in Christ, he is a new creation; the old has gone, the new has come! All this is from God, who reconciled us to himself through Christ and gave us the ministry of reconciliation." (2 Corinthians 5: 17-18). In the next verses, the discourse concludes with the statement, "that (Christ) put the word of reconciliation into us". Therefore, the redeemed by Christ have to live reconciliation in the power of Christ's Spirit. So the believer receives admonition from the Holy Scripture, Galatians 5: 1: "It is for freedom that Christ has set us free. Stand firm, then, and do not let yourselves be burdened again by a yoke of slavery".

Therefore, reconciliation with Christ leads to reconciliation with people. Only people reconciled with Christ can create peace in the areas where they are active. So the one redeemed by Christ does not pretend, that he can bring global peace to the unredeemed world.

For this reason, the one liberated from the power of the flesh refuses to gain power over the world. However, the papacy views this completely differently. As an imitation of the Biblically based faith, the old Adam is strengthened by the sacraments and connected to its powers. The subsequent misuse of power is inherent. The strengthened man of the flesh wants dominion over the whole world. These religious lusts for power are dangerous fundamentalisms, which make a peaceful co-existence of different cultures impossible. Biblical faith is to believe in the necessary salvation through Christ on a voluntary basis. This is not so with the Christian faith based on Catholic tradition which is in contrast, compulsory. Whenever compulsion is practiced, it is a sinful offense against the Gospel of grace and a relapse into the old religious constraints. However, the Roman system cannot do otherwise, than think and act out of the old structures of the flesh. Benedict XVI says, "It is the light of reason as well as of faith by which the intellect arrives at the natural and supernatural truth of love." The New Testament tells us, however, that human intellect, including reason, is equally fallen and therefore belongs to the fallen Adam. Benedict XVI says furthermore, that "truth opens the intellect of man and unites his intelligence with the logos of love". This is bloated, Luciferian, philosophical speech, which subjugates the truth. The "public" man does not have the truth of Christ; he would have to accept Christ as his savior first. Rome has neither spiritual understanding, nor truth, nor love. But it has demonic-transforming power out of the pseudo-Christian tradition. Benedict XVI wants to train man holistically. He looks for men "of good will". He looks for the "rational ones" who see that without the Catholic religion all political, technical, social, and environmental actions are doomed to fail. As described before, Benedict XVI is concerned about all unredeemed people, with whom he wants to build a social empire by strengthening them with Catholic spirit forces. Initially, it is unimportant from which culture and religion people come, for love and truth may be recognized by all people through reason. A Catholic "conversion" can be made later through baptism, which is important for the remission of original sin, through the other sacraments of penance and the Eucharist, which counts as sacrament of redemption.

In the third chapter of the encyclical, Benedict XVI explains under the title "Brotherliness", how to regard connections between economic development and civil society. He talks much about the egoism and the arrogance of man. He deplores furthermore, that man "overlooks that he has an injured nature, is inclined to evil, which leads to grave errors in the areas of education, politics, social interactions, and morality." Complaining does not help here, although some aspects of these ideas can be deemed correct. These fragments of truth however, disguise the fact that the outcome leads to religious fundamentalistic perception. Benedict XVI sees the cause for the decay of morality in sin. According to Rome, sin comes into existence, when (unredeemed) people violate moral- Western, i.e., Catholic values. Now we are stepping again on slippery grounds. The New Testament counters: "All have sinned" (Romans 3: 23). This encyclical is not concerned with underlining values of the New Testament which are independent of tradition, but the Catholic tradition claims sovereign rights of interpretation for the whole Bible. If "arrogance" of people is mentioned, it is at home in the Vatican. Benedict XVI continues, "The power of a world fellowship, which does not know barriers and borders, comes from the wellspring of love and truth. All people have received this gift. One needs only the power of goodwill to create a universal brotherly fellowship, to achieve the unity of mankind. He lacks only one thing: God's Word, who is love." However, because the Word of God (the Bible) is administered sacramentally and is subjugated to Catholic sovereign interpretation, this "Word of God" becomes a dictatorial religious alternative out of antichristian spirit. Instead of having the Word interpreted by Jesus, Rome puts itself above the Word of Jesus Christ.

The Bible tells us through Jesus Christ, who is, according to John 1, the personified Word of God, that this anticipated universal brotherly fellowship only comes into being in the expected future kingdom of Jesus Christ.

In this unredeemed world, redeemed people shall live in forgiveness and reconciliation to some degree, as an advance, in anticipation of the future kingdom of God. Only in this way will "brotherliness" spring up like a foretaste across all borders and cultures. (1 John 1: 1-7). This divine future program, was designed for redeemed people. The Vatican however, wants to use it in an unredeemed world with its unredeemed people. This leads inevitably to a renewed, Catholic religious fundamentalistic tyranny. At the end of this false path a religious tyrant, whom the Bible calls Antichrist (Instead-Christ) will await. He will assist with "regulations" so that all become people of "good will". So even today's Rome, which is a carnal, transformative way of living, wants to be celebrated with its arrogant sovereign interpretation as Christianity. It suppresses true Christian faith, which originates in the Word and Spirit of God. (Comp. Romans chapter 8). All attempts of Rome to build the kingdom of God on this earth as a kingdom of peace and righteousness is a dangerous aberration, that leads to renewed totalitarianism. Other, non-religious stray lights work just as Rome does, using fragments of truth, in order to mislead while remaining unrecognized. One asks oneself, sometimes amazedly : What does a pope have to do with themes like:

- economic development
- problems of a civil society
- particular nature of prisons
- market economy
- globalization of economy
- entrepreneurship
- systems of constitutions, justice and administration?

If this Roman Church has binding answers ready for all questions of society, where then is its religious central area?

One might think, that its religion has become secondary. However, this is not the case. It wants, as it has said, to guide mankind with its religion to perfection. It maintains, that the world will be suffused by peace and justice, if one would only listen to it. Because most people are not of "good will " and therefore unable to effect the realization of a new social and economic order, Benedict XVI. says furthermore, "... a political authority has to be promoted that is spread out and active on various levels." This "political authority" shall direct economic processes of globalization. Benedict XVI continues by saying, "The trueness of the process of globalization and its fundamental ethical criteria are given in the unity of the human family and in its progression towards the good." Then he says, that people with an open, cultural orientation are required, to include the "transcendence", in order to build a world community. Without question, he aims for a united world government with a "personalized" world authority. He sees the solution of all problems in a world government with a Catholically led, united world religion in the transcendent power of the Roman Catholic spirit. At the top will then be a world authority. The Book of Daniel in the Old Testament, chapter 7, verse 23 speaks about a coming kingdom, which will be completely different from all other previous kingdoms: "It will devour, crush, and destroy all countries." Apparently, this united world government will undertake more than it can deal with, because verse 24 reports, that 10 regions (10 kings) will arise out of it, which the Bible calls alliance of ten. Benedict XVI waits for this antichristian authority and works for it. So Benedict XVI wants to accomplish "the globalization of mankind in terms of living in connection, community, and participation."

In the fourth chapter he writes about the development of nations. His basic idea returns again and again: A development of mankind and the nations only comes to completion, when primarily Catholic transcendent powers are added as the decisive fact to political and social restructuring.

Benedict XVI warns of an immoderate arbitrariness of individual rights if these are not combined with preceding obligations. "The exaggeration of rights results in the omission of obligations." He adds, that the individual rights have to be limited by an "ethical frame". But there are no homogeneous ethics in pluralistic societies, so that here again Rome's intention comes through to transfer their ethical interpretation to suit the morals of the Vatican. This arrogance is apparent in the question: Who is a Christian and what is a Christian church? When this question comes up, the majority of the secular population has immediately the dogmas of the Roman Catholic Church in mind. The understandable rejection of the Roman Catholic Church also hits those Christians, who have distanced themselves from Rome. Because of the arrogant Roman interpretation about Christianity and church, people do not learn of the liberating Gospel of grace. This can only be apprehended away from the Catholic tradition by people who are redeemed through trust (faith) in the word of the New Testament by divine grace and thus arrive at the life of freedom. The tradition of Rome has obscured the life giving Gospel so much, that it passes for a vehicle of life negation, because of the "soul right of interpretation" of Rome. So Rome tries to enforce its arrogant "sovereign interpretation" in the areas of theology, the teaching about God, in the areas of politics, social life, environment, democracy, human rights, etc. On the one hand, Rome recognizes the evolved democracies as an accomplishment of modern times. On the other hand, Rome rejects democracy indirectly, because it implies possible changes of formerly made decisions. So Benedict XVI adds to this idea, "If however, the rights of men have their foundation only in the decisions of an assembly of citizens, they can be changed at any time." Benedict XVI considers the defense of unchangeability of ethical decisions as "duty in the service of the good". "The service of the good", according to Catholic legend, is conferred on the pope since the 9th century, who has the duty to transmit the magical power of "the blood of Christ" to him, who is found worthy to assume world dominion. If he does not find the "worthy one", he has to die like the sick fisher king. Comp. the respective article (The Grail — the esoteric, magical blood relic).

The present pope stands in the same magical tradition as well. Almost explicitly he waits for a "personified political authority", which the New Testament calls "Antichrist". So that he can establish a "kingdom of peace", pluralistic democracy has to be abolished first. The democratic civil rights with free shaping of public opinion and ethically differentiated variety would be "unified". Is the resumption of the fashistoid Order of St. Pius X into the lap of the Vatican also part of this? In any case, Benedict XVI proves himself to be a stylish worker in the vineyard of his Lord as a collector of all transcendent magical powers, which are supplied by his "Mary" and the magical

Eucharist. According to the Celtic-Catholic legend, the "sick fisher king", the pope, focuses on the arrival of a personified world authority, to which he will make available the demonic magical powers of his Grail for the establishment of dictatorial might. Now he begins with relativizing the democracies. For this he recommends "the church, which has the true development of man close to its heart."

On the one hand, Benedict XVI confesses belief in evolution (comp. article "the theory of evolution and the pope") on the other hand, he says in his encyclical in chapter four, which we have already quoted, "If nature, and ahead of it all, man are seen as the fruit of chance, or of evolutionary determinism, the sense of responsibility in the consciences weakens." And furthermore: "If this opinion disappears, in the end man will see nature either as an untouchable taboo, or conversely, will exploit it." What is one of the popular sayings? He who lies has to have a good memory. So he wants, "That the whole human family finds the necessary resources, in order to live worthily for God's gift to his children with the help of nature and the dedication of their work and their inventiveness." Again we find this "religious" arrogance: All people are called children of God, although most of them are not children of God, and do not even want to be. Benedict XVI takes the freedom away from people to decide if they want this, or not. One only becomes a child of God if one responds to the offer of God's grace voluntarily by faith. Rome does not want to know this, because they interpret the Gospel in the Light of their traditions, and put these above the testimony of Holy Scripture. Another pretension of Rome consists of speaking for all of mankind. Benedict XVI wants to strengthen the bond between man and environment, because it is a mirror of the creator love of God, "in whom we have our origin and to whom we are on the way." The Catholic sacramental God is a God of slavery. The author, as a Christian of the New Testament, does not want to be on the way to this imitated "God". And neither does the secular world want to. The Christ, who is confessed in the New Testament, is different. He is the original of grace, faith, and redemption. He is love (agape). In the Letter to the Galatians (5: 1) in the New Testament, it says: "Stand firm, then, in freedom, for which Christ has set us free, and do not let yourselves be burdened again by a yoke of slavery."

In the fifth chapter, Benedict XVI takes a stand on the topic of "The co-operation of the human family". He wants it to come to "a new impetus in thinking". He quotes Pope Paul VI, who remarked, that "the world is sick, because it lacks thoughts." The human family should not just rely on social sciences, when relationship is the issue. "It has to permit the contribution of knowledge like metaphysics and theology, in order to comprehend clearly the transcendent dignity of man." He is thinking about catholic (demonic) transcendence, or one could also say: Catholic-mysticism. Without this "his transcendency" there would be no unity. So he takes the Catholic "Trinity" as a symbol for complete unity and as a symbol for "pure relationship". This complete divine unity he wants to see applied among people. He misuses the word of John 17: 22: "That they may be one as we are one." The unredeemed "human family" has adopted the position of the redeemed people, for which these Biblical words stand, through the Catholic misuse of interpretation. "The church is symbol and tool of this unity." A church of unredeemed people become the redeemed ones through forced baptism! This is the Roman Church, which wants to include the whole world as children of the united family of mankind through the power of the Roman Catholic spirit. So this spirit is supposed to "penetrate deeply" into the people. Then these people think alike, because they were synchronized by this spirit that penetrates them. In therapeutic counseling we call this process "transformation into a synchronized consciousness". The pope continues, "The unity in the relationship connects in an analogue way (in reference to the Trinity) the truth, the rational beings and makes them think in unison by attracting them and uniting them in itself." The Roman Catholic spirit shall produce this unison. Under these conditions people allow it to rule them, e.g., through the fascination of Greek-Roman culture and the triumphalism of Roman ritual, pomp, and display of power. We live in a time of frequently broken, split up souls all the way to "multiple quanta personalities". This spirit can work very successfully in these people through invisibly launched sensations, which are nothing else but thoughts programmed by this spirit for Roman unity through fascination. Rome manipulates mankind with the Roman antichristian spirit. We determined several times, that an antichristian united world government needs an antichristian united world religion as well, in order to achieve the unity of the family of mankind. So, the pope says, "The unity of the human race presupposes a metaphysical interpretation of the 'humanum'." Benedict XVI continues and says, that also other cultures and religions teach brotherliness and peace. Therefore these religions are "of great importance for the holistic development of man." In contradiction to this he says, "That there are also some other cultures with religious backgrounds, which do not bind man to community, but isolate him in the search for individual wellness by limiting themselves to satisfy psychological expectations." Under the surface it is alleged, that through the process of globalization, economically as well as politicly, "to favour such syncretism and to nurture such forms of religions leads to the alienation of people among themselves." Rome as the "power of sovereign interpretation" interprets, that individualistic thinking, which leads to different results, is hostile to man, because it does not lead to a unified, synchronized thinking, which can be manipulated by the Vatican. As already mentioned, these Luciferian beginnings lead to the dictatorship desired by the Roman Catholic Church with a world ruler who is "nurtured" primarily by its power. Does the Vatican now want to soak up the other religions in the first attempt, so that they are only allowed to play the role of religious statistics? With Luciferian deception, Benedict XVI declares, that a fine distinction has to be made "concerning the contributions of cultures and religions for the establishment of the social community with respect to common welfare. This is especially required of the one who exercises political power." The most important criterion for him is this, that the other cultures and religions work towards "a truly universal community of man."

He determines immediately, that "Christianity (Catholicism) the religion of the God with a human face", fulfills this criterion. Through Roman interpretation one now knows, who, beside Christians who are tied to the Bible, are considered to be hostile to mankind. These are the ones, who turn against the doctrines of this aping church, which claims to be the only one that saves. Also included are those, who not only demand their democratic liberal rights for themselves, but who want to impart them to others as well. Nevertheless, these are labeled fundamentalists, unwilling to integrate, who trample human rights under foot. But the opposite is the case. If one looks for fundamentalists with dictatorial objectives, one finds them quickly and does not need to search for long. The Roman Catholic Church is plainly the most fundamental organization, because in its history of appr. 1700 years (starting with Constantine around 300 A.D.) it always pushed through its pseudo-Christian religion with political force when it had the power to do so. No religious organization with such a long history has violated so many human rights, which were formulated in the New Testament. It ostracized or even destroyed people who claimed their divinely given rights. Does this Roman Church now want to present itself as the leader of a more peaceful world? Is not the accusation of fundamentalism especially justified because of its domineering claim? Benedict XVI demands that the Roman Church should recapture more and more its position in the power of the state. The pope said furthermore: "Human rights are in danger of not being honoured, because they are either robbed of their transcendent foundation (magical esoteric) …". So, one loses "in laicism and in fundamentalism (these are the inflexible Anti-Romans for him, who protect their liberal rights) the possibility of a fruitful dialogue and a profitable co-operation between reason and religious faith." The rights of interpretation of what faith is, are Rome's of course. Could people, who demand their individual rights as human rights and pass them on inside a democratic community in the framework of their conviction of faith, be accused of fundamentalism? We do not support the views of extreme christian charismatics, who conduct morbid faith conferences. But even these do not strive for political power in general. They are wrongly called Evangelicals and insulted. But more dangerous than these are the religious organizations who try to enforce their religious conviction politicly by means of the legislature and executive powers. Here, and only here, would the name "fundamentalism" be appropriate. The Vatican attempts a maneuver of distracting from itself by redefining the term. This is slander. It would go beyond the scope of the subject of this book to elaborate on Benedict XVI's favourite topic: 'connecting reason', which only needs to be cleansed from Roman transcendence.

The pope wants to have it understood as a duty, that all people of "good will", be they believing Catholics or not, cooperate for one objective and that is to establish permanently justice and peace on this earth. Jesus Christ, as Savior, who has created the prerequisite and who will fulfill the completion of his work as king of peace no longer appears. So, Benedict XVI says, in order not to antagonize the secular world further, and he relates this to the council fathers, "It is the almost unanimous view of believers and unbelievers, that everything on earth has to be ordered toward man as his central point and pinnacle." Therefore, it is a human duty to unite "with all people of good will", which includes people of other religions and nonbelievers. Then he dissociates himself again from the elements in other religions, which have much "that is troublesome and that casts shadows, from which one has to liberate oneself and withdraw oneself." But if "the Christian faith takes shape in the other cultures and so transforms them, it can help them to grow in universal community and solidarity for the advantage of common worldwide development." Is this the Roman sanatorium as a physician for the shadows in other religions and convictions of faith? Now, in spite of this Western-Catholic arrogance, Rome is no longer strong enough to be the physician of force for all religions and orientations of faith. The "transcendency" desired by Rome through the Catholic faith would mean, that all other religions and confessions would take part in the power of the demonic transcendence of the Roman Catholic spirit. This total unification with all religions would secure the religious power of Rome as top-of-the-range of the united world church, in order to submit to the coming Antichrist as "world authority" the united religious powers as invisible elements of power, quasi as Grail.

The pope elaborates further, that "this political world authority would be acknowledged then by all, which would have effective power to enforce justice. Also, all decisions are included here, which were made by international forums. The holistic development of the family of nations requires this. This world authority has to pursue the principle of subsidiarity in solidarity, in order to control the globalization of politics and the economy. A moral social order shall be realized".

Subsidiarity is a sociopolitical concept. It means, e.g., that the state takes on only so much responsibility, which the individual can not bear or take on.

Rome's objective is also to advocate, that all Catholic work in the area of theology, politics, as well as in society has to aim at the new world order (New Age) under the leadership of a single dictatorial person, whom they call "the personified world authority". According to our knowledge, this was talked about the first time by Pope John XXIII at the Vatican Council 1962, shortly before his death. It is now easier for the readers to recognize, that the Vatican with its Babylon Harlot and its culture bearer "Mary" is the antichristian spirit supplier, who wants to put the Antichrist into power as the world authority.

In the sixth and last chapter, Benedict XVI asserts, that mankind can only be saved through reason and faith in religion. As we have determined, this "faith" gets its power from fallen and unredeemed man. However, reason also belongs to the old, unredeemed man according to the testimony of the New Testament. Genuine faith lives out of the Spirit of Christ, whereas false faith lives out of the fallen spirit of reason. When Benedict XVI talks about "spirit", he means reason. According to the New Testament, however, fallen reason is controlled by "darkness". His "honorable world authority" that he strives for as the owner of the Grail, has to be a person, that is equipped with "purified reason" and faith in Roman transcendence. So, the Antichrist will be a political, religious, i.e., also a fundamentalistic authority.

Benedict XVI misuses the Bible when he quotes it. So he testifies, that his predecessor Pope Paul VI said in his encyclical "Populorum progressio", "that man is not in a position to further his progress alone, because he cannot establish genuine humanism on his own." All people are children of God, so, people are able if they start from there, "to produce a new thinking and to unfold new powers in the service of a genuine, holistic humanism. The great power in the service of development, therefore, is a Christian (Catholic) humanism." Benedict XVI then turns against the "atheism of apathy", which represents the greatest obstacles on the path of development of mankind. Summing up he says, that "humanism that excludes God is an inhuman humanism." However, we think that the God the pope has in mind, is not the Father of Jesus Christ; for man can come to him only through Jesus Christ without other mediators (John 14: 6). We as Christians, who understand the Bible through the interpretation of Jesus Christ in the New Testament, look at the claim of the Christian imitation of the pope, that all people are God's children, as being a blasphemy.

But in John 1: 12 it says: "Yet to all who received him (Jesus Christ) to those who believed in his name, he gave the right to become children of God." One becomes a child of God, if one believes in the Jesus of the New Testament and if one lives out of him. You are not a child of God, just because you are a human being. We humans descended from the fallen, originally good creation of God. Only if people return to God by a voluntary decision of faith and believe in Jesus Christ, do they become children of God. As a Christian, who has taken this step, the author thinks it is arrogant to approach atheistic humanists with pressure to suggest to them that they are children of God, because they are human beings. According to Benedict XVI they are then still inhuman in their humanism, because they did not integrate the Catholic god. The Bible maintains decidedly, that compulsory conversion is sin, because it misses the objective of God's grace. Jesus himself did not force anyone to convert to him. He always understood his mission, just like the apostles, as an offer of life. Rome, in contrast, lures, suggests, punishes, rejects, if the Roman Catholic tradition is not accepted.

Rome wants to have the sovereign interpretation also about this topic. As we have explained already, Rome wants to recognize only a holistic humanism. It consists of the results of the social sciences in combination with the Roman Catholic religion. Rome's doctrine consists of this: to threaten, that there is no human humanism without the Roman Catholic religion. It is painful for genuine Christians, who live by the Word of God, which was interpreted by Jesus and the Apostles by the Spirit of God, that, because of Catholic forgery, they interpret the Bible according to Catholic tradition. Without this tradition no Catholic believer can, or is allowed to read the Bible. So, Rome turns itself into the supreme judge of its Catholic believers, and also into the supreme judge, who claims sovereign interpretation, above all other forms of belief, of humanism, even the whole world. This state of affairs cannot be denied by flattery aimed at the secular world: You are all children of God. The Pontifex Maximus, as supreme bridge builder, turns himself into God.

The Christian Catholic humanism is from the earth, it is temporal. Therefore it is also perishable. The concept of the Biblical Christ is "from heaven". This concept continues in the new man, who was begotten by the Spirit of Christ through grace and the response of faith. The Biblical Jesus says in John 3: 5: "Unless a man is born of water and the Spirit (from above) he cannot enter the kingdom of God."

So, you have to be born again, in order to collaborate for the coming kingdom of Christ. This is the Biblical tenor. If then the kingdom of God shall be built in the sense of a Catholic Christian humanism, this perishable program is directed against Christ, the Redeemer of the Bible. Such a program is called "antichristian". Speaking in context: It has taken the place of the statements, which Jesus interpreted in the New Testament. An instead-of-program is supported by a different spirit. This spirit is Lucifer or Satan. He is called the father of lies. This instead-of-spirit also has an instead-of-man, generated out of unredeemed "flesh". This instead-of or anti-man is also called Antichrist. In this encyclical, Benedict XVI has revealed, that he services the personified world authority, therefore, the expected Antichrist. (Comp. 2 Thessalonians 2: 3-4).

The well of papal deception bubbles out of the transcendent woman, which the Bible calls Babylon Harlot, "which sits on many waters (cultures, religions)". (Revelation 17: 1). The Catholic Western spirit-woman is the Catholic "Mary". These transcendent "spirit-women" are the "right hands" of Lucifer. They search after the man of sin and supply this antichristian system with spirit power. So, Pope Benedict XVI concludes his encyclical with the petition to his transcendent spirit-woman "Mary", that she "obtains for us through her intercession in heaven the power, the hope and the joy, that we need to furthermore devote ourselves generously to the duty of realizing the development of the whole person and of all people."

We should rather stick to the Bible and recognize it as the Word of God. About the Babylon Harlot with her cultural spirit-women, Revelation 18: 3 says this: "For all the nations have drunk the maddening wine of her adulteries. The kings of the earth committed adultery with her, and the merchants of the earth grew rich from her excessive luxuries."

It is speaking here about a mental-spiritual adultery, which, e.g., happens through the instead-of-theology of the Vatican. Corrupted religion together with corrupted financial bearings walk here hand in hand. As the supreme responsible body for this Babylonian system, the pope stands as the supreme bridge builder (Pontifex Maximus). This name comes from the old Babylonians, and it means: To have power over "the gates of the gods" (bab ilani). Verse 7 refers to the haughtiness, the arrogance of this spirit-woman: " In her heart she boasts, 'I am enthroned as queen (queen of peace); I am not a widow, and I will never mourn."

In verse 13 it talks about lucrative trade with bodies of men and souls of men. Do we have to think here only about the slave trade in the past?

The spirit from which the power of the Roman Catholic Church comes, is Babylon, and the pope, as the supreme bridge builder, is powerful enough to walk through the gate of the gods, in order to make the true Christians and the secular world hold their breath.

Appendix A

For a better understanding of our topic, we have to realize, that the Vatican and Catholic Rome plays the role of a network, that stretches over the whole globe (Ecumenism).

1. Introduction

There are four so-called patriarchal basilicas in Rome for universal Catholicism:
- St. Peter
- St. Paul before the Walls
- St. John in the Lateran
- St. Mary Maggiore

These four churches contain the "Holy Gates", which were opened for the year 2000. Now they are bricked up until the next Holy Year.

In addition, there are still three other churches in Rome, which together represent the seven main churches of universal Rome.
- San Sebastiano
- Sante Croce in Gerusaleme
- San Lorenco before the Walls

These seven churches make up Rome's power base.

Furthermore, the title and station churches serve as important power places. The location named "Titulus" refers to a house of A-Z. It passed for the houses in which the first Christians gathered. Since Constantine, with the beginning of religion from the Christian faith, these houses were reinterpreted according to the names of a genuine, or a pretended martyr. The so-called "Title Churches" came out of this. All of the approx. 130 cardinals have received such a "Title Church", in order to emphasize the common basis with early Christianity. In reality, a religious network of approx. 1500 years of demonic religious power is now established, and it is transmitted by succession. So, a picture of the respective cardinal hangs on the wall in every Title Church.

Besides the Title Churches there are still many Station Churches, in which the pope celebrates one mass according to liturgical order during the year. Therefore the seven main churches and the many title and station churches are very important for Catholics, because

Appendix A

they receive "indulgences" in them. About 40 "saints" have their graves in one of the churches. In addition, there are still the innumerable collections of relics, which can be found in each of the 400 churches of Rome. A perfect network of DEATH spreads over the whole world; it originated in the city of Rome, was kept together by all of the Roman rulers, the 265 popes, who are bridge builders into death – they build bridges from the people living in the immanence to the transcendent spirits of the macrocosm – and therefore they have the name: Pontifex Maximus.

2. The Churches

2.1. The patriarchal basilicas as parts of the main churches

<u>St. Peter (Peter Basilica)</u>

On Peter's Square is the 25.5 m high obelisk, which emperor Caligula ordered to be brought to Rome in the first century. In 1586 the obelisk was erected on the 340 m long and 240 m wide square with sacrifices of death. As a powerful Egyptian death symbol with a cross as a final decoration, which contains splinters of the cross, the obelisk represents a basic strength of the Roman religion, the death powers from Egypt.

A staircase with three times seven steps leads up to the basilica flanked with potent statues of "Peter" and of "Paul" on either side. The statues of the 11 Apostles and of "Jesus Christ" impress the visitor from the top of the 45 m high facade.

In the center of the inside of the basilica is the altar of the pope with the grave of Peter underneath. The glass casket of Pope John XXIII (beatified in 2000) was new. He initiated Vatican Council II which brought about Rome's turning point to the politics of absorption through the Ecumenical movement.

Inside the church, approximately 16 popes are buried. In the pope crypt underneath about another 130, so approximately 146 popes are buried in Peter's Church altogehter. All deliver strong demonic spirit forces, in each case those of their sinful times. In addition, there are around 60 statues and pictures. Not included are thousands of pictures in the museums. Peter's Church is the most potent power spot of Catholicism.

Appendix A

Image 21
Petrus Basilika

At the end of January 2002 I was standing again on Peter's Square when the pope opened the window of his office at 12 p.m. on the occasion of the "Angelus Prayer" and for a quarter of an hour of ritual prayer. While we were praying against this idol worship, the church people chanted hysterically, "Papa".

We should know that this Peter's Church was built upon the disintegrated Constantine-construction in the 16th and 17th centuries. The Renaissance Pope Julius II (1503-1513) had the first plans made. His successor, Paul III (1534-1549) ordered Michelangelo to manage the construction project without pay. Rafael, Michelangelo, and later on Bernini created in over 100 years of construction time the most extravagant physical evidence of the Roman religion out of the spirit of the Babylon Harlot. They chose this location for the basilica, because a huge cemetery of antiquity had been here and, according to legend, Peter met the martyr's death.

However, historically it is unlikely that Peter was in Rome at all. The first papal dwelling was built at this spot in the 6th century. The later popes resettled to Lateran Palace. Since Gregor IX returned from Avignon, after 70 years of absence of papacy, the pope's seat has always been on the Vatican's hills. The Vatican's buildings were eventually completed under Pope Pius XI (1922-1939). The whole complex of buildings contains 1400 halls, rooms, and chapels. They found during excavations from below upwards:

Appendix A

- Graves of an antique cemetery.
- Pagan Mausoleums.
- A basilica, built by Constantine in honour of Peter.
- Peter's church was erected on this site and stands there today.
- The sources of money for the basilica were primarily:
- Shares from the slave trade, especially from the Portuguese and the Spaniards.
- Money from selling indulgences.

The "Holy Brigitta" received a vision from the "Lord" in the year 1350: "Go to Rome, there the roads are paved with gold and reddened by the blood of the saints. There the heaven is open, because of the indulgences which the holy popes receive through their prayers." (Quoted from an advertisement in a Catholic travel guide of Rome).

Until today Catholics travel to Rome to receive indulgences from all punishments of sin.

So the Vatican is the world center of the Babylon Harlot. This Vatican State only exists with its present boundaries since 1929. Up until the time that Garibaldi expelled the pope from 1850 onwards, the Vatican ruled as a sovereign almost over all of the middle of Italy. Then in 1929 the Lateran Treaties were arranged with the new secular state, which established the present Vatican City, or Vatican State on the west side of the old Rome. The power consists of demonic spirit forces of the Babylon Harlot, and through pacts with the Mafia in the 1960's, the Freemasons, as well as with ultraconservative organizations like Opus Dei, by which cheerfully abundant money bubbles.[348]

St. Paul before the Walls

In the vicinity of St. Paul is the "Abbazia delle Tre fontane", the place where many Christians and also the Apostle Paul were executed through beheading at the time of the Romans. As always, several churches have unfortunately been built there. According to a pious Catholic legend which arose, the executed head of Paul bounced up three times on the stone ground. Thus the miracle occured, that

---

[348] Comp. Yallop, "Im Namen Gottes?" ("In the Name of God?"), 1988; and Urquhart, "Im Namen desPapstes" ("In the Name of the Pope"), 1995.

three springs of fresh water originated from it. This legend is retained and adored in a large painting.

A few kilometers from there, St. Paul's Church stands remotely on the southwest side of Rome, at the main arterial road Ostiense which leads to Ostia on the coast. St. Paul is the largest church after Peter's Cathedral. The Benedictines look after this church. The antique graves are suppposed to be under the basilica, thus also that of the Apostle. In January of 2000 both Orthodox and Protestant representatives walked here through the Holy Gate.

No-one pretends to be in the possession of the relics of Paul. Generally one gets the impression that this church has lost some of its importance for Rome. Very strong spirit forces were not at work here.

St. John in the Lateran

This is the third patriarchal church of the Roman system. Nevertheless, it carries unusual titles: Cathedral of Rome, Mother of all Churches of the World, Arch Basilica.

It was the first basilica that emperor Constantine built between 311 and 314.

Thus it has the privileged place of honour at all religious celebrations even before St. Peter Church.

A very close relationship exists between this church and Dominicus (13th century) the founder of the Dominican Order, which became the responsible body for the inquisition and also 100 years later the responsible body for the Counter-Reformation and all show trials and persecutions. Dominicus and the successors enforced with brutal power the Marian faith. Dominicus is buried in Bologna. He also stands for the Catholic intellectual paradigm that his spirit has initiated and which it has to protect: "Only through Mary to Jesus." At the same time Dominicus stands for the erudition of Catholic intellectuals out of which the Jesuits came. One can see in the church how Dominicus points with his outstretched right hand at Mary, the Domina of the church.

The Catholic intellect entered into a symbiosis with Francis of Assisi. So, he stands for the reconciliation with death, for a mixing up of religion through submission under Rome, for an integration of so-called folk religion with mysticism.

Appendix A

So the symbiotic union between intellect and emotionality, or between rationalism and irrationalism came into being. In a personified sense it means: Dominicus, the successor of the great erudite rabbis of the OT, and Francis, "another Christ", who experienced death and resurrection. Pope Innocent III, who was a contemporary of both and who gave St. Francis the recognition of an order, has already created this symbiosis out of Antichristian, Babylonian spirit.

The tomb of Innocent III became the crown of this church in the Lateran from whence demonic spirit power continues to operate.

Innocent III is responsible for the death of 1,1 million people because of the persecution which took place during his time in the 13th centrury.

Francis and Dominicus were the most outstanding figures during Innocent III's pontificate. Without them, even the most important Catholic theologian Thomas of Aquinas, born in 1225, and his writing "Summa Theologica" would be inconceivable. So the spirit of Thomas of Aquinas occupies a large space in this arch basilica of Catholicism. Now one understands better the title: Mother of all Churches of the World. Do we also now understand the necessity of a relentless spiritual battle against this Catholic spirit?

Another remarkable title above St. John in the Lateran: Heiress of the dignity and holiness of the temple of Jerusalem. Thus they perceive themselves as the successors of the old people of God.

<u>Santa Maria Maggiore</u>

A distinctive attribute of Catholicism is that "Mary" is placed among the Biblical patriarchs of the NT alongside with Peter, Paul, John the Baptist, and John the Evangelist. Also in this church a symbiosis was created: Mary with Pope Pius IX.

The spirit of this Mary is in reality the spirit of the Babylon Harlot. On entering the church, one discovers the kneeling and Mary worshiping pope in front of the crypt, over which the altar of the pope rises, as it is also the case in Peter's Church.

Pius IX is the pope of modern times who put in place the doctrine of Mary as "Immaculata", as "Immaculate Conception", in 1854; Mary without original sin, equal to the angels; the path leading away from man to an angelic-like being. The pope personified this with Lourdes.

Then in 1950 the final conclusion came for this spirit being of the Babylon Harlot through the doctrine of Pius XII: The ascension of Mary.

Pius IX also dogmatized the infallibility of the pope besides the "Immaculata" in 1870.

Therefore, Maria Maggiore is an explicit declaration of war against modern times and against all genuine Christians of this time.Mary – Domina, Lady, or Madonna, queen of all prophets of the Roman universal church. Through her, the Catholics come to Lucifer, but not to Jesus. By the way, the four patriarchal churches had opened the "Holy Gates" for the "Holy Year". These were walled up again after an urn had been kept safe inside. These urns, or caskets by name have transcendent power.

- Peter's Church

The casket does not contain anything. It is decorated with the theme of the years 1998-2000, i.e.: Father-Son-Trinity.

- St. Paul before the Walls

The representation: A sheet, a tree, a cross shaped sword, and a feather symbolize conversion, mission, and martyrdom of the Apostle Paul.

- St. John in the Lateran

The stylized facade of the basilica is represented there.

- Santa Maria Maggiore Annunciation of the angel, Virgin Mary, Archangel Gabriel.

2.2. *The lower-level main churches, or basis churches*

As already described, 3 other churches still exist which belong to the wholeness – the number 7 – of the power base of Rome.

Santa Croce in Gerusalem

Here the relics of the cross are kept and worshiped, which St. Helena, the mother of Constantine collected.

San Lorenzo before the Walls

A martyrs church which contains the tomb of Pius IX. In 1943 when the war turned in favour of the allies, Pius XII prayed here to the spirit of the pope of modern times for wisdom.

Appendix A

San Sebastiano
It contains the most famous catacombs and graves of martyrs. Sebastian -who was he? Historically he appears to be a nobody. The Roman Church however, puts him almost on a standing with St. Stephen because he too dispenses power out of the martyr's death as co-redeemer power.

2.3. Some title-, resp. station-churches

Santa Sabina
History: Dominicus and Francis met here several times. Catholic intellect and Catholic irrationalism coalesce here (comp. Lateran). Thomas of Aquinas (1225-1274) wrote his "Summa Theologica" here.

Santa Maria di Cosmedian
One of the oldest churches of Rome has its origin in a pagan temple. The Catholic martyrs Cyrill, Hilarius, Coronatus lie in the crypt.

St. Prisca on the Aventino Hill
The historical background originates in the Acts of the Apostles; it is the couple of faith, Aquila and Priscilla, who served the Apostle Paul. A home-based church existed here, mostly of slaves who had to serve the Roman Lords on the Aventin.

Pantheon
All gods of antiquity were united here under the Catholic Mary.

"Gesu" Church
The church of the Jesuits in which Ignatius of Loyola supposedly is buried. We did not find the tomb.

San Minerva Church
It is opposite of the Pantheon. The tomb of St. Cathrine of Siena is in here.

St. Maria d'Ara Coeli
The tomb of St. Helena, the mother of Constantine is here.

Appendix B
Assisi, the unholy place for an unholy kingdom of peace

The first inter-religious meeting took place in Assisi 1986. The last meeting in Assisi was under the leadership of Pope John Paul II on 24. 01. 2002. An additional one took place in Aachen/ Germany from Sept 7th - Sept 9^{ht} 2003. Spiritual opposition was announced here. The most important churches in Assisi/Italy are:

Basilica Franciscus
One finds the grave of Francis in it, although, according to legend, he supposedly ascended into heaven. One picture portrays him like Elijah who was taken up by fiery chariots. Another image depicts him being taken up into heaven by angels.

Francis is publicly proclaimed as another Christ, because he:
- did miracles including raising the dead
- died and supposedly rose again
- Had nail wounds on his hands and feet.

This other Christ, or Christ-substitute, read: Antichrist, is supposed to bring world peace through the peace of the religions. The pope had to take steps back because of the loss of spirit power.

The second most important basilica of the city is

Basilica S. Chiara (St. Clara)
Clara was obviously the beloved of Francis. There is a monument in Assisi that shows both of them holding hands. Later on she founded the order of the Clarissinens named after her. Another order for female Franciscans came up later. In the basilica is the tomb of the Holy Clara.

Minerva Church
in which St. Rita of Cascia is revered.

Three other churches were closed until further notice, because of damage through earthquakes in 1997. These three churches were still closed at the time of my visit in January of 2002:
- St. Appolinare
- St. Maria Maggiore
- St. Pietro

Appendix B: Assisi, the unholy place

Outside of Assisi there are another 2 important churches:

Basilica di Santa Maria degli Angeli
Mary and her angels are revered here especially.

San Damiano
Francis had a transcendent apparition here. The other, the cosmic Christ appeared to him after he had sung the famous song of the sun, the revival song of the spirit of the sun. He commanded Francis to build a chapel for his Sun-Christ, to whom he owed his nail marks. This he did.

On the 24. 01. 2002 the most unsuccessful religious leaders' conference took place which Pope John Paul II put through. Whereas formerly even the secular world was fascinated by him, this project of preparing for a united world religion encounters more and more disinterest. This time John Paul II got so much pressure from the cardinal's board, that he was not allowed to pray together with the non-Christian religious leaders, as had happened at the same place in 1986. Each of them got monastery rooms, or rooms in the church, in which they could practice their prayer-, or rather: mantra sorcery. The commonality consisted of non-binding declarations of renunciations of violence. How non-binding this was, one can see in the fact, that up to the first printing of this book, thousands of people were still dying through the hands of fanatical, fundamentalist religious people, mostly Moslems, who were rushed into terrorism by their leaders.

It makes you sad, that Protestants, even Baptists, came together for common prayer with Pope John Paul II, who has the official new title: "Mild Christ".

The following statements show the arrogant and self-confident witness of the antichristian spirit of Assisi:

"I am strong through the blood of the world,
through the ocean of tears,
through the might of the world,
through the longing of the people, only in you."

For this meeting, approx. 200 guests were invited from various religions. In addition, 2000 people from these religions were permitted as spectators at the conference. A declaration to renounce violence

Appendix B: Assisi, the unholy place

was made by all representatives. The pope summarized this with the words, "Never again violence. Never again war! Never again terrorism. In the name of God, may each religion bring to the world justice and peace, forgiveness and life, love".[349]

This proposition is a step backwards for Ecumenism, because the unification of religions no longer takes first place any more, because it is not feasible at this time. Now it should be shown to the world, "that the upright impulse to pray does not lead to confrontation and even less to contempt of the others, but to constructive dialogue, in which everyone, without giving in to relativism or syncretism in any way, becomes even stronger aware of the responsibility of witnessing and of proclaiming."[350]

At the end, the participating religions are listed:

1. Rom. Catholicism
2. Orthodox Churches, Ecumenical Patriarchy
3. Greek Orthodox of Alexandria and of all of Africa
4. • of Antioch and of all of the Orient
5. • of Jerusalem
6. Orthodox Patriarchy of Moscow
7. • of Serbia
8. • of Rumania
9. Orthodox Church of Finland
10. • of Bulgaria
11. • of Cyprus
12. • of Poland
13. • of Albania
14. - 19. all Churches of the old Orient
20. Anglican Fellowship
21. Lutheran World Alliance
22. World Alliance of Reformed Churches
23. Presbyterian Church Scotland
24. World Council of Methodists
25. Christian Church (Disciples of Christ)
26. Pentecostals
27. World Federation of Baptists

---
349 "L'Osservatore Romano", No. 5, 01,02, 2002, p. 8.
350 Ibid. p. 8.

28. European Union of Baptists
29. World Conference of the Mennonites
30. Salvation Army
31. Moravian Church (Herrnhuter Brothers)
32. Quaker
33. Ecumenical Council of Churches
34. Judaism
35. Islam
36. Buddhism
37. Shintoism
38. Confucianism
39. Jainism
40. Sikhism
41. Hinduism
42. Zoroastrism
43. African traditional Religions

Independent organizations, e.g., Fokolare Movement Italy, Taize France, Thanksgiving Square, USA.

Appendix C
Aachen, Germany, Prayer for Peace
September 7th - 9th 2003

"Between war and peace. Religions and cultures meet each other. Representatives of the Christian churches and of the great religions, delegates of various cultures, men and women on the quest for peace."

The spiritualistic Catholic fellowship Sant' Egido from Assisi/Italy organized this peace conference. As a critical observer, I visited this conference together with some of the co-workers of our organization.

What then were the most important elements which justified a get-together between the religions?

According to the desires of the organizers, the respective religions want to find ways for peace between the cultures, which had their foundation more or less in religion.

It has become obvious in the world, that most conflicts of war are justified religiously-fundamentalisticly. Especially in front of the secular world, the religious world has to prove, that it is not implicitly intolerant and murderous. However, because the atheistic world is right on this point, the religious try to veil the truth with PR measures, even worse: They try to "water down" the hard truths of their cultural history and to change darkness into light.

Three main emphases of the conference will make this clear:

1. "Ex Orient" Exhibition

A Jew named Isaac is glorified here. He travelled from Aachen to Baghdad under the orders of emperor Charlemagne (9th century) in order to enrich the empire with the great culture of Islam. The embarrassing information about oppression and heavy payments of tribute, a taxation only for Christians and Jews, was "watered down". Islam was praised as a great cultural beauty, incl. the women in harems which were taken advantage of. It was called a great power for shaping Europe, and was then transferred into our time.

Emperor Charlemagne is praised in a new book as the first European. Bible, Koran, and Thora were presented as having equivalent value. All Biblical distinctiveness of the life-giving truth is sacrificed to the equalizing religious myths – also those of history. What for? That is the question.

2. Prayers for Peace

We visited the mosque, the synagogue, various Roman-Catholic churches, incl. the cathedral, one Ecumenical, Orthodox-Roman-Catholic church: Everywhere the attempt was made to appear as peace-loving and tolerant according to PR manners. The other religions were assigned to classrooms or other places in which they held their sorcery-rituals for "peace". As critics, we visited furthermore the Buddhists, Zoroastrists (Persia, Zarathustra) Shintoists, Jainists, and Hinduists. We prayed against this idol worship to our Lord Jesus Christ. The ignorance of the participating, identity lacking protestants was the most disturbing. Did they now believe in the magic power of the religions and their sorcery after abandoning the life-giving faith in Jesus Christ?

3. Concluding Event

At the end of the all-religions conference, all religious representatives entered the podium erected behind the cathedral with great applause. The bishop of Aachen swore in all participants to the prayer of peace of the "other Christ", St. Francis of Assisi, and expressed unmistakably Rome's dominant position. Jesus was mentioned as one of the many founders and prophets of religions, which had suffered for their cause. The "proclamation" consisted of the reading of the prologue of the 34th Psalm by Benedict of Nursia (Benedictine). The Psalm itself wasn't read, of course.

So the whole event showed again out of which spirit it fed itself: The spirit of the Antichrist with his distant goal of the unified church under the leadership of the Roman religion of the Catholic Church.

Appendix D
1ˢᵗ Ecumenical Church Congress in Berlin
May 28ᵗʰ - June 1ˢᵗ 2003

This was the first church congress which was organized by Catholics and Protestants together. The preliminary goal was unity among them including the free churches. The antichristian spirit of the end-time is hard to miss.

So the Protestant Bishop Huber tried to swear in all people without distinction to the "love of Jesus", while the papal messenger related the greetings from the Vatican with the reminder, that the church split originated in Germany. The crowds were carried away by glorying in unification. Had the truth not been trampled under foot by the Vatican and the whole Roman Church, a worldwide split would not have happened. The indescribable lies and blasphemies were and are the reason, that made the church split necessary, now more than ever before.

Whereas the Christian churches formerly did mission – because of the indispensable truth question – today no mission is necessary, because the truth, and the search for it, is undesirable, in fact non-existent. So it is ignored, because it separates. Whoever brings up the question about truth today, is lined up with truth fanatics or with terrorists of fundamentalism, and he is labelled a criminal along with them. The truth becomes reinterpreted into the ability to communicate. Instead of speaking of principles for mission, we have principles of dialogue. These principles then forbid mission.

To make the dialogue even more insignificant and more empty, Thomas of Aquinas is quoted: "It is the one God, about whom we actually know nothing." A dialogue among religions without content, only dialectical rhetoric is supposed to fill the emptiness and to secure world peace. Of course, the Catholic dogmas, which had become an indispensable part in "Dominus Jesus", should remain in place. But no criticism is allowed here.

So I and a co-worker participated in a mutual symposium of Catholics, Protestants, and Moslems, which took place in a mosque.

During the symposium the Islamic representative claimed, "We do not have any missionary interest. We want to invite with wisdom and good words. The Moslem only has to be truthful." This Islamic dialectic also includes the statement, that the dialogue is not a method for mission, but a way of information with the intention of breaking down wrong information and hatred. This should be the way to peace. As long as the Moslems fulfill their religious obligations, they are peaceful, because Islam is free of violence. Because all people are children of Abraham, absolute claims shall be relativized. "The creator judges everyone according to the respective standards of the people." So far the Islamic contribution. Accordingly the theme was: "Those who worship the one God with us." The participating Protestant cleric had nothing to add, except that he confirmed this sentence.

A Catholic expert of Islam apparently saw herself provoked to contradict. She emphasized somewhat unexpectedly the indispensability of Catholic dogmas. An inter religious prayer should not therefore be arranged any more. Islam is very close to Christianity (Catholicism) as no other religion, but God in Islam is not Father and friend of man. Apart from that "the Trinity should not be put into the dark."

The son of a Protestant pastor, who had converted to Islam, responded to the Catholic contribution from the standpoint of Islam: God is the one God for all. He does not demand that we believe in the death of Jesus and in original sin, or in the Sonship of God. This type of humanistic Islam believes that man is good, and he is God's representative on earth. This Moslem hopes for world peace through eventful multi-religious cult celebrations of mass movements.

Although carried out peacefully, this dialogue solidified the individual positions of the respective representatives of the religions. At the beginning one started with generalities to enthuse the people for a nebulous unity, e.g.: "All are people of a single family of mankind of one Creator." With the statement: "All religions have the same God", the dialogue is already turning into a striking discourse for several representatives, and they feel challenged to contradict. Whereas some want to have religious unity at any price, and choke any attempt of religious profiling, others do not want to give up their basic attitude and their spirit and want to make a contribution solely for the "enrichment" of the all-religious globalization.

Appendix D: 1st Ecumenical Church Congress in Berlin

The result is that conflict arises among the unifiers about the most successful tactic.

At another panel discussion, the Jewish, Islamic, and Christian representatives tried to prove, that all so-called Abrahamitic religions have their "ascension tradition". Here again should, there is no interest in the truth; The "legends" shall unite people with God, take them into the sphere of God's influence. Apart from that — according to the lecturing Islamist — the same truths are possible through different perspectives. This view of things would bring peace. The fact that different basic perspectives have to produce the most opposing perceptions, the most contradicting "truths" does not enter into the confused heads of the mythologists. The fantastic desires replace any undesired reality.

Very extreme dreamers view themselves as "border crossers", and so this group reports about their experiences in the regularly occurring "inter religious prayer". Typically, a Protestant pastor from Wuppertal (Germany) presents himself as the moderator. He draws people together for "prayer" from Islam, Catholicism, the Protestant churches, Judaism, and the Bahai religion. The consensus they worked out together is the insight: "There is one common unknown God, who revealed himself under different names."

At another place, they hold a forum about Western mysticism. A Franciscan presents this discourse. How could it be otherwise. Through the spirit of the "other Christ", Francis of Assisi, a mixture results made up of Catholicism, Orthodoxy, Buddhistic Tantrism (erotic, sexist ritual orgasm) and Hinduism. Through mysticism as an extraordinary spirit-force of DEATH, unity of religions shall come about. The general theme, that all accepted, is finding oneself in God, finding God in oneself. So man shall become God by uniting his microcosm with the macrocosm. Therefore, it is no surprise, that even the top guru of the Tibetans, the Dalai Lama got invited to the stadium to deceive 20,000 listeners. The top guru of the Tibetans entered the stage with jubilant applause wagging the yellow-orange scarf of the ECC, "You shall be a blessing". He received a t-shirt with "Jesus ♥ you", that he blessed and put into his pocket. One cannot expect anything else of this crowd, which has become stupid through unbelief. Therefore the Dalai Lama puts them all into his all-religion pocket. The subsequent banalities during his "proclamation" did not damage the enthusiasm. Does no-one notice that the Dalai Lama acts like a clown and can't be taken seriously anymore? "Everyone wants to have happiness and a long life. Whoever lives without hope and striving for happiness will not grow old." This is an example of his "godly wisdom". Then, introducing it with "ahh" and harrumphing, some other pieces of wisdom for life follow: "Problems are everywhere. They are part of life. Mental (?) happiness is worth more than material happiness."

After these western humanistic, intellectually earthshaking observations from the psychological consultation of relevant magazines, his real motives out of the spirit of the Antichrist come through, namely those which are sectarian manipulation into irrationalism: "The spiritual attitude can see things differently through its transformation. A problem at close range looks big, from a distance small. All things are relative."

Most participants of this church conference seemed to be content with this high swell out of the mouth of the "ocean of wisdom". Our contentment however, was limited to the observation, that the Dalai Lama had become cosmically powerless by now. His best days are over and he will go a similar way as the late Pope, John Paul II.

We visited another panel discussion of the "inter religious dialogue". One marvels again about the dialectics of Rome and its ability to adjust tactically. In spite of "Dominus Jesus", in which Rome's absolute claim as sacramental steward over the complete salvation of mankind has been clearly spelled out, some Roman speakers act very moderately by presenting Rome in a relative fashion. Words like: "We are all on the way and search for the truth", appear here and are amazing for the participants. "Much more important than searching for the truth is getting to know oneself through others." The dialogue for a common consensus shall create a way, "what is not clear to anyone". Therefore, Jesus is supposed to be "communication". Faith is, actually, an internal " restlessness of "not having". Therefore, each religious person has "to reinterpret his/her divine reference point again and again". And the truth? "It is beyond all religions." So God is looking everywhere for "partners for his great project of inter religious work". In the end, this work is about "responsibility and nonviolence". Only the Vietnamese Buddhist did not agree with this dialectical-diabolic lack of substance. He became concrete and introduced his "death program". His contribution: One has to leave everything behind oneself, even Buddha. He wanted to transform all hatred, wrath, anger through inner metamorphosis of cosmic-demonic spirit power into equanimity (indifference).

The result of this would be then – according to my judgment – the end of every creative and constructive culture and manhood itself. But the death of Buddhism has nothing else to offer anyway. So the "inter religious dialogue" is called a common need. Dogmas have to be eliminated, only human experiences count. The relativity of all things should be proven by successful dialogue. By removing all religious foundations, one wants to eliminate fundamentalism, this is the simple message of deception.

Confronted with so much "thoughtfulness", we kept the refreshing critique of professor Leggewie from Cologne in our minds. He had held a talk just before this panel discussion. As the only non-religious participant, he accused the "Inter religious Dialogue", that their advocates suffered from "insufficient tolerance and insufficient profile". According to Leggewie, they go to great terms to find things they have in common, instead of carving out their differences in a contest, in order to promote the respectively better thing afterwards". If one wants to avoid the unity religion – so goes his argument – then it should be possible to say "no" in the tolerant contest "without flames and swords". But here Leggewie is mistaken: The unity of religions is the distant goal of course. It has to be really avoided – so Leggewie continues – "to press everything even, that cannot be even". Not every conflict should be avoided. Differences should be determined without violence through tolerance. So it should stop especially in Germany, that the smaller religious communities can arrogantly be called "sectarian".

In closing Leggewie said, that in his opinion religion is basically not dangerous. Danger would come, if religions did away with democracy. Attention should be paid, that politics and religion are kept strictly separated. When politics and religion are not separated and politics are used to bring religion to power then this is fundamentalism and must be rejected, for fundamentalism is the enemy of the democracy. This speech surely gave headaches to the "consensus religious". It was not part of the objectives of the organizers of ECL.

Appendix D: 1st Ecumenical Church Congress in Berlin

In 2001 the "Charta Oecumenica"[351] passed as church law by the presidents of the Conference of European Churches and by the Council of the European Conference of Bishops. It understands itself as a guideline for cooperation of the churches of Europe, and has set for itself the goal of uniting Europe's churches. The subsequent steps are dedicated for deepening the community with Judaism and upgrading the relations to Islam as well as the encounter with all religions.

---

351 Comp. Chapter III.

Bibliography

Bibliography: Chapter I

EPISCOPAL GENERALVIKARIAT TRIER (Publ..) (1995): "Holy Shroud Pilgrimage 96 'On the Way with Jesus Christ' ". Strasbourg, Editions du Signe.
BROEMMEL, Elizabeth (Publ..) : "Fire and Light" special edition 24-IV. 1996. Rees, St. Michael – bookstore.
"Liboriusblatt – Weekly Magazine for the Catholic family". 23.06.1996.
"L'Osservatore Romano", various editions 1996 – 2002.

Biography: Chapter II

ADAM, Alfred (1985): "Lehrbuch der Dogmengeschichte" [textbook of history of doctrine] (Vol. I) Gütersloh, Gütersloher Verlaghaus Gerd Mohn.
BESNER, August (1983): "Wolframs-Eschenbach". Munich and Zurich, Publisher Schnell & Steiner Ltd. & Co.
CHAFER, Lewis S. / WALVOORD, JOHN F. (1994): "Basis of Biblical Teaching". Dillenburg, Christliche Verlagsgesellschaft.
HOFFMANN, Ernst G. SIEBENTHAL, Heinrich v. (1985): "Griechische Grammatik zum Neuen Testament" [Greek grammar of the NT]. Riehen, Immanuel-Publisher.
HUNT, Dave (1990) "Global Peace and the Rise of Antichrist", Harvest House Publishers.
PIPER, D. Franz / MUELLER, D. Dr. J. T. (1946): "Christian Dogmatics". Concordia Publishing House.
ROESSLER, Andreas (1990): "Steht Gottes Himmel allen offen?" ("Is God's Heaven open for all?"). Stuttgart, Quell Verlag (publisher).
SEMLEYEN, Michael de (1993): "All Roads lead to Rome?" Dorchester House Publication.
STEIN, Walter Johannes (1986): "Weltgeschichte im Lichte des Heiligen Gral Das neunte Jahrhundert" ("World History in the Light of the Holy Grail The Ninth Century). Stuttgart, J. Ch. Mellinger Publisher GmbH, Wolfgang Militz Co. KG.

STEUBING, Hans (Publ.) (1985): "Bekenntnisse der Kirche" (Confessions of the Church) (Paperback edition). Wuppertal, R. Brockhaus Publisher.
"Die Welt" of 24. 05. 2003.
"L'Osservatore Romano", various editions from 1996-2002.

Bibliography: Chapter III

"Die Bekenntnisschriften der evangelisch-lutherischen Kirche" (The Confession Statements of the Protestant Lutheran Church) (1979) (8th edition). Göttingen, Vandenhoeck & Ruprecht.
SEKRETARIAT DER DEUTSCHEN BISCHOFSKONFERENZ (Secretariat of the German Conference of Bishops (Publ.) (16.10. 2002): "Verlautbarung des Apostolischen Stuhls – Apostolisches Schreiben Rosarium Virginis Mariae. Seine Heiligkeit Papst Johnnes Paul II. an die Bischoefe., den Klerus, die Ordensleute und die Glaeubigen ueber den Rosenkranz" ("Communiqué of the Apostolic Chair – Apostolic Writing Rosarium Virginis Mariae. His Holiness Pope John Paul II to the bishops, the clerus, the people of the orders, and the believers of the rosary") Bonn.
FISCHER-WOLLPERT, Rudolf (1982): "Wissen Sie Bescheid? Lexikon religioeser und weltanschaulicher Fragen" (Do you have wide-ranging knowledge? Encyclopedia of religious and ideological questions). Regensburg, Publisher Friedrich Pustet.
McCARTHY, James G. (1996): "The Gospel According to Rome – Comparing Catholic tradition and the Word of God." Harvest House.
"Die Welt" of 8. Oct. 2003.
"L'Osservatore Romano", various editions from 1996-2003.

Bibliography: Chapter IV

FISCHER-WOLLPERT, Rudolf (1982): "Wissen Sie Bescheid? Lexikon religioeser und weltanschaulicher Fragen" (Do you have wide-ranging knowledge? Encyclopedia of religious and ideological questions). Regensburg, Publisher Friedrich Pustet.
FONSECA, PROF. DR. (1988): "Maria spricht zur Welt" (Mary speaks to the world).Freiburg / Switzerland, Paulus Publisher.

HIERZENBERGER, Gottfried / NEDOMANSKY, Otto (1996): "Erscheinungen und Botschaften der Gottesmutter Maria Vollständige Dokumentation durch zwei Jahrtausende"(Appearances and messages of Mary, the mother of God Complete documentation throughout two centuries), Augsburg, Bechtermuenz Publisher.

IRENAEUS: "Des heiligen Irenaeus fuenf Buecher gegen alle Haeresien der Entlarvung und Widerlegung der falschen Gnosis" (The five books of the holy Irenaeus against all heresies of the exposure and refutation of the false gnosis) Publisher and translator Dr. Heinrich Hand (1872) Vol. II. In "Bibliothek der Kirchenvaeter" (Library of the Church Fathers) Publisher Jos. Koesel'sche Buchhandlung.

IRMSCHER, Johannes / JOHNE, Renate (Publ.) (1990): "Lexikon der Antike" (Encyclopedia of antiquity). Augsburg Weltbild-Verlag. (publisher).

LAEPPLE, Alfred (1995): "Die Wunder von Lourdes" (The miracles of Lourdes).Augsburg, Pattloch Verlag (publisher).

LURKER, Manfred (1984): "Lexikon der Goetter und Daemonen" (Encyclopedia of gods and demons) Stuttgart, Kroener Verlag (publisher).

SCHMITT-LIEB, Willy (1995): "Europa-Trilogi-, Madonna und Europa" (vol. I.).Muensterschwarzach, Vier-Tuerme Verlag (publisher).

SEEMANN, Otto (1869): "Die Goetter und Heroen der Griechen" (The gods and heroes of the Greek). Leipzig, E. A. Seemann.

SIGL, P. Paul Maria (1989): "Die Frau aller Voelker, Miterloeserin, Mittlerin, Fuersprecherin"(The woman of all people, co-redeemer, mediator, intercessor). Ch-9601 Luetisburg-Station, Pro Deo et fratribus – Familie Mariens der Miterloeserin.

WOODROW, Ralph (1992): "Die Roemische Kirche – Mysterienreligion aus Babylon" (Babylon Mystery Religion) Marienheide, Verlag 7000 (publisher).

"Die große Versuchung – Zeit-Ruf", No. 1/1997, Internationale Arbeitsgemeinschaft Bekennender Christen.

„The great Temptation" – Zeit-Ruf paper, No. 1/1997, International working community of confessing Cristians

"L'Osservatore Romano", various editions from 1996-1997.

"Mary's Shrine", brochures of : Basilica of the National Shrine of the Immaculate Conception, Washington D.C., USA.
Hymn: "Stand up, stand up for Jesus" by G. Duffield.

Bibliography: Chapter V

BLY, Robert (1996): "The Sibling Society", Addison-Wesley.
FONSECA, PROF. DR. (1988): "Maria spricht zur Welt" (Mary speaks to the world) Freiburg / Switzerland, Paulus Publisher.
HAACK, Friedrich-Wilhelm (1993): "Europas neue Religion Sekten-Gurus-Satanskult" (Europe's new religions Sects-Gurus-Satanic cult) Freiburg im Breisgau, Herder Verlag (publisher).
JOERNS, Klaus Peter (1997): "Die neuen Gesichter Gottes Was die Menschen heute wirklich glauben" (The new faces of God What people today really believe). Munich, C.H. Beck'sche Verlagsbuchhandlung (publisher).
MIKOCKI OFM (1982): "Fatima". Augsburg, Pattloch-Verlag (publisher).
ROSA, Peter de (1991): "Gottes erster Diener Die dunkle Seite des Papsttums" (God's first servant The dark side of the papacy). Munich, Droemersche Verlagsanstalt Th. Knaur (publisher). Request.
ROESSLER, Andreas (1990): "Steht Gottes Himmel allen offen?" ("Is God's Heaven open for all?"). Stuttgart, Quell Verlag (publisher).
SCHMITT-LIEB, Willy (1995): "Europa-Trilogi-, Madonna und Europa" (vol. I.).Muensterschwarzach, Vier-Tuerme Verlag (publisher).
URQUHART, Gordon (1995): "Pope's Armada: Unlocking the Secrets of Mysteries and Powerful New Sects in the Church". Bantam Press.
YALLOP, David A. (1984): "In God's Name" "The mysterious death of the 33-day-Pope John Paul I. Facts and backgrounds". U. K. publisher: Constable & Robinson. U.S. publisher: Carral & Graf.
OFFICE OF OFFICIAL PUBLICATIONS OF THE EUROPEAN UNION (publ.) (1996): "The budget of the European Union: What happens to your money?" Luxembourg.

OFFICE OF OFFICIAL PUBLICATIONS OF THE EUROPEAN UNION (publ.) (1995): "Luxembourg in the European Union Programs for citizens and entrepreneurs". Luxembourg.
"Focus" Magazine, No. 52. 12, 1997.
"Journal spezial" No. 13, February 2000, Marienheide, Verlag 7000 (publisher).
"Kurzbericht ueber die juengsten Ereignisse von Marpingen vom Marienwallfahrtsort"(Abridged reports about the latest events from Marpingen from the Marian place of pilgrimage) No. 8/9. Friedelsheim.
"L'Osservatore Romano", various editions from 1998-2003.
"Nachrichten" (news) (October 1990): "Vereinigung" Sonderheft. Marienheide, Verlag 7000. „Unification" special edition, publisher
"Der Spiegel" Magazine No. 3/12. January 1998.
"Topic", 18th year, No. 1 January 98/ 24. year, No. 1, January 2004.

Bibliography: Chapter VI

HUNTEMANN, Georg (1999): "Biblisches Ethos im Zeitalter der Moralrevolution" (Biblical Ethos in the Age of Moral Revolution). Haenssler.
NYGREN, Anders, "Eros und Agape" (Eros and Agape) (1955). C. Bertelsmann publ.
"Katholische Nachrichten" kat.net 9/2006. (Catholic News).
GERLACH, Horst (1999): "Leben aus dem TOD des autonomen Rationalismus", Verlag 7000 (publisher). (Life out of DEATH of autonomous rationalism).
"kreuz.net", Katholische Nachrichten 2006 (Catholic news).
"kreuz.net", 11. June 2007.
"kreuz.net", 2007.
"kreuz.net", 07. May 2008.
"sueddeutsche.de", 29. June 2009. (Newspaper)
"Frankfurter Allgemeine Zeitung" FAZ.net vom 15. May 2009. newspaper
"kreuz.net", 07. July 2006.
"Die Welt" Zeitung vom 16. June 2008. (Newspaper).
"zenit.org/article" vom 11. July 2007.

PAPST BENEDIKT XVI: Enzyklika "Deus Caritas Est" vom 25. December 2005.
PAPST BENEDIKT XVI: Enzyklika "Caritas in Veritate" vom 07. July 2009.
MAY, Georg (2007): "Die Oekumenismusfalle" (The Trap of Ecumenism) Sarto Buch (publisher).
"Die Welt" Zeitung (newspaper) 21. September 2009.
"Die Welt" Zeitung (newspaper) 14. September 2009.
"kreuz.net", 27. July 2007.
"Zeitjournal", AG fuer religioese Fragen, Feb./2007. (AG for religious issues).

Table of Figures

Figure 1: Eucharist Chalice. Das neue Dudenlexikon, Vol. 5, Mannheim, Brockhaus AG, 1991.

Figure 2: "Sangraal Knights". Besner, August (1983): "Wolframs-Eschenbach", Munich and Zurich, Publisher Schnell & Steiner Ltd. & Co., p. 17.

Figure 3: S. Rita da Cascia, Italian, postcard.

Figure 4: Rosary. "L'Osservatore Romano", 18. 10. 2002. documentations, aspotolicwriting, Rosarium Virgines Mariae, p. 9.

Figure 5: "Europa". Schmitt-Lieb, Willy (1995): "Europa-Trilogi-, Madonna und Europa"(vol. I.). Muensterschwarzach, Vier-Tuerme Verlag (publisher) p. 417.

Figure 6: "Woman for all People". Sigl, P. Paul Maria (1998): "Die Frau aller Völker, Miterloeserin, Mittlerin, Fuersprecherin" (The woman of all people, co-redeemer, mediator, intercessor). Ch-9601 Luetisburg-Station, Pro Deo et fratribus – Familie Mariens der Miterloeserin, p. 165.

Figure 7: Jesus-Mary Medal. Sigl, P. Paul Maria (1998): "Die Frau aller Voelker, Miterloeserin, Mittlerin, Fuersprecherin" (The woman of all people, co-redeemer, mediator, intercessor). Ch-9601 Luetisburg-Station, Pro Deo et fratribus – Familie Mariens der Miterloeserin, p. 184.

Figure 8: Mary as co-redeemer, cathedral in Kaunas/ Lithuania, photo.

Figure 9: Picture of grace of Jasna Gora monastery, Poland, Jasna Gora, Kuria Generalna Zakonu Paulinow I Klasztor Jasnogorski, Cover.

Figure 10: Mary with Cone of Rays. WOODROW, Ralph (1992): "Die Roemische Kirche – Mysterienreligion aus Babylon" (Babylon Mystery Religion) Marienheide, Verlag 7000, Cover.

Figure 11: Madonna of Lourdes. Hierzenberger, Gottfried / Nedomansky, Otto (1996): "Erscheinungen und Botschaften der Gottesmutter Maria Vollstaendige Dokumentation durch zwei Jahrtausende", (Appearances

Table of Figures

              and messages of Mary, the mother of God Complete documentation throughout two centuries), Augsburg, Bechtermuenz Publisher,picture part.

Figure 12: Complex of buildings of the European parliament in Strassburg. Schmitt-Lieb, Willy (1995): "Europa-Trilogi — Madonna and Europa" (vol. I.). Muensterschwarzach, Vier-Tuerme Verlag (publisher).

Figure 13: Europa with Bull. Original photo, EU Strassburg, compound of the parliament EU Strassburg.

Figure 14: Mandala. Conference magazine: "Kalachakra for World Peace".

Figure 15: Dalai Lama. Conference magazine: "Kalachakra for World Peace".

Figure 16: Madonna of Fatima. Fonseca, Prof. Dr. (1988): "Maria spricht zur Welt" (Mary speaks to the world). Freiburg / Switzerland, Paulus Verlag (publisher).

Figure 17: Original photo "Woman of all People". Sigl, P. Paul Maria (1998): "Die Frau aller Völker, Miterloeserin, Mittlerin, Fuersprecherin" (The woman of all people, co-redeemer, mediator, intercessor). Ch-9601 Luetisburg-Station, Pro Deo et fratribus Familie Mariens der Miterloeserin, p. 181.

Figure 18: The Compassionate Jesus, Krakow, tract.

Figure 19: Faustyna with the Compassionate-Jesus.

Figure 20: Medjugorje, square in front of chapel, Madonna, photo.

Figure 21: Peter-Basilica.

Subject Index

A

Abortion 195, 241, 277, 294
Absolutism 251
Adam 69, 78, 96, 97, 99, 111, 147, 149, 151, 152, 153, 154, 166, 173, 301, 302, 303
Agape-love 269, 271, 272, 273, 274, 298, 299, 300, 302
Age
  age of Ecumenism 148
  eschatological 188
  feministic 240
  Marian 221
Androcentrism 194, 195, 196, 205
  androgynous person 196, 203
Angels 64, 74, 77, 78, 79, 86, 94, 95, 111, 117, 124, 130, 135, 141, 146, 149, 154, 158, 161, 162, 165, 167, 172, 175, 232, 234, 235, 237, 244, 322, 323, 325, 326
Antichrist 8, 13, 49, 57, 60, 62, 63, 64, 65, 66, 71, 79, 88, 117, 120, 127, 137, 142, 147, 180, 186, 187, 193, 203, 214, 215, 223, 234, 235, 236, 240, 241, 249, 250, 251, 252, 253, 257, 258, 298, 305, 307, 312, 313, 315, 325, 330, 334
Apostolic succession 47, 288
Assisi 20, 206, 252, 292, 321, 325, 326, 329, 330, 333
Atheism 219, 237, 313
Awareness 200

B

Baal 143
Babylon
  big city 143, 235
  political 29, 181, 187
  religious 29, 42, 81, 181, 186, 187, 188, 189
  whore 59, 64, 89, 122, 125, 126, 129, 134, 142, 143, 144, 158, 159, 160, 164, 165, 172, 178, 203, 208, 215, 223, 226
Beatification 15, 26, 35, 36, 37, 38, 39, 246
Beatified persons 15, 37, 38, 39, 40

Subject Index

Bible 8, 12, 13, 16, 23, 27, 33, 45, 47, 49, 50, 51, 63, 72, 78, 80, 81, 82, 84, 86, 92, 93, 99, 100, 103, 111, 127, 137, 146, 151, 154, 161, 209, 214, 216, 227, 234, 240, 241, 252, 253, 257, 258, 263, 269, 272, 273, 275, 292, 295, 299, 304, 305, 306, 310, 313, 314, 315, 329
Blood of the martyrs 244, 245
Blue Army of Mary 228
bodily assumption of the immaculate God-bearer 165
Buddhism
  Kalachakra 207, 208, 212
  Mandala 208
  Tantrism 207, 333
  Tara 208, 232, 240
Bull 202

C

Caritas 264, 275, 288, 296, 297, 298
Cathedral of Peter
  Patriarchal Basilicas 286, 317, 318
  Station churches 317
  St. John in the Lateran 317, 321, 322, 323
  St. Paul before the Walls 317, 320, 323
  Title churches 317
Catholicism 11, 30, 31, 40, 52, 62, 87, 110, 132, 137, 139, 169, 190, 217, 220, 223, 224, 227, 237, 238, 264, 276, 310, 317, 318, 322, 327, 332, 333
Catholics 16, 18, 19, 21, 22, 23, 25, 32, 35, 38, 44, 52, 59, 70, 87, 92, 93, 95, 97, 98, 100, 101, 104, 106, 109, 111, 116, 119, 120, 132, 134, 135, 139, 167, 172, 175, 184, 201, 205, 213, 214, 219, 221, 222, 230, 237, 238, 248, 255, 257, 258, 259, 260, 261, 262, 263, 264, 279, 283, 285, 294, 295, 311, 317, 320, 323, 331
Celibacy 152, 231, 268
Charta Oecumenica 118, 120, 336
Church
  Catholic 12, 13, 16, 17, 18, 19, 22, 24, 32, 36, 37, 43, 44, 45, 46, 47, 49, 51, 54, 55, 57, 59, 62, 64, 65, 67, 68, 77, 82, 101, 104, 105, 107, 109, 110, 111, 115, 116, 117, 118, 125, 138, 139, 140, 141, 143, 148, 158, 172, 173, 178, 179, 205, 211, 213, 218, 223, 237, 257, 258, 261, 263, 278, 281, 290, 292, 307, 310, 311, 316, 330

Roman 12, 13, 16, 17, 18, 19, 24, 29, 31, 36, 39, 40, 43, 44, 45, 46, 47, 48, 49, 52, 55, 57, 59, 62, 64, 65, 67, 70, 77, 83, 85, 86, 88, 90, 94, 95, 99, 101, 107, 115, 116, 117, 119, 127, 139, 142, 143, 144, 148, 151, 152, 158, 161, 162, 166, 168, 171, 174, 175, 178, 180, 182, 183, 188, 204, 206, 211, 213, 214, 215, 216, 223, 224, 237, 240, 242, 251, 252, 254, 258, 264, 272, 274, 275, 278, 283, 287, 305, 307, 309, 310, 311, 316, 324, 330, 331

Churches
  Basilica of the National Shrine of the Immaculate 139, 178

Communism 19, 204, 219, 220, 228, 251, 252

Consecration
  consecration of Russia 219, 220, 221, 222
  consecration of the world 221, 222, 225
  prayer of consecration 222, 243

Contraception 195

Cosmic Christ
  Cosmic Christology 78, 79, 80
  Dominus Jesus 44, 288, 331, 334
  Eucharistic Christ 28, 41, 49, 83, 90, 94, 104, 116, 142, 144, 164, 185, 256, 257
  Jesus of Compassion 246, 247
  Mild Christ 243, 250, 326

Cosmos 9, 16, 28, 38, 57, 65, 77, 78, 79, 82, 84, 86, 87, 88, 94, 101, 104, 110, 111, 112, 116, 119, 154, 161, 175, 201, 239, 270, 279

Council
  Chalcedon 75, 76, 81, 92, 164
  Council of Constantinopel II 266
  Council of Lyon II 165
  Ecumenical 16, 165, 170
  Ephesus 16, 75, 139
  Lateran Council IV 165
  Trient 67, 97, 157, 280, 290

Counter-reformation 67, 124, 137, 157, 263, 321

Culture war 285

D

Darkness 11, 23, 26, 49, 51, 53, 65, 94, 113, 117, 139, 161, 175, 258, 266, 289, 301, 313, 329

Subject Index

Death
  eternal 56, 59, 88
Delusion 12, 13, 14
Demons 23, 34, 38, 66, 70, 77, 86, 88, 102, 111, 175
Devil 10, 23, 27, 56, 86, 103, 117, 219, 234, 299
Dichotomy 266, 267
Dogma
  dogmatizing 230, 231, 232, 236, 237, 284
  Marian 226, 230, 242, 284
Dominicans 120, 123, 124, 127, 137
Drive impulses/impulse-driven 189, 190, 192

E

Ecumenism 15, 19, 21, 25, 26, 29, 30, 34, 65, 78, 81, 86, 118, 126, 127, 133, 137, 145, 148, 187, 223, 225, 288, 289, 317, 327
Eros-love 271, 272, 273, 299, 300, 301
Esotericism 33, 205, 237
Ethnicity
  ethnocentrism 250
Eucharist 20, 35, 38, 40, 41, 47, 48, 49, 50, 52, 53, 54, 62, 63, 65, 66, 67, 68, 69, 70, 90, 95, 98, 99, 101, 102, 103, 104, 108, 119, 130, 134, 144, 145, 155, 161, 172, 173, 174, 242, 245, 249, 256, 257, 258, 265, 269, 270, 279, 289, 290, 304, 308
Europe 8, 9, 15, 20, 21, 25, 26, 31, 32, 42, 63, 118, 136, 138, 142, 155, 158, 159, 160, 178, 179, 181, 188, 189, 190, 200, 201, 202, 203, 204, 205, 207, 210, 211, 212, 213, 215, 216, 223, 227, 228, 229, 240, 241, 242, 250, 253, 254, 260, 261, 280, 293, 294, 302, 329, 336
European Commission 196, 197
European Union
  Council of the European Union 196
  EU-dictatorship 198, 200
  languages of the parliament 197, 200
  the European wind 204
  twelve stars 201
Eve 149, 151, 152, 153, 155, 240
Evolution 82, 83, 93, 149, 287, 288, 308
Exoteric 55

F

Faith 8, 9, 10, 12, 13, 14, 18, 21, 22, 23, 24, 26, 29, 33, 34, 39, 40, 43, 44, 45, 46, 49, 50, 51, 52, 53, 54, 58, 59, 61, 67, 75, 79, 81, 83, 84, 85, 87, 89, 90, 91, 93, 94, 97, 98, 99, 100, 101, 102, 104, 105, 108, 110, 111, 114, 115, 116, 117, 118, 131, 133, 141, 143, 144, 145, 149, 150, 152, 153, 154, 155, 158, 160, 161, 163, 166, 171, 180, 183, 184, 186, 203, 206, 209, 210, 212, 223, 226, 237, 238, 242, 247, 254, 255, 256, 257, 261, 263, 266, 268, 269, 271, 272, 273, 274, 275, 276, 277, 278, 280, 283, 287, 294, 295, 298, 300, 301, 303, 305, 307, 308, 311, 312, 313, 314, 315, 317, 321, 324, 330, 334

Fathers 71, 79, 80, 81, 82, 99, 104, 133, 145, 148, 150, 152, 153, 160, 161, 193, 194, 196, 200, 228, 230, 265, 269, 279, 312

Feminism 193, 196, 204, 205, 206, 237, 240, 290

Forces
  Catholic 42, 182, 239
  cosmic 20, 23, 55, 256
  demonic 22, 23, 32, 35, 38, 94, 129, 154, 175, 193, 268

G

Glasnost 252

God 11, 12, 13, 15, 16, 20, 23, 24, 25, 27, 28, 30, 33, 34, 37, 39, 43, 44, 46, 47, 48, 50, 51, 52, 53, 56, 58, 59, 61, 67, 68, 69, 70, 71, 72, 73, 74, 75, 76, 77, 78, 79, 80, 81, 82, 83, 84, 85, 86, 87, 88, 89, 90, 91, 92, 93, 94, 95, 96, 97, 98, 99, 100, 101, 102, 103, 104, 105, 106, 107, 108, 109, 110, 111, 112, 114, 115, 117, 119, 120, 121, 124, 125, 127, 128, 129, 130, 131, 133, 134, 135, 136, 137, 138, 139, 140, 141, 142, 144, 145, 146, 147, 148, 149, 150, 151, 153, 154, 157, 158, 160, 161, 163, 165, 166, 167, 168, 169, 170, 171, 173, 174, 175, 176, 177, 182, 185, 187, 189, 192, 193, 194, 201, 209, 210, 211, 212, 213, 216, 218, 219, 221, 223, 225, 226, 230, 232, 235, 237, 239, 240, 241, 244, 245, 250, 252, 253, 254, 255, 258, 259, 261, 263, 264, 266, 267, 268, 269, 270, 272, 273, 274, 275, 276, 277, 278, 284, 285, 288, 291, 292, 294, 295, 296, 297, 298, 299, 300, 301, 302, 304, 305, 308, 313, 314, 315, 322, 327, 331, 332, 333

Gods 24, 32, 54, 82, 93, 142, 184, 201, 226, 240, 246, 265, 271, 274, 285, 316

Subject Index

Grace
  sanctifying 105
Grave of Peter 318
Greece 142, 149, 185, 235
Gynocentrism 196

H

Heart of Jesus 220, 222, 223, 249
Heresies 76, 77, 104, 120, 127, 149, 151, 153, 223
Hesychasm 121, 136
Hinduism
  Western 210
Holism 88, 201
Holy Coat Pilgrimage 15, 16, 21, 22, 23
Holy Grail 60, 64, 65
Holy Roman Empire of German Nation 34, 54, 64, 159
Holy Spear 63
Holy Wafer 248
Homo noeticus 72, 79, 92, 93, 94, 95
Homo sapiens 71, 93
Host. *see* Holy Wafer
Hypostasis 75, 80, 82, 83, 84, 85

I

Immaculate 139, 140, 141, 143, 144, 145, 147, 148, 155, 157, 158, 161, 162, 163, 164, 165, 175, 176, 178, 179, 181, 182, 183, 185, 188, 215, 216, 217, 219, 220, 221, 222, 223, 228, 239, 241, 243, 244, 249, 250, 284, 322
Immanence 287, 318
Imperial Concordat 36
Incarnation 43, 59, 60, 61, 63, 72, 75, 76, 77, 78, 81, 98, 101, 120, 125, 129, 142, 174, 207, 214
Indulgence 109, 124, 134, 222, 318, 320
Infantilism 189, 190, 191, 195, 196, 240
Inheritance 44, 177, 256
Inter-religious dialogue 44, 148
Islam 90, 131, 137, 277, 285, 291, 292, 293, 294, 329, 332, 336

Sufism 136
Islamo-fascism 293

J

Jesus Christus
  Incarnation of God 43, 61, 75, 76, 77
  sacrificial death 48, 53, 55, 56, 59, 62, 68, 70, 94, 99, 103, 107, 119, 154, 174, 245, 248
  the true prince of peace 72
Jews 18, 19, 82, 160, 205, 254, 282, 293, 329
Jupiter 142

L

Liturgy 129, 131, 134, 280, 281
Lucifer 66, 86, 94, 112, 125, 126, 127, 131, 134, 141, 232, 241, 246, 247, 248, 249, 251, 254, 274, 301, 315, 323

M

Macrocosm 9, 13, 126, 166, 318, 333
Magic
  blood magic 57, 64
  magic word 50
Mary
  appearances of Mary 138, 158, 160, 182, 183, 223, 224, 232, 237, 240, 247, 249, 250
  bodily reception into heaven 239
  bodily reception of the immaculate 284
  copies of the Madonna 178, 179, 228
  co-redemptrix 146, 153, 155, 156, 161, 164, 165, 166, 170, 185, 215, 216, 230, 284, 285, 286
  Daughter of Zion 169, 170, 171
  Domina 158, 179, 215, 232, 321, 323
  everlasting virginity 165, 168
  Great Mother 16, 222, 240
  Immaculate Heart 40, 141, 216, 217, 218, 219, 220, 221, 222, 223, 225, 228, 236, 243, 244, 249, 250
  Immaculate Mother 175, 177, 284

Subject Index

Intercessor 133, 230, 231, 232, 233, 234, 285
Madonna 16, 88, 135, 136, 142, 143, 178, 179, 181, 182, 188, 200, 213, 214, 215, 216, 217, 218, 219, 220, 221, 223, 224, 225, 226, 227, 228, 229, 231, 236, 237, 238, 239, 241, 242, 246, 247, 250, 263, 284, 323
maiden motherhood 149, 166, 167, 168, 170, 173, 224
Marian Psalter 123, 124, 136
Marian revival 136, 160, 161, 164, 182, 183, 238, 250, 256, 260
Maya 232, 240
Mediatrix of all Graces 16, 28, 43, 124, 125, 138, 139, 141, 142, 145, 146, 147, 148, 161, 169, 173, 174, 175, 187, 216
Most blessed Virgin 140, 162, 165
Mother goddess 143, 214, 239
Mother of God 75, 99, 125, 138, 140, 144, 145, 146, 154, 157, 161, 168, 174, 177, 182, 216, 229, 240, 284, 285
Mother of the Church 137, 144, 172, 216, 225, 229, 263, 268, 286
primeval mother Eve 240
Queen of Heaven 28, 39, 40, 122, 125, 138, 139, 143, 144, 161, 172, 179, 202, 203, 237, 241, 249
Queen of Peace 135, 148, 161, 180, 182, 186, 214, 216, 221, 222, 223, 249, 316
Queen of the Angels 130
Queen of the Rosary 135, 222
Queen of the World 145, 177, 222
surrogate mother 72
The Woman 131, 148, 231, 232, 233, 236, 237, 238, 240
The Woman of all Nations 231, 237
vaginal intactness 149, 165, 166
Virgin 99, 122, 123, 124, 131, 134, 140, 141, 143, 147, 149, 150, 151, 152, 153, 154, 162, 164, 165, 166, 167, 168, 169, 170, 176, 186, 217, 226, 229, 230, 284, 323
Mass
  mass sacrifice 109, 279, 280
Meditation 122, 123, 124, 125, 127, 128, 129, 134, 136, 137
Method 27, 77, 120, 121, 123, 131, 133, 134, 147, 161, 252, 272, 332
Microcosm 10, 126, 166, 333
Miracle of the sun 221
Miriam 229, 232, 240

Moors 123, 136
Mutation 93, 94, 95, 146
Mysticism 49, 83, 86, 87, 88, 93, 94, 101, 112, 121, 122, 183, 254, 274, 275, 309, 321, 333
Myths 122, 134, 184, 260, 330

N

Neoevangelism 127
New-Age 19, 64, 65, 88, 94, 101, 119, 166, 209, 210, 211, 212, 218, 226, 285

O

Obelisk 318
Occident 54, 60, 140, 143, 155, 202, 203, 210, 211, 212, 286
Occult
  occult faith 209
October Revolution 220
Opus Dei 20, 38, 320
Orthodoxy 219, 333
Overshadowing 72, 73, 97, 150

P

Pantocrator 79
Paradigms 201
Pastoral care, Counseling 16, 38, 143, 144, 188, 189, 191, 197, 209, 309
Patriarchy 193, 194, 195, 196, 327
Penance 95, 96, 99, 105, 106, 107, 108, 130, 304
Perestroika 252, 253
Places of pilgrimage 20, 158, 178, 179, 185, 224, 228, 247
Places of power 178
Places of worship
  Altoetting 182
  Annaberg 182
  Banneux 182
  Czestochowa 173, 181, 182, 263
  Einsiedeln 182
  Epidauros 184

Subject Index

Fatima 128, 141, 162, 181, 182, 187, 188, 207, 215, 216, 217, 218, 219, 221, 223, 224, 225, 226, 227, 228, 229, 231, 232, 233, 236, 237, 241, 242, 243, 244, 246, 247, 249, 250, 281, 284, 285
 shepherd children 217, 244
 third mystery 223, 224, 242, 243
Guadeloupe 181, 233
Lourdes 128, 140, 141, 145, 162, 179, 180, 181, 182, 183, 185, 186, 187, 216, 217, 221, 225, 229, 232, 233, 236, 241, 242, 247, 283, 322
Mariazell 182
Medjugorje 25, 182, 186, 207, 250, 283
Santiago de Compostela 241, 242, 246
Powers
 cosmic 23, 52, 55, 77, 88, 96, 99, 101, 138, 161, 213, 216, 227, 250, 263, 283
 demonic 13, 22, 34, 52, 65, 92, 111, 161, 175
 magic 330
 of Satan 78, 90, 298
 witchcraft 13, 49, 263
Prayer 19, 21, 33, 34, 36, 41, 42, 84, 96, 106, 107, 108, 109, 112, 120, 121, 122, 123, 124, 125, 126, 128, 131, 132, 133, 134, 135, 136, 137, 172, 175, 176, 177, 182, 184, 222, 226, 227, 228, 231, 243, 247, 263, 270, 281, 292, 297, 298, 319, 320, 326, 329, 330, 332, 333
 Ave Maria 107, 122, 123, 124, 126, 129, 130, 132, 134, 137
 Formula prayers 123, 126, 131
 Short formulae 121, 122, 123, 126, 131, 136, 137
Pre-existence 73
Proto-Gospel 139, 147
Purgatory 48, 108, 109, 110, 111, 112, 113
 fire of purification 110, 111

R

Realization 83, 84, 85, 131, 170, 225, 274, 306
Re-catholicisation 127, 161, 223
Recollection 129
Reconciliation 68, 99, 101, 103, 105, 106, 107, 118, 119, 130, 205, 206, 265, 300, 302, 303, 321

Redeemership 112
Redemption
  Catholic Redemption 48, 99, 103, 110, 111, 125, 146, 169, 170, 171,
      172, 175, 213, 233, 248, 265, 300, 304, 308
Reduction 117
Reformation 20, 25, 30, 52, 57, 67, 71, 75, 76, 77, 79, 80, 81, 82, 90, 99,
      104, 127, 132, 133, 159, 160, 161, 202, 237, 275, 289, 292, 294
"Reichskonkordat" 18
Reincarnation 261
Relics 13, 15, 16, 17, 22, 38, 54, 59, 64, 87, 120, 161, 258, 318, 321, 323
Religion
  Marian religiosity 183
  religious imperialism 211
  religious unity 41, 134, 235, 332
  Roman 12, 13, 60, 318, 319, 330
  synthesis of all religions 211
Remembrance 47, 49, 53, 54, 67, 70, 102, 128, 173, 290
Remission 248, 304
Revelation 21, 41, 45, 46, 47, 64, 71, 80, 83, 90, 141, 142, 151, 159,
      203, 214, 215, 223, 225, 232, 233, 235, 241, 243, 244, 281, 282,
      284, 296, 315
Rome
  Antichristian world empire 185
  religious 8
Rosarium. *see* Rosary
Rosary 107, 120, 121, 122, 123, 124, 125, 126, 127, 128, 129, 130, 131,
      132, 133, 134, 135, 136, 137, 183, 217, 218, 222, 249, 281
  chain of pearls 134, 136, 137
Russia 219, 220, 221, 222, 228, 260

S

Sacraments
  Anointing of the Sick 95, 107, 108
  Baptism 43, 44, 95, 96, 97, 98, 99, 100, 101, 105, 109, 110, 122, 130,
      146, 217, 262, 304, 309
  Communion (firming) 20, 50, 53, 70, 101, 222, 270, 289, 290
  Consecration of Priests 114, 279
  Holy Sacrament of the Altar 101

Subject Index

Marriage 113, 114, 118, 149, 167, 168, 217, 262, 290
Repentance
  confession 30, 106
Sacrifice of Christ 49, 53, 62, 69, 70, 102
Saints 15, 16, 36, 38, 54, 64, 85, 88, 97, 116, 120, 124, 128, 130, 132, 133, 142, 158, 161, 162, 166, 172, 235, 258, 259, 318, 320
Salvation 13, 22, 33, 42, 43, 44, 45, 46, 47, 48, 49, 50, 51, 52, 53, 54, 55, 56, 57, 58, 59, 61, 62, 66, 68, 69, 73, 78, 81, 82, 86, 90, 91, 92, 94, 95, 96, 97, 99, 100, 101, 102, 103, 104, 108, 109, 110, 111, 114, 115, 116, 124, 125, 128, 129, 135, 136, 139, 145, 146, 147, 148, 149, 150, 151, 152, 153, 154, 155, 156, 157, 163, 166, 167, 169, 170, 171, 172, 173, 174, 175, 186, 187, 213, 215, 216, 217, 219, 222, 225, 235, 265, 266, 267, 272, 285, 286, 301, 303, 334
Saracens 217
Satan 13, 16, 40, 53, 55, 58, 66, 72, 78, 79, 82, 88, 90, 95, 133, 134, 142, 147, 148, 203, 233, 235, 236, 246, 251, 270, 298, 315
Sects
  esoteric 22, 192, 209, 226
  individualistic 210
Sin
  deadly sin 105, 106
  venial sin 105, 106, 109, 117
Sophia 239
Spirit
  Antichristian 19, 20, 29, 33, 34, 43, 49, 54, 64, 66, 68, 73, 78, 81, 88, 89, 90, 92, 94, 95, 99, 112, 117, 142, 154, 155, 156, 164, 196, 207, 208, 214, 229, 235, 242, 245, 249, 251, 253, 254, 263, 269, 276, 278, 298, 304, 309, 313, 326, 331
  demonic 11, 23, 35, 76, 95, 111, 227, 236, 240, 267, 318, 320, 322
  postmodern ‚Zeitgeist' (spirit of the age) 189, 206, 210, 229, 240
  'Zeitgeist' 229, 240, 245
Spiritism 144, 259
Spiritual warfare 9, 209, 227, 237, 259
Spiritual weapons 12, 161, 180, 208, 225
Splits 110, 111, 126
Star of evangelism 40
Summa theological 322, 324

Subject Index

Symbols 31, 32, 33, 34, 116, 142, 202, 260
Synergy
  Syncretism 132, 274, 310, 327

T

Threesome 76, 201
Toronto 22, 180, 192, 212, 259
Transcendence 33, 34, 48, 87, 134, 150, 207, 239, 287, 306, 309, 311, 312, 313
Transformation 23, 41, 48, 62, 70, 83, 93, 94, 111, 112, 192, 268, 272, 309, 334
Transubstantiation 21, 40, 48, 49, 52, 57, 66, 67, 69, 70, 103, 104
Trichotomy 266
Trier 15, 16, 17, 24
Trinity 16, 43, 74, 79, 80, 81, 82, 83, 84, 85, 86, 87, 88, 89, 90, 120, 128, 129, 131, 134, 139, 175, 186, 241, 266, 309, 323, 332
Truth 27, 28, 39
  love the truth 299
Two-nature-doctrine 78
Two-person-doctrine 81

U

Unification 15, 24, 46, 83, 90, 101, 120, 126, 138, 167, 172, 187, 188, 203, 205, 206, 215, 220, 226, 227, 242, 252, 253, 257, 267, 269, 270, 291, 293, 295, 312, 327, 331

V

Vaginal intactness 149, 165, 166
Vatican 13, 18, 20, 24, 32, 35, 36, 40, 41, 42, 49, 70, 120, 134, 137, 138, 141, 145, 147, 149, 158, 159, 162, 165, 166, 168, 169, 178, 181, 182, 185, 186, 190, 195, 204, 206, 214, 215, 220, 221, 222, 223, 225, 230, 231, 233, 236, 238, 239, 242, 246, 247, 248, 251, 253, 254, 270, 275, 277, 280, 281, 283, 284, 286, 287, 288, 289, 291, 293, 295, 298, 304, 305, 306, 307, 310, 311, 316, 317, 319, 320, 331
Virginal motherhood 166

W

Wafer 41, 48, 102, 104, 172, 248
Western World 50, 131, 209, 210, 232, 240, 277, 286, 289, 292, 297
Word of God 27, 50, 51, 70, 79, 137, 139, 148, 171, 177, 192, 209, 263, 271, 276, 278, 304, 305, 314, 315
Work of Redemption 169, 170, 245, 285, 286
Work of salvation 13, 53, 59, 73, 95, 115, 116, 129, 148, 153, 166, 169, 170, 171, 174, 175, 286
World
  secular 9, 237, 256, 276, 308, 312, 314, 316, 326, 329
  single world church 88
  single world government 188
  single world religion 81
  world peace 128, 207, 208, 225, 228, 229, 240, 250, 293, 325, 331, 332
Worship of the Heart of Jesus 220, 222, 223, 249

Index of Persons

A

Abraham 12, 58, 59, 73, 91, 142, 145, 150, 332
Adenauer, Konrad 228
Ahmadinedshad 293
Alkuin, Cathol. teacher 155
Anastasius I, Cathol. teacher 155
Anselm of Canterbury, Cathol. teacher 156
Arnold of Chartres, Cathol. teacher 156

B

Bernhardin of Siena, Cathol. teacher 156
Bernhard of Clairvaux 186
Bernini, Giovanni Lorenzo 319
Bonaventura, Cathol. teacher 156

C

Caesar, Gaius Julius 102
Caligula, Gaius Julius Caesar 318
Chamenai, Ali 293
Charlemagne I 31, 34, 42, 43, 54, 55, 57, 60, 61, 62, 155, 329
Colgan 228
Columbus, Christopher 178
Constantine I the Great 15, 16, 311, 317, 321, 323, 324

D

Dalai Lama 132, 194, 205, 206, 207, 208, 212, 333, 334
Dante 275
Dominic 321, 323
Drevermann, Eugen 205

E

Eadmer, Cathol. teacher 156
Ephraim the Syrian, Cathol. teacher 153

Index of Persons

F

Faustyna 247, 248
Fellay, Bernhard, bishop 278, 279, 280
Francis of Assisi 321, 323, 325, 326, 330, 333
Freud, Sigmund 11, 12, 13

G

Garibaldi, Giuseppe 320
Germanus of Constantinopel, Cathol. teacher 155
Gorbachev, Mikhail Sergejewitsh 226, 251, 252, 253, 254

H

Haack, F.W. 209, 210, 211
Helena, Flavia 15, 16, 17, 323, 324
Hieronymus, Cathol. teacher 155
Huntemann, Georg 265, 267, 271, 278, 299

I

Irenaeus of Lyon, Cathol. teacher 149, 150, 151, 152, 153, 169, 170

J

John the geometer, Cathol. teacher 156
Justin the Martyr, Cathol. teacher 149

K

Kant, Emanuel 278
Knobloch, Charlotte 282

L

Luther, Martin 53, 79, 80, 87, 132, 133, 251, 275, 279, 290

M

Michelangelo Buonarroti 319
Milone of Amando, Cathol. teacher 155

Modestus of Jerusalem, Cathol. teacher 155
Moslem Brotherhood 292

N

Napoleon I 31, 285, 293
Napoleon III 180, 183
Nimrod 142, 143
Nygren, Anders 271, 272, 275

P

Peerdeman, Ida 231
Plato 83, 274, 275
Pope Alexander VII 162
Pope Benedict XVI 44, 45, 46, 206, 212, 223, 238, 243, 245, 250, 251,
    255, 256, 257, 258, 259, 260, 261, 262, 263, 264, 265, 266, 267,
    268, 269, 270, 274, 275, 276, 277, 278, 279, 280, 281, 282, 283,
    284, 285, 286, 287, 288, 291, 292, 293, 295, 296, 297, 298, 299,
    303, 304, 306, 307, 308, 309, 310, 311, 312, 313, 314, 315
Pope Innocent III 321
Pope John Paul II 15, 19, 20, 21, 24, 26, 28, 29, 30, 31, 34, 36, 37, 39,
    42, 49, 50, 70, 82, 98, 102, 105, 120, 121, 125, 126, 127, 129,
    131, 133, 134, 135, 137, 138, 144, 145, 146, 147, 148, 157, 163,
    164, 167, 168, 170, 173, 174, 175, 187, 192, 193, 194, 195, 205,
    206, 208, 211, 212, 218, 223, 224, 225, 226, 230, 231, 237, 238,
    239, 242, 243, 244, 250, 251, 252, 253, 254, 255, 259, 260, 261,
    262, 263, 264, 276, 277, 279, 280, 283, 284, 285, 286, 287, 291,
    292, 295, 325, 326, 334
Pope John XXIII 67, 163, 164, 216, 224, 230, 295, 313, 318
Pope Julius II 319
Pope Leo the Great 16
Pope Nicolaus I the Great 266
Pope Paul VI 224, 225, 226, 230, 243, 280, 286, 295, 309, 313
Pope Pius IX 158, 162, 163, 164, 169, 284, 322, 323
Pope Pius XI 220, 284, 319
Pope Pius XII 19, 141, 163, 165, 182, 185, 186, 216, 220, 221, 223, 224,
    226, 228, 230, 242, 284, 322, 323
Pope Sixtus IV 157

Index of Persons

Prodi, Romani 241

R

Ratzinger, Joseph. *see* Pope Benedikt XVI

S

Schutz, Roger 192, 193, 194
Semiramis 143
Soelle, Dorothee 239
Soubirous, Bernadette 140, 180, 182, 183
St. Pius X-Brotherhood 279, 280, 307

T

Tammuz 143
Tertullian, Cathol. teacher 153, 265
Thomas of Aquino, Cathol. teacher 321, 322, 323, 331

W

Walesa, Lech 227
Williamson, Richard 281, 282

Books Recommended for the Topic

BUBECK, Mark I. (1984): "Overcoming the Adversary". Moody Press.

DE ROSA, Pete (2000) "Vicars of Christ — The dark side of the papacy", Poolbeg Publications.

HISLOP, Alexander (1862): "The Two Babylons" or, "The Papal Worship". Edinborough: James Wood, 130, George Street. London: Houlston and Wright.

HUNT, Dave (1990) "Global Peace and the Rise of Antichrist ", Harvest HousePublishers.

McCARTHY, James G. (1996): "The Gospel According to Rome — Comparing Catholic Tradition and the Word of God." Harvest House.

SEMLEYEN, Michael de (1993): "All Roads lead to Rome?" Dorchester House Publication.

URQUHART, Gordon (1995): "Pope's Armada: Unlocking the Secrets of Mysteries and Powerful New Sects in the Church". Bantam Press.

YALLOP, David A. (1984): "In God's Name" "The mysterious death of the 33-day-Pope John Paul I. Facts and backgrounds". U. K. publisher: Constable & Robinson. U.S. publisher: Carral & Graf.

Table of Contents

The Author 7
Introduction 8
About the origin of this book 8
Preliminary Remarks 11

Chapter I
The Activation of Invisible Powers for an Ecumenism derived from Worship of Relics and Saints 15

1. The Catholic Worship of Relics, Saints and Beatified Persons Today 15
2. The Beginning of Relic Worship in the 4th Century 15
3. The Classes of Relics 17
4. The Story of the "Holy Coat" 17
5. Problem-Solving for the Roman Church in the Face of Danger: The Pilgrimages to the "Holy Coat" 17
6. The Dangers for the Roman Church in the 19th Century 18
7. The Dangers for the Roman Church in the 20th Century 18
8. The Intentions of Pope John Paul II during His Visit to Germany from June 21-24, 1996 (Paderborn and Berlin) 24
9. The Blasphemies Hidden from the Protestant Public 25
10. The Recognizable Goals of the Papal Visit 25
11. The Deception Comes from the Falsified Source 25
12. The Devilish Method to Seduce with Fragments of the Truth 27
13. The Goal of Seduction with Fragments of the Truth: Neutralization of Spiritual Power 28
14. The Dependence of "Babylon" on Successful Religion and Politics 29
15. Ecumenism as the Basic Prerequisite for the Religious Babylon ... 29
16. The Attempt at Reviving, Activating, Reorganizing and Programming Neo-Roman Forces 30
17. Symbols being the Reality for Esoteric Spiritual Powers 32
18. The True Faith in the Triune God is Not a Religion 32
19. The Demonic Reality of Spiritual Forces out of History 34
20. First Results of the Spiritual Binding and Powerlessness of Demonic Forces 35

Table of Contents

21. The Intended Publicity Effect for Two Notable German
    Nazi Opponents 35
22. The Theological Process of Beatification and the Papal Act.....36
23. The Ecumenical Significance of Papal Beatification and
    Canonization..37
24. The Celebration of the Eucharist in the Olympic Stadium
    in Berlin on June 23,1996 38
25. Our task during the Celebration of the Eucharist...................40
26. The Speech of the Pope at the Brandenburg Gate..................41

Chapter II
The Roots of the "Cosmic Christ" 43

1. The Historical and Trend-Setting Situation at the Outset 43
2. Salvation only through the Roman Church?............................43
3. The Sacrifice of the Mass - The Eucharist 47
4. The Magic Word - The Fragmentary Dilemma 50
5. The Magic of the Roman Church..52
6. The Holy Blood and the Magic of the Blood............................54
7. Faith as Motive for Acting According to the Demands
   of the Law 58
8. The Holy Grail - the Magical, Esoteric Blood Relic................60
9. The Esoteric Fraction of Roman Catholicism in the
   Century of Charlemagne..62
10. The Close Association Between the Grail and the
    Eucharistic Chalice 62
11. The Heart of the Mass – The Holiest Sacrament of the
    Altar remains central 67
12. God became Flesh -same words different meanings!..............71
13. The Divine Glory and Pre-existence of Jesus Christ 73
14. Jesus Christ: True Man and True God in One Person 74
15. The "Incarnation" of God in Jesus Christ...............................75
16. The Cosmic Spirit – Another Characteristic of the
    Incarnation Doctrine 78
17. The Trinity and the Fathers of the Reformation 79
18. Ecumenical Cosmic Christology and the Trinity of God 80
19. The two cosmic levels through their Hypostases and the
    results of praying to pictures 83

20. The Immanent and Transcendent World 86

Chapter III
The Eucharistic Cosmic Christ and the Sacraments 90

1. Sacraments as Substitutes for Faith 90
2. Faith in Sacraments and the Eucharistic Cosmic Christ 90
3. The "New Creation" out the Roman Spirit: Homo
   Noeticus or the Enlightened Human..93
4. The Sacraments 95
5. The Sanctifying Grace in the Sacraments 96
6. Baptism...96
7. Confirmation..100
8. The Eucharist...101
9. Penance or the Sacrament of Reconciliation 105
10. Anointing of the Sick..107
11. Purgatory..108
12. The Sacrament of Orders 113
13. Marriage 114
14. The "Gospel" According to Rome; The Faith in
    Sacraments...114
15. The Sacramentaries 115
16. The "Charta Oecumenica" 118
17. The Rosary and its Significance for the Catholic Soul Today –
    The Chain of God's children that binds them to God 120

Chapter IV
Mary, the Mediatrix of all Cosmic Powers 138

1. The Queen of Heaven 138
2. The Theological Preparations and the Dogmatisation
   of the "Immaculate Conception" 140
3. Heathen Roots of the Marian Cult...142
4. Observations of an Ex-Priest in the Pastoral Care of
   Marian Believers 143
5. The Meaning of the "Immaculate Conception" for
   Pope John Paul II...144

Table of Contents

6. Rome's Theological Reasoning for the Mediatrix of all
Graces 145
7. The Continuing Development of the "Immaculate
Conception" by Rome..147
8. The Historical Development of the "Immaculate Conception"
and her Enthronement through the Marian Apparitions........148
9. The Dogma of the "Immaculate Conception"......................162
10. The Everlasting Virginity of the Roman Mary.....................165
11. Mary – the Representative and Redemptrix of Humanity 169
12. Mary – the Prototype of the Roman Church........................171
13. Mary and the Significance of her Places of Worship 178
14. The Marian place of pilgrimage in Lourdes, France –
the basis for the "Queen of Peace".....................................180
15. Lourdes – the Basis for a Religious Babylon 186

Chapter V
The Development of the European Union
and the Significance of Fatima's Madonna...................................188

1. Introduction..188
2. The Spiritual Condition of EU Citizens at the Turn of
the Century..189
3. The Infantile Half-Adult as the Product of an
Altered Consciousness...190
4. The Patriarchy — A Solution for a Feministic,
Fatherless Society? 193
5. The Structure and Goal of the European Union....................196
6. The Signifiance of a Madonna or Domina in a Post-Modern
Esoteric Europe 215
7. Summary: The antichristian preparation for the
coming of the Antichrist..241
8. The publication of the "Third Mystery" of Fatima as an
admission of Marian power loss 242
9. A new star in the cosmic heavens:
The "Jesus" of Compassion 246
10. The eschatological - antichristian character of the pope and
the finished role of the past president of the former USSR,
Gorbachev..251

Chapter VI
The Pontificate of Pope Benedict XVI..255

1. World Youth Event with Pope Benedict XVI in Cologne
   in August of 2005..255
2. Benedict XVI visit to Poland in May 2006 260
3. The Encyclical "Deus Caritas Est" of Pope 264
4. The inappropriate reactions of Benedict XVI and his
   leading clerics as a reflection of the insecurity of the pope? ...276
5. The identity crisis of the worldwide priesthood? 278
6. The Priestly Brotherhood of St. Pius X 280
7. The Trip of Benedict XVI to Israel 281
8. The Community of Medjugorje and Pope Benedict XVI 283
9. The "Woman of all Peoples" and Pope Benedict XVI 283
10. Mary, the Co-Redemptrix as Dogma? 284
11. Surrendering the papal title: Patriarch of the Occident 286
12. The Theory of Evolution and the Pope 287
13. Ecumenism and Pope Benedict XVI 288
14. Rome befriending Islam 290
15. The Christian-Ecumenical Immorality 295
16. The Encyclical Caritas in Veritas, of Pope Benedict XVI 297

Appendix A

1. Introduction 317
2. The Churches 318
2.1. The patriarchal basilicas as parts of the main churches 318
2.2. The lower-level main churches, or basis churches 323
2.3. Some title-, resp. station-churches 323

Appendix B

Assisi, the unholy place for an unholy kingdom of peace............325

Appendix C

Aachen, Germany, Prayer for Peace from the 7th - 9th of
September 2003 329

1. "Ex Orient" Exhibition 329
2. Prayers for Peace 330
3. Concluding Event 330

Appendix D

1st Ecumenical Church Congress in Berlin: 28.05.2003 –
01. 06. 2003 331

Bibliography 337
Table of Figures 343
Subject Index 345
Index of Persons 359
Books Recommended for the Topic 363

www.ingramcontent.com/pod-product-compliance
Lightning Source LLC
Chambersburg PA
CBHW021959160426
43197CB00007B/194